PITT LATIN AMERICAN SERIES

Institutions, Parties, and Coalitions
in
ARGENTINE POLITICS

Luigi Manzetti

UNIVERSITY OF PITTSBURGH PRESS

Pittsburgh and London

Published by the University of Pittsburgh Press, Pittsburgh, Pa., 15260
Copyright © 1993, University of Pittsburgh Press
Manufactured in the United States of America
Printed on acid-free paper

Library of Congress Cataloging-in-Publication Data
Manzetti, Luigi.
    Institutions, parties, and coalitions in Argentine politics /
Luigi Manzetti.
        p.   cm.—(Pitt Latin American series)
    Includes index.
    ISBN 0-8229-3755-7
    1. Argentina—Politics and government—1910– 2. Political
parties—Argentina—History—20th century. 3. Pressure groups—
Argentina—History—20th century. I. Title. II. Series.
JL2081.M36 1993
324.282—dc20   93-12872
                                                        CIP

A CIP catalogue record for this book is available from the British Library.
Eurospan, London

To Aura and Emo with all my love

CONTENTS

TABLES AND FIGURES

Tables

Figures

ABBREVIATIONS

AAA   Argentine Anticommunist Alliance

AAPIC   Association of Production, Industry, and Commerce

ACIEL   Coordinating Association of Free Enterprise Institutions

ADIM   Association of Metallurgic Industrialists

ANSSAL   National Administration of Health Insurance

APEGE   Permanent Assembly of Entrepreneurial Trade Associations

ATE   State Workers Union

BUM   Barrionueva-Ubaldini-Miguel

CAC   Argentine Chamber of Commerce

CACIP   Argentine Confederation of Commerce, Industry, and Production

CAI   Argentine Industrial Council

CAP   Corporation of Argentine Meat Producers

CAPIC   Argentine Confederation of Production, Industry, and Commerce

CARBAP   Confederation of Rural Associations of Buenos Aires and La Pampa

CAT   Confederation of Argentine Workers

CEA   Argentine Economic Conference

CES   Social Economic Conference

CFI   Independent Federalist Confederation

CGC   General Confederation of Commerce

CGE   General Economic Confederation

CGI   General Confederation of Industry

CGP   General Confederation of Production

CGT   General Confederation of Labor

CGyT   Commission of Management and Labor

CINA   Argentine Industrial Confederation

COA   Syndicalist Argentine Workers Confederation

CONADE   National Development Council

CONADEP   National Commission on the Disappeared

CONASE   National Security Council

CONES   Economic and Social Council

Coninagro   Confederation of Agricultural Cooperatives

CORA   Argentine Regional Workers Confederation

COVIARA   Cooperative of Sales of the Navy

CNT   National Commission of Labor

CRA   Argentine Rural Confederation

CSFA   Supreme Council of the Armed Forces

CTERA   Argentine Confederation of Education Workers

DGFM   General Directorate of Military Factories

DSN   National Security Doctrine

EEC   European Economic Community

ENTEL   National Enterprise of Telecommunications

ERP   People's Revolutionary Army

FAA   Argentine Agrarian Federation

FAEDCI   Argentine Federation of Entities Defending Commerce and Industry

FAP   Peronist Armed Forces

FAR   Revolutionary Armed Forces

FJL   Jusicialist Liberation Front

FNPC   National Federation of Parties of the Center

FOA   Argentine Workers Federation

FORA   Argentine Regional Workers Federation

FREJUPO   Justicialist Front of Popular Unity

GAN   Great National Accord

GOU   United Officers' Group

IAPI   Argentine Trade Promotion Institute

IMF   International Monetary Fund

ISI   Import substitution industrialization

ITLM   Tax on unused land

JMG   National Grain Board

MAS   Movement Toward Socialism

MEDI   Entrepreneurial Movement of the Interior

MERCOSUR   South American Common Market

MIA   Argentine Industrial Movement

MID   Movement of Integration and Development

MIN   National Industrial Movement

MODIN   Movement of Dignity and Independence

MRC   Movement of Renovation and Change

MUI   Movement of Industrial Unification

MUSO   Movement of Unity, Solidarity, and Organization

NAM   Non-Aligned Movement

PAMI   Comprehensive Medical Assistance Plan

PAN   National Autonomist party

PDC   Christian Democrat party

PI   Intransigent party

PJ   Justicialist party

PO   Workers party

Pronagro   National Agricultural Program

PRT   Revolutionary Workers party

PSA   Argentine Socialist party

PSD   Social Democratic party

SIDE   State Intelligence Agency

SRA   Argentine Rural Society

UCD   Democratic Center Union

UCR   Radical Civic Union

UCRI   Intransigent Radical Civic Union

UCRP   People's Radical Civic Union

UDELPA   Union of the Argentine People

UGT   Socialist General Workers Union

UIA   Argentine Industrial Union

UOM   Metallurgical Workers Union

USA   Socialist Argentine Labor Union

PREFACE

This book is an introduction to the complex nature of Argentine politics. In North America and Western Europe societal conflicts have been more or less successfully mediated by political parties. This is not the case in Argentina. Nor have parties been able to bring legitimacy to key institutions like the presidency, Congress, and the judiciary. Consequently, interest groups have taken things into their own hands, relentlessly competing against each other in their quest for power. They have also tried to further their interests through a variety of channels within which the democratic process represented one of many available options. In Argentina these groups, such as the military, the labor movement, agricultural producers, and industrialists, have acted in competition with—and often as an alternative to—parties. Because of their socioeconomic clout, they have acted like what Mancur Olson calls "distributional coalitions." Much of the instability experienced by Argentina since 1930 can be ascribed to the continuous struggle by these distributional coalitions over the most fundamental issues of political legitimacy and the distribution of economic resources. The thesis of this book is that the socioeconomic decline experienced by Argentina since 1930 can be explained by the weakness of the democratic institutions, which has allowed the military, entrepreneurial, and labor organizations to create entrenched vested interests at the expense of society as a whole. This, in turn, led to the establishment of monopolistic and oligopolistic situations that penalized economic efficiency while making political life more divisive, as any attempt to address such distortions met with the strong resistance of the distributional coalitions affected.

The chapters that follow portray the development of Argentine political institutions and highlight how the distributional coalitions' demands upon such institutions created a situation of political and economic decay. Chapter 1 sets forth the theoretical explanation concerning the relationship between democratic institutions and interest

xvii

group behavior in Argentina. Chapter 2 briefly outlines the country's political development, with particular emphasis on the last twenty years. Chapter 3 deals with political parties, while chapter 4 scrutinizes the major factors shaping public opinion and voting behavior. Chapter 5 examines the special role played by the military and its relations with the state, parties, and interest groups. Chapters 6 through 8 analyze the labor movement and the most important interest organizations in the agricultural and industrial sectors. Finally, Chapter 9 explores the prospects of the young Argentine democracy in the near future, paying particular attention to the impact that the Menem administration's policies will have on distributional struggles.

ACKNOWLEDGMENTS

The present book is the result of several field trips to Argentina between 1989 and 1993 funded by a research grant provided by Southern Methodist University and from the North-South Center at the University of Miami. During those trips I interviewed many policy makers, politicians, military officers, and scholars, whom I thank for sharing their views with me. Moreover, I appreciate the invaluable help of the Buenos Aires's office of the Economic Commission for Latin America and the Caribbean, which provided me with logistic support while I was in Argentina. I also would like to express my gratitude to several Argentine friends who arranged my interviews or found crucial data for me. They are Patricia Baxendale, Franco Castiglioni, Alejandro Corbacho, Eduardo Feldman, Andrés Fontana, Daniel Heymann, and Andrea Quiros. I am also grateful to Edgardo Catterberg and Manuel Mora y Araujo for allowing me to use their public opinion data and to Marta Valle of the Dirección Nacional Electoral who dug out unpublished electoral data. Many thanks also to Victor Bulmer-Thomas, who allowed me to use some parts of an article I published in the *Journal of Latin American Studies* in chapter 7.

While writing this book I have benefited from the comments expressed on draft chapters by some colleagues. In this regard, I owe a special debt to Carlos H. Acuña, Chris Blake, Rut Diamint, Jim McGuire, W. David Patterson, David Pion-Berlin, and John Welch. Peter Snow deserves a special mention not only because he critiqued the whole manuscript but also kindly drew the figures appearing in the text. Finally, I thank María Eugenia Musica, Jeff Stark, Holly Ackerman, and Holly Wilmot for the editing work. Of course, all errors and omissions are mine.

INSTITUTIONS, PARTIES, AND COALITIONS IN
ARGENTINE POLITICS

1

INTRODUCTION

AROUND THE TURN of the century, Argentina was regarded as one of the rising nations in the developing world. In 1895, Argentine per capita income was comparable to that of Germany, Holland, and Belgium and higher than those of Austria, Spain, Italy, Switzerland, Sweden, and Norway.[1] Endowed with abundant natural resources and a highly skilled population, Argentina seemed to resemble more a European nation than a Latin American one. Although economic growth declined after World War I, Argentina could still claim, on the eve of the Great Depression, a per capita product higher than that of Austria, Japan, and Italy.[2] However, between 1929 and 1983 per capita product grew at less than 1 percent.[3] While in 1930 Argentina was still one of the world's wealthiest nations, by 1990 it had dropped to seventieth place.[4] In 1992, the Menem administration acknowledged that 9 million Argentines, out of a total population of 32 million people, lived below the poverty line. While between 1862 and 1930 economic growth had been accompanied by the development of a relatively stable form of government, from 1930 on economic sluggishness went hand in hand with political instability.

What went wrong in Argentina? What turned a promised land into one of despair? Many scholars agree that Argentina's socioeconomic decline and political instability can be traced to the very nature of its political system. Likewise, in this book the aim is to examine how the inability of Argentine's democratic institutions and political parties to mediate interests and resolve conflicts led many interests, including the military, to act outside of institutional mechanisms and to burden the government with myriad claims, often mutually exclusive. While previous research has teased out many of the unique features of the Argentine political system, the evolution of its institutions and interest groups can be explained in more general, theoretical terms, applicable to human nature regardless of country-specific conditions. Far from being the ultimate study on Argentina, this book aims at relating the Argentine case to a broader theory of institution building and public

3

choice. The objective here is to integrate some of the findings of previous works and to put forward an explanation that links institutional weaknesses with the failure to develop collective action.

I use the concept of institutional decay to describe and explain the failure of political pluralism. Pluralism is based on the concept of the autonomous interaction of societal groups among themselves and with government. Such interaction is mediated primarily by government institutions, such as the legislature, the judiciary, the executive, and organizations like political parties that compete to gain control of such institutions. My main argument is that, in the case of Argentina, the inability of such institutions to integrate, within the framework of pluralism, an increasing number of interest groups, mobilize the support of their members, and effectively mediate societal conflicts led to the demise of pluralism. This, in turn, paralyzed collective action. In fact, as government institutions and parties grew weaker, business organizations, labor, and the military began to confront each other overtly and to articulate irreconcilable demands on governments. The result was the absence of clear-cut, widely accepted, rules of the game, which resulted in a scramble by interest groups to affect the allocation of resources by whatever means necessary often bypassing pluralist institutions. What ensued was political fragmentation and polarization, leading to anarchic behavior, chronic instability, and socioeconomic decline.[5]

Institutional Decay

Alexis de Tocqueville wrote more than a century ago, "Among the laws that rule human societies there is one which seems to be more precise and clear than all others. If men are to remain civilized or to become so, the art of associating together must grow and improve in the same ratio in which the equality of conditions is increased."[6] Indeed, in Argentina the equality of conditions did not improve gradually but instead came in great spurts in 1919–1928 and in 1946–1951. In neither period did the art of associating together grow; in fact it actually declined in each period. The result, quite clearly, has been institutional decay.[7]

Between 1862 and 1916, the Conservatives created the institutions of liberal democracy; however, these institutions, with the single exception of the presidency, were never "institutionalized." Congress met regularly, but it was clear that its function was not that of determining the political rules that governed society but rather to enact into legislation the rules decided upon by the president.[8] Similarly, the judiciary lacked appreciable independence from the executive authority. On top of that, the liberal democracy envisioned by the founding fathers of the Argentine republic was based upon elitist principles of limited pluralism, which distinguished between political rights (leading to public office), to be enjoyed by a few, and civil rights (allowing the pursuit of economic prosperity), to be enjoyed by all. Thus political institutions were, for the most part, weak to begin with, and their legitimacy was based upon a narrow interpretation of pluralism, which discredited them in the eyes of the majority of the citizenry, who were excluded from active participation. The Conservatives, who governed until 1916, more closely resembled a club of notables than a political party. Still, this low level of institutionalization was quite sufficient, given the extremely low level of participation. While the oligarchic system promoted impressive strides toward economic development, it was incapable of channeling the increasing political participation at the beginning of the twentieth century in ways that would perpetuate its hold on power. With the adoption of universal male suffrage in 1912, the Conservatives hoped to convince the emerging middle class to vote for them, but to no avail. The number of people allowed to vote increased at an incredible rate; from 190,000 in 1910 and 640,000 in 1912, it reached 1,460,000 in 1928, a growth of 750 percent in less than two decades. With each increase in the size of the electorate came a decline in the percentage of the vote received by the Conservatives.

During the Radical administrations of 1916–1930, the dramatic increase in political participation was not accompanied by increased institutionalization, not even of the Radical party. A great many of the new participants were won over not to Radicalism but to Yrigoyenism. Hipólito Yrigoyen and his lieutenants had long insisted that theirs was not a political party but, instead, a national renovating movement, hence the formal name Radical Civic Union (Unión Cívica Radical, or UCR). The Radical period was one of missed opportunities. Increased political participation made limited pluralism and the political institutions based on it obsolete and in need of redefinition and reform. Yet once in power, the Radicals practiced most of the abuses they had criticized in their Conservative predecessors. They were content to preserve the status quo as long as they benefited from it. Rather than giving new meaning to the role of the legislature and the judiciary, they kept both institutions subordinated to the presidency. The principle of federalism existed on paper only, as the central government used and abused its constitutional powers to dislodge recalcitrant governors.

In spite of passing labor legislation (scarcely enforced), the Radicals remained aloof from the working class. Many of their congressmen came from the landed aristocracy, and thus Presidents Yrigoyen and Marcelo de Alvear kept the old capitalist accumulation model based on agricultural exports. However, even this was more the result of convenience than well-thought-out strategy. The continuous emphasis on being a movement rather than a party allowed Yrigoyen and Alvear to keep tight grip on their followers, but it prevented the UCR from creating steady alliance with either labor or capital. In one area, however, the Radicals were innovators. During the Conservative period, government was relegated to a subsidiary role in line with the free-market economic theory dominant in those days. The Radicals, on the other hand, saw in government a tool to consolidate their hold on power. Public jobs were given to party loyalists, and political patronage became more endemic than under the Conservatives. The size of the state bureaucracy increased steadily under the Radicals, as did the politicization of public office. Mismanagement and corruption also increased, thus spreading the seeds of what would become in later days a gulf dividing civil society from government institutions.

With Yrigoyen's overthrow in 1930, his death three years later, and the return to power of the Conservatives by means of force and fraud, many newly enfranchised Argentines were cast adrift. Meaningful political participation was curtailed through fraudulent elections, and institutionalization was not increased; in fact it actually declined, as the Conservatives thoroughly discredited those institutions of liberal democracy that they themselves had built. By 1930, the Conservatives and the agricultural, industrial, and commercial circles tied to them had reached the conclusion that liberal democracy in its present form was unworkable in Argentina—that it had led to the mismanagement of the country and to the unbearable political mobilization of previously unenfranchised people. This was a crucial moment in Argentine history. The economic elites, unable to translate their economic power into votes, lost faith in the democratic institutions and began to look to the military in the hope of influencing public policy through authoritarian regimes. The schism between parties and business groups became the crux of political instability for the next five decades.

The second great surge in political participation came in the mid-1940s. This time it came not from newly enfranchised voters but from newly mobilized ones. In the late 1930s and early 1940s migration from rural to urban areas reached exceptional proportions. It has been estimated that in a single four-year period, 1943–1947, one of every five rural dwellers moved to an urban center, mostly to metropolitan Buenos Aires.[9] It was this urban working class, and especially recent migrants, that was mobilized by Juan Perón.[10] The Peronist vote in 1946 was channeled through the newly formed Labor party (Partido Laborista); however; shortly after his election Perón dissolved the Labor party and replaced it with the Peronist party. "With the crushing of the Partido Laborista in 1946, Perón stamped out the possibility of any incipient political organization of the workers, while at the same time ratifying their union organization—thus reinforcing the fact the political expression of the working class should pass through him."[11] Rather than using the Peronist party to give worker institutionalized access to government,

Perón saw to it that the party was nothing more than an electoral vehicle. He was fond of saying that the Peronist party functioned for a few days prior to elections and that, as soon as the votes were counted, it disappeared. Like Yrigoyenism, Peronism was an heterogeneous political movement bound together by the charisma of its leader. Mediation between the various groups within the movement, and between the government and those pressure groups excluded from Peronism, was left to Perón. The role of Congress and the judiciary was downgraded even further, the cult of personality reached its climax, and political patronage in public administration and state enterprises escalated to unprecedented levels.

The novelty of Perón's populism was not just his partisan use of macroeconomic policies. Equally important was the strengthening of the union movement, which, although subordinated to Perón's authority, was the only thoroughly organized and institutionalized element within Peronism. This introduced a new element into Argentine politics. When Perón was forced into exile, it was labor rather than the Peronist party that became the backbone of the Peronist movement. In Perón's absence, union leaders claimed to represent Peronism vis-à-vis the government and other interest groups. After 1955, with their party denied participation at the polls, the unions and the General Confederation of Labor (Confederación General del Trabajo, or CGT) were the only avenues of political action open to the Peronists. From that time on (except for the few months in 1973 and 1974 when Perón was again president), the CGT demonstrated its opposition to all administrations by means of general strikes, worker occupation of factories, and inflammatory rhetoric by union leaders. According to Gary Wynia, "What makes Argentina different from other countries with free labor movements is the persistent waging of symbolic and substantive wars between labor and government. Not only do labor leaders believe their political combat is popular among the rank and file, but they are addicted to achieving political fame by pounding on political institutions regardless of how ineffective such battering really is."[12]

If Peronism had made a mockery of constitutional democracy by downgrading the role of its institutions, the Liberating Revolution (Revolución Libertadora, 1955–1958), in its zeal to eliminate the Peronist legacy, did not enhance the average citizen's faith in the fairness of the political system. The subsequent Radical administrations of Arturo Frondizi and Arturo Illia fell victim to the political polarization between Peronist and anti-Peronist camps in the "impossible game."[13] The very proscription of the Peronists by the military created serious problems of political legitimacy for both Frondizi and Illia. Thus, while the two administrations had more or less clear policies, they had no majority to back them up nor were those policies sufficiently broad in appeal to draw new support. Moreover, the Radical presidents' partisan use of political institutions and their insulation of the decision-making process compounded the problem. The military coups in 1966 and again in 1976 were a clear sign that the military, supported by powerful interest groups (i.e., the business community, the Catholic church, opposition parties, and labor) had reached the conclusion that even the limited pluralism of the 1955–1966 period was not a feasible option. "The majority of the [political] participants reached what might be termed a 'consensus of termination': the existing political regime had exhausted its resources and had to be replaced."[14]

Both the Argentine Revolution (Revolución Argentina) of 1966 and the Process of National Reorganization (Proceso de Reorganización Nacional) of 1976 were presented as solutions to the institutional decay of pluralism. Grand plans were announced for "the wholesale reorganization of the state apparatus, the class structure, prevailing patterns of capital accumulation, and the country's insertion in the world-economy."[15] Nevertheless, the authoritarian restructuring of the society was an even bigger fiasco than the discredited pluralist regime; while agreeing on what had to be terminated, neither the military nor their civilian supporters could agree on "the new rules to be introduced and the new distribution of power and resources they should reflect."[16] Thus the restructuring rationale remained vague and contradictory at best. President Juan Carlos Onganía tried to reshape the political arena according to a vague neocorporatist model, without parties and legislatures, but his Minister of the Economy Adalbert Krieger Vasena, no matter how heterodox his stabilization plan was, relied on market forces to spur the economy. The 1976 military regime was more repressive than the Argentine Revolution but equally contradictory. Pluralist institutions were once again discarded, but they were not replaced with anything else, not even the tentative corporatist councils of the Onganía regime. Although reluctantly espousing Minister of the Economy José Martínez de Hoz's thesis for a tougher enforcement of free-market economic principles, the armed forces were too busy fighting subversives to lay down coherent plans for the creation of a new regime. What they did was to divide among the three armed services the spoils of power, thus creating a feudalization of the state, which downgraded technocratic rationality. Corruption abounded and abuse of government authority rose to a new high, making the government ineffectual in solving the country's problem. In sum, socioeconomic stagnation, which characterized limited pluralism, turned into authoritarian stagnation under the military aegis.

The collapse of the 1976 military regime raised hopes about a new, more responsive way to practice democracy. However, after their election victory in 1983 the Radicals began to talk about a Third National

Movement (the first two being Yrigoyenism and Peronism). Radical President Raúl Alfonsín had received a great deal of support from minor parties (probably seeing him as a lesser of evils), enabling his followers to claim that Alfonsín, not the UCR, had won.[17]

Shortly after the electoral debacle of 1983 a group of moderate Peronist politicians, calling themselves renovators, set out to convert Peronism into a modern political party, democratically organized, with a definite program. Most union leaders, who had dominated the Peronist movement since 1955, saw in the renovators a threat to their continued domination. The renovators' failure is largely attributable to the opposition of Peronist labor leaders. In 1990, the head of the metalworkers union (Union Obrera Metalúrgica, or UOM) said that the unions had turned the movement over to the politicians, who proved incapable of dealing with national problems. He went on to say, "What have they [the Peronist politicians] done with Perón's movement? They have carried it to chaos. Thus we [Peronist labor leaders], the backbone of Peronism, must contribute to the recreation of the Justicialist Movement."[18] The same labor leaders were crucial in Carlos Menem's election in 1989. Not surprisingly, in his presidential campaign, Menem explicitly ran as the candidate of the Peronist movement rather than of the Justicialist (Peronist) party, and after taking office, the party once again was pushed into the background. Throughout this century, then, the nation's dominant parties have insisted that they were not mere political parties but, instead, all-encompassing national movements. Of the nation's political parties, José Luis de Imaz said, "If they were not so malleable, they would be born, grow and die quickly, and if they were not so irrelevant the future they offer would be a tremendous uncertainty."[19]

The cause of the lack of institutionalization of the Congress is much the same: the fact that the entire political system revolves around the person of the president. In Congress, when the president's party had a clear majority it was willing to enact virtually any legislation from the chief executive. When it did not, the chief executive resorted to executive orders. This has been the case since 1984, with neither Alfonsín nor Menem enjoying full control of both houses. In those instances, when Radicals and Peronists were unable to strike behind-the-scenes compromises, crucial legislation (e.g., the 1985 Austral Plan currency reform and the 1990 antistrike bill) was promulgated by decree. Alfonsín well understood that this went against his initial commitment to abide by the rule of law, but as time went by, the need for quick action overwhelmed democratic purity. The pragmatic Menem, on the other hand, was quite willing to bypass both his party and Congress. His enlargement of the Supreme Court in order to appoint justices well disposed to his controversial initiatives is typical of his political style.

The Paralysis of Collective Action

Earlier, I contended that the inability of Argentine democratic institutions to aggregate and articulate societal interests and mediate conflicts was instrumental in the demise of pluralism between 1930 and 1983. This inability also prevented the achievement of a consensus on how to share the burden for the provision of public goods and hindered the development of collective action.[20] Institutional decay went hand in hand with economic decay.[21] Why was this so? I believe that the Argentine case can be explained, at least in part, by applying Mancur Olson's logic of collective action, which links economic stagnation to interest group behavior.[22] Olson's theory is primarily based on how economic rationality affects political decisions but ignores how interest groups' demands are (or are not) channeled by political institutions that are conducive to the outcomes they set forth. Thus, in this chapter, I attempt to show how his theory is linked to institutional decay.

According to Olson, the proliferation of interest groups over time is characteristic of pluralist societies. In point of fact, Argentina (as we shall see in greater detail in chapter 2) developed a political pluralism in the second half of the last century, which, although it restricted political participation, did resemble in many ways contemporary European patterns. Slowly but steadily, interest groups representing both business and labor also organized in a way similar to European groups. In Olson's view, however, interest groups seek redistributional objectives detrimental to the public good. Contrary to older pluralist theories that perceived interest groups interaction among themselves and government as leading to positive policy outcomes for society, Olson views interest groups as primarily interested in reaping distributional advantages from government, their efforts are aimed at creating or maintaining monopolistic or oligopolistic positions "harmful to economic growth, full employment, coherent government, equal opportunity, and social mobility."[23]

Moreover, Olson posits that "those groups that have access to selective incentives will be more likely to act collectively to obtain collective goods than those who do not, and . . . smaller groups will have a greater likelihood of engaging in collective action than larger ones" (34). More to the point, he argues that, "if the group that would benefit from collective action is sufficiently small and the cost-benefit ratio of collective action for the group sufficiently favorable, there may well be calculated action in the collective interest even without selective incentives" (29). Following this rationale, small homogeneous groups can easily agree on what collective good to pursue and will enjoy a higher cost-benefit ratio than larger groups or groups lacking access to selective incentives. Thus "in the absence of selective incentives, the incentive for group action diminishes as group size increases, so that large groups are less able to act in their common interest than small ones" (27). This leads eventually to the paradoxical phenomenon of the exploitation of large groups by small ones. Based upon this rationale, Olson posits that "members of 'small' groups have disproportionate organization power for collective action, and this disproportion diminishes but does not disappear," and that "on balance, special interest organizations and collusions reduce efficiency and aggregate income in the societies in which they operate and make political life more divisive" (74).

These statements fit the early development of Argentine interest groups quite nicely. For instance, the Argentine Rural Society (Sociedad Rural Argentina, or SRA) was the country's first interest organization (in the modern sense of the word), gathering together since 1866 the most powerful elements of the landowning elite. From the start, the SRA experienced high cohesiveness, unity of purpose, and a high cost-benefit ratio, all of which made its organization possible even in the absence of selective incentives. Furthermore, in spite of its smallness, the SRA quickly became the dominant association in Argentine society. Its domination of Argentina's economic development in the second half of the nineteenth century supports Olson's position that, under these conditions, a small group can eventually exploit much larger ones by lobbying for favorable legislation. This can be seen not only in the adoption of an economic model that furthered the vested interests of SRA members but in politics as well: the politicians who ruled Argentina until 1943 were often members of the SRA. In practice, the SRA and its members constituted the core of the Conservative governments that dominated Argentine politics between 1880 and 1916 and 1930 through 1943. Besides, many of the Radicals who ruled between 1916 and 1930 were SRA members. It is then no surprise that several administrations either hired SRA members as consultants or appointed them as government officials. Thus, under such conditions, the SRA enjoyed a monopolistic power of representation. Olson also postulates that "Oligopolists and other small groups have a greater likelihood of being able to organize for collective action, and can usually organize with less delay, than large groups. It follows that the small groups in a society will usually have more lobbying and cartelistic power per capita . . . than the large groups. The fact that small groups can usually organize with less delay than large ones implies that this disproportion will tend to be greatest in societies that have enjoyed only a brief period of stability and least great in those societies that have been stable for a long time" (41).

Again, not only was the SRA the first interest group worthy of this name to be organized in Argentina but its fortunes coincided with a brief period of political stability under Conservative administrations. The SRA was unopposed and took advantage of the institutional and organizational vacuum at a time of great, yet convulsive, development to occupy the central stage in the country's political arena. To a large extent there was a symbiotic relation between the SRA and the government, in which the Conservative administrations prior to 1916 enacted policies to the almost exclusive benefit of the landowning aristocracy.

It is in this light that we can explain how the SRA, in spite of its smallness, remained the most prominent organization of the agricultural sector, although over time its hegemonic role declined as a result of the emergence of contending interest groups. Moreover, following the same rationale, we can explain the slow start of industrial interest groups and labor associations. The former were subordinated to SRA interests for a long time. Compounding their lobbying strength was the fact that industrial interests were more heterogeneous, often lacking selective incentives, and several organizations competed for hegemonic representation. Although the Argentine Industrial Union (Unión Industrial Argentina, or UIA) became the most important interest group in the industrial sector, it had to face the competition of a host of rival associations created later, among which the most important was the General Economic Confederation (Confederación General Económica, or CGE).

Labor, on the other hand, was until 1943 repressed by the same Conservative governments that embodied the interests of the SRA and remained deeply divided. Only under Perón did labor gain an important socioeconomic status. In fact, from the mid-1940s until the mid-1970s the high percentage of unionized workers and the establishment of collective bargaining regulations reinforced the contractual power of labor leaders. As unionism began to encompass a large part of the working force and exercise almost a monopoly on the supply of labor, its lobbying power increased as well. The selective incentives provided by individual unions in the form of welfare and health benefits, along with a host of other privileges, diminished the impact of the free-ride problem.[24] Nonetheless, in spite of its large membership and rank-and-file loyalty, the labor movement was debilitated by factionalism, which prevented it from acting in a unified way. A compounding factor was the role of the military, which in Argentina is both a government institution and a vested interest. Indeed, from the 1930s on the military was not only a referee, ready to intervene when civilian politicians were unable to tackle mounting socioeconomic problems; it was also a powerful interest group, owning a vast military-related industrial complex and articulating its own political and economic demands, which at times were compatible with those of the socioeconomic groups mentioned above. As a result, agricultural, industrial, and labor organizations, as well as the military, began to create distributional coalitions, whose main goal was to obtain benefits from the government and its institutions (commonly referred to in Argentina as the state), with little or no interest in competitiveness and economic growth.

Distributional coalitions are, according to Olson, interest groups that struggle over income distribution to maintain or increase their economic rents and, it should be added, political privileges. Thus, the longer an interest group has existed, the more cohesive and encompassing it is and the more entrenched it becomes. The negative consequence of this state of affairs is that interest groups having such characteristics are more inclined to find ways to carve themselves a larger slice of the country's economic pie rather than to look for ways to increase the size of the pie itself. This is precisely because distributional coalitions tend to channel economic resources away from their optimal use to satisfy their narrow interests. In the case of Argentina, as we shall see, distributional coalitions increased in number across time, and as postulated by Olson, political life grew more divisive and economic growth turned into prolonged stagnation. The only solution to the problem would have been, in Olson's view, an external shock, like the foreign occupations after World War II that wiped out many distributional coalitions in Germany, Japan, and Italy and that are credited with the strong economic growth of these countries after 1945. However, Argentina, like the United Kingdom, did not have any foreign occupation, and its distributional coalitions tightened their grip.

Olson argues that long periods of political and economic stability are conducive to the creation of new interest groups and the consolidation of older ones.[25] However in Argentina, after 1930, the scenario has been one of not only political instability but also the emergence of new interest groups and the strengthening of older ones. This is because instability "diverts resources that would otherwise have gone into productive long-term investments into forms of wealth that are most easily protected, or even into capital flights to more stable environments.[26] Thus, the outcome has been disastrous, as distributive conflicts have increased and hindered economic growth. Indeed, in discussing the implication of his theory to unstable societies, Olson argues that "the most substantial and wealthy interests are relatively better organized . . . [and] they often own an unrepresentative mix of the country's productive factors. They obtain policies that favor themselves and work in different ways against the interests of the larger unorganized groups in the society, thereby making the distribution of income even far more unequal (ibid., 170). Thus, in unstable developing countries, in the absence of an external shock *and* protracted socioeconomic instability, distributional coalitions are fewer, leading to even worse results than in developed ones. What could explain the variance in performance between Argentina, on the one hand, and Chile, Mexico, and Uruguay, on the other, is the ability of political institutions in the latter countries to channel and restrain the demands of distributional coalitions.

One more point deserves attention. Olson postulates that distributional coalitions use democratic procedures in their lobbying effort. However, in the case of Argentina this is just one of several options. Military coups have often been perceived by business and labor as just as effective a means as elections to get an advantage over their competitors.

Let us now return to the rise of interest groups in Argentina and their impact on the political system. The emergence of new distributional coalitions threatening the interests of older, more established groups is a common pattern in the evolution of modern societies. As long as the groups are few and the emerging distributional coalitions make demands that can be accommodated through the mediation of pluralist institutions, conflict is avoided. This is, more or less, the scenario that characterized Argentina up until 1930. Until then, Conservative parties could well represent the interests of the dominant landowning elites. The political institutions of the limited pluralism set up by the Conservatives mirrored the needs and political orientation of Argentine landowners. By the same token, up-and-coming industrial groups accepted the complementary role that the landowning oligarchy had reserved for them. The radical administrations of the 1916–1930 period did not challenge this state of affairs. However, Yrigoyen was unable or unwilling to meet the demands of agricultural, industrial, and military circles for quick policy responses to ameliorate the consequences of the Great Depression. This plus mounting social unrest (which ensued from the increased political mobilization of the lower strata of Argentine society) provoked the first breakdown of the pluralist system.

The creation of a powerful union movement under Perón and of new economic interest groups that arose from the import substitution industrialization (ISI) process (e.g. the CGE) increased the number of distributional coalitions challenging the economic interests of the landed and industrial elites. This increase in political mobilization and proliferation of interest groups was not met by the creation of new institutions to mediate the conflicts arising from mounting demands upon the state.[27] The problem was exacerbated by the fact that, while more and more groups were demanding part of the pie, the pie itself had shrunk and the ability of the state to sustain redistributive policies was progressively exhausted. Agricultural producers wanted the end of taxes on their exports, industrial sectors linked to foreign interests and dependent on foreign technology pressed for the opening of the economy to favor the importation of capital equipment, while the industrial sector that had flourished under economic protectionism was vitriolicly opposed to such an opening. The latter was supported by the labor movement, which saw in economic protection a means to keep full employment (even in inefficient industries) and high wages.[28] Finally, economic protection was also endorsed by sectors of the military wishing to shelter their poorly run industries. These interests had grown too strong, and the capacity of any government to promote change without triggering a political backlash had diminished considerably, and after Perón's ouster, it became virtually impossible.

In the meantime, lobbying efforts by one sector or the other forced first the Conservative governments of the 1930s—and more so the Peronist administrations of the 1940s and 1950s and the Radical administrations of the late 1950s and early 1960s—to create a web of regulations that strangled the economy and gave greater authority to the state to intervene. Industrial exporters received subsidies and tax breaks; agricultural producers, while being taxed for their exports, never faced land reform or a serious tax on their properties or incomes; and domestic industrial producers were able for a long time to thwart the entry of foreign competitors while receiving fat government contracts under special legislation (thus maintaining their monopolistic or oligopolistic status). Moreover, the foreign multinationals that came in the late 1950s enjoyed tax breaks and monopolistic conditions, and labor exerted pressure on the government to have state companies provide basic services at prices well below their cost and to maintain high wages regardless of productivity. The result was the creation of a closed and heavily subsidized economy where markets operated under monopolistic conditions that dampened business opportunities and growth. To compound matters, the fiscal requirements of subsidizing the private economy and an inefficient entrepreneurial state dramatized distributive struggles, since none of the interest groups concerned was willing to finance a growing budget deficit. Repeated attempts by different political regimes to have specific distributional coalitions shoulder part of the deficit financing were short-lived. Invariably, these regimes ended up in severe socioeconomic crises and political polarization, which led almost invariably to military coups. Thus, Olson's suggestion that "the accumulation of distributional coalitions increases the complexity of regulation, the role of government, and the complexity of understandings, and changes the direction of social evolution" seems to fit Argentina quite well.

From 1955 on, political and economic clashes reinforced each other, with no apparent room for institutional mediation. The claims of too many distributional coalitions constituted a crucial problem, because they created a situation that tempted each coalition to not make a decision with immediate costs to itself, even though the decision would eventually benefit it. Each coalition wanted, for the same reason, to encourage other coalitions to make decisions that brought itself immediate benefits, even though it recognized that the decision would eventually harm all of them. "The results . . . [were] immobility and incoherence—in brief, a paralysis of public choice."[29] Political instability turned into stop-and-go economic cycles characterized by increasingly longer recessionary periods and high inflation, briefly interrupted by spurts of economic recovery and price stability. Albert Hirschman depicted the Argentine business cycle as based on three pressure groups: the industrial bourgeoisie, landowners, and the urban working class.

> The pivotal group is the industrial bourgeoisie: it tends to make a common cause with the urban masses in a recession when both groups can agree on a strongly expansionary economic policy and on holding down the price of Argentina's principal export product, meat, which also happens to be its principal wage good. But exports tend to decline under those circumstances and to do so fairly rapidly both because the workers, with their increasing incomes, literally eat up the country's exports and because the cattle breeders, unlike Brazil's coffee planters, can react to a price squeeze by liquidating their herds. As a result the industrialists soon experience supply difficulties for their imported inputs and capital goods. With meat prices, among others, starting to rise, the workers make demands for higher wages; soon industrialists find their allies too demanding. At this point they join the agricultural elites and this new coalition can now agree on holding real wages down and on raising prices for agricultural output. Policies directed to this end, and to fight inflation in general, cause a recession which eventually leads to a new switch by the industrial bourgeoisie so that the play starts over again. The different phases of the play are marked by different kinds of political regimes: during the expansive, inflationary phase an uneasy coalition is maintained between populist forces and certain sectors of the business community; the military takes over when these sectors become concerned about the excessive inflation and ally themselves with the land- and cattle owners.[30]

In the 1955–1983 period, the rapid change in political regimes and rules of the game that this business cycle introduced enhanced the tendency for maximizing short-term benefits. While individual interest groups did not have the ability to impose either by themselves or in coalition with others long-lasting policies for the reasons mentioned by Hirschman, they could veto policies that negatively affected them. This veto power rested on the exclusive possession of resources indispensable for a normal functioning of the economy. The withdrawal of such resources could easily paralyze the implementation of any coherent policy. Unions, thanks to their extensive control of the labor force, could retaliate against policies they opposed by striking. Agricultural exporters, upon which the government relied to finance its operation through taxation, could, by cutting down output, bring any administration to its knees. Industrialists, who employed a large part of the working force, could threaten to [divest and] lay off workers, with predictable negative consequences for the economy and for social harmony. Last but not least, the military possessed the coercive means to protect its vested interests.

With parties and Congress too polarized to mediate, interest groups struggled to get or to remain ahead of the competition, which in the longrun was self-defeating. The "scrambling" logic is fairly simple: the large number of distributional coalitions made it impossible for any one of them to make a difference. Therefore, under conditions of high inflation and a government unable to make groups abide by the rules of the game, self-restraint brought no tangible benefits. Quite the contrary, it presented any distributional coalition with potential losses if other groups engaged in self-maximizing behavior. Consequently, even though each group understood the importance of all groups restraining their claims, the payoff for noncollaborative behavior was too great. Although rational from the perspective of each group, this led to irrational political and economic behavior. Two outcomes arose from this zero-sum mentality, where one's gain is the other's loss: first, an ever accelerating inflationary cycle, with each distributional coalition trying to pass the cost of economic stabilization on to other groups, and second, the disappearance of cooperative behavior.

Argentine distributional coalitions constantly struggled to affect the reallocation of resources by going to the ultimate source of policy making—the executive and the public bureaucracy. While the bypassing of Congress and political parties to press demands directly upon the president is most noticeable in the case of organized labor, it is certainly not limited to that group. In fact, virtually all of the nation's interest groups have at some point followed this course. Actually, at the turn of the century several presidents and key cabinet ministers were members of the SRA and, of course, looked after the interests of the landowning elites. This established a tradition within which interest groups did not limit themselves to lobbying but actually tried to privatize public policy by placing their people in strategic government positions. However, since 1943 the country's economic elites lacked a political party with any prospect of gaining power at the polls. They thus felt compelled to take their demands directly to the president and, failing there, to the armed forces. The rationale behind this behavior was that capturing government or being able to influence its policies allowed a coalition to impose the cost of resource allocation on others.

The net result of this scrambling was that virtually everyone lost. Why? Because, during authoritarian rule, labor and industrialists producing for the domestic market invariably shouldered the burden of stabilization attempts, while agricultural exporters and domestic conglomerates tied to the international market soon found that the authoritarian regimes' policy agendas often contrasted with theirs. The paradox of this situation was that, "in order to pursue projects for restructuring the economy to benefit capital, these regimes [were] frequently led to exclude the dominant classes' political representatives from participating in decision making."[31] The authoritarian regimes' economic failures and the insulation of the decision-making process greatly disappointed those distributional coalitions, headed by the SRA and the UIA, that had endorsed the military in the hope of being allowed to influence public policy. When these groups concluded that the military no longer served their interests, they withdrew support for the regime and eventually openly opposed it, leading to the demise of the authoritarian experiment.

By the time Alfonsín assumed office in 1983, the Argentine economy was on its knees and so was the state and its institutions. Although the Alfonsín period (1983–1989) was characterized by unusual political tolerance, government policies were ineffectual in bringing economic stability, as distributional coalitions continued their constant struggle for income shares. In this regard, following Olson's theory, Mueller suggests that "an economy with a well-developed interest group structure that has been experiencing some inflation and suddenly undergoes a deflationary shock can be expected to continue inflationary price increases while unemployment rises—stagflation—or perhaps to collapse into a deep recession, as occurred during the Great Depression."[32]

Indeed, all these symptoms can be found in Argentina. High inflation remained a constant, and many shock therapies were tried since the early 1950s by democratic and authoritarian regimes alike. Each attempt worked at best temporarily only to end in a renewed price increase spiral of greater proportions. Alfonsín made a few efforts himself, but the burden of a huge foreign debt, his indecisiveness in pursuing needed socioeconomic structural reforms, and faulty economic policies exacerbated the scrambling among distributional coalitions and doomed his administration to failure. At the beginning of his administration Alfonsín made it clear that he was going to defend the public good against the pressure of the country's distributional coalitions, which in his view had with their lobby destroyed the national economy. Indeed, during its first year in office the Radical administration tried to keep interest groups at bay. As Minister of the Economy Bernardo Grinspun stated, "we have been elected to rule, not to make pacts."

However, as the economic situation kept worsening, Alfonsín found it increasingly difficult to stick to his promise. He eventually gave way to the various distributional coalitions, depending on the circumstances of the moment. Between 1985 and 1986 the first major austerity program, the Austral Plan, was launched, with the support of the country's major economic conglomerates, since they played a key role in setting benchmark prices. From 1987 to mid-1988 the administration switched partners by making major concessions to agricultural and labor distributional coalitions. Finally, in mid-1988 with the launching of the last stabilization program, the Spring Plan (*Plan Primavera*), Alfonsín's economists moved toward a pact with industrial and commercial distributional coalitions in a last attempt to bring inflation and public spending under control. At every turn, the administration became more the captive of narrow interests.[33] This severely limited its capacity to maneuver but also triggered severe distributive conflicts as those economic interests left out of government-business strategic alliances fought back by sabotaging public policy. By July 1989, Argentina had fallen into stagflation. "The fierce pursuit of short-term payoffs (a high discounting of the future) strongly shaped the microeconomic behavior of private-sector firms, public enterprises, labor unions, and individual investors, thus generating extraordinarily high levels of distributional conflict. With the state in virtual financial collapse, the market became, progressively, the principal mechanism for allocating income and regulating social conflict."[34]

Under President Menem, the government's alliance with some of the country's most important distributional coalitions became overt. Having inherited a bankrupt state, Menem believed the only way to solve the crisis was to give even greater shares of the national income, via privatization and deregulation policies, to the rural producers of the SRA and to the entreprenurial groups represented by the largest domestic conglomerates. The role of political institutions like Congress, the judiciary, and the parties was once again downplayed as Menem chose to rule not with them but in collaboration with the most important representatives of big capital. Consequently, the economic reform of the Menem administration, as in a natural selection process, allowed the strongest distributional coalitions in the agricultural, industrial, and service sectors to fill the power vacuum produced by the retreat of the state to more basic socioeconomic functions. However, this inexorably penalized the weaker distributional coalitions, like small industrialists and the unions, which were forced to bear the cost of the economic reforms. Although hailed at home and abroad as the beginning of sound economic management, Menem's market reforms did not end monopolistic and oligopolistic practices. Thus, while redesigning the rules of the distributive struggle, they made it possible for the surviving distributional coalitions to acquire greater socioeconomic power. Disguised as free-market initiatives, the restructuring reforms, far from thwarting the pursuit of special interests and collusion, simply raised the stakes of the distributive game. The consequences will be possible to assess only in the years to come.

2

POLITICAL DEVELOPMENT

ARGENTINA WAS FIRST discovered by the white man when Spanish sailors, looking for a southern passage to the Far East, reached the estuary of the Río de la Plata in 1516. However, once the Crown of Spain found that the area had few precious metals and Indians, it paid little further attention. Thus colonization was slow, as only a few thousand Spaniards ventured into a region offering such doubtful prospects for quick riches. The colonists came from two directions. The first arrived from the Atlantic and settled along the Río de la Plata and Río Paraná, founding the cities of Buenos Aires (1536, 1580), Santa Fe (1573), and Corrientes (1588). The second wave came from Peru and Chile and set up communities in Santiago del Estero (1553), Mendoza (1561), San Juan (1562), Córdoba (1573), Salta (1582), San Salvador de Jujuy (1593), La Rioja (1593), San Luis (1596), and San Miguel de Tucumán (1685). The cities in the northwest were basically an appendix of the silver mines of Potosí, in what was then Upper Peru (today's Bolivia). With Potosí quickly becoming one of the largest cities in the Americas in the seventeenth century, the Argentine northwest became its supplier of food, textiles, and wine. On the other hand, Buenos Aires and the other towns along the Paraná River established close commercial ties with the Portuguese colonies in Brazil and only later began to trade with Potosí and Upper Peru. Thus, until the eighteenth century contacts between the two streams of colonization were only a function of commerce and for all intents and purposes the two regions were quite separate. However, in both regions society was shaped by the hierarchical, elitist, and bureaucratic patterns imposed by the Spaniards.[1]

The Spanish Crown's interest in Argentina rose again in the eighteenth century as a result of the Portuguese attempt to gain control of Uruguay and the estuary of the Río de la Plata. As a result, Buenos Aires ceased to be part of the viceroyalty of Peru and in 1776 became itself the site of the new viceroyalty of the Río de La Plata. Buenos Aires benefited immensely from that decision. The Spanish monarchs of the Bourbon dynasty made a concrete effort to strengthen not only the Spanish military presence but also the economic well-being of the new viceroyalty. The Crown granted to Buenos Aires the right to expand its trade with other Spanish colonies and impose custom duties on all the trade through its port from the northwest provinces and Upper Peru. The *porteño* (port dweller of Buenos Aires) bankers and merchants soon acquired a wealth that was comparable in Spanish America only to that of their counterparts in Lima and Mexico City.

The economic boom spurred the development of the agricultural economy of the pampas, one of the most fertile plains in the world, forming a 500-mile inland semicircle around Buenos Aires. Between the 1750s and the 1790s, cattle exports expanded fourfold, and the porteño population grew from 12,000 to 50,000.[2] With the creation of the viceroyalty, Spanish bureaucrats, judges, and military officers arrived to staff the royal administration, creating animosity between the Spaniards and the Argentine-born elites (*criollos*) of Buenos Aires. The latter, who until 1776 had enjoyed great autonomy and socioeconomic prestige, resented being considered second-class citizens by the Spaniards and being excluded from government. Furthermore, the Spaniards established new taxes and trade monopolies. Eventually, porteño merchants began to defy Spanish authorities by smuggling goods to Britain and France.

In the early 1800s, the British decided to take advantage of the weakened Spanish empire and to occupy Buenos Aires. However, while the Spanish troops were easily defeated, the porteños, after a brief British occupation in 1806–1807, drove the British out. The final blow to Spanish authority over the colony came in 1808, when French troops invaded Spain and replaced King Ferdinand VII with a brother of Emperor Napoleon I. Two years later, on 10 May 1810, the city council of Buenos Aires deposed the last viceroy, and the *criollos* began their rule of the city, marking the beginning of the independence movement. In 1816, delegates from different parts of the country convened in Tucumán to sanction the declaration of independence of the United Provinces of the Río de la Plata. A second constitution was signed in 1819, when the national convention moved to Buenos Aires.

The basic problem facing the independence movement was that the only cause binding the various provinces was the common threat posed by the Spanish armies in Upper Peru. When this menace became less compelling, Argentines busied themselves fighting the Paraguayans, Uruguayans, Brazilians, and most often, each other. Between 1810 and 1819 a number of weak governments, in the form of supreme directors, juntas (ruling councils), and triumvirates, alternated rapidly, in an attempt to hold the United Provinces together—without any appreciable success. The real driving force behind the independence movement was General José de San Martín, who took a porteño-dominated army across the Andes and defeated the last Spanish troops in Chile and Peru. While victorious on the battlefield, San Martín, a sincere democrat, failed to convince the criollo elite of the provinces and Buenos Aires to promote meaningful political reforms and, in 1923, left for Paris, where he remained until his death.

The basic split plaguing the young republic was between Buenos Aires and the rest of the provinces. The latter, resentful of their subordinate role since Buenos Aires had become the capital of the viceroyalty, wanted to create a federal government. The Federalists, as they came to be known, believed that federalism was best suited to promoting democracy and liberty and to protecting the social and political diversity of the interior provinces from interference by Buenos Aires. On the other hand, the Unitarians, most of whom were porteños, contended that without a strong central government the republic would fall apart.

The split also had an economic basis. Since commerce was disrupted with Upper Peru and Chile, Buenos Aires was the only port through which the provinces could trade with the external world. However, porteño authorities reaffirmed their colonial rights to impose heavy duties on all goods traded by the provinces. The Federalists of the provinces were also worried that opening the country to unrestricted trade with the rest of the world after independence would enable Buenos Aires to import goods from abroad, in direct competition with their own. Thus, the Federalists supported local autonomy and economic protection, the Unitarians strong central government in Buenos Aires and free trade.

In 1826, the Unitarians seemed to prevail when their leader, porteño Bernardino Rivadavia, was elected the first president of the United Provinces of South America and a constitution was drafted reflecting unitarian principles. However, Rivadavia's success was short-lived: the oligarchy of the provinces rebelled, and a year later Rivadavia was forced to resign. From 1827 until 1862 Argentina fell into a state of virtual continuous civil war. Caudillos (strongmen) commanding armed bands of gaucho cavalrymen monopolized politics during this period, and caudillismo came to symbolize a political leadership that gained popular compliance by personal charisma and the arbitrary use of force. Caudillismo was the antithesis of institutionalization. Relationships between the caudillo and his following were based on *personalismo*, that is, a personal bond between the leader and his subordinates, which distrusted the mediation of impersonal organizations. Therefore, personalismo manifested itself as "the exaltation of, and identification with the leader—el 'caudillo'—at the expense of principles and party platforms."[3] Personalismo and charismatic leadership remained dominant traits of Argentine political life in the decades to follow.

Among the many caudillos who dominated political life in the twenty years following Rivadavia's resignation, Juan Manuel de Rosas was undoubtedly the most important. In 1829, the Buenos Aires provincial legislature appointed Rosas governor. In 1833 he momentarily stepped down, preferring to lead a military expedition to exterminate the Indian population in order to open new territory for grazing and farming in the south. The chaos that followed his departure convinced the Buenos Aires legislature to recall him and grant him dictatorial powers. Rosas was essentially a "conservative autocrat dedicated to the aggrandizement of his own province."[4] His regime was based on conservative values and interests dating back to the colonial era and tried to erase the liberal legacy of the independence war period. Consequently, Rosas's support came from ranchers (*estancieros*), exporters of salted meat (*saladeristas*), the Catholic church, and the gauchos of the pampas, many of whom served in his army. Although a self-proclaimed Federalist, Rosas imposed a centralized and autocratic rule on Buenos Aires. To gain compliance from the caudillos of the surrounding provinces, he gave them autonomy but, at the same time, retained control of the national revenues coming from import-export duties levied at the Buenos Aires port. To strengthen his power, Rosas created an infamous secret police force that terrorized the population, instituted tight censorship, and tortured suspects at will; when he did not publicly execute or assassinate his enemies, he forced them into exile. Rosas did not hesitate to crush those provincial caudillos who defied his authority. In this way, he held the United Provinces of South America together and set the stage for the creation of a nation-state. At the same time, he routinely engaged in wars against Brazil, Uruguay, and Paraguay.

Rosas's protectionist policies clashed with the trading interests of European powers. In the second half of the 1840s, British and French naval vessels set up a blockade to force Rosas to reinstate free trade, but with little success. However, the continuous state of war depleted government finances and disrupted economic activity. In the end, the Tyranny, as Rosas's period was called, ended as it had begun, through violence. In 1851, the caudillo of Entre Ríos, General Justo José de Urquiza, broke his longtime alliance with Rosas and formed a coalition with exiled unitarians, Brazilians, and Uruguayans. A year later, Urquiza's forces defeated Rosas in the battle of Caseros.

After seizing power, Urquiza convened a new constitutional assembly. In 1853, delegates from all the provinces except Buenos Aires signed a new constitution crafted after the U.S. model. With Buenos Aires claiming its independence and retaining trade revenues, conflict with the rest of the country became inevitable and ended in renewed civil war. In 1861 the army of Buenos Aires, commanded by its governor, Bartolomé Mitre, scored a narrow victory over Urquiza's federal forces at Pavón. Finally, both Federalists and Unitarians arrived at a compromise. The provinces watered down their demands for autonomy and accepted free trade in return for revenue sharing and an overrepresentation of the interior in the Senate. For their part, the porteños ratified the 1853 constitution after introducing some minor amendments. In 1862 Buenos Aires became the capital of the new Federal Republic of Argentina, with Mitre as its first president.[5]

With Mitre's inauguration, Argentina entered a new era. The political chaos that had marked the country's history after the declaration of independence ended. From 1862 until 1930 Argentina witnessed unprecedented political stability and economic development. Mitre and his successors devoted their greatest efforts to the building of political institutions, a capable bureaucracy, and modern infrastructures. The post-1862 political elite adopted European positivism as its guiding principle in developing the new nation. In the realm of politics this meant an "enlightened" elitist rule and restricted political participation. Regional caudillos and gauchos represented those Hispanic values believed to be an impediment to progress. In the eyes of President Domingo Sarmiento, who succeeded Mitre, Hispanism was tantamount to barbarism and therefore had to be eliminated. Accordingly, when caudillos and their gaucho bands tried to resist the changes introduced by the new regime, they were crushed without hesitation.

Economically, Argentina was to embrace the export-led development model based on the comparative advantage theory postulated by David Ricardo and John Stuart Mill. The theory, which gave great impetus to the United Kingdom's domination of the world economy, argued that countries should specialize in the production of those goods in which they had an advantage over their competitors and trade them in the international market for goods that were too expensive to produce domestically. As long as all countries concerned put no obstacles on the free flow of goods and services, comparative advantage was expected to work to everyone's benefit. Based upon this rationale, Britain in the nineteenth century began to foster industrialization, in which it had a comparative advantage, and to trade manufactured products for food and raw materials. Argentina quickly fell into this scheme. Although unable to conquer Argentina militarily, the British did so economically in the last quarter of the century, by which time Argentina had become an integral part of the British economic empire. Argentina traded beef and grain for manufactured goods, primarily from the United Kingdom. With the help of British investment and technology, Argentina began to build roads, railways, ports, telegraphs, schools, and slaughterhouses.

Economic progress was halted from 1865 to 1870 by a long and expensive war with Paraguay but after 1880 was resumed at an even greater pace. In that year the city of Buenos Aires became the Federal District, and a new generation of politicians renewed their efforts to stimulate economic growth. This attitude was exemplified by President Julio Roca, who said "Commerce knows far better than government what is in its own best interests; true politics, then, must consist in granting commerce the widest possible freedom. The state should limit itself to establishing the means of communication . . . holding up high the public credit abroad [and] as for immigration, we must protect it at all costs."[6] The results were striking. Between 1862 and 1912 railway tracks increased from 2,000 to 20,000 miles, farmed land expanded from 1.5 million acres to over 60 million, and cattle and sheep ranches were expanded.[7] Industry also flourished in offshoots of the export economy, such as meat packing. Despite several recessions between 1860 and 1930, Argentina had one of the fastest growing economies in the world. It was estimated that the GDP increased yearly at least 5 percent between 1864 and 1914 and a significant 3.5 percent between 1914 and 1930.[8] Most of this spectacular development took place because of the opening up of new land in the pampas. On the other hand, the northwest was hardly touched by these events, because its subsistence agriculture failed to be integrated into the export-oriented economy.

During this same period, Argentine governments, aware that no economic progress could be sustained without a substantial population increase, provided strong incentives to European immigrants. Juan Bautista Alberdi, the father of the 1853 constitution, had said, "To govern is to populate," and his successors took his advice literally. Appreciable immigration started in the 1850s; and it became a serious factor between 1871 and 1914, when 5.9 million foreigners arrived, of whom 3.2 million stayed on. The bulk came from southern Europe: 50 percent were Italians, 25 percent were Spaniards, and the rest were Germans, Swiss, French, Portuguese. eastern Europeans (especially Russian Jews), and Ottomans.[9] Between 1869 and 1929, immigration was responsible for 60 percent of the nation's population growth.[10] Only a few of these people became farmers (through federal grants). Most of the good land had already been taken by large estancieros, and the economic boom of the 1880s made landownership by recent immigrants almost impossible, as land values had appreciated many times. Thus the majority of the immigrants settled in Buenos Aires, Córdoba, and other cities along the Paraná River, where they became shopkeepers, artisans, traders, peddlers, and blue-collar workers. In 1869, Argentina had only 1.8 million inhabitants, but by 1910 the population had risen to 7.8 million, 1.5 million of whom were in Buenos Aires. Urbanization went hand in hand with immigration. The population living in towns with more than 2,000 inhabitants rose from 28.6 percent in 1869 to 52.7 percent in 1914. In the pampas, where most of the immigrants settled, urban dwellers accounted for 62.1 percent in 1914. In that year, half of the Buenos Aires population was foreign. By contrast, the northwest remained rural, and the percentage of foreigners living there was much smaller.[11]

The First Conservative Era

Although during this first Conservative era (1862–1916) the population, both Argentine-born and foreign, found in the thriving economy an opportunity to quickly improve its economic well-being, it remained at the margins of the political process. The founding fathers of the Argentine Republic believed in an elitist democracy where political rights and civil rights were two separate concepts.[12] Political rights, entailing voting and office holding, were restricted to an "enlightened" upper class that appreciated their significance and could translate them into good government. On the other hand, civil rights (the rights to improve one's economic status) were given to the entire population in order to encourage immigration. The ruling elites, afraid that the immigrants could weaken their hold on power once they became citizens, made the naturalization process extremely difficult.[13] The first waves of immigrants, however, saw Argentina as a place to make money quickly before they returned home. Even those who eventually stayed were content that Argentine authorities neither required them to become citizens nor forced them into military service—which was compulsory in most of Europe.

The early years of the conservative era were dominated by a variety of loosely organized political parties. After 1862 most of the conflicts dividing Federalists and Unitarians became obsolete, and other national or autonomist parties appeared. However, these were cliques representing different groups of the upper class—or the *oligarchy*, as it was dubbed in Argentina. The expression of elitist, oligarchic rule took a new form when the National Autonomist party (Partido Autonomista Nacional, or PAN) was created in 1874.[14] In practice, the PAN merged previous conservative groups of provincial and porteño politicians. Throughout its history, the PAN was more a movement of loosely organized political cliques representing provincial notables than a real party. Within it the representatives of the pampas estancieros occupied a progressively more dominant role. The PAN was the embodiment of patronage politics. Starting in 1880 with Julio Roca, its leaders began to occupy the presidency, which made the PAN the "official" party of the new conservative regime. The objective of the PAN was to further the socioeconomic interests of the dominant elites, using the state as its primary vehicle. "The concern of the elite for control over the State was dictated by the role of the national government as a major source of credit and as a bridge for lucrative contracts with foreign capital."[15] At election time, party candidates were selected through backdoor agreements among provincial bosses. Until 1889, the PAN ruled virtually unopposed by co-opting political foes through favors or government jobs. When co-optation failed, physical intimidation and electoral frauds were used to discourage political opposition.[16]

Biased Political Institutions

The federal constitution of 1853, still in place today, justified the elitist rule that followed. However, its ambiguous nature created many contradictions, which later would allow populist and authoritarian governments to interpret it in ways that would legitimize their undemocratic rule. As the constitution was crafted after the U.S. model, it called for separation of powers among the presidency, the legislature, and the judiciary; in practice such separation was ignored. Elected for a six-year term (but without the possibility of a second consecutive term), the president has the authority to declare a state of siege (Article 23) when "internal disorder" threatens the constitutional government. A state of siege automatically suspends all constitutional rights, allows for the deportation of political opponents, and permits the president to rule by decree, thus bypassing congressional approval. Because the constitution does not specify what constitutes internal disorder, Article 23 has often been invoked to crack down on political opposition. Because the constitution also gave the president control over the bureaucratic apparatus and government appointments, his power was further strengthened.

The contradictions of the Argentine republican system were evident not only in practice but on paper as well. Nominally a federal republic, Argentina referred to its different components not as states but as provinces, that is, administrative subdivisions characteristic of some of the highly centralized European monarchies of the nineteenth century. The provinces, despite having their own legislatures and appointing their representatives to Congress, had in reality limited powers. In fact, governors could rig local provincial elections, and thus local legislatures were often subservient to the governors. The governors in turn usually complied with the president due to his powers of intervention. Moreover, the provinces lacked not only political autonomy but fiscal independence as well. Most of their revenues came from the federal government, which had almost absolute control over tax collection. With the oligarchy in control, revenues did not come from property or income taxes but rather from the taxation of consumer goods, licenses, and imports. In the end, elite rule was self-perpetuating; presidents and governors from elite circles were elected and supported in office through political alliances based upon clientele agreements, force, and fraud.

As for Congress, aside from the 1912–1930 and 1983–1993 periods, it has hardly played a meaningful role. Many presidents regarded it as a mere rubber stamp for their bills. When Congress refused to acquiesce, presidents simply declared a state of siege and sent its members home. During the conservative era, "decisions tended to be made by the president and a small group of friends and advisers; some of the members of this group may have been congressional representatives, but it was their socioeconomic status that made them members of the political elite, not the offices they held."[17]

The Argentine judicial system was equally weak. Although empowered with the right of judicial review, the Supreme Court, with few exceptions, sanctioned the biased laws the Conservative administrations kept proposing. Later on, when Supreme Court justices tried to exercise their independence, supposedly guaranteed by their life appointment, they were fired and replaced by colleagues more pleasing to the government of the day. This happened in 1946, 1955, 1966, and 1976. (As recently as 1990, President Menem "packed" the Supreme Court by appointing five additional justices to ensure that his reform policies would not be overturned.) Another fact damaging the Supreme Court's prestige was its inclination, after 1930, to acknowledge the legitimacy of de facto governments that had resulted from military coups. Moreover, the Argentine Supreme Court, like that of the United States, has traditionally refused to hear "political questions." Yet a crucial difference was that, in Argentina, any time a case might pit the Supreme Court against the ruling administration, the justices refused to hear it on these grounds. Furthermore, the politicization of judges in lower courts added to the general perception that the legal system was biased and ineffective. Legal proceedings were often "merely . . . a figleaf to cover the predations of state-sanctioned lawbreakers."[18]

The combination of all these factors allowed political power to be concentrated in the presidency; to a large degree, this is still the case. Perhaps President Sarmiento put it best when he said that a president "does and will do what he wants, because this is a republic without citizens, without public opinion, educated by tyranny."[19] In such a climate, the president is all-powerful but, conversely, is perceived by interest groups and common citizens, alike, as all-responsible. With parties merely transitory phenomena supporting the ambitions of upper-class politicians, interest groups pressed their demands directly on the president rather than on Congress. "Those speaking for most groups were well aware that the president could meet their demands by issuing an executive decree, by bringing pressure to bear on the bureaucracy, or, if necessary, by obtaining the enactment of legislation by Congress."[20]

From Conservative to Radical Hegemony

The PAN's use and abuse of constitutional provisions and its political patronage worked as long as the landowning elites were cohesive enough to overcome their internal differences and the vast majority of the citizenry could be kept socially and economically subordinated. However, those two conditions began to disappear at the turn of the century. Contrary to what the elitist ideologues of the 1853 constitution had believed, economic opportunities could no longer satisfy the lower strata of society. Instead, the economic boom had brought with it an increasing awareness among the emerging middle and working classes that they were getting only the crumbs of the country's prosperity. Now they were demanding not only a bigger slice of the economic pie but also a say on how the pie was divided. The PAN's exclusionary practices under which the oligarchy thrived were no longer to be tolerated. The political mobilization of these sectors created, in turn, deep divisions among the elites. Some thought that a greater dose of repression was the only remedy; others, like former President Carlos Pellegrini, were convinced that the answer rested in opening up the political system and incorporating the middle sectors into a new conservative party.[21]

To be sure, the leadership of the protest movement came primarily from estranged elements of the privileged class. In 1889, upper-class university students began to denounce the corruption of the PAN's administration, and a year later they organized the Civic Union (Unión Cívica). Students quickly found a common cause with other unsatisfied members of the landowning elite (e.g., former President Mitre), young military officers, ambitious urban politicians (e.g., Leandro Alem), and those Catholics who resented the separation of church and state advocated by the regime. Yet the Civic Union's support remained slim. In 1890, it launched an unsuccessful revolt against the government. Soon afterward the Civic Union was dissolved, and from its ashes Alem formed the UCR. The UCR ideology remained vague; it campaigned for universal male suffrage, a more representative political system, and greater local autonomy. At the same time, the Radicals believed that as long as the electoral process was in the hands of the Conservatives there was no reason to play a loyal opposition. Accordingly, under the motto of Revolutionary Intransigence, the Radicals boycotted elections and, instead, cultivated the idea that power could be achieved only through violence and by opposing any compromise with the Conservatives. In 1893 and again in 1905, the UCR launched armed revolts with the support of some young officers, but on both occasions it was defeated.

In 1896 Alem committed suicide, and UCR leadership was taken over by Hipólito Yrigoyen, his nephew. Yrigoyen was an enigmatic figure, who cultivated an image of mystery. Allegedly, he had a very austere life-style and hardly ever appeared in public or addressed large crowds. Instead, he strengthened personal loyalty among fellow Radicals through one-on-one contacts. With time, this enabled him to rely on a party organization that was hierarchically structured and controlled by his followers. Such an organization took the form of local committees, which executed his decisions and popularized his ideas. Like the Conservatives, Radical ward bosses used patronage networks to gain votes. The crucial difference was that the Radicals made a concerted effort to engage the support of the urban middle classes, while the Conservatives did not. As in the 1890s, after 1905 the Radical leadership still drew heavily from the upper class, but by then it had appreciably broadened its support to include large numbers of middle-class, first-generation Argentines. The latter, usually employed in government and other service sector activities, were eager to gain access to higher status employment, which they perceived the oligarchy as having kept for itself. Since the Radicals pledged to replace the oligarchy as Argentina's new ruling elite and to use the state to reward their followers, they appealed to these emerging middle sectors. Ironically, the content of the Radical propaganda, in spite of luring many children of immigrants, was highly xenophobic. A partial explanation for this stance can perhaps be found in Yrigoyen's preoccupation with strengthening the young Argentine state; this could not be achieved if children of immigrants continued their parents' habit of looking back to Europe for self-identity and allegiance. Thus Yrigoyen's appeals were directed to Argentine citizens. Recent and old immigrants were purposely ignored in the Radicals' call for the universal franchise.

Since Yrigoyen kept Radicalism ideologically vague, it was easy to transform it into a vehicle of personal politics. In Yrigoyen's view, Radicalism was a political movement, since, like the PAN, it pretended to be the expression of national unity. Using a rationale similar to other movements that followed, Yrigoyen equated Radicalism with the "harmony of classes," "distributive justice," and a "national renovation," of which he was of course the true interpreter.[22] Thus Radicalism quickly became identified with Yrigoyenism.

There was an additional element of intolerance in Yrigoyen's rhetoric: because the Radical quest for greater political participation was tantamount to the "cause" for which the whole nation was striving, any opposition to this cause was regarded as antination. Thus, the deep-seated intolerance for diversity manifested earlier by the Conservatives was now manifested by the very people advocating greater democratic participation. Ascribing to national opinion, what today we would label "political correctness" became a dominant and unfortunate trait of the Argentine political discourse. Like his Conservative predecessors, Yrigoyen strove for political hegemony rather than democratic debate.

Under Yrigoyen's leadership Radicalism upheld an uncompromising commitment to popular democracy and to the principles of government accountability and honest administration. However, the group lacked a constructive or detailed plan for reform and tended to present democracy as a panacea. Behind the rebellious exterior most Radicals were largely conservative in orientation, their attitudes for the most part falling within a continuum between conservative paternalism and liberal laissez faire. The doctrines of Radicalism also betrayed more corporatist influences. Radicals proclaimed their ethical superiority to their political rivals. They were less concerned with the instrumental significance of popular democracy than with its normative functions to promote the common good.[23]

At the beginning of the twentieth century, socialists, syndicalists, and anarchists started to organize the poor working class of Buenos Aires into unions. Between 1902 and 1910 the country was hit by a wave of strikes that further deteriorated the Conservatives' political leadership. In 1909, the PAN ceased to exist, splitting into a number of provincial conservative parties. In 1912, hoping to convince the Radicals to ease their opposition and join forces against labor and left-wing parties, the Conservative-dominated Congress approved a sweeping electoral reform. The Sáenz Peña electoral law (named after the president who introduced it) established universal and obligatory suffrage for all males, the secret ballot, and minority representation in Congress. In promulgating the law, the Conservatives' intention was one of "sharing" power with the Radicals from a position of strength in order to prevent a socialist revolution.[24] In fact, the Sáenz Peña Law discriminated against foreigners, who were barred from voting. This certainly pleased the Radicals, whose electorate drew heavily from the middle sectors. The rationale for this exclusion was that most foreigners were in the working class, which was now perceived as the main threat to oligarchic rule. However, the Sáenz Peña Law increased voter participation (from 190,000 in 1910 to 1.4 million in 1928) beyond the Conservatives' expectations. More important, most of the new voters were no longer from the upper class.[25] In 1916, Yrigoyen was elected president with 46 percent of the popular vote, as opposed to 26 percent for all the conservative parties' candidates combined. Never again would the Conservatives win office at the ballot box through honest elections. Their reform had backfired, and their electoral hegemony had collapsed.

Between 1916 and 1930 Radical administrations ruled Argentina, establishing themselves as the country's new dominant party. However, once in power, they made only marginal changes in the existing capital accumulation system. Although the UCR's electoral support came primarily from the middle sectors, its leadership remained in the hands of members from the landowning and commercial elites. Yrigoyen himself was a property owner, and his successor, President Marcelo T. de

Alvear, was a direct descendant of one of Argentina's wealthiest ranching families. Moreover, a large number of Radical congressmen and cabinet ministers were members of the landowning elites. Thus, it is no surprise that first Yrigoyen and then Alvear promoted the free-trade economic policies of the previous conservative administrations that had benefited the landed elites. In 1919, Yrigoyen ordered that a tenant farmers' strike be crushed and during his two terms in office ignored the plea of rural laborers for land reform. Radical presidents were moderate reformers whose aim was to maintain the allegiance of their constituency through the use of political patronage. State jobs were created way beyond government needs to please the middle class, industrialists were granted some protectionist legislation, and students obtained reform of the university system.

Yrigoyen also made some attempt to incorporate the working class in his movement by having Congress pass some labor legislation—which, however, was hardly ever enforced. Workers' unrest built up during Yrigoyen's first administration due to high unemployment, poor pay, and miserable working conditions. Beginning in 1916 a wave of strikes hit Buenos Aires particularly hard, culminating in the bloodshed of the Tragic Week (Semana Trágica) of 1919, during which hundreds of workers and innocent Jewish immigrants were killed by right-wing, xenophobic, vigilante gangs. The 1919 events put an end to labor militancy and discouraged Yrigoyen from further pursuing the working class electorate for the rest of his first term.

Contradicting many of their proposals for clean government, made when in the opposition, the Radicals proved to be as corrupt as their predecessors. Clientelism and corruption under Yrigoyen rose to a new high, and the president himself ignored democratic procedures when they became obstacles to his policies. Although federal intervention had been an established practice in the Conservative era, taking place eighty-two times between 1862 and 1911, Yrigoyen set a new record during his first term, intervening in twenty provinces to demote Conservative governors and local legislatures. In so doing, the president hardened the opposition in Congress. However, probably more destructive was the fact that the Radicals, like their predecessors, weakened democratic institutions whenever they saw fit.

During President Alvear's term (1922–1928) the greatest concerns were in the economic sphere. As the international demand for Argentine agricultural products dropped, the economy began to experience difficulties. To make things worse, Yrigoyen's clientelistic policies had created a substantial fiscal deficit, and Alvear's budgetary cuts hurt many of Yrigoyen's supporters. By 1924, Alvear had lost the support of Yrigoyen and his loyalists, and the party split in two. Those loyal to Alvear, usually from the conservative sectors of the party, named themselves antipersonalists, a label that was an explicit denunciation of

Yrigoyen's highly personalized, autocratic style. The power struggle between antipersonalists and personalists (Yrigoyen's supporters) ended in favor of the latter when, in 1928, Yrigoyen won a second term. Although losing ground in upper-class districts, Yrigoyen more than compensated for the loss by increasing his following in working class districts. By 1928, the middle-class nature of Radicalism became more evident, allowing Yrigoyen to capture 60 percent of the popular vote.[26]

Yrigoyen's second term would not last long, though. The renewed political patronage exercised by his administration led again to a fiscal deficit on the eve of the Great Depression. Political opposition also stiffened in the face of the mounting corruption of government officials. The impact of the world depression was devastating to the Argentine economy and hardened social confrontation. Commercial and land-owning elites put pressure on the government to cut its deficit and redirect funds from social programs to subsidies for business. The middle class, on the other hand, demanded greater government spending to sustain employment levels and the purchasing power of wages. Caught in between, an increasingly senile Yrigoyen fell victim to his own mistakes as much as to the incompatible demands that the depression had triggered.

The Conservative Restoration

In September 1930 a military coup put an end to the chaos that political polarization had created. The coup was a turning point in Argentine history for a number of reasons. It set a precedent in justifying military intervention, making the armed forces the ultimate arbiter of how the political game was to be played. Although military officers had been courted before by Radicals and Conservatives alike, the coup institutionalized the involvement of the military in political matters. This set in motion a pernicious trend, which would eventually disrupt not only the political system but also the internal cohesion of the armed forces.

Equally important, the coup demonstrated that conservative political and economic groups had lost faith in the democratic process and had concluded that the old elitist, authoritarian approach was the only way to govern what they believed to be an unruly citizenry. The year 1930 saw the end of the golden age of Argentine socioeconomic development. Whereas from 1862 to 1930 the country had attained a degree of political stability and economic development unprecedented in Latin America and southern Europe, after 1930 political instability and sluggish economic growth would go hand in hand, exacerbating further societal conflicts.

Soon after the coup, the right wing of the military took control of the government, and its leader, General (retired) José Uriburu became provisional president. Uriburu was an ultraconservative officer coming from one of the most prominent landowning families of the interior. As a strict Catholic and nationalist, Uriburu openly expressed his intention to create a corporatist, authoritarian state resembling Italian fascism. However, his project quickly collapsed due to the opposition of the bulk of the military and their civilian supporters. Consequently, in 1931 Uriburu called for a new election, won by General Augustín Justo, an antipersonalist Radical. His administration put back in power those conservative elements of society that had ruled before 1916.

Between 1932 and 1943 a coalition of the conservatives of the National Democratic party, antipersonalist Radicals, and Independent Socialists (a moderate splinter group of the Socialist party) supported what came to be known as the Concordancia regime. Following the Justo administration, subsequent presidents of the Concordancia were forced to rig elections to prevent Radicals and socialists from defeating them. The period was dubbed, depending which side one was on, as either the Era of Patriotic Fraud or the Infamous Decade. In spite of its tarnished democratic record, the leaders of the Concordancia proved to be imaginative policy makers. They pulled Argentina out of the Great Depression and promoted important economic reforms, although their foremost concern was to protect the interests of the landed and commercial elites. An independent Central Bank was created, the budget was balanced, the foreign exchange system was reformed, and Argentina honored its external debt, the only South American country to do so. Dropping the dogma of free-trade economics, Concordancia administrations made a concerted effort to use state regulation to revive the economy. Counter cyclical measures were enacted to offset the negative effects of the depression. Government subsidized agricultural production, funded infrastructure programs, and protected domestic industry to put people back to work. In so doing, it created the basis for the ISI policies, which would be greatly expanded in the decades that followed.

The industrialization process had profound consequences not only for the structure of the whole economy but for the country's social structure as well. In the 1880–1916 period, economic development had been carried out by foreign immigrants, but in the late 1930s and early 1940s the growing demand for industrial workers was met by Argentine-born children of immigrants and poor people from the north and northwest who flocked to the cities in search of a better living.[27] The new urban working class differed from that of the predepression period in at least two respects. First, most of its members were citizens and, hence, potential voters. Second, communist, socialist, and syndicalist labor activists had been successful in organizing workers, so by 1943 the Argentine labor movement was the largest in Latin America.

The early 1940s put additional strains on the Concordancia: the outbreak of war in Europe created additional economic difficulties, as world trade was again disrupted, and more important, as time went on, both the Allies and the Axis put pressure on Argentina to take sides. While the rest of Latin America had little problem giving token support to the Allies, in Argentina the predominantly pro-Axis military establishment prevented such a choice. By 1943, the situation had once again reached a political stalemate. Working class unrest grew, while in Congress the Radicals blocked any government initiative. In response, the unpopular and autocratic President Ramón Castillo imposed a state of siege, ruling by decree more often than not. The use of electoral fraud and of emergency presidential powers had, in the eyes of the military, delegitimized the Concordancia. This conclusion reinforced the idea held by many officers that the liberal democracy was not viable in Argentina and that what was needed was a strong authoritarian government like those in contemporary Spain, Italy, and Germany. Indeed, what tipped the balance was Castillo's decision to support the candidacy of a pro-Allies politician in the upcoming presidential elections. At that point, the military intervened for the second time in two decades, and in June 1943 they deposed Castillo. Once again, the nation's political institutions had failed to adapt to the changing times. It had ignored the demands of new emerging groups of political participants, particularly the working class, which had increased in size but still did not benefit from the capitalist economy.[28]

As in 1930, the provisional military government was nationalistic and right wing. Organized labor was repressed, many unionists and left-wing politicians were jailed, and press censorship was enforced. However, following a pattern that would repeat itself in the years to follow, military officers could agree on removing an unpopular administration but not on what to do next. Rather dramatic squabbles developed, leading to a rapid succession of three military administrations between 1943 and 1946. During this period an obscure army colonel, Juan Domingo Perón, would acquire such a following and political power as to make him the gray eminence behind the military government and the master of Argentine politics for the next thirty years.

The Rise of Peronism

Perón, better than anyone else at the time, perceived how much the nature of Argentine society had changed and realized that the opportunity was there for him to make the difference. Neither the old party system nor the military had proved capable of meeting the challenge that industrialization had brought. Whereas many of his fellow officers viewed working class demands as destabilizing, Perón reasoned that the pleas of workers could no longer be ignored and, if not addressed, would be exploited by communists.[29] However, if properly channeled, the working class pleas for better wages and standard of living would not only avert a revolution but would also enhance the power of whoever was capable of articulating such demands. "Perón was not the originator of social change: he merely capitalized on existing trends."[30]

Perón was a conservative at heart and an outspoken admirer of Italy's Mussolini, whom he observed closely when he was a military attaché in the Argentine embassy in Rome during the late 1930s. He envisioned the creation of a new conservative coalition to thwart the communist threat, but there did not seem to be a constituency for it at the time. The existing conservative parties were too discredited and too tied to the interests of the landed and commercial elites. The Radicals, divided and intransigent as ever to compromise, refused to join Perón. The working class, which both Conservatives and Radicals had neglected, was the only societal sector whose leadership had not been won by any party. Perón recognized the political potential of the working class and quickly proceeded toward its politicization.

From the unheralded post of head of the Labor and Social Welfare Department, Perón skillfully pursued his quest for power. He regrouped the weak and divided Argentine unions into the regenerated CGT, the equivalent of the U.S. AFL-CIO, which had been created in 1930 by socialists and syndicalists. Union leaders who resisted Perón's favors were repressed. Between 1944 and 1945 Perón established collective bargaining and social welfare programs, set up labor courts, and granted a month's extra pay and paid vacations. Moreover, the requirement of only one union per branch of activity and mandatory union fees greatly enhanced labor's strength. Perón did not stop here. Besides gaining control over most unions, he unionized marginal workers who had recently arrived in the cities, the *descamisados* (shirtless ones), who had been previously left out of the labor movement. Perón gave these people for the first time a political identity, self-respect, and most important, tangible material benefits.

The labor movement, greatly enlarged and strengthened, became Perón's strongest supporter and from then on played a role in Argentine political life that no government could ever again ignore. Thus, while in Western Europe the working class movement gained its status through a sequence of struggles with government and entrepreneurs, in Argentina social benefits were granted from above, thanks to the paternalism of a charismatic leader. After 1943, the working class came to identify itself with Perón and his *justicialista* (social justice) rhetoric. In practical terms it meant an income distribution toward the lower middle class and the working class through high wages, cheap social services, and full employment. *Justicialismo* pretended to represent a "third position," steering the middle ground between the two contending ideologies of the time—free-market capitalism and Marxism-Leninism. Based on some of the corporatist themes of fascism and nazism, Perón's third position, announced in 1944, postulated that the state "should harmonize the interests of employers and employees and thereby promote true social justice."[31] From then on, it was the state, rather than the market, that decided how economic resources were allocated. Indeed, under Perón state interventionism through regulation of business activities, the creation of monopolistic state companies, and interference in business-labor relations reached an all-time high. In foreign policy, the third position saw Argentina as the leader of the nonaligned countries; this would entail rejecting the cold war mentality established by the U.S.-USSR confrontation and would fulfill Argentina's destiny as a regional power. Yet the third position never gained much support, as many Latin American neighbors remained suspicious of Perón's hegemonic intentions. Worst of all, it angered the United States, which had replaced the United Kingdom as Argentina's trading partner of industrial goods. Already upset by Perón's sympathies for fascism, Washington after 1946 looked upon Argentina's defiant attitude in international affairs with anxiety. As a result, relations between the two countries remained strained.

By August 1944 Perón had acquired enormous power. Besides being secretary of the Department of Labor and Social Welfare, he soon became minister of war, chairman of the Postwar Council, and vice president. His astonishing political career created resentment and opposition among more senior officers. Many of them despised Perón's overture to labor and his relationship with María Eva Duarte (Evita), who had been instrumental in rallying popular support for the new caudillo. Perón's companion, who later became his wife, was an actress whose humble origins and doubtful moral reputation were viewed as unacceptable for an army officer by many of his colleagues. On October 9, 1945, a palace coup removed Perón from all his positions and sent him to a prison on a remote island.

To the amazement of coup leaders, union leaders rallied enormous popular support for Perón, which reached its climax on 17 October when a quarter million people staged a mass demonstration in front of the presidential residence demanding Perón's release. Fearing bloodshed, anti-Peronist officers gave up, and Perón was freed. This event constituted a personal triumph for Perón and legitimized his quest for the presidency, whose election had been scheduled for the following year. Unionists offered Perón the head of the Labor party (Partido Laborista) ticket, a political formation they had created after the 17 October demonstrations. In February 1946, Perón was elected by a broad coalition marked by strong nationalist overtones, which in addition to labor included large sectors of the armed forces, the Catholic church (which appreciated Perón's endorsement of the reintroduction of Catholic teachings in public schools), and some professional and business associations. If the enfranchisement of the middle class was fundamental in helping the Radicals gain political supremacy between 1916 and 1930, the urban working class and petite bourgeoisie were responsible for the election of Perón.

Perón's political style was often referred to as populist. Lacking any coherent ideological content, his populism took the form of "a movement led by dissident members of the elite who bid for the support of the lower class through promises of benefits."[32] Robert Kaufman and Barbara Stallings define populism as a phenomenon involving "a set of *economic policies* designed to achieve specific *political goals*. These political goals are: (1) mobilizing support within organized labor and lower-middle-class groups; (2) obtaining complementary backing from domestically oriented business; and (3) politically isolating the rural oligarchy, foreign enterprises, and large-scale domestic industrial elites. The economic policies to attain these goals include, but are not limited to: (1) budget deficits to stimulate domestic demand; (2) nominal wage increases plus price controls to effect income distribution; and (3) exchange-rate control or appreciation to cut inflation and to raise wages and profits in nontraded-goods sectors."[33]

Many of these characteristics applied to Peronism. In an era of mass mobilization, Perón resorted not to crude force, as was characteristic of the old caudillos, but to a variety of means to gain public acceptance. The most important means were a strong nationalistic and antioligarchic rhetoric, emotional appeals, mass rallies, economic policies that emphasized income distribution in favor of supporting groups (i.e., labor, sympathetic businessmen, political cronies) rather than economic rationality, and political participation by previously marginal social sectors. Moreover, like caudillismo, populism's main feature was strong charismatic leadership and a direct bond between the leader and the population without any institutional mediation (e.g., party structure or Congress).

During his first administration Perón continued his pro-working-class policies. The ISI strategy received renewed emphasis. For Perón and his economic advisers, ISI would free Argentina from its reliance on agricultural exports, since the country would produce the manufactured goods it had previously imported and hence would become economically independent. By the same token, the industrialization process would absorb the labor force that Argentine agriculture could not employ. This new labor force would become, in turn, part of the Peronist movement through the unionization process.

Between 1946 and 1948, Perón's effort concentrated on income distribution. During this period real wages increased by 62 percent, double the rate of inflation. The large wage increases enabled new consumers to buy goods, many of which were now produced domestically. Perón also greatly expanded government expenditures by enlarging the public bureaucracy, nationalizing utility companies, railways, and domestic and foreign manufacturing industries, and creating new industry and commerce under state ownership. The large employment that these initiatives generated was used to reward followers and consolidate Perón's support among the working class and white-collar workers. Overstaffing and corruption in the public sector, which had marked the patronage approach to policy making of Conservative and Radical administrations, reached an unprecedented high under Perón. Expenditures to sustain the ever expanding public sector were funded in part by substantial gold reserves that the Argentine Central Bank had put aside during World War II and by revenues coming from the Argentine Trade Promotion Institute (Instituto Argentino de Promoción del Intercambio, or IAPI). The IAPI established a monopoly over the commercialization of agricultural goods by purchasing beef and grain from producers at very low prices and selling them at much higher prices to foreign customers. Perón refrained from promoting land redistribution, but through the IAPI he saw to it that a large part of the landed elites' profits financed his populist policies. From using the state to increase its wealth and political power, the old oligarchy was now being used by the same state it had helped corrupt. The manipulation of the economy to satisfy political needs became an overt feature of Peronism, although it alienated the landed elites. It created a "hybrid economic system in which a welfare state without a plan and capitalism without a free market uneasily coexisted."[34]

Although Perón had been elected in honest elections, his regime became increasingly authoritarian. The Peronist party, which later replaced the Labor party, was essentially an electoral machine used at election time and played no role in institutionalizing the movement. In order to remain in power, Perón had Congress pass a new constitution so that he could run for reelection, which he did successfully in 1952. Political intimidation became endemic to the point that many anti-Peronists referred to Perón's rule as "the second tyranny" (the first one being that of Rosas). For Perón democracy made sense when it enhanced his grip on power but not when it could be used to challenge his leadership. In his view, when pluralism was used to criticize him it became sectarianism.[35] Widespread censorship made freedom of speech and of the press virtually impossible. In the name of social justice and class harmony, he purged the federal judiciary, packed the Supreme Court with Peronists, violated the independence of the university system, fired many professors, and harassed, jailed, and often drove into exile opposition leaders. Another aspect of Peronism was its demagoguery. Although Perón can be credited with granting women the right to vote (1949) and for the construction of schools, hospitals, and affordable housing, he and Evita started a cult of personality typical of dictatorial regimes.[36] When faced with specific crises, the Peróns used mass rallies to turn their followers against those who dared to criticize the administration. These rallies often ended in acts of violence by the Peronist rank and file. In 1953, when the church began to criticize Perón's decision to introduce bills in Congress legalizing prostitution and divorce, the president's response was to turn loose his followers. Peronist activists set churches on fire, triggering Pope Pius XII's excommunication of all who had ordered and carried out violent action against the church.

The expansionary, redistributive policies came to an end in 1949, when the country suffered a serious balance of payments deficit. With the Central Bank and the treasury's coffers depleted, Perón took a more pragmatic approach to economic policy and in 1952 adopted some stabilization measures with the compliance of the labor movement. Perón asked the workers to be patient and to tighten their belts for a while, and they did. By then, though, most other sectors of society had become outraged with the president's authoritarianism. Former allies like the Catholic church and large segments of the armed forces joined the political opposition, made up of most parties and business interest groups. A first coup failed in 1951, but in September 1955 the anti-Peronist coalition headed by army and navy officers was strong enough to depose Perón, who fearing a civil war, went into exile.

The Peronist Proscription Period

The coup leader, General Eduardo Lonardi, wanted to avoid further political backlash. He thought that the best solution was to compromise with the Peronists and told the nation that there would be "neither victors nor vanquished." However, the more hard-line groups within the coup coalition believed that the only solution was to get rid of not only Perón but Peronism. When Lonardi stood firm in his plan for national reconciliation, he was tossed out after only fifty days. General Pedro Aramburu was sworn in as provisional president in his place.

The Liberating Revolution regime headed by Aramburu set out to erase any Peronist legacy. Many Peronists employed in the federal bureaucracy were dismissed, and the Peronist party was banned. Schools, squares, streets, and so on named after the exiled president or Evita were renamed. Many union leaders were jailed and the labor movement "democratized," which meant that the CGT and most unions were taken over by government bureaucrats. Later, a new labor law tried to favor the election of non-Peronist candidates more willing to collaborate with the new authorities. However, this effort was to no avail. Years of mass mobilization had made unions very well organized and politically skillful. In the face of harsh repression by the military, Peronist labor leaders and their followers closed ranks and boycotted the new authorities. Thus the political spectrum became further polarized. In the realm of economics, Aramburu was unable to reverse many of Perón's interventionist policies due to the opposition of the UCR and powerful distributional coalitions. The half-way measures implemented during Aramburu's tenure achieved no tangible lasting results, and by the time a civilian president stepped in, the economic situation had further deteriorated.

In early 1958, when Argentines went to the polls to elect their new president, the country was deeply divided. Before withdrawing to their barracks, the military had vetoed any Peronist candidacy in the upcoming elections. This meant excluding the political representation of about a third of the electorate, thus creating serious legitimacy problems for the winner. With the Peronists outlawed, the Radicals were left to contest elections against a number of smaller, regionally based conservative parties. However, in 1957 the Radicals had split over the Peronist problem. Party leader Ricardo Balbín wanted to run on a platform of vague economic nationalism and a refusal to deal with the Peronists. His deputy Arturo Frondizi reasoned that, to promote economic growth and political stability, it was necessary to incorporate the Peronists into the political system. The conflict between the two Radical leaders was irreconcilable. Half the party went with Balbín, renaming itself the People's Radical Civic Union (Unión Cívica Radical del Pueblo, or UCRP), and half with Frondizi, taking the name of Intransigent Radical Civic Union (Unión Cívica Radical Intransigente, or UCRI).

Thanks to a secret pact with Perón, in exile in Venezuela, Frondizi captured most of the Peronist vote and became president. This pact, though, discredited Frondizi in the eyes of the armed forces, business groups, and the UCRP, which regarded his administration as illegitimate. Frondizi soon found out that, had he maintained his promises to Perón, he would have triggered a military coup. After increasing wages by 50 percent and allowing Peronist leaders to retake control of their old unions, Frondizi thought he could count on labor support. He was wrong. Unions quickly made more demands, which the president could not meet, and after only five months in office Frondizi had to reverse most of his economic policies. His adoption of deflationary measures cost him union support, yet it did not gain him the support of the military, business, and the opposition parties. For four years Frondizi struggled to govern a country in which opposition forces were constantly creating the conditions for a military takeover. Although an ambitious plan was carried out to give the country modern heavy industry, political polarization doomed Frondizi to failure. In March 1962, the president made his last gamble when he allowed Peronist candidates to run for the midterm and gubernatorial elections. Contrary to his expectations, it was the Peronists, not the UCRI, that came out victorious, although by a narrow margin. A few weeks afterward, the commanders in chief of the armed forces deposed Frondizi, who had by then lost most of the popular backing he had enjoyed in 1958.

For the remainder of 1962 the country fell into chaos as rival military factions battled each other. The hard-line faction within the armed forces (*colorados*) wanted to establish a pure military dictatorship devoted to the eradication of Peronism. More moderate elements of the military (*azules*) believed, on the contrary, that their best option was to concentrate on professional matters, leaving to civilians the task of tackling the socioeconomic crisis. Eventually, the latter group prevailed, and in 1963 new elections took place. Once again the Peronists were banned from participating.

The new president, Arturo Illia, came from the ranks of the UCRP. Elected with only 26 percent of the popular vote, Illia was a minority president from the start. Moreover, since he was unwilling to form coalitions with other parties and had no congressional majority, his policy agenda was severely crippled. Thus, only a few months into his term, Illia found himself attacked from all sides. To make things worse, labor unions staged a wave of strikes to discredit the administration. Although isolated and harassed by political parties, business, and labor, Illia refused to use repressive measures to silence his opponents. His economic policies tried to protect domestic industry and compensate the working class for some of the losses it suffered under Frondizi—but that was not enough. The military, witnessing a deterioration of the socioeconomic situation, interpreted Illia's moderation as a refusal to act. In March 1966, the top brass of the armed forces removed Illia from power and asked the former commander in chief of the army, General Juan Carlos Onganía, to take charge.

The Argentine Revolution

The 1966 coup had been a foregone conclusion for almost a year, and it received widespread support. In the minds of many Argentines, the situation had reached a point of no return. Some drastic action had to be taken, although nobody, not even the commanders in chief of the armed forces, knew exactly what to do. This is probably why they decided to urge Onganía out of retirement. Onganía had been the army commander until 1965, when Illia forced him to quit. He enjoyed great respect among the officer corps due to his high professional standards and personal integrity.[37] It was due to Onganía's effort that military hard-liners had been defeated in 1963 and the country returned to civilian rule.

The Argentine Revolution, as the new regime presented itself, was meant to be a watershed. In his government, Onganía claimed to represent the concern of all Argentines to break the political impasse of the post-Peronist period. Such an impasse, according to Onganía, demonstrated the unworkability of the democratic system. Democracy had failed to promote political stability and economic development, which were the country's top priorities. Onganía promised to achieve those goals by instituting a new brand of authoritarian regime, whose policies would be based upon technical rationality as opposed to the "political" reasoning of the previous Peronist and Radical administrations. In practice, the leaders of the armed forces reluctantly gave Onganía a blank check, entrusting him with the power to do whatever he felt necessary.

Ambitious plans were announced for the creation of a new political system based on corporatist principles, but as time went by, the new regime seemed to concentrate more on destroying than on creating. In fact, Congress was dismantled, provincial legislatures and municipal councils were dissolved, governors were removed, the Supreme Court was packed, state universities were purged of "leftist" faculty and administrators, and political parties were dissolved. Notably, Onganía stopped short of an all-out confrontation with labor, still the most formidable political force; on the contrary, he tried to establish a working relationship with those union leaders willing to collaborate, while repressing those who did not.

Throughout Onganía's tenure there was little revolutionary change to speak of. The new regime seemed to be unclear about what kind of political institutions should replace the discredited pluralist model. In part, this was due to the lack of consensus among Onganía's closest advisers and the socioeconomic groups supporting the administration in identifying the problems that were at the root of the Argentine crisis. Rather naively, Onganía came to the conclusion that the enforcement of law and order and the achievement of economic stability would solve all the country's ills. The latter task was given to Adalbert Krieger Vasena, a distinguished economist who earlier had served as minister of the economy under President Aramburu.

While Krieger Vasena remained in office (from 1967 to mid-1969), Argentina experienced an economic stability that it has not achieved since. By 1969 growth had resumed substantially, inflation had dropped to 7.3 percent (the lowest since 1954), real wages purchasing power and their share of the GDP were above the 1965 average, unemployment had fallen, and the budget deficit was reduced significantly.[38] Unlike the 1964 Brazilian military government, whose stringent monetarist measures had induced a major recession, Krieger Vasena successfully combined stabilization and growth without affecting employment. This was achieved by combining fiscal austerity and exchange and price controls with moderate monetary expansion, export promotion, and a balanced income policy. (See table 2.1.)

For a time, Onganía seemed to succeed. On the political front, most political forces were disbanded, but the problem was that they never completely disappeared. In fact,

> the nation's political parties were dissolved (as they had been dissolved before), yet the major parties, with all their defects, were not really destroyed, but rather forced into temporary hibernation; those parties taking part in the 1973 elections behaved in a manner almost indistinguishable from the behavior of those taking part in the 1963 elections. The organized labor movement was neither unified nor depoliticized; the cleavage between the official CGT and the CGT of the Argentines was as deep as the former split between Peronists and Independents, and the followers of Augusto Vandor. Student organizations were closed, yet student political activity during the last year of the Onganía administration may well have been at an all-time high, and certainly the students were engaged in violent activity to a greater degree than ever before. Even the Catholic church had begun to choose sides to an unusual degree. Within the armed forces, the azul-colorado cleavage of the early 1960s was virtually eliminated, but only to be replaced by a struggle between liberals and nationalists. And, as was demonstrated by the military coup of June 8, 1970, which overthrew Onganía, the armed forces were not removed from the political arena.[39]

As a matter of fact, the higher echelons of the military, particularly army commander in chief General Alejandro Lanusse, became more and more frustrated with Onganía, who had removed the armed forces from actively participating in the decision-making process. Lanusse, who had personal ambitions to become president himself, feared, along with his colleagues, that Onganía could become an Argentine Franco (General Francisco Franco ruled Spain from 1939 to 1973). This could

TABLE 2.1
The Economic Performance of the Onganía Regime, 1966–1970

Factor	1966	1967	1968	1969	1970
GDP growth (%)	0.6	2.7	4.3	8.6	5.4
Investment change (% of GDP)	4.5	10.6	21.4	7.3	10.5
Real wages (1970 = 100)	98.9	96.6	91.7	96.4	100.0
% of GDP going to wage earners	46.5	48.4	48.1	48.8	49.5
Unemployment (%)	6.1	6.5	5.1	4.5	5.0
Inflation (%)	31.9	29.2	16.2	7.6	13.6
Trade balance (US$ million)	468.9	369.0	198.7	36.0	79.1
Current accounts (US$ million)	252.5	174.2	−48.6	−226.3	−158.9
Foreign debt (US$ billion)	2.6	2.6	2.8	3.2	3.8
Fiscal deficit (% of GDP)	4.7	4.1	1.9	0.9	2.4

SOURCE: Guido Di Tella and Rudiger Dornbusch, eds., *The Political Economy of Argentina, 1946–1983* (Pittsburgh: University of Pittsburgh Press, 1989), pp. 326–37.

mean relegating the armed forces to a junior role for an extended period of time, something they were not willing to accept. In mid-1969 riots started in Córdoba (and were known as the Cordobazo) and several other cities of the interior, and urban guerrilla groups began to organize. In the aftermath of the Cordobazo, Krieger Vasena resigned. His departure coincided with a steady deterioration of the economy. By 1970 it was clear that the military was accomplishing very little, that public acquiescence had eroded almost totally, and that the nation was experiencing an intolerable level of political violence. In June 1970 Onganía was deposed by his former colleagues.

Terrorism

The Cordobazo ignited the flame of terrorism. Although Argentina had witnessed the emergence of terrorist organizations prior to 1969, most of them lasted for only brief periods and had negligible consequences. Usually, these guerrilla groups were modeled after the Cuban revolution and created *focos* (cells) in the countryside as the bases for a popular uprising. The Cuban strategy appealed to many young revolutionaries not only because it was the only successful Latin American example readily available but also because Ernesto "Che" Guevara, one of its masterminds, was an Argentine. In 1959 a first foco was set up primarily by university students in the province of Tucumán, but it was easily put down in a few weeks. Another foco was destroyed in 1962 in Salta. During 1963, urban guerrilla activity replaced rural activity in newspaper headlines when the Tacuara terrorist group successfully robbed a bank in Buenos Aires. Nonetheless, like its predecessors, the Tacuara lived a short life, as its leadership either was captured by security forces or left for Uruguay. The political orientation of the terrorist groups ranged from Marxism-Leninism, Castroism, and Guevarism, to left-wing Peronism or combinations of all of the above.

In many ways, the political repression exercised by Onganía played into the hands of terrorism, particularly after 1969. Many young leftists forced to go underground became convinced that only through an armed struggle could they, the "vanguard of the proletariat," lead the masses toward a socialist revolution. Among the terrorist groups that emerged in the late 1960s, a substantial number of them were of Peronist orientation. This was true of the Revolutionary Armed Forces (Fuerzas Armadas Revolucionarias, or FAR), the Peronist Armed Forces (Fuerzas Armadas Peronistas, or FAP), and the *montoneros* (the name given to the gauchos who fought in the war of independence and, after 1962, against the national government).

Incidentally, many of these young leftists, most of them in their twenties, belonged to the Peronist Youth Movement and Catholic Action (the Catholic church youth organization). Their backgrounds were primarily middle and upper-middle class, and many were university students or young professionals. Dismayed by the repeated failure of the Argentine left and fearful of the consolidation of the Argentine Revolution regime, they believed that socialism could be achieved only through violent means. Of all the guerrilla groups that gained prominence in Argentina between the late 1960s and the late 1970s, the montoneros were the most visible. In 1973 they were joined by other Peronists.

The montoneros ideology was an odd synthesis of Peronism, Catholicism, and Marxism. The historical leaders of the group came from Catholic organizations.[40] The montoneros in their revolutionary fervor came to idealize Perón and his "social justice." This was partly due to the fact that most of them were just children when Perón was deposed and had not seen firsthand the authoritarian face of Peronism. All they saw, or wanted to see, was the working class base of Peronism. Given that their ultimate goal was freeing the working class from the oppression of capitalism and that Perón was the undisputed hero of the working class, they assumed that Perón was a true revolutionary. Thus, Peronism was tantamount to revolution, and the quicker Perón returned, the sooner the revolution would start.[41] The young montoneros were not the only Catholics to think so. During the same period radical Catholic priests belonging to the Third World Priests' Movement openly endorsed Peronism, backed labor strikes, and allegedly collaborated with the montoneros in their terrorist activities. The montoneros hit the spotlight when they kidnapped and later executed former President Aramburu in 1970. Subsequently, they robbed banks and assassinated army and police officers and conservative Peronists who collaborated with Onganía and the military governments that followed him. They kidnapped wealthy Argentines and managers of multinational corporations as well. On several occasions, the montoneros used Robin Hood tactics to win popular support: to release their abducted personnel, multinationals were forced to distribute food and other basic goods to shantytown dwellers as symbolic "reparations" for their exploitive ventures.

The other major guerrilla organization was the People's Revolutionary Army (Ejército Revolucionario del Pueblo, or ERP). The ERP started out as the armed branch of the Workers Revolutionary party in June 1970. Originally Trotskyite in orientation, the ERP eventually split from the party and in 1973 dropped its Trotskyite affiliation to become a Guevarist insurgency movement.[42] Unlike the montoneros, the ERP did not believe that Peronism was the true representative of the working class. In their view, Perón, if not a fascist, was surely a right-winger and an ally of the Argentine bourgeoisie. Thus, while the montoneros' primary objective was to create the conditions for Perón's return, the ERP had greater plans in mind. Their leaders seemed to believe that a Marxist-Leninist revolution in Argentina was tied to the Latin American struggle against U.S.-led imperialism. They thought that "a high level of political violence would push the military government toward indiscriminate repression, which would increase popular dissatisfaction and eventually lead to a civil war, which, in turn, would result in the creation of a socialist state."[43]

The ERP differed from the montoneros in another way. While the montoneros were strong in Buenos Aires, the ERP had its strongholds in the non-Peronist unions of Córdoba and in the countryside of Tucumán. Thus, while the montoneros concentrated on urban warfare, the ERP emphasized the creation of rural focos. To finance its activities, the ERP, like their Peronist counterparts, robbed banks and kidnapped large landowners and executives of multinational corporations.

Perón's Return

Onganía was replaced by a little-known intelligence officer, General Roberto Levingston, supposedly a mere spokesman for the armed forces. When Levingston, like Onganía, showed no signs of moving toward elections, he was tossed out after only eight months in office. Finally, in March 1971, army commander in chief General Alejandro Lanusse assumed the presidency and announced that he would hold office only long enough to stop the violence and hold elections. To regain support for the regime, Lanusse ushered in a new political phase, the Great National Accord (Gran Acuerdo Nacional, or GAN). The GAN's short-term objective was to form an alliance among the military, anti-Peronist political parties, and business interest groups to fend off economic instability. In the long run, the GAN was expected to be the focus for the creation of a conservative bloc that would endorse the presidential ambitions of Lanusse once the military decided to withdraw from power. In fact, the leaders of the armed forces decided that they had no choice but to hold elections and return to constitutional government. There was evidently some hope that the return to democracy would relieve the frustrations that were contributing to the violence and also a feeling that, even if this hope was not borne out, the armed forces would be relieved of responsibility for political events. However, Lanusse's ambitions were quickly struck down, and the conservative bloc he envisioned never materialized.

In 1973, a discouraged Lanusse let political parties decide for themselves, and the Peronists were allowed their first presidential candidate (but not Perón) in seventeen years. Knowing that the Peronist candidate could easily win the plurality, Lanusse decreed that the winner had to receive the majority of the vote cast, otherwise a runoff election was to be held. This was done on the assumption that, after the first ballot, the anti-Peronist forces would unite and win. In his Spanish exile, Perón ordered that one of his left-wing lieutenants, Héctor Cámpora, would head the Peronist ticket. It was clear that voting for Cámpora meant voting for Perón's return: the Peronist campaign slogan was Cámpora to the Presidency, Perón to Power. In March 1973, Cámpora polled 49.6 percent of the popular vote. Reluctantly, Lanusse acknowledged the defeat of his electoral engineering and announced that 49.6 percent was enough for Cámpora to take office. Once in power, Cámpora drifted to the left; most of his cabinet appointments went to left-wing Peronists. Many terrorists were freed through an amnesty, which angered the military.

Cámpora's tenure did not last long. After less than eight weeks in office he resigned and called for new elections to allow Perón to take charge, as had been planned all along. The following September Juan Perón defeated his main opponent, Ricardo Balbín of the UCR, by a landslide (62 percent of the vote). Perón's third wife, María Estela Martínez de Perón (more frequently referred to as Isabel), became vice president, something that the more popular Evita had been unable to achieve in 1951 due to the military's opposition.

Upon starting his third term in office, Perón swung the political pendulum decisively to the right. A power struggle had been going on within the Peronist movement pitting against each other left-wingers and montoneros, on the one hand, and conservatives and most union leaders, on the other. As a consequence, most of Cámpora's ministers were replaced by conservative ones and the left-wing administrators of state universities were purged and replaced with neofascists. Perón's decision to side with the right-wing elements of the movement provoked a dramatic internal split. In May 1974, the montoneros, who had momentarily abandoned the armed struggle to work in election campaigns, ceased to support Perón after he publicly accused them of betraying the Peronist movement. However, while the montoneros did not resume guerrilla activities after their "excommunication," the ERP stepped up its attacks against military bases and its assassinations of conservative Peronists (like the CGT general secretary), hoping to provoke the aging Perón to adopt repressive measures. In the eyes of the ERP leadership, this should finally convince the montoneros and the working class that Perón was indeed a neofascist.

The tenuous socioeconomic balance that Perón had kept alive while in office collapsed when he died in July 1974. While in office, Perón gained acceptance for a "social pact" designed by Minister of the Economy José Gelbard that forced labor and business to temporarily restrain their demands in order to bring about economic stability. With Perón gone, his wife did not have the same authority, nor was she prepared for the task she had to face. More troublesome, she surrounded herself with incompetent advisers, who tarnished the image of her administration. Accordingly, labor and business no longer felt obliged to observe the social pact and made a series of redistributional demands, which led to economic disaster.

To further compound the problem, the montoneros accused Isabel Perón of having sided with the right wing of the party, and they joined the ERP in terrorist attacks against the administration. Left-wing terrorism began to be matched by an equally violent right-wing movement, the Argentine Anticommunist Alliance (Alianza Anticomunista Argentina, or AAA). The AAA indiscriminately killed and kidnapped not only "Marxist subversives" but whoever stood in their way. Among their most illustrious victims were Carlos Mujica, who was the leader of the Third World Priests' Movement, the brother of former President Frondizi, and Peronist politicians. Allegedly, the AAA was organized by Minister of Social Welfare José López Rega, a right-winger and Isabel Perón's closest advisor. Its ranks were made up of off-duty police and military officers and civilians of neofascist tendencies. Not surprisingly, after the 1976 coup the AAA disappeared. By 1975, Argentina was undergoing an undeclared civil war, as the montonero, the ERP, and the AAA were killing people at a rate of one every eight hours.[44] While "the most publicized of these murders" were "prominent lawyers, politicians, liberal journalists . . . the great majority" were "rank and file trade unionists, community workers, priests, students, and teachers.[45]

In 1975 the 100 percent devaluation, decreed by Minister of the Economy Celestino Rodrigo to stop speculative operations and make exports competitive again, had contrary effects. The CGT's stiff opposition to the minister's measures forced the government to decree large wage increases and to fire both Rodrigo and López Rega. From the second half of 1975 on, union bosses and particularly the leader of the UOM, Lorenzo Miguel, became the gray eminence behind a president who no longer commanded any appreciable authority. The continuous policy reversals led to a public loss of confidence in the economic authorities. By early 1976, hyperinflation, a severe balance of payments crisis, a bloody terrorist insurgency, and a scandal-ridden administration had led Argentina, in less than two years, to a state of chaos. (See table 2.2.) When the commanders in chief of the armed forces concluded that there was overwhelming public support for bringing this state of affairs to an end, they deposed Isabel Perón and assumed direct power.

The Process of National Reorganization

The 1976 coup encountered no opposition. For many Argentines this was the country's last chance to defeat terrorism and solve its chronic

TABLE 2.2

The Economic Performance of the Military and Peronist Regimes, 1971–1975

Factor	1971	1972	1973	1974	1975
GDP growth (%)	3.6	1.6	3.4	6.5	−0.9
Investment change (% of GDP)	21.2	22.1	19.6	19.3	10.5
Real wages (1970 = 100)	105.2	99.0	107.2	126.4	123.7
Unemployment (%)	5.9	6.6	5.5	6.2	7.7
Inflation (%)	34.7	58.5	60.3	24.2	182.8
Trade balance (US$ million)	−127.7	36.4	1,030.7	295.8	−985.2
Current accounts (US$ million)	−388.7	−222.9	714.9	127.2	−1,284.6
Foreign debt (US$ billion)	4.5	5.7	6.2	7.9	7.9
Fiscal deficit (% of GDP)	3.1	4.0	7.9	9.5	15.3

SOURCE: Guido Di Tella and Rudiger Dornbusch, eds., *The Political Economy of Argentina, 1946–1983* (Pittsburgh: University of Pittsburgh Press, 1989), pp. 326–37.

socioeconomic instability. The military immediately took drastic measures. Congress was closed down, strikes were outlawed, the CGT was put under military control, and its financial assets frozen (along with those of most individual unions), labor courts were abolished, the death penalty was reintroduced, political parties were dissolved, the administration of state universities was taken over by government officials, and students were banned from participating in political activities. The commanders in chief of the army (General Jorge Videla), navy (Admiral Emilio Massera), and air force (Brigadier Orlando Agosti) set up a military junta that would henceforth rule the country. General Videla was later selected for a three-year term (until early 1981) and was replaced as army commander by General Roberto Viola. Aware of the consequences of leaving one man in sole charge of government, as had happened under Onganía, the junta made sure that the new president would behave as first among equals and would act only after receiving the others' approval.

Unlike previous coups, the military did not intervene long enough to reestablish order and allow new elections. This time, following the military coups in neighboring Brazil (1964), Uruguay (1973), and Chile (1973), the armed forces were going to establish what Guillermo O'Donnell defined as a bureaucratic-authoritarian regime.[46] The junta set for itself a number of goals, which were announced on March 24, 1976, and were known as the Act of the National Reorganization Process (Acta Para el Proceso de Reorganización Nacional). The document represented the political manifesto of the Proceso, as the military regime would be referred to thereafter.

The government devoted most of its energies to three basic objectives: the improvement of the economy, the elimination of subversion, and the creation of a new institutional framework. While the armed forces took charge of the "dirty war" against terrorism, Videla appointed as new Minister of the Economy José Alfredo Martínez de Hoz—a member of one of the country's oldest and wealthiest oligarchic families. The new minister "nurtured within the government the concept of a farsighted and remote authoritarianism, possessed of a morality and a discipline higher than that of a surrounding society made sick by years of mismanagement. In this way he both met the political objectives of a military government aiming at social transformation, and at the same time turned the interlude before political life was to be restored to his advantage, by steering the regime in a direction compatible with his own vision of conservative democracy."[47]

Between 1976 and 1980, Martínez de Hoz employed a series of neoconservative economic policies.[48] In the first two years (1976–1977), through the assistance of the International Monetary Fund, Martínez de Hoz implemented a fairly orthodox stabilization program, which succeeded in reestablishing a positive balance of payments and in strengthening Central Bank reserves, which had been depleted by the Peronist administration. Inflation, on the other hand, although declining substantially, proved much more difficult to attack. This fact induced Martínez de Hoz in December 1978 to switch to an expectation management approach to price stabilization based upon an overvalued exchange rate and periodic minidevaluations. At the same time, the capital market was deregulated, and many sectors of the economy were exposed to foreign competition on the assumption that this would make local industry more efficient and push prices down. The plan, instead of creating a new economic order, led the country to bankruptcy. Wealthy Argentines, taking advantage of the lax exchange policies, bought cheap dollars; but instead of investing them at home, they deposited them in Uruguayan, U.S., or European banks. A large number of small and medium-sized manufacturing producers, unable to compete with foreign companies, went out of business, taking with them many banking institutions they had borrowed from.

In March 1981, Videla, who had defended Martínez de Hoz's policies for five years, was succeeded by General Roberto Viola in the first orderly transition of power by an Argentine military regime. Viola, perceiving the imminence of the economic collapse, named a new economic team headed by Lorenzo Sigaut to rescue the situation. Viola's decision was supported by some simple but revealing data. (See table 2.3.) During the years Martínez de Hoz held office, the country's foreign debt rose from $8 billion to $36 billion, the cost of living increased approximately 18,500 percent, and some of the largest banks and industrial conglomerates went under, spreading panic among investors and bystanders alike.[49]

TABLE 2.3
The Economic Performance of the Military Regime, 1976–1983

Factor	1976	1977	1978	1979	1980	1981	1982	1983
GDP growth (%)	−0.2	6.0	−3.9	6.8	0.7	−6.2	−5.2	3.1
Investment change (% of GDP)	19.5	21.5	24.4	22.0	22.0	22.8	20.1	15.3
Real wages (1970 = 100)	79.2	75.6	77.2	86.2	100.0	91.2	79.3	102.6
Unemployment (%)	9.0	5.4	4.9	5.3	6.8	10.8	9.3	8.0
Inflation (%)	444.0	176.1	175.6	159.9	100.8	104.5	164.8	343.2
Trade balance (US$ billion)	0.9	1.4	2.5	1.1	−2.5	−0.3	2.2	3.3
Current accounts (US$ billion)	0.6	1.2	2.0	−0.5	−4.7	−4.7	−2.3	−2.4
Foreign debt (US$ billion)	8.2	11.7	12.4	19.0	27.1	35.6	43.6	45.3
Fiscal deficit (% of GDP)	11.7	5.1	6.8	6.1	7.5	13.3	14.9	15.6

SOURCE: Guido Di Tella and Rudiger Dornbusch, eds., *The Political Economy of Argentina, 1946–1983* (Pittsburgh: University of Pittsburgh Press, 1989), pp. 326–37.

The Dirty War

Even though the economic objective was missed, the armed forces could claim that the elimination of terrorism had been achieved. By 1978, the ERP had virtually ceased to function, and relatively little was heard from the montoneros after 1979. This was accomplished, however, by unrestrained government violence. Unlike contemporary military regimes in Brazil, Chile, and Uruguay, which chose a "surgical" strategy to combat "subversives," their Argentines colleagues were indiscriminate in their effort. More often than not, the army, navy, and air force carried out their own separate extermination campaigns with little government supervision and even in competition with one another. The result was one of the most savage political repressions in Latin America's modern history. General Luciano Menéndez, commander of the Córdoba military region and one of the most extreme military hard-liners, said, "While Videla rules, I kill";[50] and General Ibérico Saint Jean, commander of the Buenos Aires military region, reportedly said, "First we will kill all the subversives; then we will kill their collaborators; then their sympathizers; then those who are indifferent; and finally, we will kill all those who are timid."[51]

The assassinations carried out by the montoneros and the ERP dropped dramatically from about 1,500 in 1976, to 700 in 1977, to 30 in 1978.[52] In the meantime, the government kidnapped, tortured, and killed thousands of people. The repression began under the Perón administration: in February 1975, the military was called in and given a blank check to eliminate the ERP guerrilla groups in the Tucumán province. The following October, after guerrilla attacks were stepped up, the president of the Senate Italo Luder (who had been sworn in as ad interim president while Isabel Perón was in Spain) issued a decree that allowed the armed forces to take over the fight against subversion using "all necessary means." In 1984, the National Commission on the Disappeared (Comisión Nacional sobre Desaparición de Personas, or CONADEP), after hearing the testimony of hundreds of witnesses, reported to President Alfonsín that thousands of people had been kidnapped and illegally detained by security forces in about 340 detention prisons. Of those abducted, 8,960 were still missing. (Other human rights organizations believed that the total was much higher, ranging from 15,000 to 30,000.) The CONADEP described the military repression as follows:

> The abductions were precisely organized operations, sometimes occurring at the victim's place of work, sometimes in the street in broad light. They involved the open deployment of military personnel, who were given a free hand by the local police stations. When a victim was sought out in his or her home at night, armed units would surround the block and force their way in, terrorizing parents and children, who were often gagged and forced to watch. They would seize the persons they had come for, beat them mercilessly, hood them, then drag them off in their cars or trucks, while the rest of the unit almost invariably ransacked the house or looted everything that could be carried. The victims were then taken to a chamber over whose doorway might well have been inscribed the words Dante read on the gates of Hell: 'Abandon hope, all ye who enter here.' Thus, in the name of national security, thousands upon thousands of human beings, usually young adults or even adolescents, fell into the sinister, ghostly category of the *desaparecidos* [disappeared].[53]

Some of the victims were subversives, collaborators, and sympathizers. However, most often they were innocent people whose ideas did not conform with those of the military or who were friends, relatives, or acquaintances of people on the black list of the security forces. According to the CONADEP, "all sectors fell into the net: trade union leaders fighting for better wages; youngsters in student unions; journalists who did not support the regime; psychologists simply for belonging to suspicious professions; young pacifists; nuns and priests who had taken the teachings of Christ to shantytown areas; the friends of these people, too, and the friends of friends; plus others whose names were given out of motives of personal vengeance, or by the kidnapped under torture. The vast majority were innocent not only of any acts of terrorism, but even of belonging to the fighting units of the guerrilla organizations: these latter chose to fight it out, and either died in shoot-outs or committed suicide before they could be captured. Few of them were alive by the time they were in the hands of the repressive forces."[54]

Of the 8,960 people officially disappeared, blue-collar workers made up 30.2 percent; students, 21 percent; white-collar workers, 17.9 percent; professionals, 10.7 percent; teachers, 5.7 percent; the self-employed and others, 5 percent; housewives, 3.8 percent; military conscripts and members of the security forces, 2.5 percent; journalists, 1.6 percent; actors and performers, 1.3 percent; nuns and priests, 0.3 percent. Once abducted, the desaparecidos—including the elderly, children, and pregnant women—were viciously tortured. Many of those who survived were killed, their identity concealed, and their bodies buried in mass graves or simply dropped into the ocean. The CONADEP also underscored that, although the military junta had estimated that the terrorists had some 15,000 members plus 10,000 collaborators, only 356 of them were actually tried and convicted. This discrepancy led the commission to conclude that, with the excuse of fighting terrorism, the armed forces had tried to purge from society all those they did not like for whatever reason.[55] The regime denied for a long time that abductions were taking place or that detainees were being killed. However, in 1979, it issued a decree (Decree Law 22.068) regulating the judicial and patrimonial matters of those who had "disappeared," which implicitly acknowledged that those people were to be considered dead.

Having been incapable of creating a viable political system or of producing a sustained economic recovery, Viola reasoned that the military had only two options to justify its hold on power, either to use more repression or to gradually open up the political system, as the Brazilian military had done in 1974. Reeling under the accumulated pressure of five years of harsh dictatorship, Viola began to talk, in rather vague terms, about plans for political liberalization. Viola's moderate plans almost immediately encountered opposition from the army's commander in chief, General Leopoldo Galtieri, and other military hard-liners. While armed forces factions squabbled, leaders of the dissolved political parties took advantage of the more tolerant climate and organized the Multipartidaria (Multiparty), a broad opposition front whose main objective was a return to free elections in 1984, when Viola's term was scheduled to expire.[56]

In the meantime, the economic bubble artificially inflated by Martínez de Hoz burst in Sigaut's hands. The latter had no choice but to resort to three large devaluations within eight months to remedy the distortions created by his predecessor's policies. A positive balance of payments and low inflation remained, as in the past, the highest priorities of the military regime, but they were pursued through a protectionistic approach based on a two-tiered exchange control system, heavier import tariffs, and export promotions. Indeed, the trade balance was reduced, but the budget deficit, business failures, capital flight, unemployment, and the foreign debt began to accelerate at an alarming pace.

In December 1982, Galtieri seized the initiative and deposed Viola. His ascendancy to power meant a return to old-style authoritarianism, associated with economic orthodoxy. In fact, Roberto Alemann, a conservative business consultant, was appointed to head the Ministry of the Economy. Although striving to give an impression of resolution by declaring that "the period of words and promises is over, now is the time for firmness and action," Galtieri was unable to turn back the clock. Many high-ranking officers resented the continuation of the neoconservative experiment and asked for a policy reversal.[57] With support for the Proceso fading away, not only among once enthusiastic entrepreneurial groups, but within the armed forces as well, Galtieri expressed his intention to form "a political force which will represent, in organic fashion, an independent current of national opinion which until now has remained diffused."[58]

In other words, Galtieri aimed at creating a political coalition beyond the barracks that could assure his election in an "open" presidential contest to be held later.[59] Contacts were established with labor and political party representatives to sound out the feasibility of the project. This initiative openly contradicted Galtieri's 1981 stand and indicated how much the armed forces' confidence in their original project had disintegrated. However, in the early months of 1982 the further deterioration of the economic situation fueled mounting public unrest, particularly among labor. On April 2, 1982, Argentine troops invaded the Falklands/Malvinas islands in the south Atlantic, one of the last remnants of the British Empire. Argentina had claimed the islands since the British had taken them over in 1831, but due to the strong economic ties that had developed between the two countries thereafter, the issue remained unresolved. Why did Galtieri go to war? Explanations have run the gamut from creating popular support for his electoral debut and closing ranks within a divided military to distracting attention from the worsening economic crisis. To this day it is still unclear why Galtieri and the junta decided to act so hastily.[60]

Although virtually all Argentines were delighted at the "recovery" of the islands, they were also totally disillusioned by the time the Argentine task force capitulated to the British on June 14. This rather ignominious defeat was Galtieri's and the Proceso's political coffin. The conflicts existing before the war between the army, on the one hand, and the air force and navy, on the other, exploded in a virulent way after the debacle. To save face, the junta, under mounting civilian pressure, set up a provisional government headed by retired General Reynaldo Bignone, whose only purpose was to hold elections and to return to constitutional government. Despite a desperate attempt to negotiate its exit from power and secure immunity for the crimes committed during the "dirty war," the military was unable to gain any concession from political parties. In fact, although in 1970 the armed forces could ascribe the failure of the Argentine Revolution to Onganía, in 1983 the demise of the Proceso had no culprit but the military. Aside from the defeat in the south Atlantic, most of the 1976 goals of the Proceso remained unfulfilled. Indeed, subversion was eradicated but at such a high price that it tore society apart for many years to come. Both the institutionalization of a "stable, republican, and federal democracy" and its instrument, the "movement of national opinion," remained ill-defined declarations of intent.

In the end, the policies of the 1976–1983 regime were essentially ad hoc responses to unfolding crises. Moreover, the regime never completely succeeded in eliminating opposition forces, particularly labor. On the economic front, the Proceso led the country to ruin. By 1983 domestic industry was devastated by Martínez de Hoz's erratic policies. Many small and medium-sized manufacturers were wiped out, the banking system was crippled, foreign debt ballooned to $45 billion, wages and salaries lost a third of their 1975 purchasing power, unemployment and underemployment remained high, the budget deficit continued to grow, and the recession was accompanied by galloping inflation (the peso reached 260,000 to the dollar). The beneficiaries of the economic model chosen in 1976 were the local conglomerates and a few multinational corporations, which increased their share of the national economy, and the financial speculators who had exported $20 to $30 billion abroad.[61] The losers were the middle and lower classes, who saw their economic status worsening even further.

The Alfonsín Administration

Unlike similar experiences of transition from military to civilian rule in neighboring countries (Brazil, Uruguay, and Chile), in Argentina a pact between opposition forces and the military, regarded by many analysts as a prerequisite for a smooth process of redemocratization, never materialized. As noted earlier, the Multipartidaria was just a temporary accord aimed at speeding up the military withdrawal. Neither Peronists nor Radicals had a real incentive to form a pact because they believed that a go-it-alone approach, which made compromise unnecessary, was in their best interest. For instance, the claims for justice by many civilian sectors with regard to military crimes made any pact that compromised this matter electorally unpopular. Moreover, the military had fallen into such public discredit and was so divided among itself that it had no means of negotiating its exit.[62]

On October 30, 1983, Argentines went to the polls for the first time in more than a decade and, to the amazement of most observers, chose as their new president a Radical, Raúl Alfonsín. For the first time since the party's formation in 1946, the Peronists lost a presidential election— and lost decisively, as their presidential candidate, Italo Luder, received only 40 percent of the popular vote, while Alfonsín obtained 52 percent. The coming to power of Alfonsín was welcomed both in Argentina and abroad with great optimism and expectations. Alfonsín's political discourse—focusing on the enforcement of the democratic principles of the 1853 constitution and respecting individual freedoms, human rights, and minority points of view—generated enthusiasm among a frustrated population, which had witnessed all kinds of abuses. Even the labor and business distributional coalitions that had been crucial in supporting authoritarian solutions in the past seemed now to embrace democratic principles without major reservations. For some observers, however, the changed attitude of labor and business elites was more the consequence of a lack of viable options to democracy. Since 1930 alternatives based upon exclusionary pluralism, populism, corporatism, authoritarianism, and direct military rule had been tried to no avail. According to this argument, labor and business elites were now embracing democracy by default. "As a result of Argentina's own experience with authoritarianism and guerrilla warfare, and of lessons drawn from Latin American and Eastern Europe, nondemocratic models of the Right and the Left had lost their attractiveness. Moreover, there was a realization that the old principles of liberal democracy, enshrined in an Argentine constitution that had been systematically violated, were, after all, the only road not tried in the previous century."[63]

The new president simultaneously faced three problems that would have overwhelmed most officeholders in Europe or North America. First, he was under pressure to revitalize a sluggish economy burdened by a huge foreign debt (the world's third largest) created for the most part under the military dictatorship. Second, he was committed to bringing to justice those officers and civilians guilty of human right violations during the 1970s. Third, he had to create a consensus on the basic rules of constitutional democracy, the lack of which had been largely responsible for the protracted political instability that had plagued the country since 1930. For most of his term, Alfonsín gave priority to the second and third problems; he paid less attention to economic issues. The president's bias—that all problems, regardless of their nature, had a political solution—was decisive in shaping his administration's early policies. Unfortunately, this approach turned out to be disastrous in the end.

Once in office, Alfonsín still saw no need for a pact either with the military or with opposition parties and distributional coalitions. A number of factors accounted for his decision. First, the UCR traditionally refused institutionalized accords with interest groups, which it perceived as selfish and unreliable. Since the Radicals considered themselves the representatives of the common citizen, as opposed to special interests, they failed to include business and labor demands in the party platform.[64] Second, socioeconomic pacts in Argentina were closely associated with Perón's corporatist schemes, which were opposed by the UCR. Third, the factionalism that affected the Peronists until 1985 made it impossible to have a reliable interlocutor in the Justicialist (Peronist) party (Partido Justicialista or PJ). Fourth, the large victory of October 1983 was interpreted by Alfonsín and his advisers as a clear mandate to act unilaterally. Fifth, the president probably thought that Peronism was disintegrating, a process that could be accelerated through a divide-and-conquer strategy. Had Alfonsín been successful, the UCR would have had no real competition and would have become the hegemonic political force of the postmilitary era.[65] Alfonsín's divide-and-conquer strategy, however, suffered a serious setback from the start, when a new law, presented by Labor Minister Antonio Mucci, aimed at breaking the power of Peronist union bosses over labor organizations, was defeated by a narrow margin in the Senate in March 1984. As a result, Mucci was replaced by Juan Manuel Casella, one of Alfonsín's closest associates, who was given the task of exploring the possibility of an agreement with both unions and entrepreneurial groups.

In the meantime, the president's foreign policy enjoyed favorable results. Although negotiations with The United Kingdom on the Falklands/Malvinas stagnated, a longstanding feud with Chile finally came to an end. In 1978, the two countries almost went to war to solve a territorial dispute over three deserted islands along the Beagle Channel in the South Atlantic. Through mediation by the Vatican, a preliminary agreement was reached in January 1984 awarding Chile the islands while Argentina obtained access to the eastern entrance of the Magellan Straits. Although the treaty was subject only to Senate approval, Alfonsín asked his fellow citizens to express their opinion in a referendum the following November. In spite of the vitriolic opposition of the right-wing Peronist leadership and other nationalist groups, 77 percent of the voters supported the treaty's ratification. The results marked another personal victory for the president and put the Peronists even more on the defensive.[66]

On the human rights front, Alfonsín acted with caution. As noted earlier, he began by appointing the CONADEP—made up of twelve distinguished civilians chaired by Ernesto Sabato, a world-renowned writer—to determine the extent of the crimes committed during the "dirty war." The commission's results were expected to provide an impartial document for the courts' use. Alfonsín first charged the Supreme Council of the Armed Forces (a military court) with the task of trying former members of the military juntas. When the council discounted most of the major accusations, the president turned the trials over to civilian courts. In December 1985, Videla and Massera were sentenced to life, and Viola was given seventeen years for human rights violations. Shortly afterward, a military court sentenced Galtieri to twelve years, Admiral Jorge Anaya (the architect of the Malvinas invasion) to fourteen, and Brigadier General Lami Dozo to eight years for their mismanagement of the war against Great Britain. For the first time in Latin America, former members of military juntas were tried and convicted. Trials were also extended to field commanders.

On the economic front, Alfonsín relied upon the old guard of the UCR to revitalize a sluggish economy. Minister of the Economy Bernardo Grinspun adopted a gradualist, neo-Keynesian approach under enormous redistributive demands from all socioeconomic sectors, which were asking for compensation for the losses suffered under the military regime. Grinspun simultaneously pursued three related goals: income redistribution favoring salary earners, low inflation, and economic growth.[67] By the end of 1983 Argentina suspended interest payments on its debt and shortly afterward fell into arrears. Grinspun's personal opposition to the IMF's recipe for economic stabilization made relations between the Alfonsín government and the Washington-based lending organization extremely tense. Although a standby agreement was finally signed with the IMF in December 1984, Argentina soon fell out of compliance and the IMF promptly withdrew its financial support.

In the meantime the economic situation went from bad to worse. Grinspun's policies emphasized a state-led market expansion through government investments and subsidies and industrial protectionism. While such a model had proven viable under the Illia administration, it seemed out of step with the realities of the 1980s. In 1984 alone, inflation increased by 668 percent. Moreover, Grinspun's hostility to any policy consultation with distributional coalitions not only aroused the animosity of the latter but also deepened the conflicts with Interior Minister Troccoli and Labor Minister Casella, who were actively pursuing an accord. In February, Alfonsín ended the feud and replaced Grinspun with a team of independent economists, headed by Planning Secretary Juan Sourrouille. The failure of consultation talks between March and May hardened the opposition of key distributional coalitions and particularly of the CGT, which under the leadership of General Secretary Saúl Ubaldini (a Peronist) took a defiant stance.

With the country in a situation of de facto hyperinflation, the president cut short the brief overture toward consultation and switched again to unilateral decision making. On June 14, 1985, he announced the implementation of the Austral Plan, a bold stabilization program that Sourrouille and his team had been preparing for some time. The innovative aspect of the plan was its attempt to combine some of the main tenets of orthodox monetary and fiscal policy advocated by the IMF with a heterodox shock treatment of inflation. Its main features were (1) a price and wage freeze, (2) increases in taxes and public utility rates to reduce the fiscal deficit, (3) the commitment by the Central Bank to avoid printing money to finance the deficit, (4) the replacement of the peso with the austral, a new currency whose parity was fixed at US$1.25, and (5) the implementation of a financial mechanism that could establish positive interest rates and increase banks' lending capacity.[68] At the same time, Argentina renegotiated its standby agreement with the IMF and received additional support from the U.S. Treasury.[69]

The Austral Plan was an instant success, going beyond the rosiest expectations. Inflation, which had increased by 30 percent in June, dropped to 3 percent in December, nominal interest rates fell likewise, government tax revenues rose substantially, and employment levels remained fairly constant. The president tried to capitalize on the good results by making the November election for a partial renewal of the Chamber of Deputies a plebiscite on his policies. The UCR was able to gain one seat. On the contrary, the PJ, which along with the CGT bitterly criticized the Austral Plan, recorded its worst performance ever by losing ten deputies. Alfonsín's popularity reached its peak during this time and reinforced the belief held by many in the UCR (including the president) that Radical hegemony was just around the corner, which would lead to the creation of a Third Historical Movement, a multiclass coalition like the ones previously assembled by Yrigoyen and Perón.[70]

Alfonsín's early achievements in foreign policy, human rights, and economics made him one of the most visible and respected Latin American leaders, thus enhancing Argentina's international standing, which had been badly tarnished by the military dictatorship and the debacle in the Falklands/Malvinas war. However, by early 1986 the unilateral decision-making approach through executive decrees, adopted with the Austral Plan, ran out of steam. It was seen as an obstacle in the long run to social cooperation and the consolidation of democracy. Distributional coalitions (industrial, agricultural, and financial interest groups, and unions) therefore demanded to be consulted on key economic issues when talks were begun again.[71] Moreover, the president also came under pressure from interest groups and Radical leaders alike to promote policies emphasizing economic growth over fiscal and monetary restraint. In April 1986, on the assumption that a reactivation of the economy could be compatible with a tolerable inflation rate, the administration switched to a system of administered prices, and the IMF standby agreement was not renewed when it expired in June. Unfortunately, the economy overheated again, and in February 1987 Sourrouille had to impose a wage and price freeze for four months, which was to be accompanied by reform plans aimed at restructuring both the state and the capital market sector. The new stabilization package, commonly referred to as Australito, brought only momentary relief. By the time the freeze period expired, inflation began to climb again, but the structural reforms never got off the ground. On the political front, in April 1987, Alfonsín tried to divide the Peronists by naming Carlos Alderete as the new labor minister. Alderete was a prominent leader of the Group of 15, a sector of the union movement that defied Ubaldini's authority and that had previously collaborated with the military regime. Alderete's inclusion in the cabinet turned out to be a Trojan horse. In fact, the labor minister's open criticism of Sourouille's plan fueled uncertainty over the general direction of the administration's policies.

In September 1987, gubernatorial and congressional elections were held. Alfonsín again presented the contest as a plebiscite. Unlike 1985, this time he asked Argentines for a vote of confidence not on the administration's economic performance—which was rather poor—but on his effort to build democracy through his new proposals for a European-style parliamentary constitution and the relocation of the Federal District. The only problem was that by that time most Argentines were more concerned with the erosion of their salaries' purchasing power than with democracy, which seemed to many to be an accomplished fact. Reversing the trend begun in 1983, the PJ scored a clear victory over the UCR. The Radicals lost their absolute majority in the Chamber of Deputies and, equally important, the governorship of Buenos Aires, the second-most important public office in the country, where Casella was defeated by Peronist Antonio Cafiero. The 1987 elections marked the end of the rhetoric about a Third Historical Movement. Alfonsín, personally devastated by the setback, never regained the political initiative, which was taken over by the more aggressive and confident PJ.[72]

To make things worse, the military became increasingly restless. In December 1986, fearing an escalation of the confrontation between the military and civil society, the president had Congress pass the Full Stop Law (Punto Final), according to which a time limit was set for filing charges of human rights abuses. However, the law had the unexpected side effect of leaving junior officers, rather than their senior colleagues, exposed to judicial prosecutions. Openly challenging the armed forces' upper echelons, two maverick colonels (Aldo Rico, twice in 1987, and Mohammed Ali Seineldin, in 1988) led young officers in three military mutinies. These mutinies were generally interpreted as an expression of the profound dissatisfaction of many field commanders over the prosecutions of officers for crimes committed during the "dirty war," over the lack of appreciation by civilians for the elimination of terrorism, and over poor salaries and military equipment. While the government held out against the rebels' wish to vindicate the role of the military against terrorism in the 1970s, concessions were made through bipartisan support in Congress. In the name of national reconciliation, military salaries were increased, the Due Obedience Law (Obediencia Debida) was passed halting prosecutions for all but twenty higher officers, and a score of senior generals, whom the mutineers regarded as having sold out their subordinates to civilian justice, were retired (including two army chiefs of staff).[73] Such concessions weakened the president's prestige and clearly showed his inability to deal with the military problem. To complicate matters, left-wing terrorism, which was assumed to have disappeared after the tragic experience of the 1970s, surfaced again when, in January 1989, a commando group attacked an army base in the outskirts of Buenos Aires.[74] While the reason for this suicidal attack remained obscure, it gave the armed forces new political ammunition to obtain more concessions.

The demise of the Austral Plan convinced the Radical administration that a middle-of-the-road approach to economic stabilization was unworkable. Thus, greater emphasis was given to reform of the government bureaucracy and state-owned enterprises and the opening of the economy. However, it was too little, too late. In August 1988, in a last attempt to gain control of the economic situation, the administration launched a last, desperate, austerity package called the Spring Plan. The 1989 presidential elections were scheduled for May, six months before the expiration of Alfonsín's term in the hope that by then economic stability would have been achieved, thus enhancing the chances of a UCR victory. The Spring Plan was made possible through an agreement made by the government with the UIA and the Argentine Chamber of Commerce (Cámara Argentina de Comercio, or CAC). The latter agreed on a 180-day price freeze in return for some concessions.[75] The feasibility of the plan hinged upon the maintenance of high interest rates and a steady exchange rate. At the same time, the government pledged to slowly open the economy to more imports but failed to address the problem posed by the fiscal deficit.

Interestingly enough, whereas the IMF refused to support the plan, the World Bank granted the Alfonsín administration $1.25 billion to sustain the exchange rate. (Because Argentina had stopped making payments on its debt in April of that year, the IMF judged the plan as insufficient to address debt payments and the budget deficit.) Domestically, the CGT and the SRA and other agricultural producer organizations resented the fact that the government had left them out of the agreement and began to work for its demise. Export-oriented agricultural and industrial coalitions that felt damaged by the Spring Plan actively worked to sabotage it. In fact, these groups (whose remittances in dollars were crucial for the administration to keep a steady exchange rate) not only stopped exchanging their dollars for australs but actually engaged in financial speculations by purchasing massive sums of foreign currency. Once these efforts were known, other business groups made a run on the dollar before the government would be forced to devaluate. Indeed, the government depleted most of its foreign reserves to defend the austral against savage speculations, but in the end it had to devalue. After some initial success, the plan fell apart in February 1989.[76]

Alfonsín found himself increasingly isolated; he was attacked by most interest groups and opposition parties. As election time neared, it was apparent that Alfonsín had failed to solve the military problem and, most of all, to bring economic stability to a country again on the verge of hyperinflation. Aware of these shortcomings, Eduardo Angeloz, the candidate selected by the UCR to succeed the outgoing president, distanced himself from the policies of the Alfonsín administration. In an effort to find a scapegoat and to save his campaign, Angeloz forced a reluctant Alfonsín to dismiss Sourrouille (and his technocrats) and to replace him with Speaker of the Chamber of Deputies Juan Carlos Pugliese, who had occupied the same position under Illia. This decision proved to be the most damaging to Alfonsín, as it destroyed whatever credibility the administration had left. As uncertainty increased so did the value of the U.S. dollar, which from seventeen australs in February reached the one-hundred mark just before the May election. On 14 May 1989, Carlos Menem, the Peronist candidate, obtained 47 percent of the popular vote, against 37 percent for Angeloz. In the aftermath of the election, a hyperinflation spiral took off, triggering a wave of riots. Hundreds of poor people, who were now over a third of the population, looted grocery stores. As a lame duck president with five months still left in his term, Alfonsín found it impossible to give credibility to any policy initiative. In July he resigned so that Menem could restore some calm and confidence in an economy where inflation had reached 200 percent a month.

What went wrong? How could a man who had enjoyed so much respect and popularity in the first three years of his mandate leave office on such a sour note? To be fair, it must be said that Alfonsín inherited problems of great magnitude. However, he proved naïve in believing that the restoration of democracy would cure all wounds. It did not, but working on that assumption made things even worse. Both the president and his first cabinet came to power not fully aware of the complexity of the crisis they were expected to tackle, and they proved to be ill prepared to solve it. Not until 1985 was the administration able to design a consistent economic plan. Probably one of Alfonsín's greatest shortcomings was his inability to take advantage of the short-term benefits that ensued from the Austral Plan, which although unpopular could have turned the economy around. While repeatedly raising the flag of reform, pledging fiscal austerity, and promising drastic changes through market economics, he kept postponing the implementation of such crucial policies to avoid alienating key distributional coalitions. He hoped that positive results could be attained by a less traumatic ad hoc approach. An Alfonsín economic adviser acknowledged that the momentary "stability that ensued after the Austral [Plan] lulled the willingness to reform."[77]

Alfonsín also failed to some extent in sticking to other campaign promises. His pledge to respect Congress and make it a forum for the debate of national problems was abandoned. Lacking a congressional majority, the president more and more used executive orders to bypass Congress. A typical example was the monetary reform creating the austral, which though it required congressional approval was enacted by executive order. Moreover, his administration was marred by corruption scandals, which made a mockery of the campaign promise of clean government. As a matter of fact, the Radicals rewarded political clienteles with government jobs and contracts, thus worsening an already precarious fiscal deficit.[78] Moreover, the president underestimated the military's political muscle and thus failed to design a coherent policy. He also overestimated his personal popularity. In the end, too many broken promises cost Alfonsín and the Radicals dearly at the polls in 1989, as the country entered its worst economic crisis ever. (See table 2.4.)

However, Alfonsín's errors should not be overemphasized, for he had little room to maneuver. Although his performance disappointed the high hopes of many Argentines, Alfonsín could claim that he had restored democracy. For the first time since 1928 a civilian president had been replaced by a democratically elected successor, and the rules of constitutional democracy could now count on the consensus of the vast majority of citizens. Moreover, never before had Argentines enjoyed so much freedom nor had their parties shown a greater sense of political responsibility.

The Menem Administration

During his presidential campaign, Menem pledged that if elected he would faithfully adhere to the Peronist creed of economic nationalism, strong state regulation of the economy, economic growth through government financing (productive revolution, or *revolución productiva*), and social justice in the form of income redistribution in favor of salary and wage earners (the so-called *salariazo*). Moreover, in foreign policy he promised to fight, if necessary, for the recovery of the Falkland/Malvinas islands and to enforce a five-year moratorium for the repayment of the country's foreign debt.[79] Such rhetoric gained him the support not only of the traditional Peronist constituency centered on the labor movement but also of those middle-class sectors that had voted for Alfonsín in 1983 and had been frustrated by five and a half years of unfulfilled

TABLE 2.4

The Economic Performance of the Alfonsín and Menem Regimes, 1984–1992

Factor	1984	1985	1986	1987	1988	1989	1990	1991	1992
GDP growth (%)	2.7	-4.4	5.7	2.2	-2.6	-4.5	0.0	8.9	8.7
Investment change (% of GDP)	14.1	12.5	17.5	17.0	-10.8	-27.0	-14.0	27.5	34.3
Real wages in manufacturing (1970 = 100)	117.5	99.5	101.2	94.3	89.1	76.4	73.2	69.5	68.8
Unemployment (%)	4.7	6.3	5.9	6.0	6.5	8.1	8.6	7.6	7.8
Underemployment (%)	5.4	7.5	7.7	8.2	8.9	8.6	9.3	8.5	8.3
Inflation (%)	627.5	672.2	90.1	131.3	343.0	3,079.2	2,314.0	84.0	17.5
Trade balance (US$ billion)	3.9	4.8	2.4	1.0	4.2	5.7	8.6	4.5	-2.8
Current accounts (US$ billion)	-2.4	-.9	-2.8	-4.2	-1.5	-1.3	1.7	-2.8	-5.0
Foreign debt (US$ billion)	48.8	50.9	52.4	58.4	58.7	64.7	61.1	56.2	58.0
Fiscal deficit (% of GDP)	-12.6	-6.1	-4.7	-7.3	-7.9	-8.0	-4.9	-1.8	0.2

Sources: Interamerican Development Bank, *Economic and Social Progress in Latin America: 1992 Report* (Washington D.C.: Interamerican Development Bank, 1992), p. 23; Central Bank of Argentina; and Argentine Industrial Union. The figures for 1991 and 1992 are preliminary.

promises and economic disasters. Although Menem skillfully avoided any specifics about concrete policy plans, few questioned his real intentions. After all, his Peronist credentials were impeccable. A three-time governor of La Rioja, one of Argentina's poorest provinces, the flamboyant Menem had put half of that province's work force on the state payroll. When the Radical government curtailed disbursement of federal subsidies, he even printed his own money. However, with the country in its worst economic crisis of the century and the treasury's finances depleted, he realized in the weeks before assuming office that no room was left for the redistributive measures he had promised. Thus, if the consolidation of democracy had been all-important for Alfonsín, the solution of the economic crisis became the top priority of the Menem administration.

In the most stunning policy reversal since Frondizi, Menem came to the conclusion that the recipe for turning around the economy no longer rested on the adoption of the old populist, nationalistic, redistributive approach but in the reestablishment of a free-market economy through a sweeping market-oriented reform program worthy of Thatcher and Reagan. Oddly enough, it took a Peronist president to undo most of Perón's reform policies of the 1940s. What provoked such a decision? An economist who served under Alfonsín argued that "Menem simply had no choice." However, Menem's adoption of a neoconservative economic approach was not an isolated case in Latin America but part of a regional trend. Old time proponents of state interventionism and economic nationalism like Acción Democrática's President Carlos Andrés Pérez in Venezuela, Christian Democratic President Patricio Aylwin in Chile, and populist President Alberto Fujimori in Peru, not to mention Mexican President Carlos Salinas de Gortari, once elected, became enforcers of free-market economics.[80]

Four major factors induced such a policy reorientation in the late 1980s, in Argentina as well as in the rest of the region. First, the old Keynesian model based upon state-led ISI, economic protection, and strong regulation of the private sector had exhausted its capacity to promote sustained growth. It had created a large and inefficient government bureaucracy, money-losing state enterprises, and huge fiscal deficits. Resources were channeled from the private sector into an unproductive public one, while import barriers protected inefficient state and private industries. Thus, when the state became incapable of pumping up the economy with fresh money and the private sector proved unable or unwilling to pick up the slack due to lack of incentives, Latin American economies began to experience growth rates from sluggish to negative. Second, and closely related, was the escalating foreign debt. The IMF, the World Bank, the U.S. Treasury, European governments, and foreign banks all admonished Latin American governments that the renegotiation of their debts was dependent upon the reduction of government intervention in the economy, the opening of the domestic market to foreign competition, and the adoption of an economic model that gave the role of promoting economic development to market forces rather than government manipulation. Third, the failure of neo-Keynesian, middle-of-the-road attempts tried in the 1980s in most of the region, along with the collapse of Marxist and socialist states around the world, left policy makers with no viable alternatives. Fourth, large sectors of the public had grown disenchanted with the old populist, interventionist model and were now receptive to free-market economics, which promised better services, less taxes, low inflation, and greater economic opportunities.[81]

Menem first formed a center-right coalition with a longtime political foe of Peronism, conservative Alvaro Alsogaray, leader of the Democratic Center Union (Unión del Centro Democrático, or UCD), who was asked to serve as personal adviser to the president for the renegotiation of the foreign debt. Alsogaray's daughter, María Julia (a UCD politician herself), was appointed trustee of the state telephone company, with the explicit mandate to privatize it. Other UCD members were appointed to government posts later on. Menem left the solution of the economic crisis in the hands of a team from Bunge and Born, the country's largest conglomerate, which, like Alsogaray, had opposed Perón's policies during the 1950s. In July 1989 Bunge and Born economists announced an orthodox stabilization plan described by Menem as "surgery without anaesthetic." The immediate aim was to stop hyperinflation through a massive devaluation of the austral and a major fiscal adjustment. Menem's alliance with big business constituted an event of historical proportions in the country's history. For the first time in the country's history, a coalition was established between a populist movement and the most influential economic groups.[82] When he was in the opposition, Menem had witnessed how powerful the distributional coalitions of large agricultural and industrial conglomerates could be when, through financial speculations in February 1989, they had forced the collapse of the Spring Plan. Thus, with the state in virtual bankruptcy, only the domestic private sector and foreign investors could resurrect the Argentine economy.

The Bunge and Born economic team, headed by Minister of the Economy Nestor Rapanelli, was able to achieve positive results in the short term by causing inflation and interest rates to drop significantly. This was done by cutting the fiscal deficit, reducing subsidies to the private sector, increasing tax revenues, and gaining the cooperation of important entrepreneurial groups to refrain from price and wage hikes. The long-term objective of the Bunge and Born plan was to set in motion a number of radical structural reforms that were not possible under

Alfonsín, in order to channel economic resources from financial speculations into productive investments. This, however, meant clashing with powerful distributional coalitions that had blossomed under the interventionist, closed-economy model.[83]

> While applauding the central role allocated to agriculture in the new economic model, rural producers attempted to force Rapanelli to reduce export taxes by refusing to exchange their hard-currency earnings for australs. Industrialists also had strong misgivings about Rapanelli's declared intention to modify entrepreneurial strategies. They were particularly concerned about the priority given to agriculture and the petroleum sector as part of the plan for Argentina's reinsertion into the world economy as a major commodity exporter. Meetings with the *Grupo María*, the *Unión Industrial Argentina* (UIA), and the *Consejo Empresario Argentino* (CEA) gave public vent to the fears of the leading "captains" that industrial interests (including those firms capable of exporting to world markets) would be sacrificed on the altar of fiscal austerity if state subsidies to the private sector were eliminated across the board.[84]

Small and medium-sized business, negatively affected by Rapanelli's policies, also cried foul and gained the support of big conglomerates like Techint that resented Bunge and Born's newly acquired political clout. A combination of entrepreneurial opposition and policy mistakes led to the downfall of the Bunge and Born plan after only six months. The resurgence of inflation in December 1989 led Menem to replace Rapanelli with a little-known accountant, Antonio Erman González, a Christian Democrat who had previously served as economy minister in the province of La Rioja. Yet the reform effort was continued with even greater energy. In little more than a year the mild-mannered González did more to free the market of its distortions than any of his more illustrious predecessors had done working under military regimes. He started by eliminating price and exchange controls (one of the few times this has happened) and by drastically reducing import duties.

In early January 1990 he converted, by decree, seven-day deposits yielding interests above the inflation rate into ten-year bonds (BONEX Series '89), which at maturity would be paid in U.S. dollars (but at a six percent interest rate, well below the inflation level). In practice, this amounted to an outright confiscation of $3 billion. The following October, he applied the same recipe to $8 billion of outstanding government debts to the private sector. This internal moratorium took a substantial amount of liquidity from the market. The positive consequences of these arbitrary measures were that the inflation rate was reduced substantially and so was the government's quasi-fiscal deficit.

The deflationary policies forced many people to sell their dollars to buy the few australs still in circulation. Consequently, the domestic currency that a few weeks earlier everyone wanted to sell greatly appreciated in value against the dollar and remained unusually stable all through 1990. By the same token, the financial markets suffered a severe blow, credit operations plummeted, and capital flight resumed. Most of all, economic growth remained anemic (see table 2.4). The following August, Menem granted González broad powers in economic matters, which enabled him to take control of the Central Bank and to cut the expenditures of federal agencies and state corporations and the transfers to provincial governments. This centralization of the decision process made him a de facto "super minister" or, as he was labeled in Argentina, "Super-Erman." To streamline government operations, González planned to lay off 122,000 public employees—a fifth of the government bureaucracy. In an effort to rationalize and improve the tax system, a new law was enacted creating a value-added tax.[85] Both corporate and income taxes had proven hard to collect in the past.

Despite these efforts, the administration failed to cut its budget deficit, putting pressure on an overvalued exchange rate and fueling inflationary expectations again. In early 1991, a new inflationary upsurge led to the resignation of González. His place was filled by Foreign Minister Domingo Cavallo, a well-known economist, who quickly introduced a more coherent and managerial approach to the government's economic policy.

A cornerstone of Menem's neoconservative agenda was sweeping reform of the state sector. At the beginning of his presidential term, the Peronist-controlled Congress approved the president's State Reform Law authorizing the executive branch to place trustees in charge of all state companies for 180 days. The law allowed the privatization of many of the 400 state enterprises, whose deficit in 1988 alone totaled $3.7 billion. A second bill, the Economic Emergency Law, gave the president the right to suspend costly industrial subsidies and tax breaks. By the end of 1991 the first round of privatizations had been accomplished, with the telephone company, two television stations, the national airline, some secondary oil fields, railway tracks, highways, gas and water companies, chemical plants, shipping companies, and port authorities being transferred to private ownership. The Argentine privatization process was the most sweeping in Latin America since the one carried out by General Pinochet in Chile in the 1970s. It brought to government coffers some $5.4 billion in revenues and $12.9 billion in debt reduction (many companies preferred to pay by purchasing debt equity papers issued by the Argentine government and foreign banks).[86] At the end of 1992 Menem announced the sale of most of the remaining state companies, for an expected $17 billion. Privatization policies stemmed from the realization that the economy could not be reconstructed without new foreign investments, which were lured to Argentina by granting them equal status with domestic investments and by selling assets well below their book value. After all, Menem answered his critics, the state could no longer guarantee many public services, anyway.

Important departures from the original campaign platform occurred in foreign policy as well. Menem made it clear that he wanted to bring Argentina back into the First World. In 1990, Foreign Minister Guido Di Tella put it in these terms, "We want to belong to the First World, to the Western alliance. They are our allies. . . . We are implementing the same policies, the policies that have led 10, 15, or 25 countries to prosperity."[87] This was a clear break from Alfonsín's emphasis on making Argentina a leading member of the Non-Aligned Movement (NAM) and a champion of Third World countries against "economic exploitation" by the capitalist countries of the north (meaning North America and Western Europe). The administration's tough austerity measures and privatization policies responded to the foreign creditors' demand to put the country back on track by adopting sound management criteria and by negotiating the rescheduling of its external debt. The international financial community welcomed Menem's policy U-turn and Argentina was able to secure a new IMF standby loan and additional help from the World Bank, the United States government, and European nations.

To gain closer ties with the United States, Menem broke with the Argentine tradition of neutrality in foreign affairs and dispatched two frigates to the Persian Gulf to enforce the embargo against Iraq in 1990.[88] Knowing that this initiative could not count on legislative support (which was required by the constitution) nor on public opinion (about 70 percent of the people interviewed were opposed to it), Menem bypassed Congress and resorted to an executive order to send the naval squad to the Gulf. Menem's strategy rested on the assumption that Argentina needed a closer relationship with the United States to receive its help in reducing its foreign debt, to attract U.S. investments, and to improve trade with that country. Here again was a sharp contrast with the previous Peronist administrations. Whereas Perón in the 1940s, starting from a position of relative strength, had challenged the United States by advocating an independent "third position" during the cold war years, a much weaker Menem found it more appropriate to show a cooperative spirit. As a matter of fact, Argentine-U.S. relations had never been better.[89] Argentina left the NAM (which it had joined in 1974, during the third Perón administration), repeatedly denounced Castro's regime in Cuba, and terminated the Condor middle-range ballistic missile project, against which the U.S. State Department had lobbied strongly.[90]

Relations with Europe improved substantially as well. Argentina resumed diplomatic links with the United Kingdom in February 1990 and signed preliminary accords dealing with the status of the Falklands/ Malvinas islands. This rapprochement was perceived as the key to securing greater exports to the European Economic Community (EEC), Argentina's largest commercial partner, and in fact, months later, Argentina and the EEC signed new commercial and technological accords. Continuing Alfonsín's early policy of closer ties with Latin American neighbors, Menem gave new impulse to the South American Common Market treaty (MERCOSUR) with Brazil, Paraguay, and Uruguay. Further, the president tried to diffuse border disputes with Chile by subjecting them to the arbitration of the Organization of American States.[91] On the military front, despite strong opposition from Radicals, human rights organizations, and public opinion, Menem attempted to defuse tensions between the armed forces and civil society through the use of special presidential powers: in October 1989 he pardoned about 280 people, some of them military officers and left-wing terrorists convicted of human rights abuses; and after crushing a military coup in December 1990, he pardoned the military officers still in jail and the former leader of the montonero terrorist group.

All these changes gained the president the approval of many business circles, conservative political parties, foreign governments, and international agencies, but they left the traditional Peronist constituency in disarray. As the consequences of the president's policies began to unfold, many who voted for Menem felt cheated, leaving the legitimacy of his mandate in doubt.[92] The Peronist party was torn between presidential supporters and those who thought Menem was a traitor. The labor movement was equally split. In the first month of his administration, Menem engineered the ouster of the CGT General Secretary Ubaldini, who opposed his measures, and replaced him with a person more willing to collaborate. The ouster was only partially successful, because the CGT then split into two rival factions, one loyal to Menem and the other supportive of Ubaldini, each claiming to be the legitimate representative of the labor organization. Not surprisingly, the unions endorsing Ubaldini were those in the public sector and thus most affected by the privatization plans, while the pro-Menem faction represented unions in the private sector. To weaken labor opposition to his policies, the president sent to Congress a stringent antistrike bill. When congressmen (including many Peronists) showed no intention of passing the bill, Menem enacted it into law through an executive order. His use of the executive order to break strikes by telephone, steel, and railway workers underscored the president's resolve to ignore union demands when they got in his way.

For their part, the Radicals after their 1989 electoral defeat had fallen into internal squabbling, which discredited them politically; the conservatives of the small UCD, while happy to see many of their ideas translated into action, felt that Menem was stealing their constituency, which furthered long-standing conflicts among their leadership. Opposition to

Menem's sweeping economic reforms also came from the provinces, including the seventeen Peronist governors. Traditionally, the provinces were heavily dependent on the federal government to fund their operations. However, when González tightened up outlays, governors were told to do the same and to slash expenditures. This meant laying off thousands of workers in depressed regions like the northwest, where the public sector constituted the largest employer. As local authorities found themselves unable to pay salaries, retirement pensions, and local suppliers, a deep crisis developed in Santa Cruz, Chubut, Jujuy, and La Rioja, leading to the resignations of their governors. In other provinces the crisis brought about civil unrest, forcing the central government to send federal interventors to reestablish law and order in Tucumán, Catamarca, and Corrientes, the first such actions since 1983. While the interventions were necessary, the end result was widespread public dismay with not only local authorities but also the Menem administration, which came to be perceived as the source of many ills.[93]

Finally, some distributional coalitions in the business community, and particularly state suppliers who had grown accustomed to fat government contracts (the so-called *patria contratista*), began to criticize Menem's recessionary policies. This was most ironic, since the same companies had often advocated reform of the government sector and had promoted free-market policies. However, once Menem cut subsidies, tax breaks, and contracts, they rose up against what they described as government abuse. More surprising, perhaps, was the formation, at the end of 1990, of a group partly made up of businessmen who had previously advocated economic austerity and reform but who now thought Menem's reforms went too far, too fast. The so-called Colón group gathered together prominent union bosses as well as highly visible business figures, like Guillermo Alchourón, former president of the powerful Argentine Rural Society, Gregorio Pérez Companc of the Companc conglomerate, Richard Handley of Citibank, and even former ally Jorge Born of Bunge and Born. Nonetheless, such opposition failed to coalesce: surprised by the speed of reforms, the labor movement, opposition parties, and negatively affected industrial, financial, and agricultural coalitions remained divided, disorganized, and unable to put forward any credible alternative.

Going into his second year, Menem stood by his reform plan. Without doubt, his policies had no precedent in recent Argentine history: they undermined powerful vested interests that even Martínez de Hoz had not dared to endanger. In 1990, three ministers of the economy and nine economic packages, Menem could claim that the foreign debt was declining, industries were improving their efficiency and reorienting their production toward the export sector, and the country was experiencing a record-breaking $8.6 billion trade surplus.

However, inflation remained volatile, unemployment and underemployment were at an all-time high, salary earners' purchasing power in relation to 1985 was down 65 percent (making a mockery of Menem's presidential campaign promise of a "productive revolution"), and 40 percent of the national income, according to the president himself, still evaded taxation. Moreover, the unraveling of some privatization schemes and the lack of improvement in services by newly privatized companies made many wonder about the soundness of the free-market approach. The president's popularity sagged, mirroring citizens' increasing disenchantment with not only the country's economic performance but also presidential pardons, corruption, and the dispatch of warships to the Persian Gulf.[94] After reaching an unprecedented 81 percent in August 1989, Menem's February 1991 approval ratings plummeted below 20 percent.[95] To complicate matters, Menem, who during his campaign had promised an honest and clean government, saw many of the most prominent people in his administration resign under allegations of corruption. Among the first to go was union leader Luis Barrionuevo, an early Menem supporter and fund-raiser, who had been in charge of the powerful state agency dispensing welfare benefits. Similar charges of corruption prompted the resignation of Public Works Minister Roberto Dromi, who was in charge of the privatization program, and María Julia Alsogaray, who had grossly mismanaged the privatization of ENTEL, the telephone company. A further blow to the president came when relatives of his estranged wife, Zulema Yoma, were accused of using their high posts in the administration to their personal advantage.[96]

Fortunately for Menem, the economic situation turned unexpectedly positive in mid-1991. In March new Minister of the Economy Domingo Cavallo launched the most audacious stabilization plan yet. He had Congress approve legislation creating a "dollar standard" regime in Argentina. Accordingly, the Central Bank pledged to back with foreign currency and gold reserves all australs in circulation at an exchange rate of 10,000 australs per U.S. dollar. This measure prevented the government from running a fiscal deficit, thought by many to be at the core of the inflationary cycle. In other words, from now on the Argentine government would spend only what it earned, without resorting any longer to the old trick of printing money. An important feature of the new plan called for the elimination of indexation clauses from salary agreements and labor contracts, which tended to perpetuate inflation. Cavallo also persuaded some industrial and farm producers to cut their prices in return for tax reductions.

After only six months, the plan paid off: inflation dropped to its lowest point in over two decades, and interest rates plummeted to their lowest level in thirty years. The unexpected price stability spurred a bullish stock market, which posted the largest profits worldwide.[97] In turn, many sectors began to experience an economic recovery. Wages began to improve, unemployment decreased, and public opinion polls showed strong support for Cavallo's economic policies. Cavallo enjoyed greater approval ratings than Menem and, as a matter of fact, slowly became the virtual prime minister, with powers greater than those enjoyed by Erman Gonzáles before him. In early September, the PJ scored a landslide victory in the mid-term congressional and gubernatorial elections, capturing ten of twelve governorships at stake, including the most important one, Buenos Aires. The Radicals, on the other hand, were badly defeated. Although many analysts contended that the victory was a vote of confidence for Cavallo rather than Menem, the government as a whole came out greatly strengthened.

Following the electoral results, Cavallo announced yet another important measure aimed at dismantling the old state intervention structure. A sweeping deregulation decree lifted all restrictions on prices, business hours, export and import taxes, and import quotas, scrapped many remaining subsidies to the private sector; and eliminated ten government monopolies and regulatory agencies. Once one of the most regulated and closed economies in the world, Argentina turned into one of the most open. Menem and Cavallo were hailed abroad by foreign governments and multilateral agencies as examples of a new brand of Latin American leadership.[98] In 1992, thanks to a new tax reform, the privatization of state enterprises, lower inflation, and stricter control over tax evasion, the government showed a fiscal surplus for the first time since the 1940s. The profitable business climate created by privatization and deregulation lured into Argentina $7.8 billion of foreign and Argentine capital once invested abroad.[99]

The big strides made on all these accounts and the excellent relations established with the Bush administration opened to Argentina the long-sought incorporation into the Brady plan.[100] The Brady plan allowed Argentina to wipe out $2.5 billion owed to creditor banks and to reduce its outstanding debt from $64 billion in 1989 to more manageable proportions. Although the interest burden would increase, as now payments were higher, Argentina's creditworthness and international standing improved. The plan, in fact, cleared the way for additional lending from the IMF ($3.15 billion) and the World Bank and the Inter-American Development Bank ($1.2 billion).

Thus, with all his contradictory statements and policy reversals, Menem in the first half of his term displayed an uncanny ability to weather any kind of political storm. He survived attacks from his enemies by exploiting the deep divisions among labor, opposition parties, and interest groups. To his critics within the Peronist movement, Menem pointed out that even Perón had limited the right to strike and had granted concessions to U.S. petroleum companies to exploit Argentine oil. He also added, "Current Peronism is a totally updated Peronism. . . . If the world changes, the political parties must change. I would be a fool or a slow-witted person if I wanted to practice in 1991 the Peronism practiced in the 1940s."[101]

However, the most troublesome aspects of Menem's presidency—those in the social and political spheres—remained. First, despite being elected with the strong backing of the working class, Menem's policies had completely neglected this sector. The dramatic swing toward capital accumulation, favoring the most affluent members of society, pointed up the conditions of the poor, as income inequalities increased. While in 1960 the wealthiest 10 percent of the population shared 39 percent of the gross domestic product, by the end of the 1980s this share had jumped to 46 percent. Of a population of 32 million people, over a third lived in poverty.[102] Moreover, 9 million people lacked running water and 17 million proper sewage disposal.[103] Most disturbing, however, is that many of these poor once belonged to the lower-middle and working class but, as a result of the prolonged crisis, had lost their jobs and fallen into poverty. Between 1984 and 1989 unemployment and underemployment doubled and the purchasing power of wages dropped 61 percent. The trend became more acute under Menem, as austerity measures cut many social programs that had eased the life of the poor. Such a state of affairs prompted Pope John Paul II, the Argentine Catholic church, opposition parties, and human rights organizations to denounce Menem's capital accumulation model, which inevitably excluded so many once integrated social groups from the economy. Ironically, "The general thrust of Peronist social programmes has been towards self-help and away from welfare."[104]

A second problem was Menem's attempts to legitimize government actions by personal charisma rather than institutions. Unlike Alfonsín, torn between a commitment to uphold the rule of law and his use of presidential decrees to get things done, Menem did not disguise his intention to achieve his goals regardless of the means. In his first half of his administration, Menem deemphasized the role of political institutions to legitimize government action and in many ways downgraded the role of Congress and the judiciary. He not only used—some would say abused—his powers extensively, as in the case of presidential pardons and the use of decrees to bypass Congress, but also added justices to the Supreme Court to ensure the court's loyalty. While he defended these measures as necessary, they constituted a severe blow to constitutional democracy. Depending on presidential charisma rather than on institutions to solve socioeconomic conflicts places an unbearable burden on the chief executive. This could end in a stalemate like that of 1976, or of May 1989, if presidential leadership fails. The final chapter returns to these issues and discusses in more detail the problems of democratic consolidation, political stability, and social equity, which are at the core of the Argentine riddle.

3

THE POLITICAL PARTY SYSTEM

E. E. SCHATTSCHNEIDER SAID about democracy that it would be "unthinkable save in terms of parties."[1] Wildenmann added that "party government is the crucial agency of *institutional legitimation*." Among other things, parties shape the popular vote, create political identities, mobilize and channel popular participation, aggregate and articulate societal interests, provide political leadership, and design—and once in office, carry out—public policy.[1] Indeed the role of parties in a democratic setting is to act in a way that will bring legitimacy to the institutional setting, a setting that citizens perceive as fair and responsive to their demands and that promotes a sense of self-efficacy. For Alessandro Pizzorno: "if creation and preservation of political trust is to be considered the ultimate function of political parties in a representative regime, we may conclude . . . that political parties are thriving when other bases of trust . . . are lacking or politically dormant, and citizens are in need of stable structures to which they can trustfully refer to orient themselves not only in their utilization of political machineries but also in their acquisition of new social identities. Parties *decay* when these conditions do not obtain."[2]

A cross-country study of Latin American democracies in the 1980s stresses the importance of the party role: "An important element in the institutional resilience of democracy has been the strength of the party system and the high degree of institutionalization and popular loyalty achieved by the major parties. . . . All of our cases call attention to the institutional strength and weakness of parties as a determinant of success or failure with democracy."[3] A later cross-country analysis emphasizes that, although parties by themselves do not determine "the entire foundations of stable democracies, an examination of the evidence concerning the various dimensions of party institutionalization should provide at least one significant clue as to whether . . . democracy has a more solid *potential* for survival in Latin America . . . compared to the situation of a generation ago."[4]

Unfortunately, in Argentina, parties have failed as an agent of democratic legitimation, have been unable to create political trust, and have remained weakly institutionalized. The result has been the decay of democratic institutions and of the parties themselves. One analyst goes as far as to say that "democratic institutions have just not been where the action is. . . . Democracy never had a chance in Argentina."[5] We have seen (chapter 2) how early in their history Argentine political parties were incapable of (or unwilling to practice) legitimate government action. As time went on, with society becoming more complex and the distributional coalitions discussed in chapter 1 becoming stronger, parties were increasingly, incapable of representing and articulating the demands of interest groups. The cause of this phenomenon rests on the very nature of Radicalism and Peronism, the country's two major political forces, which resembled movements more than parties. Despite their claim to represent the "national opinion" and the interest of "all Argentines," both movements purposely ignored the demands of the most important economic interest groups. This, for instance, is the case of the Radicals, whereas the Peronists became too identified with the interests of one group (labor), thus alienating contending distributional coalitions.

The very fact that interest groups developed independently of political parties was counterproductive for democracy. The economic strength of agricultural, financial, and industrial distributional coalitions, on the one hand, and labor, on the other, gave all of them a veto power. Such a veto power restricted the ability of Radical, Peronist, and authoritarian administrations to pursue long-term policies and accomplish the needed socioeconomic changes. In this regard, "because political decisions are entirely the outcome of negotiations between separate interests, political parties have to adapt their structure to the needs of the real actors, the interest groups."[6] Yet this did not happen precisely because the *movimientista* nature of Radicalism and Peronism prevented them from acting as effective mediators of contending interests. Instead, distributive conflicts came to be resolved in open confrontations, often adjudicated by the military. These conflicts ended in power alignments that were only temporary and were usually overturned at the next crisis.

The Development of Argentine Political Parties

Until the last quarter of the nineteenth century, the evolution of Argentine parties resembled that of some southern European countries. The crucial departure from this pattern came at the turn of the century, when the rise of socialism in Europe ushered in the era of mass parties whereas mass movements became dominant in Argentina. Although many scholars preceive Argentine parties as embedded in the Hispanic, Catholic, and other domestic political traditions, Argentina's case is not sui generis.

In describing European elite participation in party politics, one writer distinguishes three forms: the elite "have participated from the outset, slowly learning to share power with newer groups; they have participated in the party system but only half-heartedly and with reactionary intentions; or they have stayed outside altogether, seeking to maintain their influence through other power structures."[7] If we apply this classification to the evolution of party politics in Argentina in the second half of the nineteenth century, we can see that Argentine elites played the second and third roles to some degree. We saw in the previous chapter how the landed and commercial elites of Buenos Aires and the provinces came to dominate politics through a wide variety of conservative parties from 1862 until 1916. However, they remained extremely reluctant to incorporate the emerging urban middle classes until 1912, and by then it was too late. Throughout the second half of the nineteenth century the conservative parties that represented them were more reactionary than conservative, since their main goal was the preservation of the status quo—in spite of occasional attempts to co-opt the Radicals.

That the elites participated in the party system only half-heartedly is testified to by the fact that the conservative parties remained elusive political formations, coming into play only at election time and becoming dormant again afterward. Moreover, the elitist principles they defended made a mockery of representative democracy. In other words, although democratic institutions and parties did exist on paper, in practice they operated a political system based upon exclusion. Thus what was true of early conservative parties in Europe—that they "tended to remain little more than outward appearances, democratic fig leaves . . . for entrenched power positions that had their basis elsewhere"—can also be said of Argentine conservative parties.[8] By the same token, the Radicals—who in the beginning represented elite members estranged by the power arrangements established by more prominent groups—stayed outside the party system until 1916, preferring either abstention from electoral politics or violent revolutions (with the support of young military officers).

Similar to the agrarian liberals of Europe, Argentine conservatives preached the virtues of authority, tradition, and conformity to the established order.[9] These conservative parties were initially created by local notables, and, as in France and Italy at about the same time, their organization in Congress often reflected special provincial interests or geographic proximity to assure control over government policy.[10] Initially, these parties lacked any organization in the modern sense; due to the fact that most of the population was still to be enfranchised. Their basic unit was the local caucus, which comprised a restricted number of notables—those with control over the patronage system. Party caucuses came into play during electoral periods. Thus, conservative parties were at best loose political formations. Party systems prior to the emergence of mass parties "are typically fragile if not evanescent parties; they reflect 'coalition linkage,' at best a confederal linkage, among self-sufficient units, i.e., among notables or popular leaders elected in their own right. Therefore the elite-notability parties amount to loose, if not shifting, systems of alliances. In other words, in the pre-mass stage the leaders stand above the party; in a very literal sense, the party consists of the leaders."[11]

This thesis seems to closely describe Argentine events. In 1874, many provincial and porteño conservative parties were merged into the PAN so that the president and his governors could exercise personal control. In fact, the president and the governors selected the PAN's candidates for Congress and other public offices. Splits among the Conservatives prior to and during the PAN's dominance were not so much over policy content as over political patronage and the shares of the spoils of power. "Such particularistic, kin-centered 'ins-outs' opposition are common in the early phases of nation-building; the electoral clienteles are small, undifferentiated, and easily controlled, and the stakes to be gained or lost in public life tend to be personal and concrete rather than collective and general."[12]

The demise of Argentine conservatism was the direct consequence of its inability to change from an agent of elitist representation to one of popular representation. The first challenge to the PAN came from those estranged members of the elites that first organized in the Civic Union and later in the Radical Civic Union. As the "outs" of the political system, the Radicals opted for an antisystem stance and advocated violent revolution. The other "outs" were the anarchists and syndicalists, who were concentrated in the working class. Like their counterparts in Southern Europe, Argentine anarchists and syndicalists shared the conviction that working within the framework of electoral participation and the existing "democratic" institutions was useless.[13] In this, at least, they agreed with the Radicals. In this rejection of party politics by the emerging social sectors of society we can find the seeds of the problems that plagued parties and democratic institutions thereafter. Thus, although the elites had created a supposedly democratic system (albeit half-heartedly), the middle and working classes refused to work through that system, since they did not believe in it.

Argentine socialists, on the other hand, tried to organize the working class and to promote change within the system by participating in electoral politics. However, their support remained relatively small, as anarchists and syndicalists commanded the loyalty of the majority of the working class (see chapter 6). This fact turned out to be of critical importance. At the turn of the century, European socialist parties entered electoral politics, and through their mobilization and organizational skills ushered in a period of mass politics that dramatically changed the way party politics was played. Party caucuses based upon loosely organized alliances of notables began to be challenged by tightly organized, ideologically minded, and well-financed mass parties, forcing the conservatives to do the same. "In contrast to the coalition party, the mass European party is a linkage party; not only is it a suprapersonal entity that stands above its leaders, but the party consists of its organizational linkage. In a very real sense the linkage *is* the party."[14] In Argentina at roughly the same time mass political movements emerged in the form of Radicalism. Thus, if mass European parties were the creatures of mass democracy and its main stabilizing force, in Argentina as well as other countries of Latin America mass movements, or movimientismo, were born outside of it and retained certain features detrimental to the democratic process.

Why is this so? Before I answer the question I should clarify that, when talking about mass movements and movimientismo, the reference is to those movements that mobilize their supporters to gain office through elections and, to this end, may also take up the formal name of parties although they are not.[15] This clarification is necessary because movements in Latin America and elsewhere have also appeared within business, labor, and even environmental groups, which do not necessarily seek office. According to David Rock, movements are "usually erected upon *caudillos* and often exemplify the peculiarly Latin American politico-cultural tradition known as 'personalism.' "[16] But while Rock is quite correct in identifying the caudillo and personalism roots of Latin American movements, it is also necessary to stress that movements by themselves are not just peculiar to countries with Hispanic and Catholic backgrounds. Movements like fascism and Qualunquismo in Italy, nazism in Germany, and Poujadism and Gaullism in France are examples of non-Hispanic phenomena. In the United States, Robert La Folette in the 1920s, Huey Long in the 1930s, and Ross Perot in 1992 also tried to lead popular movements challenging the existing party system.[17]

One of the problems of movimientismo that affect democratic institutions stems from the way movements are organized. Radicalism, for instance, although it began to organize itself in local and national standing committees that remained active even after electoral campaigns, still resembled a cadre party: the goal of cadre parties is the "grouping of notabilities for the preparation of elections, conducting campaigns, and maintaining contact with the candidates; . . . what the mass party secures by numbers, the cadre party achieves by selection."[18] Not until 1908 did Radical "clubs" organize themselves into "committees," often at the ward level. Well-defined programs, typical of mass parties were absent and were replaced by fiery slogans. Radical committees were usually closed circles, which enlisted new members primarily through selective cooptation rather than enrolling new people which is typical of mass parties. Not surprisingly, committee chairmen acted more like bosses and worked more at strengthening electoral loyalties based on patronage politics than on being delegates. Indeed, the whole structure of Radicalism resembled a loose top-down organization.[19] Like other movements that evolved into cadre parties, Radicalism tended to appeal to the masses while keeping them in a passive role. The same applies to Peronism. During Perón's first two terms, the Peronist movement was organized into corporatistlike associations, which, however, "were assembled in such a way under authoritarian Peronist bosses so as to filter and limit . . . demands. The system also obliged groups seeking government responsiveness to their sectional demands to enter into a relationship of formal subordination."[20]

Several elements of electoral mass movements can be identified. One is *movimientismo*, which has been a vehicle for dissenting members of the ruling elites to gain power in times of crisis when existing institutions loose their legitimacy. While giving the masses the impression of having a say in how things are run, mass movements actually limit mobilization. It is not by chance that both Radicalism and Peronism have traditionally been strongly anti-Marxist. Moreover, in its beginnings, Radicalism remained aloof not only from the working class but also from foreigners. Yrigoyen tried to attract the working class, yet only in 1928 were his overtures met with success, and that was temporary. However, after the rise of Peronism, Radicalism's appeal, save for the 1983 elections, was primarily confined to the middle classes. While Peronism made organized labor its "vertebral column," it did so in a paternalist, conservative fashion, seeing communism as a deadly enemy.

Another element of mass movements has to do with the external world; the movement is based upon the distinction between friend and enemy, we and they. The relationship between these two parts of a dichotomy is open conflict. In turn, this produces a zero-sum-game approach to problem solving. The purpose of the movement is to defeat the enemy. There is little or no room in this relationship for mediation, negotiation, or compromise.[21] A further element of mass movements is the relationship between the individual and the movement itself, a relationship of identity. As "the individual 'believes' in the movement, identifies with it, his/her personality loses individuality and acquires a group dimension."[22] The central element of mass movements is charismatic leadership. Charisma can be defined as an influence relationship marked by asymmetry, directness, and, for the follower, great passion. Asymmetry means that the leader has profound influence on attitudes and behavior of the following but that the opposite is not true; the following does provide the all-important empowering responses . . . but its other influence on the leader is muted. Directness means the absence of significant mediation of the relationship, by either formal structures or informal networks. Great passion is a little more difficult to define. It is much more than the feeling an audience associates with "popular" public figures—although the term charisma is often (and almost always, wrongly) applied to such figures. Indeed, it is much more than many of us have ever experienced in dealing with leaders of one kind or another. Great passion means intense devotion to and extraordinary reverence for the leader. Of the three defining elements, it obviously is this which is most distinctive of charisma.[23]

Although charisma is valued as an essential component of political leadership regardless of the country, in electoral movements it becomes all-important. The leader asserts himself as the founder, the undisputed master, the embodiment, and the sole interpreter of a set goals and political symbols. "The logic of the movement is such that the stronger the loyalty, the devotion, the surrender of the movement to its leader, the greater the leader's capacity to defeat his enemies. The leader, due to his extraordinary capacity, interprets and expresses the *feeling* of the masses. For this reason, movements provoke more passion than rationality. The relationships of authority that develop within it are of a personal type, and are not framed into clear and defined institutional rules, precisely because the fundamental function of the movement is to break a specific institutional setting. The movement creates its own values which give it unity, while the rules of conduct are flexible, informal, and not regulated."[24]

Thus, the creation of strong, long-lasting institutions and organizations goes against the very nature of mass movements, because institutions establish rules and procedures that would limit the discretionary decision-making power of the charismatic leader and his interpretation of the "popular feeling." The longer the movement remains loosely organized, the greater chance the leader has to do what he wants. Thus, the vested interest of charismatic leaders and their movements in democratic institutions exists as long as the latter serve the goals of the former. The mass movement's antiregime, antistatus quo origins have much to do with their antiparty character.[25] In Argentina, their formation outside of Congress and traditional party politics—similar to some of the externally created mass parties of Western Europe—often induced mass movements to be antidemocratic and plebiscitary and to discount the existing political, social, and economic institutions.[26] Yrigoyen, and more so Perón, downplayed party politics. Instead, they referred to their political creatures as movements, and once in power, they further downgraded democratic institutions.

The looseness of mass movements' ideological stands is another of their major elements. Interestingly enough, Argentine movements claimed to be true representatives of the "people" while downplaying the class cleavages that communism and socialism point up. Movements appealed to the "citizens" and the "national community." A typical example is the Radical profession of faith, which reads as follows: "The Radical Civic Union is not a simple political party, it is not a group that struggles for its own benefit. . . . It is instead the patriotic mandate of our national solidarity, of the intransigence with which the radical sentiment of Argentine civic dignity can be fulfilled." Radicalism is thus a concept of the total life of the people. "The Radical revolution, based on man and his liberty, is composed of all aspects of life from religion to economics. Radicalism is not partial to social classes, races or offices; it looks upon man as a man, with dignity. For Radicalism the ends are inalterable: liberty and democracy for the integration of man. The means may very because they are only instruments, and because the social conditions of the national reality will themselves vary."[27] Both Yrigoyenism and Peronism rallied people around nationalistic, xenophobic themes and, at the same time, claimed to strive for the "harmony of classes" and the achievement of "social justice" through a more equitable distribution of income across social sectors. Indeed, what counts for the charismatic leader is the control of the state and its resources. This leader, having been supported by a heterogeneous coalition of societal groups previously excluded from the spoils of power, finds it essential to dispense government jobs and contracts to the political clientele making up the movement.

There are several differences among the various movements that emerged in Argentina in the last hundred years, because their emergence was a response to crises brought about by the social and economic changes in distinct historic periods. Peronism, for instance, upscaled the mass movement tradition by bringing innovations; under Perón, movimientismo turned into a more extreme form, populism. With populism, "new political actors were incorporated in the political arena. But they lacked ideological and organizational autonomy. In addition, the expanded participation in no way meant a strengthening of the *political system*. Instead, opposing forces fought for the occupation and the appropriation of the State, which became paradoxically more and more the embodiment of the interests of those sectors which controlled it and at the same time more and more powerful and autonomous with respect to the excluded interests."[28]

This way of governing—for the benefit of previously marginal socioeconomic sectors and to the detriment of previously dominant groups—

alienated the latter. Moreover, this problem was coupled by the movements' structural inability to mediate among contending interests inside and outside the movement itself, save perhaps for the charismatic leader. This scenario set in motion a vicious cycle. After 1946 many agricultural, industrial, financial, and commercial interest groups that did not share the goals of either the Radicals or the Peronists did not have a strong conservative party to represent their interests. As a result, they began to look to the military to end their exclusion from power and thus became known as the military party.[29] The failure of the Argentine party system in this century has indeed been this lack of linkage between conservative economic interests and mass-based electoral movements.

In the absence of effective mediative political institutions and clear-cut rules of the game, it is no wonder that conflict among the various distributional coalitions increased in intensity and produced the effects described in the first chapter. Since the real source of power rested not with parties but with the presidency, the state bureaucracy, government agencies, and the military, interest groups devoted their lobbying efforts to these.[30] This tendency was strengthened after 1930 as authoritarian governments began to banish parties altogether. The unstable nature of the political system after 1930 taught distributional coalitions that their interests were best served by ad hoc nonbinding agreements or coalitions to achieve short-term objectives, since "getting stuck" with the "wrong" party would spell economic disaster. This short-term behavior, in turn, made it very difficult for parties to make inroads among economic interest groups. In the 1980s, political parties found themselves ill equipped to reverse this trend [due to ideological stands,] and were unable to present a unified leadership with whom interest groups could deal. In 1988, a survey based on open-ended interviews with businessmen and union leaders concluded that they did not trust political parties as an effective means of interest mediation.[31]

Movimientismo remained a dominant characteristic of Argentine politics even after Perón's downfall. Actually, electoral movements flourished in even greater numbers than before. First Frondizi, with his Movement of Integration and Development (MID), and later Aramburu, Levingston, Lanusse, Massera, and Galtieri had plans for the creation of popular movements to back their presidential ambitions; all failed. With Peronism and Radicalism claiming the bulk of the electorate, such attempts were easily frustrated. Both of these movements had mobilized previously unorganized social sectors and had retained, to some degree, their loyalties. The movements that followed after 1955 found "all the bases loaded." This partially explains the failure of Peronism without Perón in the 1960s.[32] What can explain the longevity of Radicalism and Peronism in comparison to other movements? As we saw, mass movements are based on a charismatic bond with their leader. However, charisma is often volatile and must be constantly reinforced by both ideological and material incentives. Max Weber theorized that "pure" charismatic movements are most likely to disappear after a brief existence unless charisma becomes "routinized."[33] After the initial euphoria, charismatic movements are faced with two possibilities: "(1) the movement . . . fails to beat the enemy and consequently loses support, strength, and loyalties, which can drive it to extinction; (2) the movement transforms the existing order and enters into a mature phase, which corresponds to the process of institutionalization [and] the 'routinization' of charisma. From a situation of exceptionality [the movement] goes into one of normalcy."[34]

We have seen that charismatic movements, almost by definition, are averse to institutions and institution building, since it is the best interest of the leader to maintain freedom of action. The reason many movements quickly disappear is precisely that their founding leaders try to obstruct the institutionalization process. The routinization of charisma involves a "transfer of loyalties from the leader to the organization . . . a growing divergence between the party's organizational identity and the leader's personal political fortune . . . a movement from a solidarity system towards a system of interests, and the adaption of the original goals to the daily organizational needs."[35] In simple words, this entails a process wherein the mass movement acquires the features of a political party. The initial uncoordinated mobilization process mastered by the charismatic leader begins to be coordinated and structured according to some rules. From being the means of the charismatic leader's ambitions, the movement becomes an end in itself, with its own interests and loyalties. The movement can be held together by the provision of two types of incentive: collective and selective. Collective incentives usually refer to the reinforcement among the movement's rank and file of an identity with the ideals set forth by the charismatic leader. This identity helps them keep their loyalty to the movement. Selective incentives, on the other hand, have to do with patronage politics. This means the prospect of careers for notables who see in the movement a springboard for their own ambitions, and, at the rank-and-file level, various jobs and favors. If selective incentives are appealing enough, supporters will try to institutionalize the movement to enable it to survive the eventual eclipse or death of the movement's founding father. By institutionalizing itself into something resembling a party, the mass movement establishes its autonomy with respect to its external environment and creates the basis for its preservation.

Most movements do not survive beyond their initial stage, and even those that do survive do not institutionalize in the same way. Among those that succeed, some create stronger party organizations than others. Radicalism and Peronism are cases in point: both survived the deaths of Yrigoyen and Perón, respectively, by institutionalizing themselves into organizations resembling cadre parties. Yet they did not do so in the same way. Their differences can be explained by using Angelo Panebianco's model of party institutionalization. The degree of institutionalization of a given movement trying to become a party is dependent upon two dimensions: the movement's autonomy with respect to its external environment and its systemness—that is, "the degree of interdependence of its different internal sectors."[36]

Let us examine the first factor. Autonomy is accomplished when the party can control its collateral associations, can draw upon its own finances, has a strong central bureaucratic organization that dominates peripheral party branches, has national party leaders who dominate local ones, and has a party leadership selected from within the party. Autonomy is weak when the party depends on member organizations, like trade unions, for funds, campaign organization, and the mobilization of the rank and file. This seems to be true of Peronism, within which the labor movement constituted what Perón called the vertebral column. Unions played the major role in all the presidential elections where Peronist candidates participated. According to Panebianco, the greater the organizational boundaries between the party and external groups, the greater the autonomy. In the case of the PJ, the opposite is true, because many groups and associations formally outside the party are in fact part of it and have kept their ties with internal factions within the party. As for the Radicals, union dependence does not exist; the UCR enjoys greater autonomy from its external environment than does the PJ.

Systemness, on the other hand, is concerned with the autonomy of subgroups within the organization.[37] The less systemness the organization has, the more heterogeneous it is. Both the UCR and the Peronists have exhibited chronic factionalism and have had subgroups that used their financial and mobilizational resources to defy central authority. This is particularly true of the Peronists in the mid-1970s and the late 1980s: many union bosses resisted party leaders' attempts to diminish their authority. The centralization of the UCR is a little greater than in the PJ. The chairman of the UCR national committee often, although not always, is the recognized party leader and the probable presidential candidate when the party is in the opposition. However, committee chairmen at the local and provincial levels have substantial autonomy in times of unclear political leadership. The powerful electoral machines of Córdoba, and to a lesser extent Misiones, Río Negro, Mendoza, Santa Fe, and Entre Ríos, have routinely tried to establish their bargaining position vis-à-vis the party leadership from the Federal District.

Thus, party institutionalization has been greater for Radicalism than for Peronism, but from an organizational standpoint, both parties remain quite weak. The unwillingness of both the UCR and the Peronists to embark upon full-fledged party institutionalization and their determination to retain many movimientista features has much to do with the personal ambitions of middle-ranking leaders concerned with keeping their options open. Although some party organization has emerged, the overall trend has been one of "atomized individualism" within the party, which has created a situation "in which the incumbents do not fight across party lines, but are primarily engaged in internecine 'list' battling."[38] For instance, in the 1985 congressional elections, rival Peronist leaders presented several lists of candidates. The same happened in 1991 when the Peronist CGT leader Saúl Ubaldini ran for governor of Buenos Aires against the official party candidate. Ironically, whenever a strong leader arises as the clear front-runner, the institutionalization process stops. Both Alfonsín and Menem, at the peak of their success, downplayed the role of their parties while revitalizing the movimientista tradition.[39] This is because a strengthening of the party structure would have limited their room for maneuvering, while the return to strong charismatic leadership could keep their internal enemies at bay.

During the early period of the transition to democratic rule (1983–1984), there seemed to be a genuine interest from many quarters of Argentine society to claim the role of political parties and Congress. However, these good intentions faded quickly. First Alfonsín and, later, Menem purposely relegated their parties to marginal roles. This centralization of the decision-making process, which took place during 1983–1992, emphasized the president's direct mediation with key distributional coalitions and left parties completely out of the action. The UCR and Peronist presidents merely allowed the different factions of their respective parties to divide the spoils of power among themselves, which in turn fueled widespread corruption. Congress, as well, failed to gain a crucial role for itself. On the contrary, congressional representatives came to be perceived by the public as corrupt and whose sole interest was to look after the interests of powerful lobbies. By the early 1990s the "downgrading of parties, politicians, and Congress, implied that the majority of the Argentine society perceived with frustration and disgust those institutions that had been re-evaluated during the transition of 1983." As a consequence, people began to act politically outside the party system and to "exercise the protest vote without feeling obliged to party loyalties or ideological stands."[40]

The Radicals

The 1955 military coup that established the Liberating Revolution regime drew the support of most opposition parties. President Aramburu's executive order dissolving the Peronist party and banning Peronism from electoral participation left the UCR as the only major party competing with many small, often regionally based, parties. The political scenario that ensued was one of extreme polarization. The only common cause bringing conservatives, socialists, and Radicals together was the demotion of Perón from power. Once this was achieved, differences over political and economic issues surfaced almost immediately. Moreover, opposition parties had been so engaged in their vendetta against Perón that they had neglected concrete policy programs to tackle the unfolding economic crisis of the mid-1950s. The UCR was a typical example of this situation. Balbín, the party leader who had unsuccessfully challenged Perón in the 1951 presidential elections, was an old-style, unimaginative politician. His ideas were still anchored to the old Radical doctrines of intransigence (that is, a refusal to compromise or to form electoral alliances with the other political forces), strong government regulation of the economy, and opposition to "foreign imperialism." Balbín was bitterly anti-Peronist and openly supported President Aramburu's project to thoroughly de-Peronize Argentine society.[41]

One politician who seemed to diverge from the dominant witch-hunting attitude of those days was Arturo Frondizi, Balbín's running mate in 1951. Frondizi reasoned that in order to promote economic growth and political stability it was necessary to reincorporate the Peronists into the political system. This stand provoked a split within the UCR in 1957, leading Balbín to form the UCRP, while Frondizi organized his own party, the UCRI.[42] The UCRP had slightly greater support than the UCRI, averaging, between 1957 and 1965, 20–30 percent of the vote, as opposed to the UCRI's 20–25 percent. The UCRP's stronghold was primarily Buenos Aires, whose delegates had voted for Balbín at the 1957 UCR convention in Tucumán. Conversely, the UCRI did better in most of the less developed provinces.[43]

With Aramburu supporting Balbín, Frondizi's attempts to co-opt the Peronists became a necessity. Such attempts intensified after 1957, when the UCRI was defeated by the UCRP in elections for the constitutional assembly, which was convened by Aramburu to replace Perón's 1949 constitution. Allegedly, in early 1985 Rogelio Frigerio, Frondizi's closest adviser, met with Perón in Venezuela and presented him with an agreement already signed by Frondizi. The document proposed an electoral pact according to which Frondizi promised to legalize Peronism and return unions to their old Peronist leaders in return for electoral support. Perón accepted. Although Frondizi always denied that such a pact was ever made, his landslide victory in the 1958 election over Balbín could not have taken place if a substantial number of Peronists, who had cast blank ballots in 1957, had not voted for the UCRI.[44]

In the months preceding the 1958 elections, Frondizi ran a campaign based on many of the themes of Peronism and blasted the anti-Peronist policies of the Aramburu administration. Initially, Frondizi ran on a

"National and Popular" platform offering nationalist, statist, and redistributive policies blended with populist rhetoric; one Peronist leader said that the UCRI's "discourses, their pronouncements, their postulates, their declarations, their watchwords sustained and even repeated in essence the principles of our doctrine."[45] However, right after being elected, Frondizi abandoned the nationalist, statist overtones of the National and Popular Front's plan in favor of a more pragmatic approach. Since May 1, 1958, two themes characterized his reform program: integration and development.

Integration meant luring the Peronist constituency into the UCRI by adopting some of the social policies of Peronism, which meant the recreation of a new class alliance linking the urban middle and working classes. However, while for Perón labor was to be not only protected by, but subordinated to, state authority, for Frondizi labor had to become a more autonomous political actor.[46] Frondizi recognized the close identification of the labor movement with Peronism and promised a number of measures to win it over: the reinstatement of the Peronist labor legislation suspended by Aramburu, the legalization of the CGT, the drafting of a new law of professional associations regulating collective bargaining agreements with capital, and the return of Peronist leaders to the helm of their unions. Furthermore, Frondizi guaranteed that the Peronist party would be allowed to compete again in honest elections at a later time.

Development, or *desarrollismo*, was Frondizi's economic program and complemented his integration strategy.[47] Like Perón, Frondizi believed that the country's future rested no longer on the agricultural sector but rather on the encouragement of ISI. However, Frondizi argued that Perón's ISI policies had been poorly planned and implemented and had centered upon the production of consumer goods. Because the country was still dependent on the importation of capital goods, the argument went, the consumer goods industry exacerbated the country's balance of payments problem. In fact, the consumer goods industry, unable to export because of its high production costs, remained dependent upon the revenues of the agricultural sector to continue to import capital equipment. Unfortunately, agricultural exports could not keep pace with the industrial sector's demand for foreign capital goods, since (1) agricultural exports' capacity to expand was constrained by the fluctuating demand of world markets, (2) a substantial share of beef and grain production was now consumed by the Argentine middle and lower classes, whose purchasing power had increased under Peronism and who demanded that food be affordable and plentiful, and (3) prices of agricultural goods rose less rapidly than those for imported industrial goods. The end result was inflation, sluggish growth rates, and an ever increasing foreign debt. To solve these problems, Frondizi proposed the creation of a domestic heavy industry (petrochemicals, steel, paper, automotive machinery, etc.) and basic transportation infrastructures (highways and airports) to better link Buenos Aires with the regional economies. It was hoped that by switching from consumer goods to capital goods production, Argentina would eventually be self-sufficient. To finance its program—given that the treasury's finances had been depleted—Frondizi had no choice but to lure foreign companies through very lucrative incentives to invest in Argentina. While this exposed him to the criticism of the UCRP and other nationalists, he claimed that it was the only possible way to acquire modern technology. To his Peronist critics Frondizi also pointed out that Perón himself, before being ousted, had begun to encourage foreign investments in the petroleum and telecommunications sectors.

The development program appealed to many constituencies. Unions approved of increasing state management of the economy and of the creation of new jobs through the ambitious investment program. Domestic entrepreneurs were assured that foreign capital would not constitute a menace because it would be concentrated in new economic activities. And agricultural producers were told that once the industrial sector had become self-sufficient the government would lower the tax burden of farm exports.[48]

Indeed, upon taking office in May, Frondizi decreed an amnesty for all those Peronists jailed by Aramburu, raised wages 60 percent, and allowed Peronist labor leaders to regain possession of their unions; but stopped short of legalizing the Peronist party. The long-term goal of Frondizi's integration strategy was to convince Peronist supporters to permanently switch to his side. He believed that, once they realized that Perón would not be able to return due to the military veto, they would conclude that the UCRI was the only party that could represent their interests. Unfortunately for him, the Peronist leadership, and particularly the union leaders, wanted to use Frondizi as much as Frondizi wanted to use them. After the first concessions were made, the Peronist unions, instead of restraining their demands as Frondizi had hoped, asked for more. The executive order assigning to U.S. oil companies the right to exploit Argentine oil fields in Patagonia created further tension. Union leaders charged Frondizi with "selling off" the country to the Yankees and with contradicting his early nationalist stand on the issue. Unable to bend—both because the economic situation soon began to get out of hand and because the military gave clear signals of an impending coup if further concessions were made—Frondizi saw his electoral alliance with Peronism crumble after only seven months in office. As 1958 drew to a close, the president was forced to call in the army to enforce the state of siege and break strikes. By December 1958, his integration strategy suffered a severe blow and was pursued inconsistently thereafter.

That same month, the president signed a highly controversial agreement with the IMF, which while preserving his development projects, reversed his campaign promises of expansionary policies. On the contrary, an austere stabilization plan was enforced, which outraged the unions. In the meantime, business circles that months before had asked for the implementation of deflationary measures remained aloof. In part this happened because Frondizi reapproached the Peronist unions when he saw fit and also because the president refused to involve business distributional coalitions in the design and implementation of policies important to them.[49] Even with respect to his own UCRI, Frondizi seemed to be unwilling to involve it in the day-to-day policy process. For instance, Frigerio and the team that had designed the development program were party outsiders. The president saw his party primarily as an electoral machine to be set in motion around election time. In Congress the UCRI was almost exclusively used to rubber-stamp executive legislation.

In the end, Frondizi's unwillingness or inability to use his party to forge new alliances once the Peronists had turned against him doomed his administration to failure. The president kept the UCRP and the other small parties in Congress at arm's length, they in turn, stepped up their opposition to the UCRI.

The economic situation did not help Frondizi, either. To placate the military, from 1959 on he was forced to ask conservative economists, with whom he did not personally get along, to enforce the stabilization policies agreed upon with the IMF. Argentina enjoyed unusual economic stability between late 1960 and 1961, but in 1962 things began to unravel. The development program so cherished by Frondizi turned out to be grounded on faulty assumptions. First, most of the new industries were capital-intensive rather than labor-intensive and did not increase employment significantly, as had been hoped. Second, the new industries once installed kept requiring new and expensive foreign inputs to operate. Thus, instead of making Argentina self-sufficient they worsened the foreign debt situation. By the end of 1961 the bubble burst. Diminished business confidence led foreign and domestic entrepreneurs to divest, foreign reserves vanished with the flight of capital and wage concessions to striking railway workers added to the budget deficit.

The final blow to Frondizi came in March 1962 when gubernatorial and midterm congressional elections were held. With two years left of his term, the president took his last gamble and honored his old promise to allow the Peronists to run their own candidates under the Popular Union (Unión Popular) label.[50] Although in 1959 he had banned neo-Peronist candidates from the 1960 midterm elctions, in 1962 he felt confident that he could win at the ballot box honestly. In fact, local elections in the provinces of Formosa and La Rioja early in 1962 had been favorable to the UCRI.[51] Consistent with his past ambivalent behavior, Frondizi tried to pit the anti-Peronists and the Peronists against each other. He lured conservative voters by assuring them that he was their only hope against a return of Peronism, while with the Peronists he argued that only he could save them from a new wave of purges. This double-talk did not work out, as the Peronists defeated the UCRI, both at the gubernatorial and the legislative levels.[52] In a last-minute attempt to save his presidency, Frondizi turned to the UCRP and the conservatives to form a coalition government, to no avail. They were still resentful about Frondizi's decision to defy the anti-Peronist bloc in 1957 and actually welcomed the military coup that deposed him at the end of March.

During the brief tenure of President José María Guido (who as speaker of the Senate had been forced by the military to assume the presidency ad interim), political polarization grew. In May 1963, Frondizi, still detained by the military, ordered his followers to join forces with the Peronists of the Popular Union and with other minor forces in the National and Popular Front. However, a sector of the UCRI defied Frondizi's order and named former Buenos Aires governor Oscar Alende as the party candidate for the upcoming election. The chances of the National and Popular Front to win the election ended when the military vetoed the participation of Peronist candidates and UCRI candidates linked to Frondizi. When in July 1963 Argentines went to the polls to select the next president their choice had furthered narrowed. The UCRP, Alende's faction of the UCRI, and a conservative movement supporting the candidacy of former President Aramburu, were the only major contenders. Arturo Illia, a country doctor from the province of Córdoba, headed the UCRP ticket in order to capture some independent and Radical voters who had supported the UCRI or minor parties in the past and were not particularly fond of Balbín.[53] With many Peronist and Frondizi supporters staying home or casting blank ballots (19 percent), Illia won with only 25 percent of the total vote, leaving behind Alende (16 percent), Aramburu, and forty-five minor parties. (See table 3.1.)

Nationalism and intransigence against alliances with other parties remained the hallmarks of the UCRP administration. After assuming office, Illia reversed most of Frondizi's policies. The contracts with foreign oil companies were canceled, despite the fact that they had been instrumental in making Argentina almost self-sufficient in oil production by 1963, and the stabilization program with the IMF was terminated. Illia's nationalism could also be seen in Argentine foreign policy. While relations with the United States remained cordial, the president made a point of keeping an independent agenda in foreign relations. Under his tenure, Argentina strengthened ties with neighboring Latin American countries (mainly its archrival Brazil) and backed the Non-Aligned

TABLE 3.1
Election Results, by Party, 1957–1965 (percentage)

Party	1957	1958	1960	1962	1963	1965
People's Radical Civic Union	23	25	24	20	25	29
Intrasigent Radical Civic Union	21	42	21	25	16	4
Socialist party	6	6	8	5	6	4
Conservative parties	6	3	9	6	6	5
Christian Democratic party	5	4	4	2	5	3
Progressive Democratic party	3	2	3	2	2	3
Justicialist (Peronist) party				32	7	35
Movement of Integration and Development						6
Other parties	11	10	7	6	11	8
Blank ballots[a]	25	9	25	3	18	3

SOURCE: Electoral Department, Ministry of Interior.
a. In 1957 and 1960 the vast majority of the blank ballots were cast by Peronists. In 1963 most of the blank ballots were cast by Peronists, but many were cast by Intrasigent Radicals.

Movement, which was led by developing countries in Asia and Africa and rejected the East-West confrontation arising form the cold war.[54] Moreover, diplomatic and commercial ties were established with communist countries.

Illia was a committed democrat. During his presidency he tried to uphold the rules of the democratic game even in the face of opposition by his political foes, who resorted to any means to discredit him in order to trigger a military takeover. In 1964, the Peronist-dominated labor movement launched a major wave of strikes and factory occupations under the name of Battle Plan (*plan de lucha*), which severely disrupted economic activity. Similar circumstances under Frondizi had led to a military repression of the strikers, but Illia refused to set the military loose. While Frondizi had tried to capture labor support through under-the-table deals with the Peronist leadership, Illia tried to achieve the same goal by giving workers material incentives. He believed that his expansionary economic policies—emphasizing full employment, moderate income redistribution to benefit wage earners, price controls, tax reform, the promotion of ISI, control of foreign investments, and regulation of the domestic market—would sway workers to support him.[55] Yet, like Frondizi, Illia grossly underestimated working class loyalty to union bosses and Perón. A second instance of Illia's tolerance came in 1965 when he allowed neo-Peronist parties to compete in midterm legislative elections. Although the UCRP was soundly defeated by the neo-Peronists, Illia accepted the results.

However, Illia remained determined to avoid compromise. As a president elected with only a quarter of the popular vote (thanks to the exclusion of the country's major political movement), Illia faced a serious crisis of legitimacy. Moreover, his party in Congress had only a plurality. Such circumstances would have led another politician to form legislative alliances with minor parties, but Illia, loyal to the old Radical doctrine of intransigence, preferred to remain a minority president. Without a legislative majority, the president's policy agenda was either delayed or blocked in Congress, leaving the country in a dangerous political vacuum. In the end, the contradiction between Illia's commitment to liberty and his unwillingness to compromise doomed his administration to failure. The president reacted to mounting opposition to his policies, or lack thereof, by insulating the decision-making process from even his own party. Economic policy making was left to a team of technocrats from the Economic Commission for Latin America who had no ties with the UCRP. Trapped in his own contradictions and unable to generate any meaningful party support for his administration, Illia was incapable of solving his country's problems. It was this inability to act that convinced the military, business groups, unions, and large sectors of the public that parties and democracy had to go if Argentina were to catch up with the developed world—a conclusion exactly opposite to what Illia had envisaged. After the hibernation into which they were forced to by the Onganía regime, the Radicals began to regroup, as first General Levingston and later General Lanusse, acting as provisional presidents, began to discuss the timetable for the return to constitutional government.

Once Lanusse called for elections in 1973, squabbling arose among UCRI factions. In 1972 the party ceased to exist, with Frondizi and Frigerio reorganizing their followers under the banners of the MID. The MID offered nothing new to voters. Its platform retained most of the 1950s, economic program of the UCRI, with an emphasis on developing the regional economies of the interior through state-sponsored industrialization. Politically, Frondizi began to drift to the right.

In 1973 the MID joined the Peronists and several minor parties in creating the Justicialist Liberation Front (Frente Justicialista de Liberación, or FJL). Oscar Alende set up his own party, the Intransigent party (Partido Intransigente, or PI). The PI became a left-wing, nationalistic party, using political rhetoric and advocating policies somewhat reminiscent of socialists parties in southern Europe. In 1973, Alende joined with the revolutionary Christians and the communists to form the Revolutionary Popular Alliance (Alianza Popular Revolucionaria). The old UCRP dropped the word *people* and, once again, became the Radical Civic Union, with Ricardo Balbín as its undisputed leader. The percentages of votes the parties received in the March and September elections are reported in table 3.2.[56]

Balbín, once bitterly opposed to Perón, had by December 1970 decided to adhere to the Hour of the People (La Hora del Pueblo), a mul-

TABLE 3.2
1973 Presidential Election Results (percentage)

	March	*September*
Justicialist Liberation Front (FREJULI)	49.6	61.6
Radical Civic Union	21.3	24.5
Federal Popular Alliance	14.9	12.1
Revolutionary Popular Alliance	7.4	
New Force	2.0	
Democratic Socialist Party	0.9	
Workers Socialist Party	0.6	
Popular Left Front	0.4	

SOURCE: Electoral Department, Ministry of Interior.

tiparty agreement aimed at creating new political institutions and overcoming the anti-Peronist ostracism that had polarized the Argentine political system since the mid-1940s. In Balbín's view La Hora del Pueblo was the first step toward the creation of a stable two-party system, wherein the Peronists would finally be recognized as a legitimate power contender. In practice, this meant that if the Peronists were to win an honest election, the Radicals would become the loyal opposition, even at the cost of accepting a subordinate role.[57] Balbín lived up to his commitment. When Perón won his third term by a landslide in 1973, Balbín refrained from harassing the government in Congress or through the media. On the contrary, he preferred to affect government policy by frequent personal contacts with Perón, who had by then chosen Balbín as his preferred interlocutor, out of the public eye. The Perón-Balbín axis, while ensuring stability and tolerance for a while, impeded the creation of mediative political institutions since the emphasis was on the charismatic leadership of the two men rather than on the UCR and the PJ, which remained on the fringes of the political debate. The shortcomings of this situation were made apparent at Perón's death in 1974. The ineptitude of Vice President Isabel Perón, who succeeded her husband to the presidency, made it impossible for Balbín to continue the same working relationship he had with Juan Perón. Unable to influence the new administration through informal channels and unwilling to mobilize the UCR to force Isabel to change her policies (in the fear that this would destabilize the democratic system), Balbín had no option but to stand by as a military coup nullified all his efforts.[58]

Political parties were officially disbanded following the 1976 coup. Only after General Viola succeeded General Videla as president in 1981 did the military allow a timid dialogue with political leaders. With Perón gone, Balbín became the recognized leader of the civilian opposition to the authoritarian regime. This opposition took the form of the

Multipartidaria, a broad coalition of political leaders created in May 1981, whose main goal was to develop a common front to deal with the military and to return Argentina to constitutional democracy. The Multipartidaria was in a sense a continuation of the political reconciliation between the Radicals and the Peronists begun with La Hora del Pueblo.[59] Therefore, by the time of his death, Balbín's political battle had come full circle. While in the 1940s and 1950s he was instrumental in leading the Radicals into the anti-Peronist camp, toward the end of his career the polarization that such behavior had created, along with Perón's willingness to compromise, convinced Balbín that democracy was best served by working with the Peronists rather than by ostracizing them. As a consequence, confrontation gave way to dialogue. This constituted an important change and paved the way for more tolerant and constructive political behavior.

Soon after the creation of the Multipartidaria Balbín died. The leadership vacuum was quickly filled by Raúl Alfonsín, Balbín's protegé in the late 1960s. However, dissent over political strategy between the two led Alfonsín to form his own Movement of Renovation and Change (Movimiento de Renovación y Cambio, or MRC) in 1972 and to challenge Balbín and his faction, National Line (Linea Nacional), to head the UCR ticket for the 1973 presidential election.[60]

Alfonsín continued to criticize Balbín after the Radicals were defeated. Although he shared Balbín's conciliatory approach toward Perón, Alfonsín contended that Balbín's new strategy had deprived the UCR of maneuvering space, since the party had failed to convince the electorate that it was a credible alternative to Peronism and that Balbín's conservative political discourse had ignored the profound changes in Argentine society. However, Alfonsín's proposal to move the party to the left of Peronism in order to satisfy new demands by young voters fell on deaf ears.

With the coming to power of the military, Alfonsín put aside his criticisms for the sake of party unity, but he kept cultivating support among fellow MRC members. At the same time, he gained a name for himself by becoming a prominent human rights lawyer. When the military government called for primary elections in 1982 to select presidential candidates, Linea Nacional, still in control of the party machinery, was plagued by internal rivalries. Alfonsín took advantage of this situation: he allied himself with the powerful Córdoba faction (Linea Córdoba), headed by Victor Martínez and Eduardo Angeloz, while the MRC enlarged its influence nationwide. As the primary campaign took off in early 1983, Alfonsín toured the country with a simple message: he was the only Radical with any hope of beating the Peronists in the fall. In June, Alfonsín easily won the UCR nomination over his main opponent, Fernando de la Rúa, a moderate Radical—who, after a bitter internal struggle, had emerged as the Linea Nacional's candidate.

Securing the UCR nomination was, however, quite a different task from beating the Peronists, who had won all presidential elections they had been allowed to participate in since 1946. Aware of his underdog status, Alfonsín devised a campaign with broad electoral appeal, in which political rhetoric was supported by a shrewd campaign strategy. Unlike Balbín in 1973, he opted for a confrontational style, which put the Peronists on the defensive. He began in April 1982 by denouncing an alleged pact between the military and a future Peronist government, according to which the military would support the Peronists in return for the Peronists' refraining from investigating human rights violations committed during the repression years.[61] He also mobilized the party to breach the working class, traditionally a stronghold of Peronism, by denouncing the illegal practices of union bosses and by promising a better standard of living and social reforms. Alfonsín reminded the middle and upper classes that the military dictatorship was made possible by the incompetent and corrupt Peronist administrations that had preceded it and that there was little to hope for from a Peronist victory, which would only bring back to power the political class responsible for the 1973–1976 fiasco.

The choice was clear: the decision was between the pseudocorporatist, authoritarian, populist model proposed by the PJ and a new Argentina in which Alfonsín would strengthen democracy through the rule of law, civil liberties, and human rights—by making political institutions responsive not to the particularistic needs of vested interest groups but to the demands of the average citizen.[62] Democracy based on ethical and moral principles became Alfonsín's formula for a new society. This formula gained the support of voters of all social classes eager to break the authoritarian cycle that had doomed Argentina to a socioeconomic stalemate. Last but not least, Alfonsín's strong leadership in a country where charisma is tantamount to political success played a central role in the outcome.[63] Although toward the end it was clear that the presidential contest would be close, Peronists and Radicals alike were stunned when, on October 30, 1983, Alfonsín received 52 percent of the popular vote, to 40 percent for the PJ candidate. The UCR also captured the majority of seats in the Chamber of Deputies but not in the Senate, where the Radicals obtained eighteen of forty-six seats and were, therefore, forced to make alliances with small provincial parties to ensure approval of legislation.

The 1983 election results were a remarkable event in Argentine history. For the first time since 1928 the UCR had won a competitive election: it had more than doubled Balbín's 1973 vote (24 percent), the average party support after the appearance of Peronism. The UCR thus returned to its hegemonic party status last enjoyed under the leadership of Yrigoyen in the 1916–1930 period. Conversely, the political equation that had allowed the Peronists, beginning in 1946, to be the hegemonic political force was upset; the PJ was now relegated to a minority role. Moreover, the victory seemed to ratify Alfonsinism as a new and enduring political phenomenon. Members of the Coordinating Board (Coordinadora), an internal left-wing faction of the MRC with university roots dating to the late 1960s, began to talk of Alfonsinism as the Third Historical Movement (Tercer Movimiento Histórico). In their view, the multiclass basis of Alfonsín's electoral support made it the natural heir to the great popular movements that had shaped the nation's history earlier in the twentieth century: Yrigoyenism and Peronsim.[64] The movimientismo advocated by Alfonsín was, however, closer to "Yrigoyen's idea that a party should organize itself to become a national movement [rather than] the Peronist idea of a great national movement that includes the party, but subordinates it."[65]

Movimientismo was at odds with Alfonsín's repeated intention to transform the UCR into a European-style social democratic party: Alfonsinism, at any rate, escaped any clear-cut classification. It was a political phenomenon in which the personal appeal of its leader was the common denominator binding a wide variety of often clashing interests and ideologies. Movimientismo as well as liberal and social democratic ideas could all be found in some form in Alfonsinism, but no one of them emerged as its distinctive feature. The emphasis on personalism was even more evident when the old Radical internal rules—which, unlike the PJ, regulated the selection of representatives within the party hierarchy—were changed so that Alfonsín and his closest associates in government could retain their positions in the UCR.[66] The party then became even more hierarchically organized and heavily subordinated to the president's initiative. The UCR rank and file willingly stayed in Alfonsin's shadow in view of the fact that for most of his term he was more popular than the UCR.[67] Having obtained an indisputable electoral mandate—which was strengthened by the successful referendum over the ratification of the border treaty with Chile—Alfonsín early on established a direct relationship with the population, a relationship that eluded party mediation. Following the movimientista tradition, his style was one of plebiscitary democracy, according to which the leader appeals for support of his policies through the skillful use of the mass media, public rallies, and political ideals and symbols. The process of democratic consolidation thus became identified with presidential leadership, as shown by Alfonsín's famous statement, "I am democracy!" Moreover, by dividing the spoils of government among UCR factions, Alfonsín kept dissent under control during the first part of his term.

The 1987 electoral defeat marked a downturn both for the administration and the UCR. The hegemonic ambitions of the Third Historical Movement came to an end, as did Afonsín's retention of the political initiative: having lost the majority in the Chamber of Deputies, Alfonsín was unable to create lasting coalitions with minor parties to counter a confident and aggressive PJ. On the contrary, he was forced to make concessions to the Peronists on issues like labor laws and the redistribution of federal money to the provinces. To compound matters, factions within the party (particularly the Coordinadora), while not openly attacking the president, criticized the technocrats of the economic team and the intellectuals outside the UCR upon whom Alfonsín relied for political advice.

As the economic situation grew worse, so did party infighting, and, Alfonsín found himself increasingly unable to control party politics. Eduardo Angeloz, nominated as the 1988 UCR presidential candidate, had little in common with Alfonsín's political and economic views and distanced himself from the administration's policies. As governor of Córdoba, Angeloz had proven a capable administrator who emphasized pragmatism over ideology. His low-key approach and conservatism contrasted with Alfonsín's charismatic style and social democratic rhetoric. Angeloz proposed free-market economic policies and the redefinition of the state's role in the country's development. Plans were drawn to privatize public services and companies and to stimulate private investments in areas previously monopolized by state corporations through deregulation. Although one of Alfonsín's closest associates, Juan Manuel Casella, was Angeloz's running mate, the nomination of the Córdoba's governor testified to the disillusion of many of the UCR rank and file with Alfonsín's performance. Further evidence of the party's move to the right came when Angeloz formed an electoral alliance with María Cristina Guzmán's Independent Federalist Confederation (Confederación Federalista Independiente, or CFI), which comprised a number of conservative provincial parties. This last effort, in the end, was to no avail, as Angeloz was soundly defeated by Menem.

On 14 May 1989, the UCR realized how dangerous it had been to rely on one person's fortunes. Alfonsín's prestige was shattered and, with it, the UCR's hegemonic dreams. Alfonsinism, in the end, was a transitory phenomenon; it failed to translate an initial multiclass electoral support into a long-lasting coalition that could create a new political realignment, as Yrigoyenism and Peronsim had done.[68] The UCR came out of the polls badly split, as Angeloz ascribed his electoral failure to Alfonsín's mistaken policies. Although defeated, Angeloz could claim that, even under adverse conditions, he had retained 37 percent of the popular vote. He could therefore challenge Alfonsín's leadership within the UCR, which had fallen into a severe identity crisis.[69] In the end, Alfonsín managed to retain his post of party chairman and the support of the largest party faction, but he came increasingly under fire by contending groups within the UCR. The major issue was Alfonsín's strategy vis-à-vis President Menem's policies: Alfonsín denounced these orthodox policies and turned down Menem's repeated offers for a multiparty pact to overcome the crisis. Alfonsín stood firm in his position that no pact was possible unless Menem dropped his orthodox economic policies and his alliance with the conservatives of the UCD that had inspired them. Angeloz criticized Alfonsín's sterile opposition and was more sympathetic to Menem's economic policies given that he had advocated many of them during the 1989 campaign. On the other hand, the center-left Coordinadora faction believed that Alfonsín had not acted tough enough with Menem and made tactical alliances in Congress with anti-Menem sectors of the PJ.

In the 1991 midterm elections, Alfonsín suffered his last blow. The UCR vote dropped to 28 percent, its worst performance since the country's return to democracy. The great popular appeal of the UCR in the mid-1980s had evaporated. Even more damaging was the fact that the defeat of most UCR candidates close to Alfonsín corresponded to the victory of his conservative opponents within the party. In fact, the traditional strongholds of Radicalism, Córdoba and the Federal District, elected Angeloz for a third term as governor and Fernando De la Rúa as congressman. The UCR collapse prompted Alfonsín to step down from the party's National Committee chairmanship in favor of Misiones Senator Mario Losada, an Alfonsín backer. Unexpected victories in later gubernatorial elections gave the UCR control of Chubut and Catamarca, in addition to Córdoba, Río Negro, and the Federal District; but the overall picture within the party remained one of continuous infighting. By early 1992, although Alfonsín was trying to resurrect his career by launching a social democratic movement, former collaborators were openly distancing themselves from him.[70] Within the party, the conservative wing, headed by Angeloz and De la Rúa, teamed up with the left, led by Federico Storani, a former Coordinadora member, to remove pro-Alfonsín leaders from control of the National Committee and to decide who would get the UCR nomination for the next presidential election. Yet despite all these maneuvers behind the scenes, the UCR was incapable of putting forward a credible alternative program to Menem's. While accusing Menem of lack of concern for the devastating consequences his policies had on the poorest social sectors, Angeloz and De La Rúa still agreed on the philosophy behind the administration's restructuring program.

The Peronists

Prior to Perón's overthrow, the PJ had three main branches: union members, the old party elite, and the women's organization. Although each branch had the right to select a third of the delegates to the party congress, in practice Perón exercised all the power, particularly when it came to nominating candidates for legislative and gubernatorial elections.[71] Of the three branches, the unions were the strongest as they had a well-established organization and economic resources of their own, which the other two lacked. The party was a heterogeneous group with often conflicting demands: (1) a professional and intellectual sector from the right and from among Catholic reformists, (2) a sector of predominantly small business owners producing for the domestic market who had benefited from Perón's early protectionist policies, (3) a large, mobilized, but not unionized popular sector in the urban areas, and (4) in the provinces, another unorganized sector of peasants, rural laborers, small farmers, small-town workers, public employees, and shopkeepers all more conservative than their urban counterparts and whose participation in politics was mediated by clientele relationships with local notables or powerful families.[72] The female branch of the party, created in 1949 by Eva Perón, who chaired it until her death in 1952, was, although theoretically important, the weakest of the three.

Politicians, senators, cabinet ministers, high-ranking bureaucrats, judges, and the above-mentioned provincial notables constituted the party elites. They were the link between the various constituencies and its leader. Nonetheless, unlike union bosses, party elites usually did not have an institutionalized power base of their own. Thus, the Peronist party remained institutionally weak and welded together only by Perón's personal charisma. "First, [it] played a relatively minor role in carrying out two tasks for which other political parties are renowned: mobilizing voters and dispensing patronage. Second, the party failed to generate a stratum of middle and upper-level leaders capable of managing the party on their own. Third, party members and supporters tended to identify more with Perón himself than with the party organization."[73] With the party so loosely organized and its officials so dependent upon Perón for guidance and funds, Aramburu had little difficulty in disbanding it.

He had a different experience with the unions, which successfully resisted his repressive measures and retained substantial support from the working class. Indeed, Aramburu's acknowledgement of his failure to de-Peronize the labor movement led him to hasten the return to civilian government. By the time the Liberating Revolution regime came to an end, the Peronist unions had substantially strengthened their position with respect not only to Aramburu but also to the existing political parties.[74] More than before, they could claim to be the backbone of Peronism, with or without their charismatic leader.

In spite of being banned from electoral competition most of the time, Peronism continued to be the country's major political force between 1955 and 1966. This was demonstrated in different ways depending upon the circumstances of the moment. When prevented from competing, Perón's followers, following Perón's orders, cast blank ballots in 1957 and 1960. In 1958, Peronism was instrumental in the election of Frondizi. When Peronists filed candidates under disguised party banners in 1962 and 1965, they again outpolled both the ruling parties, the UCRI and the UCRP. On both occasions, Peronist victories set in motion the military coups that ousted Presidents Frondizi and Illia.

During the 1955–1966 period the composition of Peronism was altered to some degree. Some segments of the industrial bourgeoisie and middle-class and lower-middle-class members in a few provinces were temporarily lured away by Frondizi; but the industrial working class of the Federal District and its suburbs continued to pledge allegiance to Perón and to their Peronist union bosses.[75] The internal dynamics of Peronism was influenced as much by the policies adopted by Presidents Aramburu, Frondizi, and Illia to break it or co-opt it as by the absence of Perón. His absence encouraged maverick Peronist leaders in the labor movement and the provincial patronage systems to pursue their own political agendas, create personal power bases, and compromise with the government of the day. According to some scholars, the post-1955 period saw a reconfiguration of Peronism and the emergence of factionalism. Perón himself fueled disagreements and squabbles within the movement, as he had done when he was in power, as a means to keep his subordinates in check. He usually sided with the weakest groups against the strongest in order to prevent the emergence of potential contenders. He thus acted simultaneously as a partisan and a mediator: being the only one who could reconcile internal strife, Perón assured for himself the position of ultimate arbiter of the movement's fate.

The old party elite remained the most loyal to Perón.[76] Its members—former government officials and legislators—described themselves as orthodox, to stress their total devotion to their leader and his orders. Their devotion is not surprising, given that their status previous to 1955 had been acquired through the direct intervention of Perón— without whom, even within Peronism, their legitimacy and influence was quite limited.

During the 1957 CGT convention sixty-two Peronist unions organized as a separate faction of the labor movement, calling themselves the "62 organizations." Peronist unionism remained fairly united against the perceived threat posed by Aramburu's policies. However, as government repression lessened during the Frondizi and Illia administrations, internal splits increased. A hard-line faction formed around José Alonso, the secretary of the state workers union (ATE), who had been elected to head the CGT in 1963. Alonso was in some ways similar to orthodox Peronist politicians: he pledged loyalty to Perón and advocated his return, so that the policies of the "good old days" (1946–1949), during which unions had flourished, could be restored. The crucial difference between Alonso and orthodox politicians was that Alonso could count on the vast financial resources and organizational skills of the CGT and on its member confederations, which could mobilize hundreds of thousands of workers. Reasoning that the quicker Perón returned the better, Alonso took a tough stand against the Illia government. This opposition invariably translated into strikes and the occupation of factories, such as the Battle Plan of 1964, which paralyzed the country. While the official excuse for the strike was to protest Illia's economic policies, in reality Alonso hoped to so discredit the government that a military coup would be the only way out of the chaos. Although the 1966 coup did not return Perón to power nor bring unionists any short-term benefits, Alonso and his followers were satisfied with the armed forces' decision to intervene.

A more moderate posture was taken by Augusto Vador, leader of the powerful UOM. While never attacking Perón openly, Vandor began to slowly challenge his leadership. If Alonso's ultimate loyalty was to Perón, Vandor's was to the workers. Vandor was an astute and pragmatic labor leader who had mastered the strike-and-then-bargain art of negotiation, which often led him to compromising with potential enemies. He established close links with business leaders and military officers, hoping to gain their support for Peronism without Perón,—a more responsible brand of Peronism. Indeed, after 1966 a working relationship developed between the military-supported Onganía regime and Vandor, provoking a split within the labor movement. Unionists loyal to Perón challenged Vandor's project, which, however, ended with Vandor's assassination in 1969.

Although he played a crucial role in the organization of the Battle Plan of 1964, Vandor used more moderate means to achieve his goals. Central to Vandor's quest for power and political recognition was the creation of a labor-dominated Peronist party independent of Perón, relegating him to a figurehead role. This project materialized when Vandor's Popular Union party won the 1962 and 1965 elections. In 1964, Vandor gained control of the PJ, the stronghold of orthodox Peronism. The PJ had been a Peronist party since 1958 but was banned from electoral contests that year due to its direct ties with Perón. After 1964, although Perón remained PJ chairman, the real power rested with Vandor.[77]

Neo-Peronists of the interior provinces, particularly the poorest ones like Chaco, Neuquen, Río Negro, Salta and Santiago del Estero had no formal ties with the CGT and its unions, as in the period before 1955. Usually organized around prominent provincial notables, these parties of the interior were independent of Perón, and some of their leaders began, like Vandor, to advocate "Peronism without Perón." These "neo-Peronists lacked the class consciousness of the hard-line group. In many

provinces the neo-Peronist movement was more personalist than ideological, and the personality involved in some instances was the local political leader, not Juan Perón."[78] Many of these neo-Peronists contested
the 1963 election despite Perón's order to cast blank ballots. Their moderation and their willingness to work within the new system induced
both the Radical administrations and the military to tolerate their existence. However, neither the neo-Peronist leaders of the interior nor Vandor succeeded in legitimizing Peronist political participation. Vandor
failed to build a Peronist party independent of Perón, who undermined
Vandor's plans. Afraid of losing his authority over the movement, Perón
built key alliances with union leaders jealous of Vandor's increasing political clout within Peronism.[79] Eventually, Vandor abandoned his
project. He was not driven out of the movement, however: Vandor was
important in Perón's chess game; he could be used to thwart future
mavericks within the movement.[80] The infighting enabled Perón to remain on top, but it unleashed centrifugal forces within the movement
that later tore Peronism apart.

In the late 1960s and early 1970s the Peronist youth group and the
montoneros became the most dynamic and radical sectors of Peronism.
Historic Peronism, which was represented by the unions, the neo-
Peronists of the provinces, and the old party elite, was ideologically
weak, conservative, and at times even reactionary. Ideological Peronism, which had in the montoneros its most violent proponents, was
revolutionary and stubbornly against union bosses that the montoneros
believed had sold out the workers for their own personal benefit. Perhaps it is not by chance that Vandor and Alonso, who dominated the
political scene in the 1960s, were both assassinated under mysterious
circumstances (in 1969 and 1970, respectively).

The cleavage between historic and ideological Peronism became
more acute when Lanusse allowed the Peronists to participate in the
1973 presidential election. By 1972, the only thing these two factions had
in common was their desire to bring Perón back from his Spanish exile.
Perón had fostered many expectations among his diverse constituency.
He had assured union delegates who traveled to Madrid that he would
reestablish a labor-based government; he had told the old party elite
that they would enjoy a privileged status within the movement; he had
assured the neo-Peronist notables of the provinces that he would dis-
burse federal funds to sustain their personal clienteles; and he had
promised the Peronist youth movement a *trasvasamiento generacional*
(meaning a generational transfer of power from the old guard to the
new) in order to accomplish a socialist revolution like those of Castro in
Cuba and Allende in Chile. He referred to the montoneros as the "special formations" of Peronism and, in a sense, justified their terrorist acts
(i.e., he condoned Aramburu's assassination) as a means to gain con-

cessions from the outgoing Lanusse administration.[81] These promises, though contradictory, successfully gained support for Perón from a range of political groups. His drift to the left in the early 1970s was dictated, as in the past, by tactical reasons. Perón planned to use the young radicals "to counter the growing influence of politicians and labor chieftains who were challenging him"[82] Following this rationale, Perón chose as the Peronist candidate for the 1973 election a long-time but mediocre party politician, Héctor Cámpora.[83] Revealing of the changed balance of forces within Peronism, it was the left of the movement—particularly the young militants of the montoneros and the Peronist youth movement—that was the driving force behind the 1973 electoral campaign; the labor sector played an unusually small role. Once in office, Cámpora was increasingly influenced by the Peronist left.

The several interpretations of Peronism and the factional cleavages that Perón had encouraged and precariously managed while in exile came to a dramatic showdown on the day of his return to Argentina after seventeen years of exile. About 400,000 people gathered at the international airport in Buenos Aires to welcome the old leader. Unfortunately, prior to his arrival montoneros and union members had engaged in a bloody shoot-out to gain control of the welcoming ceremony, leaving 200 people dead.[84] Once back in power, Perón abandoned his left-wing rhetoric and returned to his pragmatic, conservative politics. The Peronist left was swiftly purged from his administration, and historic Peronism returned to center stage.[85]

After Perón's death, the montoneros went underground to topple the right-wing government of Isabel Perón. This event left the battle for the control of the movement between the party archconservatives, headed by Social Welfare Minister José López Rega and the union bosses, led by Lorenzo Miguel, who had succeeded Vandor at the helm of the UOM.[86] The internal struggle finally ended in mid-1975 with the departure of López Rega from the cabinet. Miguel and labor came finally to control the Peronist movement, but it was a Pyrrhic victory. In fact, the country had fallen into such chaos as to prompt a new military takeover a few months later.

Peronism ceased to be an active political force after the 1976 coup; many Peronist union leaders and left-wing activists were the target of military repression. The PJ surfaced in 1982 by joining the Multipartidaria but found itself divided into rival factions. This was hardly new. However, while Perón had been able to reconcile contending groups in the past, his death left the party not only leaderless but in complete disarray. The responsibility for this state of affairs can be ascribed to Perón himself: he openly distrusted politicians and refrained from giving the PJ clear rules and a party structure. By keeping Peronism an undefined political movement, he could make arbitrary decisions and avoid delegation of power. Isabel Perón, still nominally the party president in her Spanish exile, was so much in disrepute that most Peronist leaders found it wise to distance themselves from her.

As 1983 began, five main factions developed. *Verticalismo* represented the Peronist old guard. It consisted of a heterogeneous group of politicians, among whom Herminio Iglesias, the party boss controlling the country's most important electoral machinery (the working class suburbs of Buenos Aires) emerged as the front runner. The second group was represented by the Peronist union movement headed by the resuscitated Miguel. The third faction, the *ultraverticalistas,* consisted of a small group of right-wing provincial caudillos who pledged loyalty to Isabel but who had little political weight. The Movement of Unity, Solidarity, and Organization (Movimiento de Unidad, Solidaridad y Organización, or MUSO) proposed the candidacy of Antonio Cafiero, a longtime Buenos Aires party leader running on a vague reformist program. The fifth faction, the Intransigence and Mobilization (Intransigencia y Movilización) claimed to be the left of the party, but more than anything else it served the ambition of Catamarca's caudillo Vincente Saadi— whose support, however, never extended beyond that province.[87]

The profound divisions afflicting the party were momentarily overcome by the nomination of Italo Luder to head the Peronist presidential ticket. Luder, an upper-class politician who had presided over the Senate in 1975, was, however, a compromise candidate, as he had no power base of his own. Whatever respectability he could bring to his ticket was tarnished by Iglesias, his running mate, whose vicious campaign tactics and public slanders against Alfonsín reinforced the public's impression that the authoritarian nature of Peronism had not changed. Moreover, the CGT and, most of all, the heavy involvement in the campaign of its Peronist faction—the "62" organizations led by Miguel—strengthened the perception held by weary voters that, behind the scenes, Miguel was indeed the person in command. In fact, Miguel had been instrumental in creating the coalition behind Luder's nomination by cutting deals with other Peronist leaders. He had also gained control over the nomination process of many candidates running for Congress and secured for himself the position of party vice president, which, due to the absence of party president Isabel Perón, gave him virtual control of the PJ. Therefore, both Iglesias and Miguel constituted more of a liability than an asset for Luder, as they reminded voters of the gloomy legacy of the last Peronist administration. To complicate matters, Luder, unable to achieve party cohesiveness on any specific policy, reiterated the old "social justice" rhetoric, which had little to offer the many Argentines looking for a new way to tackle the very profound socioeconomic crisis afflicting the country.

The 1983 defeat destroyed the myth of Peronist invincibility at the polls. The electoral debacle was particularly embarrassing for both Iglesias and Miguel, who lost decisively in their own districts. Regional caudillos, particularly in the poorest provinces, were the only ones to save the day by capturing several governorships and most of the PJ's Senate seats. Nonetheless, Iglesias and Miguel teamed up and, due to their control of the party apparatus, rebuffed the attacks of a divided opposition unable to capitalize on their bankrupt leadership. In December 1985, a new faction was created, which took the name of Renovation (Renovación). Its original leaders were Cafiero (who had dissolved the MUSO a year earlier), Carlos Grosso (a prominent politician of the Federal District), Carlos Menem, and José Manuel de la Sota.[88] The *renovadores*, or renovators, were a loose coalition of ambitious PJ leaders. Their common goal was to democratize Peronism by transforming it from a movement into a real party through the establishment of clear internal rules. In a sense, the Renovation was to the PJ what the MRC had been earlier to the UCR. Similar emphasis was placed on modernizing the political discourse, respecting the rule of law and ethics, and criticizing the antidemocratic path taken by Peronism since Perón's death. This, of course, was in direct contrast to Iglesias's neofascist stance and, most of all, to Miguel's interests in keeping the traditional supremacy that unions had enjoyed in the party since 1946. The situation within the PJ remained very volatile, and squabbles followed in rapid fashion—testified to by three party congresses between late 1984 and mid-1985, which in the end reaffirmed the leadership of the "orthodox" Iglesias-Miguel bloc.

With the further defeat suffered in the November 1985 congressional elections, the PJ crisis reached its climax. However, while orthodox candidates lost badly in crucial districts, the renovators, many of whom had run on independent tickets, scored important victories. In view of such results, Iglesias and Miguel soon fell into disgrace, and by early 1986 the Renovation had seized control of the PJ. In the meantime, while sitting on the opposition benches, the renovators, particularly their younger cohort, skillfully used the Congress as an arena to show their potential for leadership and their commitment to democracy.[89] The renovators were instrumental in passing UCR-sponsored bills such as the National Food Plan, the Beagle Treaty with Chile, and the military-related Full Stop and Due Obedience laws, either by voting in favor or by abstaining. Furthermore, they provided essential support for Alfonsín when the president faced three military uprisings between 1987 and 1988. In so doing, the renovators showed that they could play the loyal opposition role necessary to build a healthy democracy, although they wasted no occasion to attack the government, particularly on economic issues.

From 1986 on, Cafiero and other prominent renovators reorganized the party structure and diminished the influence of labor bosses within the PJ. This process received the important electoral and financial backing of the Group of 25, a left-wing Peronist faction within the labor sector that challenged Miguel's leadership and that was willing to subordinate itself to the party. The renovators' stated objective was to regain the political initiative by defeating the UCR in the upcoming gubernatorial and congressional elections. They cleverly exploited popular dissatisfaction with UCR economic policies. Moreover, they were able to project a new democratic image of the PJ to appeal to those moderate voters lost in the 1983 election. The victory in the September 1987 election was a boost for the renovators, in particular Cafiero—who, after capturing the governorship of the Buenos Aires province and later (January 1988) the presidency of the PJ, could aim for the PJ's nomination for the 1989 presidential contest.

Surprisingly, it was Menem not Cafiero who won the Peronist primaries in mid-1988, the first in the party's history. Menem was in many respects the stereotypical Argentine caudillo. A three-time governor of La Rioja, one of the country's poorest provinces, Menem built his power base through patronage. With the bulk of the renovators supporting Cafiero, Menem left that faction in early 1986 to create one of his own. His strategy for the presidential bid was multifaceted. In terms of alliances, Menem faced an uphill battle, as the party apparatus and most Peronist governors endorsed Cafiero's candidacy. Thus, he eluded the party and went straight to the traditional source of Peronist power. To begin with he made a key pact with labor and in particular with the Group of 15, which not only mobilized votes but also heavily financed Menem's campaign. Miguel also joined the Menem bandwagon toward the end of the primaries, as he resented Cafiero's unwillingness to compromise and the secondary role to which the renovators had relegated the unions. Other components of Menem's alliance were a few provincial notables like the Saadis in Catamarca (who feared that a Cafiero victory would further strengthen Buenos Aires in the PJ) and Eduardo Duhalde, a Federal District politician who was estranged from Cafiero.

The second element of Menem's strategy was to package his campaign in a way that could be readily understood by the average citizen. While Cafiero talked of transforming the PJ into a Christian democratic party to counter Alfonsín's overtures to social democracy, Menem downplayed ideology. His was a pork barrel approach to politics. He portrayed himself as the true heir of Perón and adroitly presented the primaries as a competition not between Menem and Cafiero but between the movement and the party, adding that the latter notion was alien to Peronism. In addition, taking advantage of the decreasing popularity of politicians, Menem claimed to be the "outsider," the man not compromised by party politics and interest groups, the man who cared about the poor, the workers, and the impoverished middle class. While Cafiero preached the virtues of democracy and tolerance, Menem promised more "social justice" and higher salaries, the kind of rhetoric that many Peronist rank-and-file members wanted to hear. Third, Menem contended that not much change could be expected from Cafiero, who was, in his view, heavily involved in the Alfonsín government's ineffective policies. (In fact, Cafiero agreed with Alfonsín on a number of laws to be passed by Congress on taxation, union regulations, and federal financing of the provinces after 1987.) Last, Menem's personal charisma, together with an uncanny ability to communicate with people and cut deals, contrasted with Cafiero's more conventional, boring style and greatly helped him in his quest for the party's nomination.[90]

During the 1989 presidential campaign, internal squabbles were momentarily set aside and an alliance was formed with the Christian Democrats, the Intransigent party, the MID, and some provincial parties under the banner of Justicialist Front of Popular Unity (Frente Justicialista de Unidad Popular, or FREJUPO). Noticeably, Cafiero and the renovators kept a low profile during the months preceding the elections. Since the party apparatus had opposed his presidential bid, Menem relegated the PJ to a marginal role. During the presidential campaign, Menem added to the old populist themes his plan for a "productive revolution," a nebulous concept to reactivate the economy through a social pact between capital and labor. After all, it was easier to point out the Radicals' failure than to make alternative proposals, which could have gotten him into trouble. "The prophet," as Menem was nicknamed due to his messianic campaign style, easily won over the UCR's Angeloz.

His victory signified a reversal of the renovators' project of making Peronism a true party. His emphasis was now on movimientismo and conservative populism through the reinclusion of labor and right-wing groups in his coalition. Menem himself, coming from La Rioja, fell well into the conservative tradition that had previously characterized the Peronist movement in the provinces. In other words, with Menem, Peronism was back to square one.[91] More than Alfonsín, Menem stressed elements of plebiscitary democracy over institutional consolidation. His initial cabinet appointments were a clear indication of old-fashioned personalismo. Following Perón's old idea that the economy should be run by businessmen, Menem selected as minister of the economy first Miguel Roig and, after his sudden death, Nestor Rapanelli, both former executives of the Argentine conglomerate Bunge and Born. Similarly, the Labor Ministry was given to a unionist from the Group of 15, Antonio Triaca, as a reward for that faction's electoral support. Although Triaca was a Peronist, he had been instrumental in undermining the renovators' party project. The only two Peronists left in the cabinet occupied the defense (Luder) and social welfare (Julio Corzo) ministries, but by early 1990 they were both gone. The Foreign Ministry was given to an independent, Domingo Cavallo, and the appointments of conservatives Alvaro and María Julia Alsogaray as presidential adviser and ENTel trustee, respectively, testified to the insignificance of the party in Menem's calculations. In subsequent appointments he stressed criteria ranging from personal loyalty to technocratic ability but paid scant attention to party links. The fact that former rivals like Cafiero and other renovators were still in control of the most important PJ posts discouraged him from appointing party members to government posts. Besides, many of these members were voicing their opposition to his policies. In fact, Menem's adoption of free-market economic policies and his alliance with the political right not only forced the PI, the Christian Democrats, and the MID to leave the FREJUPO by September 1990 but also aroused bitter protest from large sectors of the Peronist movement.

The collapse of the FREJUPO coincided with the unraveling of the latent contradictions of Peronism, which, while subdued during the presidential campaign, exploded in 1990, giving birth to several splinter factions and subgroups. The most vocal of Menem's critics was the Group of 8, composed of young, left-wing deputies who claimed to adhere to the principles that had inspired the moribund Renovation. As time went on, they forged tactical alliances with Trotskyites and sectors of the UCR to torpedo in Congress the president's legislative agenda, which they believed betrayed the principles of Peronism. The biggest casualty of this new party scrambling was Cafiero. In 1989, with the support of the UCR, many union leaders, and a lukewarm Menem, Cafiero asked citizens to vote on a referendum aimed at amending the constitution of the Buenos Aires province. Among other things, the amendments allowed the governor to run for a second term and empowered him to levy new taxes and expropriate land.

The referendum was openly rejected, and Cafiero soon afterward stepped down from the position of PJ chairman. This gave Menem the opportunity to seize control of the party. First he made it possible for his brother, Senator Eduardo Menem, to become party vice president. Then, through under-the-table negotiations, he managed to be elected PJ president without the consent of the party congress; soon afterward he took a leave of absence, claiming to be busy with government responsibilities, thus enabling Eduardo to run the party. The bottom line is that Menem, thanks to the divisions plaguing his critics, was able to divide and rule, although his Menemista supporters were an odd mix of people, with little or nothing in common. Furthermore, his takeover of the PJ did not seem to show an intention to use the party structure to revive support for his administration. Rather, it looked as if it were designed merely to deprive potential rivals of an institution that could challenge Menem's leadership within the Peronist movement.

Menem's ability to take advantage of his opponents weaknesses was further attested to by events in the labor movement, in which he played both instigator and peacemaker. The CGT, as the PJ had, split between the unions supporting government policies (Menemistas) and the unions under the leadership of Ubaldini (Ubaldinistas) opposing them. The inability of either faction to prevail enabled Menem to act as a broker, which strengthened his position. Ubaldini's failure to gain the support of the Group of 8 and other dissenting Peronist groups in early 1991 for his bid for the governorship of the Buenos Aires province made plain once more the disorganization and heterogeneity of the anti-Menem forces.

On the other hand, the president's strategy as the 1991 midterm congressional and gubernatorial elections approached seemed to again downgrade the role of the party. This could be seen in his recruitment of candidates outside the PJ and his simultaneous call for a "rectification" of the Peronist doctrine.[92] Menem had a double objective: to attract the conservative constituency that had voted for Alsogaray and Angeloz in 1989 but that now sympathized with his policies and to justify his policy U-turn to long-time Peronist backers, who had voted for him hoping for a very different outcome. His strategy seemed to have worked in the September 1991 elections, when Menemista candidates scored important victories while the Group of 8, Ubaldini, and the UCR all suffered defeat.

Menem also consolidated his grip on the PJ delegation in Congress. In the Chamber of Deputies, a substantial number of the new Peronist representatives were people outside the party (i.e., businessmen and professionals) who had embraced the president's neoconservative policies and were loyal to him rather than to the party. Conversely, the Group of 8 lost three deputies and was forced out of the PJ, while several other potential enemies—union leaders, orthodox Peronists, and left-wing Peronists—failed to be reelected. Although Menem still did not have the necessary majority to pass legislation in the House of Deputies, he could count on the votes of sympathetic conservative provincial parties and of the UCD. In the Senate, the situation was even rosier. With the Menemistas in control of many provincial legislatures (which elect senators), Menem could expect to gain up to thirty-five senators in the midterm election of 1993. Taking credit for the improved economic situation, Menem used the September results to strengthen his power within and outside of Peronism. By early 1993, he talked more and more of Menemism as a new conservative movement, whose Peronist roots were rapidly blurring. With the opposition in disarray and himself enjoying high approval ratings, President Memen could now push—as Alfonsín had and failed—for a constitutional change that would allow him to run for a second term.

Minor Parties

Radicals and Peronists have so dominated politics at the national level that many observers describe Argentina as essentially a two-party system. However, smaller parties have had, at one time or another, a disproportionate influence on national politics, at times dominating the ideological debate and providing ideas and policies that eventually were taken over by the two major groups.

The Right

Provincial parties have been able to create legislative alliances in Congress due to their overrepresentation in the Senate; since the country returned to democracy in 1983, provincial parties have often held the balance between the UCR and the PJ. After 1853 they dominated the political scene as long as they could rig elections. The adoption of a fair electoral system ended their hegemony in 1916. The brief interreign of the Concordancia gave them another chance to rule the country—both fraudulently and in collaboration with other parties. However, after 1943 they were never able to win meaningful representation in Congress. Their nadir was reached during 1943–1955, when only three conservatives were elected to Congress.[93]

Even during its heyday, Argentine conservatism was little more than a loose alliance of provincial parties with their counterpart in Buenos Aires.[94] Electoral coalitions continued to be a trademark of Argentine conservatism after 1916, but these coalitions barely survived once elections were over, since conservatives differ a great deal from one another in economic policy and ideology.

Provincial parties defend the interests of their local elites and their regional economies against what they perceive to be the abuses of the central government in Buenos Aires, much like the Federalists of the previous century, whose leaders tried to shelter their local economies from competition from abroad and from Buenos Aires. They have a pork barrel approach to politics, aimed at obtaining financial transfers from the federal government through industrial, infrastructural, and agricultural policies. They attempt to maintain the social status quo and the traditional patterns of life that will ensure the dominance of important provincial families and the continuation of the patronage system. By the same token, their commitment to the preservation of the local culture is the secret of their longevity. The conservatives of Buenos Aires, on the other hand, although as opposed to social mobilization as their provincial cousins, advocate free trade, close links with the external world, and a leading role for Buenos Aires (particularly the Federal District) in the national economy. The crucial difference between the provinces and Buenos Aires is that parties from the smaller provinces have had more representatives in Congress, particularly the Senate, than parties from Buenos Aires due to the constitutional provision that allows local legislatures to elect two senators. After the appearance of Radicalism and Peronism, the small conservative parties of Buenos Aires found it virtually impossible to gain seats in the Senate, and only on occasion were they able to elect representatives to the Chamber of Deputies. The rise of Radicalism and Peronism deepened the split among conservatives. Some joined Yrigoyen and Perón in the early stages of their movements, but most remained part of the opposition and supported the military coups of 1930 and 1955.

The absence of a strong right-wing party after 1916 contributed to Argentina's political instability; the economic right (landowners, industrialists, financiers), having no real hope of success in the electoral field, tried to "readdress things in its favor via the armed forces."[95] Internal divisions continued during the proscription of Peronism and the political stalemate after Perón's downfall. Instead of taking advantage of the opportunity offered by the proscription, Argentine conservatism was plagued by squabbles. Most conservative parties were bitterly anti-Peronist; they temporarily united under the banner of the National Federation of Parties of the Center (Federación Nacional de los Partidos del Centro, or FNPC), while a minority group, the Popular Conservatives (Conservadores Populares) believed, like Frondizi, that the best way to deal with the Peronists was to lure them away from their charismatic leader by reincorporating them into the political system.[96] Neither of them gained appreciable electoral support, particularly the Buenos Aires conservatives headed by former Minister of the Economy Alvaro Alsogaray, who advocated a return to the socioeconomic policies of the pre-1930 period. During 1955–1966, the only conservative parties that fared well in local elections were Mendoza's Democratic party and the Liberal Autonomist party of Corrientes.[97]

In 1963, some conservatives formed the Union of the Argentine People (Unión del Pueblo Argentino, or UDELPA) to support former President Aramburu's presidential ambitions. Aramburu styled himself as the Argentine De Gaulle, the man who could bring about law and order and revamp democratic institutions through strong leadership. He managed to bring together conservatives of both the Federal District and the provinces. Nonetheless, he finished a distant third, after Illia and Alende. After the montoneros executed Aramburu in 1969, UDELPA ceased to exist. In the 1973 presidential elections two of Aramburu's closest associates made one more bid to unite Argentine conservatism. Julio Chamizo was named the candidate of New Force (Nueva Fuerza), a newly created party that could count on important financial support from Buenos Aires economic circles. New Force spent lavishly to create an image of a modern liberal-democratic party like those of continental

Europe. Its platform included the pledge to abide by the rules of the democratic process and to foster "neo-liberal business oriented policies."[98]

The other major conservative party was the Federal Popular Alliance (Alianza Popular Federal) of Francisco Manrique. Manrique's party was an alliance of provincial and neo-Peronist parties that had refused to join the New Force. Unlike the New Force, the Federal Popular Alliance employed the old themes of conservative and paternalist Argentine populism common in the interior of the country.[99] Manrique's more traditional appeal enabled him to finish third, with almost 15 percent of the vote, whereas Chomizo polled a disappointing 2 percent.

The UCD, founded by Alvaro Alsogaray in 1982, gave new life to the right in the 1980s. It provided a political home to those conservatives who had traditionally turned to the armed forces: the 1976–1983 military experiment had convinced many of them that the alleged affinity between conservative and military ideals just did not exist, as the latter still clung to statist and corporatist policy-making patterns. Of the post-1983 parties, the UCD was one of the most ideologically grounded. The core of its platform was the reestablishment of liberalism (conservatives in Argentina, as in Europe, usually refer to themselves as liberals) based upon the free-market economic system that had been in place until 1930. The novelty of the UCD's discourse was that, unlike past conservative parties, which wanted freedom in the marketplace but restricted participation in the political realm, it pledged to respect the principles of constitutional democracy.[100] The UCD soon became the fastest growing party in the province of Buenos Aires, rising from 1.1 percent of the vote in the 1983 congressional elections to 9.9 percent in 1989.[101] Its constituency was concentrated in the middle and upper-middle classes of the Federal District, where by 1989 it obtained 22 percent of the vote, a net gain of 13 percent over the 1983 congressional results.

As the UCD enhanced its strength, tensions arose within its leadership. Alsogaray came increasingly under fire for his autocratic decision-making style, nepotism (his daughter María Julia and his cronies controlled key UCD posts), and elitism. UCD student organizations, prominent in university politics, and young party leaders asked for the democratization of the internal party structure and a less ideological, more accessible, political message so that the UCD could gain the support of the working class. The "popularization of liberalism" became a main concern of intellectuals like Manuel Mora y Araujo and Buenos Aires councilwoman Adelina D'Alessio de Viola.[102] De Viola adopted a populist, door-to-door campaign style to appeal to the working class and the poor of Buenos Aires when she ran for Congress in 1989, breaking with Alsogaray's patronizing attitude typical of the Argentine upper class (de Viola came from the middle class). The ascendancy of women within the UCD was further shown in the crucial role that María Julia Alsogaray played in creating the Centrist Alliance (Alianza de Centro), an alliance between the UCD and the conservative provincial parties for the 1989 presidential elections.[103] The Alianza polled a little more than six percent, while de Viola, although defeated, received 35 percent more votes than in the congressional elections of 1987.

The negative results were attributed to several factors: Alvaro Alsogaray's aloof style, the polarization of the presidential contest between Menem and Angeloz, the UCD's failure to attract the vote of important conservative constituencies, right-wing Catholics' resentment of the party's secularism, the industrial bourgeoisie's opposition to its free marketeers, middle-class state employees' fear of the party's sweeping privatization plans, the party's inability to expand beyond the province of Buenos Aires, and its resistance to de Viola's attempt to popularize conservatism among the lower social strata. To complicate matters, the CFI, which turned down the Alianza in favor of Angeloz, scored significant advances on the UCD's home turf, the Federal District, by attracting conservative voters uneasy with de Viola's overtures to the poor.[104]

Menem's surprising adoption of many UCD economic policies and inclusion of the two Alsogarays, de Viola, and other UCD figures in key government posts in his administration were a partial vindication of the electoral disappointment—and a historical event. Peronists and conservatives, once enemies, had become allies. Equally important, their alliance underscored the fact that the ideas of a small ideological party could be important in shaping the Argentine political debate.[105] Yet the UCD found itself virtually co-opted by presidential policies, creating an identity crisis within both its leadership and its constituency, which cost the party votes in the 1991 midterm election. As Alvaro Alsogaray mused, "It is paradoxical that when our ideas are implemented, we lose votes."[106] At the end of 1991 both Alsogarays formally stepped down from their party posts. However, they again dragged the UCD into a renewed alliance with Menem by backing his hand-picked candidate for the Senate seat of Buenos Aires, independent Avelino Porto, in the July 1992 election. This left many wondering about what future the party could have.[107]

Conservative provincial parties also experienced a revival by the late 1980s. They fared best in midterm elections, when polarization between radicals and Peronists played a smaller role in voter's decisions. In 1991 ten provincial parties were represented in the Chamber of Deputies, with twenty-five seats, compared to four parties in 1983, with five seats. The Liberal Autonomist party, the Bloquista party, and the Neuquén Popular party have kept small but important delegations in the Senate since 1983 (table 3.8). The strengthening of provincial parties in 1991, apart from long-standing factors such as caudillismo and clientelism, may be explained by the profound socioeconomic crisis that hit the rest of the country more severely than it did metropolitan Buenos Aires. The disillusion with both Radicalism and Peronism probably convinced many to vote for provincial conservatives, even though provincial parties have been closer to Peronism than Radicalism on national issues.

Between the late 1980s and the early 1990s, right-wing populist movements grew, headed by former military officers. The first to appear was the Republican Force (Fuerza Republicana) in Tucumán, the electoral vehicle of retired General Antonio Bussi. Bussi had been the military governor during the Proceso and was credited with eliminating the ERP from Tucumán. Bussi effectively exploited public resentment of the corrupt administration of the Peronist governor of Tucumán (which had led Menem to send a federal trustee to run the local government). In the context of a depressed and scarcely diversified economy and an unemployment rate of about 25 percent, Bussi ran an antiparty campaign and reminded people that while he was governor law and order reigned and full employment was maintained. This earned him four representatives to Congress, although his bid for the governorship of Tucumán was frustrated by a former singer running as an independent Peronist.

A more surprising phenomenon was the Movement of Dignity and Independence (Movimiento de Dignidad y Endependencia, or MODIN) created by former *carapintada* leader Aldo Rico. This ex-colonel promoted himself as the defender of the common people, who had been forgotten by political parties. He vigorously attacked Peronists and Radicals alike for their corruption. He charged Menem of selling off Argentina's interests to please the United States and the IMF. Most of all, he capitalized on the fact that the burden of stabilization policies was borne by the poorest sectors of society. Among Buenos Aires working class suburbs and shantytowns, MODIN garnered 532,000 votes, enabling it to send three representatives to the Chamber of Deputies.[108] Both Bussi's and Rico's protest movements took advantage of the malaise of the lower classes, but their potential to turn negative campaign slogans into credible alternative programs was very much in doubt. These personalized movements were too dependent on their charismatic leaders and specific socioeconomic ideas to become lasting political phenomena. In explaining his success, Rico acknowledged, "It is not because we are good but because the others are simply worse."[109]

In sum, both conservative provincial parties and right-wing populist movements had gained momentum by 1991 by exploiting the dissatisfaction of specific constituencies with some of the Menem administration's policies. Nonetheless, once in Congress, most of their representatives, with the exception of the MODIN, seemed willing to back Menem's legislative agenda. For the most part, they agreed with the thrust of the president's neoconservative policies as long as their provinces could reap some of the benefits.

The Center

Most centrist parties, once the Peronists were allowed to compete again in national elections in 1973, were unable to survive unless they formed electoral alliances with either Peronists or Radicals. This was true of Frondizi's MID, which in 1973, along with Vincente Solano Lima's Popular Conservatives and the Popular Christian party, supported the Peronist-dominated FJL. In the late 1980s a deep disagreement between Frondizi and Frigerio forced Frondizi's resignation, leaving Frigerio and his sons in control of the party, but by that time the MID was no longer a meaningful player in Argentine politics. In 1983 and 1989 it again joined the Peronist electoral alliance (FREJUPO), giving it a small representation in Congress. After Menem's victory, the MID was rewarded with the appointment of one of Frigerio's sons to the state oil company (Yacimientos Petroliferos Fiscales) chairmanship. However, the president's economic policies soon clashed with those supported by the Frigerios; in 1990 the MID abandoned the FREJUPO, only to rejoin it in order to back Menem's senatorial candidate for Buenos Aires in 1992.

Catholic parties have been important in neighboring Chile and in Venezuela but always failed to gain appreciable support in Argentina. The Christian Democratic Party (Partido Democrata Cristiano, or PDC) was created in 1955. Similar to its counterparts in Italy and Germany, the PDC started as a moderate, center-right party that campaigned for parliamentary democracy based on proportional representation and the establishment of Catholic schools.[110] The PDC, however, never came close to become a multiclass, catchall party as in other Latin American or European countries, nor was it able to become a clear alternative to either Radicalism or Peronism. It remained fundamentally a party of ideas, appealing to the Catholic middle and upper-middle class of the Federal District, with little following in other provinces. Additional support came from Catholic youth organizations like university students and Catholic Action (Acción Católica), but in a country where Catholicism is not pervasive, such associations failed to make the difference. The PDC, like other parties, was soon torn apart by internal disagreement about how to deal with Peronism. Right-wing and left-wing factions battled for control of what still was a small political party.

In the early 1960s, frustrated by their inability to capture a large mass following, some leaders became convinced of the necessity to find common ground with the neo-Peronists. The social content of Peronism also coincided in many ways with the objectives of many young party members who believed that Christian democracy should steer a middle course between capitalism and socialism. This move was rejected by the more conservative elements of the PDC, who eventually abandoned the party. The Christian Democrats welcomed the 1966 coup, and some of them served in Onganía's first cabinet. The alliance lasted only a few months. Soon after the appointment of Krieger Vasena (who replaced a Christian Democrat) to the Ministry of the Economy, the PDC withdrew its support from the regime, although many right-wing members of the party remained loyal to Onganía until the end.

In 1973, internal conflicts were no longer between the left and the right but rather between the moderates and the left, as the right had fallen into disgrace after Onganía's removal. The moderate faction, under the name of the Christian Popular party (Partido Popular Cristiano), joined the FREJUPO alliance, while the leftist Christian Revolutionary party (Partido Cristiano Revolucionario) united with the Intransigent party in the Revolutionary Popular Alliance. These two parties combined gained three seats in the Chamber of Deputies and one in the Senate.[111]

With the return of democracy in 1983, the Christian Democrats again reunited in the PDC but, similar to the MID, were forced into electoral alliances with the Peronists to compensate for their lack of popular support. Ideologically, the PDC in the 1980s was a center-left party, advocating strong state interventionism in the economy, tight regulation of the private sector, and redistributional policies to promote "social justice" for the less privileged social classes. The PDC also supported the integration of the grass-root movements that emerged from the military dictatorship: environmentalism, women's rights, squatters' rights, and human rights. Menem's drift to the right forced the PDC to leave the Peronist alliance, but without causing many governability problems, given that the Christian Democrats had only one seat in Congress in 1991. Some conservative Christian Democrats, on the other hand, decided to stay with Menem and be elected under the Peronist banner. The most visible among the pro-Menem Christian Democrats was Erman González, who served in various cabinet posts after 1989.

The Left

The Argentine Socialist party (Partido Socialista Argentino, or PSA) was organized early in the twentieth century. From the start, Argentine socialists were moderates and engaged in a tough competition with the anarchists to gain control of the labor movement. Their platforms included income redistribution, progressive income taxes, the forty-hour workweek, legalization of divorce, improved elementary education and first among Argentine parties, the electoral enfranchisement of women.[112] In 1930, the Independent Socialists, an offshoot of the PSA, handed the UCR its first defeat in the Federal District and later allied itself with the conservatives in supporting the Concordancia. The PSA, on the other hand, remained in the opposition during the 1930s and won over an appreciable part of the labor movement. By moderating its demands and compromising on a number of issues, the PSA gained the acceptance and respect of the UCR and the conservatives as a legitimate political opponent. However, for some observers, such moderation proved fatal to the party, making Peronism more appealing to the working class in the 1940s.[113] As it was for the Radicals, conservatives, and Christian Democrats, Peronism was a thorny issue for the socialists. Some socialist leaders eventually joined Perón, but the bulk of the party continued to oppose him. In 1959, the most anti-Peronist, right-wing faction of the party abandoned the PSA and formed the Social Democratic party (Partido Socialista Demócrata, or PSD). Like its Italian counterpart, the PSD was a moderate if not conservative party, with few socialist ideals. While the PSA ceased to exist for all practical purposes by the late 1960s, the PSD ran its own candidate in the 1973 presidential elections; it polled less than 1 percent.

In the 1980s, the socialists were again divided into several groups, among which Socialist Unity (Unidad Socialista) and the Unified Socialist party (Partido Socialista Unificado) were the largest. These two parties were centered primarily in the provinces of Buenos Aires and Corrientes, long strongholds of Argentine socialism. The socialists experienced an unexpected rise in popularity when in 1990 the Alianza Socialista won the election for the mayor of Rosario, the country's second-largest city. However, this result seemed more a vote of no confidence in Menem's policies than a long-lasting party realignment. In 1991, Socialist Unity captured 2.4 percent of the vote and three seats in the Chamber of Deputies. Within the left, the socialist parties constituted its moderate sector and have, on occasion, sought electoral alliances with the UCR in the Federal District.

Alende's PI reorganized again in 1983 and positioned itself to the left of the PJ. After a further drift to the left that helped it score some impressive gains in the 1985 congressional elections at the expense mostly of Peronists, the party suffered a serious setback in 1987. Following a severe internal split, the PI joined the FREJUPO in 1989, only to leave it again a year later, accusing Menem of selling out the country to the interests of the United States and the IMF. Tough opposition to Menem's neoliberal economic policies and its proposal to revive the old policies emphasizing economic nationalism did not pay off for the PI. In the 1991 midterm elections, it polled less than 1 percent. The fundamental problem of the PI was its hybrid nature. Neither a Marxist nor a social-democratic party, the PI often used Marxist class analysis blended with left-wing populism, which failed to capture either Marxists or Peronists. Without a clear identity, the PI fell into obscurity by the early 1990s.

The Communist party soon after its creation experienced severe splits between supporters of Stalin and Trotsky. In the late 1930s it acquired some prominence when several of its members gained control of important unions in the manufacturing sector. In 1946, most communists joined the opposition front that contested Perón's presidential bid. With the labor movement thoroughly Peronized, the communists were deprived of their main constituency and never again were capable of drawing a mass following. Even after Perón's ouster, the Communist party remained small, with many of its members and sympathizers coming from the urban middle class of the Federal District rather than from the working class. In the 1960s, Argentine communism was divided among Maoists, Castroists, Guevarists, and supporters of Soviet communism. A Trotskyite offshoot of the communists formed the Revolutionary Workers party (Partido Revolucionario de los Trabajadores, or PRT), whose armed branch in 1970 turned into the ERP terrorist organization. The 1980s saw the flourishing of many new Marxist parties, all small, all ineffective. Two groups, the Workers party (Partido Obrero, or PO) and the Movement Toward Socialism (Movimiento al Socialismo, or MAS), with some support among students and the urban working class, contended for leadership among Trotskyites. The MAS and the Communist party (the two largest leftist parties) joined with minor left-wing groups in the United Left Alliance (Alianza Izquierda Unida) in 1989. The coalition received only 2.4 percent of the presidential vote and won only one seat in the Chamber of Deputies. In the 1991 midterm election, the Alliance collapsed due to ideological and personal differences among its leaders. The split further weakened the left's performance, with both the MAS and the Communist party (with its allies) polling barely more than 1 percent each.

A number of factors account for the left's lack of success. Factionalism, more than capitalism or imperialism, seems to be its worst enemy. In 1989, five different center-left and leftist tickets vied for congressional seats; in 1991 their number increased to seven, leading however to only one seat in the Chamber of Deputies.[114] The electoral performance of the left averaged a meager 5.75 percent in the Chamber of Deputies elections during the 1983–1991 period. (See table 3.3.) To complicate things, most left-wing support comes from urban centers, where the number of votes necessary to elect a representative is much greater than in rural areas. For example, in 1989, 573,583 votes were needed for the United Left Alliance to elect a representative, compared to 48,596 for the Neuquén Popular Movement.[115] This prevents the left from translating its votes into greater congressional representation. The more radical leftist parties still advocate a class struggle, which finds little response in a society like Argentina's that is more receptive to populist rather than doctrinaire rhetoric. The Communist party, PO, and the MAS receive their greatest support from intellectuals and university students, while most workers support Peronism. A few issue-oriented parties have appeared, like the Greens (Frente Humanista Verde) and the Retirees (Blanco de los Jubilados), but only the latter gained appreciable votes (1.9 percent in the 1989 presidential elections).

TABLE 3.3
Chamber of Deputies Election Results, 1983–1991 (percentage)

Party	1983	1985	1987	1989	1991
Major parties					
Justicialist party and allies	38.47	34.60	41.46	44.68	38.84
Radical Civi Union and allies	47.39	43.20	37.24	28.29	27.40
Total	85.86	77.80	80.20	72.97	66.24
Minor parties					
Right-wing and provincial parties	4.48	10.00	12.00	17.94	22.62
Left-wing and center-left parties	5.19	9.80	6.26	6.11	5.57
Other parties	0.96	0.47	0.50	0.91	0.42
Total	10.63	20.27	18.76	24.96	28.61
Blank or invalid ballots	3.51	1.93	1.04	2.07	5.15

SOURCE: Data based upon Liliana De Riz and Gerardo Adrogué, "Democracia y elecciones en la Argentina: 1983–1989, "*Cuaderno CEDES*, no. 52 (1990):21, 50. Data for 1991 (Tierra del Fuego is not included) are from the Electoral Department, Ministry of Interior; preliminary figures.

1983–1992: A Two-Party or a Multiparty System?

The Argentine electoral system, according to the 1853 constitution, establishes that the president be elected by popular vote through an electoral college. The Chamber of Deputies is also elected by popular vote. Since 1983, midterm congressional elections have taken place every two years, renewing half of the Chamber's seats. Seats are assigned according to proportional representation criteria based upon the D'Hondt system, which favors the two largest parties in any given district. As in the United States, to balance the greater representation in the Chamber of Deputies of the most populous provinces, the Senate allocates two seats to each province. (See table 3.4.) However, senators are selected by the provincial legislatures for a nine-year term. The president is elected, as in the United States, through an electoral college to avoid the most populous provinces deciding the final outcome beforehand.[116]

The Argentine Congress has powers similar to the U.S. Congress. Its approval is needed on legislation regarding foreign treaties, the budget, war, taxation, state corporations, external debt, and the currency. Bills must be approved by both branches of Congress. Traditionally, most legislation has been pushed through by the executive and sponsored by backbenchers. Since 1983 deputies and senators have been more active in presenting their own bills, although their rate of success has been much lower than that of executive-sponsored legislation.

Between 1946 and 1976 Peronism dominated Argentine politics. Yet there are differences of opinion regarding the evolution of the party system after 1983. Catterberg, for instance, argues that Argentina turned into a "bipolar," or a "dominant two-party" system between 1983 and

TABLE 3.4
Seats in the Chamber of Deputies, by Province, 1983

Province	Seats	Population
Buenos Aires	70	6,567,298
Catamarca	5	182,308
Chaco	7	449,824
Chubut	5	145,205
Córdoba	18	1,631,287
Corrientes	7	439,798
Entre Ríos	9	621,449
Federal District	25	2,341,791
Formosa	5	166,651
Jujuy	6	215,074
La Pampa	5	142,988
La Rioja	5	107,344
Mendoza	10	749,248
Misiones	7	312,945
Neuquén	5	129,662
Río Negro	5	195,344
Salta	7	388,567
San Luis	5	147,100
San Juan	6	290,040
Santa Cruz	5	54,974
Santa Fe	19	1,676,080
Santiago del Estero	7	397,068
Tierra del Fuego	2	15,349
Tucumán	9	612,446
Total	254	17,929,951

SOURCE: Liliana De Riz and Gerardo Adrogué, "Democracia y elecciones en la Argentina: 1983–1989," *Cuaderno CEDES*, no. 52 (1990):47.

1989. Drawing upon the works of Sartori and Lijphart, he maintains that the lack of ideological, religious, racial, and linguistic cleavages, the absence of an antisystem party and of centrist minor parties, the presence of weak left-wing and right-wing parties, and the unimodal distribution of the electorate indicate that Argentina has moved toward bipolarism. Furthermore, undecided Radical and Peronist voters are most likely to switch to the other major party rather than to minor ones, according to opinion polls taken after the 1987 elections.[117] On the other hand, Zuleta Puceiro contends that in the 1983–1989 period the share of the PJ and UCR combined vote dropped. To him, Argentina is a system of "moderate pluralism" in which two major, but not dominant, parties battle over an electorate greatly concentrated at the center while facing the competition of smaller but consistent parties.[118]

A strong electoral polarization took place in the presidential elections of 1983 and (to a lesser degree) 1989. (See table 3.5.) In those two elections the combined PJ-UCR presidential vote averaged 8.9 percent higher than the congressional vote. However, polarization has diminished since 1989. Taking the whole 1983–1991 period, which is a better indicator of a party's strength than only two presidential elections, we see that the 1983 election was exceptional (extremely good for the Radicals and unusually poor for the Peronists). By 1991, both the PJ and the UCR had returned close to their traditional levels. In fact, if we discount the contribution of electoral allies (indeed, the practice by the PJ and the UCR to form electoral alliances with minor parties poses further questions about the real strength of these two parties), the Peronists were below 40 percent, while the Radicals obtained 27 percent of the total vote (a little more then their historical average of 25 percent since the

TABLE 3.5
Presidential Election Results, 1983 and 1989 (percentage)

Party	1983	1989
Major parties		
Justicialist party	40.1	47.3
Radical Civic Union[a]	51.7	32.4
Total	91.8	84.2
Minor parties		
Socialist Democratic Alliance	0.3	0.0
Christian Democratic party[b]	0.3	0.0
Intransigent party[b]	2.3	0.0
Movement Integration and Development[b]	1.2	0.0
Democratic Center Union	0.3	0.0
Centrist Alliance[c]	0.0	6.2
Movement toward Socialism	0.2	0.0
Popular Socialista party	0.2	0.0
Línea Popular Movement	0.1	0.0
Workers party	0.09	0.2
Alliance of the Popular Left	0.0	2.4
Socialist Unity Alliance	0.0	1.3
White Flag (Pensioners)	0.0	1.9
Independent Federal Confederation	0.0	4.5
Greens	0.0	0.2
Other parties	1.1	1.4
Blank ballots	2.3	2.5
Voter turnout	81.1	84.6

SOURCE: Electoral Department, Ministry of Interior.
a. In 1989 includes the Independent Federal Confederation.
b. In 1989 allied with the Peronists in the FREJUPO.
c. Includes the Democratic Center Union.

1950s). Conservative parties in the provinces (but not in the Federal District where the UCD lost ground) strengthened, and the left declined, over the same period. As polarization eroded, small parties gained in strength both in terms of percentage of the vote and in number of seats. This depolarization trend is seen best in elections for provincial legislatures. (See table 3.6.)

To test the two-party thesis, the Laakso and Taagepera's index was used to ascertain the "effective number of parties" based upon the num-

TABLE 3.6
UCR-PJ Control of Provincial Legislatures, 1983–1989 (percentage)

Polarization	1983	1985	1987	1989
100–90%	Córdoba	Catamarca	Catamarca	Formosa
	Chaco	Chaco	Córdoba	La Rioja
	La Rioja	La Rioja	Chaco	
	Misiones	Misiones	Entre Ríos	
	Santa Cruz	San Luis	Formosa	
			La Pampa	
			Misiones	
			Santa Cruz	
			Santiago del Estero	
89–80%	Buenos Aires	Formosa	Buenos Aires	Catamarca
	Entre Ríos[a]	Santa Cruz	Chubut	Chaco
	Mendoza	Tucumán	Mendoza	Misiones
	Río Negro[a]			Santa Cruz
	Santa Fe[a]			
	Tucumán			
79–70%	San Luis	Buenos Aires	Jujuy	Buenos Aires
	Federal Capital	Mendoza	Río Negro	Mendoza
	Santiago del Estero[a]	Salta	Salta	San Luis
	Catamarca		San Luis	
	Chubut[a]		Santa Fe	
	Formosa		Tierra del Fuego	
	Jujuy			
	La Pampa[a]			
	Salta			
–70%	Corrientes	Corrientes	Corrientes	Corrientes
	Neuquén[a]	Federal Capital	Neuquén	Jujuy
	San Juan[a]	Jujuy	San Juan	Salta
	Tierra del Fuego	Tierra del Fuego	Federal Capital	Federal Capital
			Tucumán	Tucumán
			Tierra del Fuego	Tierra del Fuego
				Santiago del Estero

SOURCE: Liliana De Riz and Gerardo Adrogué, "Democracia y elecciones en la Argentina: 1983–1989," *Cuaderno CEDES*, no. 52 (1990):59.
a. Provinces that elect their legislatures only every four years.

ber of seats in Congress.[119] According to this index, two equally strong parties leads to a score of 2.0, a two-party system with one party having 70 percent of the seats and the other one 30 percent has a score of 1.7, while a system with three parties sharing roughly the same number of seats scores 3.0.[120] This index when applied to the Argentine Chamber of Deputies confirms the initial conclusion. In 1983, Argentina seemed to fall into the category of two almost equally strong parties, much like Austria. However, as time went on the trend reversed, and if one considers the whole period, the mean score is 2.5 (the same as Australia's). This suggests that Argentina, between 1983 and 1991, did not have a two-party system, especially in 1991, when the index reached 2.9 (see table 3.7). Of course, the time series is too short to be conclusive, but if one takes into account the exceptional nature of the 1983 elections, the two-party system argument is questionable.

TABLE 3.7
Mean, Lowest, and Highest Effective Number of Legislative Parties in Twenty-three Democracies, 1945–1980

Country	Mean	Lowest	Highest
United States	1.9	1.8	2.0
New Zealand	2.0	1.9	2.0
United Kingdom	2.1	2.0	2.3
Austria	2.2	2.1	2.5
Canada	2.4	1.5	2.9
Australia	2.5	2.4	2.7
Argentina[a]	**2.5**	**2.2**	**2.9**
Germany	2.6	2.2	4.0
Ireland	2.8	2.4	3.6
Japan	3.1	2.0	5.8
Sweden	3.2	2.9	3.5
Norway	3.2	2.7	4.1
Luxembourg	3.3	2.7	4.1
France (V)	3.3	1.7	4.6
Italy	3.5	2.6	4.4
Iceland	3.5	3.2	3.9
Belgium	3.7	2.5	6.8
Denmark	4.3	3.5	6.9
Israel	4.7	3.4	6.0
France (IV)	4.9	4.2	5.9
Netherlands	4.9	3.7	6.4
Switzerland	5.0	4.7	5.5
Finland	5.0	4.5	5.6

SOURCE: Arend Lijphart, *Democracies: Patterns of Majoritarian and Consensus Government in Twenty-One Countries* (New Haven: Yale University Press, 1984). After World War II, France adopted a parliamentary system that was eventually replaced with a presidential system in 1958.

a. For Argentina only, years are 1983–1991; the lowest number was in 1983 and the highest in 1991.

Moreover, while most of the factors listed by Catterberg as characterizing the Argentine polity seem reasonable, the interpretation of such factors, using Sartori's typology, is arguable. If anything, following Sartori's typology, it is safer to describe today's Argentina as a "moderate multiparty" system, in which party fragmentation is high and ideological distance is low.[121] That political fragmentation exists can be seen in the number of parties represented in Congress, parties whose support became crucial to the Radicals once they lost their majority in 1987 and to the Menem administration from its outset in 1989. (See tables 3.8 and 3.9.) Indeed, two of Sartori's key factors in establishing the relevance of minor parties is their coalition and blackmail potential. Not surprising, Menem, lacking a congressional majority during his first three years in power, made an explicit effort to co-opt both the UCD and the provincial parties in return for positions in his administration and special consideration for the needs of the provinces. Without the support of provincial parties in the Senate, Menem's legislative agenda could not pass. By 1992, Argentine conservative parties enjoyed both coalition and blackmail potential.

Argentina also fits Sartori's typology in its lack of ideological cleavages. The antisystem party, which according to Sartori is a key indication of ideological distance, has not been present in Argentina since 1973, when the Peronists were fully reincorporated into the political process. The data collected by Catterberg in major urban centers seems to confirm such a conclusion: the bulk of the Argentine electorate lies in the center-right of the ideological continuum (figure 3.1). This partly explains why ideological parties, particularly those on the left, have had difficulty making electoral inroads. On the other hand, most Peronist and Radical voters are center-right. Both parties have mass-based and loose political formations, which strive for support from diverse constituencies, downplaying ideological issues and emphasizing pork barrel politics. It is too early to say whether these trends may indicate a shift of the PJ and the UCR toward the catchall party model. Indeed Argentines are not divided by linguistic and racial cleavages; moreover, as a 1991 Gallup poll shows, religious, ideological, and political differences are far less relevant in Argentina than in Chile and Mexico.[122] Argentina thus appears to fall into the "moderate multiparty" type characterized by numerous but essentially nonideologically polarized parties. (Figure 3.2).

How do we explain the fact that Radicalism and Peronism— although originating as antiregime mass movements—were by the 1980s in the mainstream of Argentine politics? Scholars who have examined political cleavages in Western Europe and North America argue that in their beginnings, parties or mass movements representing previously excluded social groups emphasize their differences from the es-

TABLE 3.8
Chamber of Deputies Seats, by Party, 1983–1992

Party	1983	1985	1987	1989	1991
Justicialist party	111	101	105[a]	120	120
Radical Civic Union	129	130	117[b]	90	84
Democratic Center Union	2	3	7	11	10
Intransigent party	3	6	5	2	2
Liberal Autonomist Pact	2	3	4	3	3
Christian Democratic party	1	2	3	3	1
Progressive Democratic party		1	2	3	3
Neuquen Popular Movement	2	2	2	2	2
Salta Renovating party		1	2	2	4
Movement of Integration and Development		1	1	1	1
Bloquista party		1	1	1	1
Mendoza Democratic party		1	1	1	1
Socialist Unity			1	1	3
Río Negro Provincial party			1	1	
White Flag (Pensioners)			1	1	1
Provincial Action			1	1	
Jujuy Popular Movement	1	2	c	2	2
Pampas Federal Movement	1				
Humanismo and Liberation				1	
Federal party				2	1
Republican Force				2	4
United Socialist party				1	
Movement toward Socialism				1	1
Renovating Crusade Alliance				1	2
Movement of Dignity and Independence					3
Group of "8"					5
Chaco Action					1
Tierra del Fuego Popular Movement					2
Total	254	254	254	254	257[d]

SOURCE: Liliana De Riz and Eduardo Feldman, *Guía del Parlamento Argentino* (Buenos Aires: Fundación Friedrich Ebert, 1990), and *Buenos Aires Herald*, 29 October 1991.
a. Includes and independent deputy, Domingo Cavallo.
b. Includes two members of the Jujuy Popular Movement, two of the Partido Federal, and one of the Solidarity for Change.
c. The Jujuy Popular Movement allied itself with the UCR.
d. In 1991 Tierra del Fuego became a new province and was granted three representatives.

tablished parties in order to make clear their separate identities. Thus they adopt an outright opposition posture based upon non-negotiable political demands. However, once these parties or movements finally decide to participate in electoral politics and are accepted by the old parties, they are socialized into the system, where the need for the original identity fades. The longer the party or mass movement is entrenched in the system, the more it becomes aware of the limits on radical change, and the more it appeals to marginal voters. As moderation begins to

TABLE 3.9
Senate Seats, by Party, 1983 and 1989

Party	1983	1989
Justicialist party	21	26
Radical Civic Union	18	14
Liberal Autonomist Pact	2	2
Neuqén Popular Movement	2	2
Bloquista party	2	2
Movement of Integration and Development	1	
Total	46	46

Source: Liliana De Riz and Eduardo Feldman, *Guía del Parlamento Argentino* (Buenos Aires: Fundación Friedrich Ebert, 1990).

prevail, there is a tendency for the old radical demands to be dropped in favor of demands not so far from those of the older parties. This brings about a situation of "policy convergence."[123]

Thus, the convergence reached by the Radicals and Peronists by the late 1980s is not surprising. By the same token, when the convergence process reaches a point where voters can no longer distinguish what parties stand for, schisms or new antiestablishment parties or movement may arise. In other words, when most distinctions are blurred, there is a renewed interest by parts of the electorate to reestablish their

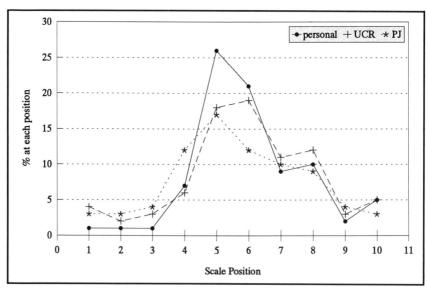

FIGURE 3.1   Ideological Location Scale
Source: Estudios Survey, 1988

	Fragmentation	
	Low	**High**
Low	**Two Party** **Canada** **United States** **United Kingdom** **Austria**	**Moderate** **Multiparty** **Netherlands** **Denmark** *Argentina*
Ideological Distance **High**	**Predominant** **Norway** **Sweden**	**Extreme** **Polarized** **Finland** **Italy**

FIGURE 3.2   Party System Typology

SOURCE: Sartori *Parties and Party Systems* (Cambridge and New York: Cambridge University Press, 1976) p.314

separate identities. An alternative can be "to shift to personalities for the task of representing alternatives. Choice among parties, ideologies, and programmes . . . is then replaced by choice among images of personalities in which the electors are asked to put their trust. Here the choice is dissimilar from the choice between programmes . . . in that it is not binding on the specific policy of the elected, and therefore allows the governing groups to adopt very similar policies even if their images are distinct enough to make choice possible."[124] This fact can help us understand Menem's victory over Cafiero in the 1988 Peronist primaries. Cafiero's political discourse and program had come to be perceived by many Peronist rank-and-file members as close to what Alfonsín had preached for five years. For these people, it was necessary to reinstate the old Peronist identity, which was just what Menem offered. By voting for what Menem represented rather than what he had to say (that is, his program), Argentines allowed the new president to interpret his mandate as he saw fit. Once in office, although still claiming to abide by Perón's doctrine, Menem implemented policies much more drastic than Alfonsín's.

4

POLITICAL CULTURE, PUBLIC OPINION, AND VOTING BEHAVIOR

THE CONCEPT OF political culture, based upon aggregate measures derived from survey research, has been a powerful tool in explaining why and how a given political system evolves the way it does. Although the political culture concept has come under attack for its lack of theoretical consistency it is still helpful in casting light on behavioral patterns related to political institutions and collective action. This chapter first focuses on traditional interpretations of what has often been labeled the Argentine national character and explores how individual-level traits have shaped the country's political culture. We will also examine public opinion trends since the return of Argentina to constitutional government. Finally, we will analyze the impact of socioeconomic and political factors in shaping voting trends in Argentina—historically as well as more recently.

The Argentine National Character

Although many judgments have been passed on the true nature of Argentine behavioral patterns, such judgments were, for the most part, impressionistic accounts based upon the personal experiences of individual writers and therefore lacking any scientific grounding. Yet in 1960 Tomás Fillol felt sure enough to depict the typical Argentine as apt "(1) to put undue emphasis on personal, short-run advantage without adequate consideration of the future consequences that his actions may bring about for himself and the community; (2) to respect and [to] confer prestige [upon] what is considered to be born with the individual, and to assert it against other interests within the society as a right and a prerogative; . . . (3) to preserve at all costs what he has already gained or achieved for himself and his own family, and to value gains accrued to the community only insofar as he and his family are likely to profit from them; (4) to blame other individuals or groups for the sorrowful consequences of his own act."[1] These cultural traits are thought to prevent the development of social relationships based upon cooperation and the pursuit of "common goals and interests." Argentina is described as a "conglomeration" of individualistic people, rather than an "organic community." People seek public office not for the public good but for self-aggrandizement and personal wealth.[2] Others argue pretty much the same, stressing the absence of a civic culture across all social classes and rampant social hostility, indifference, factionalism, selfishness, apathy, and deceit.[3]

Much of the blame for these character traits has been ascribed to the lack of leadership in the Argentine upper class, whose backbone has traditionally been the pampean landed oligarchy. The oligarchy looked to Europe as a model, played down its Hispanic heritage, and regarded Argentina as a European outpost in Latin America. Much like its nineteenth-century European counterparts, the Argentine oligarchy viewed the lower social classes with contempt and paternalism. Such elitism has provoked resentment and impeded the process of nation building. Interestingly enough, the new industrial and financial elite that emerged in the twentieth century (see chapter 8), instead of challenging the landed elites' standards, simply tried to get into the "club" by accepting their values, joining their exclusive clubs, and acquiring large estates. Thus, even if the ranks of the upper class diversified, the elitist attitude did not change much. "The wealthy never advanced from exploitation and consumption to productive investment, remaining smugly immune to reform. They came to power through exclusion and they remained exclusive, never willing to share political power freely with other economic groups."[4]

The rise of Peronism, however, ended the exclusionary model that the upper class had preserved even after the advent of Radicalism. The exclusion from political power for prolonged periods weakened the leadership qualities of the Argentine oligarchy. A conservative observer comments:

The upper class lost the notion of what constitutes a managerial culture . . . after the 1940s, and it has retreated into an exclusionary, provincial, parochial life style little oriented to the achievement of leadership. [The upper class] accepted the decline of the nation, whose leadership had been exercised by its fathers and grandfathers, without its pride being hurt. The upper class stopped instilling civic values, being inspiring models (except for ostentatious consumption), and feeling responsible for the destiny of society. It stopped being a ruling class and perpetuated itself as the subculture of the affluent, condoning power abuse [and] obstructing the progress of society.[5]

For its part, the middle class, as in the rest of Latin America, remained amorphous, lacking a specific class consciousness and values of its own. Indeed, the middle class (or the *middle sectors,* as some authors label it to underscore its heterogeneity), although resenting the oligarchy's elitism, looked to it as a model.[6] In particular, the middle class aspired to the status symbols and material benefits enjoyed by the upper class but remained relatively unconcerned with more substantive matters. Thus, the Argentine middle class remained anchored to conservative, traditional values; it was a "culture of consumption rather than production, of social mobility rather than personal achievement."[7] At the same time, it manifested contempt for the working class, deepening social polarization.

While these generalizations contain some truth, they have often been used to create a simplistic and stereotyped version of reality. Several observers stress that corruption and clientelism is institutionalized in both the public and private sectors and is taken for granted by citizens.[8] However, far from being a peculiarity of Argentine or Hispanic societies, corruption is also endemic in the more advanced societies of North America. One thing that differentiates the Argentine from the North American citizen is that, while the latter still professes aversion to this phenomenon, the former has long given up fighting back and has learned to live with it. While it is true that corruption, selfishness, deceit, and apathy are widespread in Argentina, these cultural traits are not typical of Argentina or of all Argentines: As one observer points out, "It is impossible to identify a single culture that adequately describes, in any useful way, the world of such a diverse citizenry."[9]

One thing on which most analysts agree is that the Argentine culture is not plagued by racial or linguistic problems. About 90 percent of the population is of European descent, and Spanish is uniformly spoken across the land. Moreover, despite being over 90 percent Catholic, religion does not seem to influence the Argentine national character to any appreciable degree. The old cleavage between clericals and anticlericals affecting the country in the nineteenth century is basically absent today. The legalization of divorce in the 1980s, for instance, did not create a political uproar. As in many other Catholic countries, church attendance has decreased since the 1970s and has primarily been confined to women. Moreover, evangelical churches have made some significant inroads among the middle and lower social classes. The attitude of many Argentines toward the Catholic church has been one of pragmatism, which can be summarized by the old adage, Do what I say, not what I do.

Anti-Semitism is another feature often ascribed to Argentines. Undoubtedly, Jews were the target of attacks, which reached their low point in the Tragic Week of 1919. Jewish emigration to Argentina, primarily from eastern Europe, contributed significantly to the country's development. Whereas a minority settled in the pampas, giving birth to the famous *gauchos judíos* (Jewish cowboys), the bulk of the Jewish population, estimated at 400,000 to 500,000, remained in the cities. At the end of World War II, Buenos Aires had the second-largest Jewish community in the world, after New York City. Besides enjoying great success in business, Jews became prominent in the liberal professions and academia. However, their presence in the military and among landowning elites has been meager, if not nonexistent, thus leading to allegations of discrimination in these groups. The same has been said about political elites, but during the 1980s this myth seems less tenable than in the past. Since 1983 a number of Jews were elected to Congress, and there were many Jews among Alfonsín's ministers and advisers—to such an extent that people in Buenos Aires referred to them as the *cúpula judía* (Jewish hub). One hears occasional racist remarks, but it is impossible to ascertain how anti-Semitic Argentine culture actually is; Jews themselves disagree about the extent of anti-Semitism. Some argue that Jews were one of the groups singled out for repression during the Proceso, but others deny that their fellow Argentines discriminate more than other people around the world. "Yet, the mere fact that it troubles some of them indicates that anti-Semitism cannot be dismissed as casually as many people try to do."[10]

Distrust, cynicism, and intolerance are three dominant attitudes often mentioned as shaping the Argentine national character. Distrust and cynicism are believed to have their roots in the civil wars following national independence from Spain, when provincial groups battled with groups in Buenos Aires to establish regional autonomy: since then, people from the provinces have resented the arrogance of the porteños, who have politically and economically overpowered the rest of the nation. Most analysts, though, believe that distrust and cynicism became endemic in the 1930s when the Concordancia began to manipulate public office and that these traits deepened with the controversial policies of the Peronist era.

In the early 1940s, José Ortega y Gasset observed that "there is a relative justification to the defensiveness of the Argentine. His wealth, social position, or public office . . . are in constant danger due to the pressure of the appetites surrounding him, unchecked by any other rule. Where impudence is the common trait of social relations, it is necessary to be perpetually on the alert." In 1965 Jeane Kirkpatrick's survey of public attitudes in Argentina found that 84 percent of the respondents agreed with the statement, "People will take advantage of you," which led her to claim that Argentines expressed very high levels of distrust and cynicism. In 1971, Ezequiel Martínez Estrada concluded that these traits originated in the individualism typical of Hispanics; in his view, the introduction during the last two centuries of European values like democracy and social cooperation created an odd mix, whose outcome was the worst of both worlds. Similarly, in 1989 Susan and Peter Calvert argued that "Argentine politics has been seen as dominated by individuals" and Argentines have exhibited little "confidence in impersonal organizations and [in] people they do not know personally." The Calverts contended that the inability of either the Hispanic or the European culture to prevail led to a political stalemate, because the fundamental contradictions arising from the uneasy coexistence of the two backgrounds were never resolved. On the other hand, Schoultz pointed out that, when asked the same questions, Italians and Germans showed a level of distrust similar to Argentines', and Mexicans were even more distrustful.[11] Thus in Schoultz's view, neither distrust nor cynicism, with regard to government, appear to be Argentine traits. And if one takes into account the tendency of Argentine politicians to ignore their promises once in office, as happened particularly under the Frondizi and the Menem administrations, there is little reason for Argentines not to be distrustful and cynical.

My main contention is that these patterns of behavior are common in Argentina but are not typical of that country alone. The individual-level attitudes discussed above are believed to be responsible for the lack of a sense of community and national solidarity and the zero-sum approach to problem solving. Laura Randall summarizes: "It seems justified to say that in Argentina more than in most countries social groups tenaciously cling to their acquired situations and vested interests, strive to maximize their own short-run material advantage to the exclusion of larger ends, and insist that all other social groups are doing the same."[12] From a political standpoint, such group behavior leads to a situation where coalition building becomes very difficult, compromise is almost impossible to reach, and "intransigence becomes widespread and in turn creates isolated (and often embattled)" political groups behaving in a feudalistic and anarchic fashion.[13]

One outcome of this state of affairs has been the general lack of consensus on what rules should be used to play the political game. Argentines have conformed to different and often conflicting formal and informal rules, depending upon their personal interests and the interests of their socioeconomic groups. As time went on, people began to adhere to the rules of not only limited democracy, but also competitive pluralism, authoritarianism, and corporatism. When the rules of the group in power were not accepted by those in opposition, political conflict was exacerbated. Thus, elections became only one of many means to gain power: military coups, charismatic leadership, public protest aimed at undermining authority, and guerrilla warfare were also used in various combinations. Succinctly put, "The leitmotif of Argentine politics [has been] the quest for political legitimacy in a culture that lacks a consensus on many of the most fundamental issues of power and privilege."[14] A similar lack of consensus has affected the rule of law. Public officials have often used the law to further the interests of specific constituencies and to bless illegal practices or privileges. "In the popular perception, policemen are corrupt, judges are biased, and attorneys unscrupulous [and] legal proceedings often have merely provided a fig leaf to cover the depredations of state-sanctioned lawbreakers."[15]

Part of the problem rests with the 1853 constitution which, as we saw in chapter 2, contained contradictory provisions, sanctioning democratic ideals while leaving the door open to authoritarian practices. The Supreme Court, which was entrusted with the authority to keep in check the abuses of the executive and legislative branches of government, began to lose prestige in the 1930s when it acknowledged the de facto constitutionality of the 1930 military coup. Subsequently, the purging and "packing" of the Supreme Court became a widespread practice under Peronist and military administrations. Not only has the Supreme Court been politicized, but many of its members have often acted in a very disreputable way. For instance, in 1991, at a time when the government virtually froze public employees' salaries, the Supreme Court awarded its own members a pay hike of $11,500 a month; and later some justices hired their own relatives as staff members, claiming that they needed people they could "trust." These events damaged public confidence in the legal system and in the enforcement of the law. Many citizens and interest groups, while agreeing that uniformity of treatment is paramount in inspiring compliance, believe that exceptions are justified when it comes to their own well-being.[16]

This free-ride attitude, far from being exclusive to Argentine political culture, deepened as time went on. Argentines commonly say that theirs is a society of "neither reward nor punishment."[17] However, a reward does seem to exist for those who break the law. A typical example is income taxes: in 1989 tax authorities estimated that only half of the individuals legally required to pay income taxes actually did. Tax evasion can be described as a national sport. Although stiff penalties do exist for tax evaders, seldom have governments enforced them. On the contrary, amnesties by money-starved administrations have been so frequent as to create the belief that evasion pays off better than compliance.[18]

Another outcome of this scenario is that almost all aspects of public and private life assume political meaning. Citizen participation in politics has long been characteristic of Argentina, and it has expressed itself in the coming and going of political movements. What is most intriguing, however, is that the strong participatory nature of the Argentine political culture has not been matched by an equal emphasis on ideology. In effect, as noted in chapter 3, ideology is sorely missing from the country's most important political movements of the twentieth century: Peronism and Radicalism. As in other Latin American countries, Argentines have been receptive to foreign ideologies, like liberalism, social democracy, fascism, Christian democracy, Marxism-Leninism, Maoism, and Castroism. However, the overwhelming tendency by political groups has been to disassemble such ideologies and adopt only those parts that appealed to them and fit their domestic situation. Consequently, "Argentine belief systems are only vaguely related to the formal ideologies that have developed" elsewhere.[19]

Public Attitudes Toward Parties and Political Issues

In the 1960s and 1970s reliable national public opinion polls were unavailable, and therefore our knowledge about public perception of parties and key political issues is based on sketchy data. Even today, the only true national public opinion survey is the one carried out in 1965 by Kirkpatrick.[20] Other surveys were mostly confined to metropolitan Buenos Aires and only occasionally included some provincial capitals. In addition, these surveys were often flawed by their sampling procedures. Until the early 1980s, aside from Kirkpatrick's study, survey questions on parties and political issues were rare.

In 1963, a survey conducted in Rosario showed that two-thirds of the people interviewed voted because they were required by law to do so (voting is mandatory in Argentina). Others also mentioned that the ban on Peronism and the lack of credible alternatives put forward by the Radicals and minor parties presented them with only negative choices.[21] The complaint about the lack of representativeness of political parties in the 1960s was particularly common among the elites. José Luis de Imaz, in his survey of the Buenos Aires upper class, found that 66 percent of his respondents felt unrepresented by the existing parties. About 30 percent mentioned that parties lacked concrete programs; 11 percent contended that parties put their own interests above those of the nation; 9 percent believed that parties were too demagogic; and the remaining 7 percent thought that parties did not have competent leaders.[22] This situation presumably explains why Kirkpatrick in 1965 found that subjective party identification was quite low. In fact, only 3 percent of her respondents admitted to belonging to party organizations, whereas 54 percent expressed no party preference at all.[23] A further reason for public disillusion was due, according to the Rosario survey, to the parties' inability to keep their campaign promises or to their lack of ideological principles.[24] If one considers that Frondizi a few months after being elected reversed most of his economic policies, it is easy to understand such public disillusion.

In 1963, a survey taken in metropolitan Buenos Aires, Mar del Plata, and Bahia Blanca indicated that, among the most important institutions of the country (unions, universities, political parties, congress, and the army), only the army was regarded as worse than parties as a factor preventing progress:

> There appears to be little doubt that political parties, between the 1950's and the early 1970's, were not held in high repute by the general public. A more important question in 1966 and again in 1976, as far as the leaders of the armed forces were concerned, must have been "Is the public amenable to the complete abolition of the political party system?" In this connection it might be noted that a survey carried out shortly before the 1966 coup showed 60 percent of the Buenos Aires working class in complete agreement with the statement: "We have too many platforms and political programs; what we need is a strong man to lead us." Another 23 percent agreed "more or less," and only 17 percent were in complete disagreement. At about the same time a survey of all Argentines showed over 40 percent in agreement with the statement: "A few strong leaders would do more for this country than all the laws and talk."[25]

How did public attitudes toward parties, democracy, authoritarianism, populism, statism, and the role of Argentina in the world today change after the country returned to constitutional government in 1983? Most of the discussion that follows is based on survey research carried out in the 1980s and early 1990s by two of Argentina's most important pollsters, Edgardo Catterberg and Manuel Mora y Araujo. It should be emphasized that their data, as well as the others mentioned here, are not true national samples as they are based on a limited number of urban centers; nor were they carried out systematically over time due to the fact that they were collected mostly for ad hoc purposes. Therefore, no definite conclusions can be drawn from their findings. Nonetheless, they do provide, more than past studies, useful insights into postauthoritarian Argentina.[26]

Let us begin from where we left off, that is, with public perceptions of political parties. The last year of the military regime in 1983 coincided with a positive image of the role of democratic institutions in general. (See table 4.1.) Between 1982 and 1983 Argentina experienced an unprecedented revival of interest in parties, which surprised the politicians themselves. Formal party membership reached three million for the Peronists and one million for the UCR that year. This means that 20 percent of the eligible voters were formally affiliated with a party organization. However, by 1988 things had turned sour; the evaluation of politicians deteriorated most of all. By June 1988 only union leaders and military officers were evaluated more negatively. Political parties experienced the same trend but to a lesser degree. Subsequent public opinion polls in early 1991 showed that the politicians' credibility, including President Menem and opposition leaders, was at its lowest point since the restoration of democracy.[27]

TABLE 4.1
Evaluation of Institutions and Leaders, 1983–1988 (percentage)

	May 1983	May 1984	April 1985	August 1985	April 1986	Sept. 1986	April 1988	June 1988
Political Parties								
positive		84	80	77	77	77	70	63
negative		14	17	21	21	21	27	35
Politicians								
positive	38	61	59	58	50	50	29	30
negative	54	36	38	39	48	47	68	67
Entrepreneurial groups								
positive		75	74	79	76	77	72	72
negative		19	17	16	20	17	21	22
Entrepreneurs								
positive	32	33	43	47	44	42	37	43
negative	57	62	50	49	53	53	57	52
Unions								
positive		81	77	67	71	72	66	59
negative		16	18	32	26	26	31	38
Union leaders								
positive	23	30	43	36	34	33	25	24
negative	55	67	52	62	64	64	72	73
Armed forces								
positive		55	52	54	54	59	55	53
negative		42	42	43	43	38	39	42
Military officers								
positive		12	16	20	22	22	22	24
negative		85	78	77	71	73	72	73

Source: Edgardo Catterberg, *Argentina Confronts Politics: Political Culture and Public Opinion in the Argentine Transition to Democracy* (Boulder: Lynne Rienner, 1991), p. 56.

Similar conclusions were reached by Mora y Araujo, who, however, contended that although the parties' positive image declined after its peak in 1982, 40 to 50 percent of the population continued to express confidence in them.[28] In Mora y Araujo's view, what people really questioned was not parties per se but their leaders and internal organizations. The disrepute in which politicians and parties had fallen was not peculiar to Argentina; by the early 1990s the same phenomenon was affecting other countries in Latin America (e.g., Mexico, Venezuela, and Brazil), North America, and Western Europe. For Mora y Araujo the reason for such a disillusionment rested on the fact that "in the Argentina of the past few years the political class became just another vested interest. It looked for and obtained privileges and asked society to grant it immunity in return for the provision of an important public service: upholding the democratic order—that is, preventing the military from ruling again. While society hoped that other services would follow, linked to the exercise of government, it accepted all this. However, this lasted only a short time."[29]

Thus, as the public perception of public officials deteriorated, so did that of the institutions they represented. A 1991 cross-national survey shows that Argentines had lower levels of confidence in their institutions than Chileans and Mexicans. Somewhat disturbing was the fact that the score indicating the public's level of confidence in the military, although low, ranked higher than opinions of the legal system and Congress (see table 4.2). The only bright spot is the lack in Argentina of significant demographic and attitudinal cleavages such as are found in Chile and Mexico.[30] (See table 4.3.)

In terms of political culture, Catterberg's study confirmed previous works that found Argentines to be a highly individualistic people who place great importance on social mobility based on competence and material incentives. However, in Catterberg's view, this translated into support for moderation and gradualism, as opposed to radical change, since people believed that the Argentine socioeconomic structure, despite all its defects, was best suited for the pursuit of individualistic goals. The discrepancy between this conclusion and those of earlier

TABLE 4.2
Institutional Confidence Rankings in Argentina, Chile and Mexico, 1991[a]

Rank Order	Argentina	Score	Chile	Score	Mexico	Score
1	Church	−10	Church	52	Education System	52
2	Education System	−23	Education System	47	Church	52
3	Military	−43	Congress	27	Legal System	5
4	Media	−45	Police	18	Media	−3
5	Police	−48	Business	15	Social Security	−3
6	Business	−51	Social Security	7	Military	−7
7	Legal System	−53	Civil Service	−2	Business	−9
8	Social Security	−61	Unions	−6	Unions	−23
9	Congress	−67	Legal System	−11	Congress	−30
10	Unions	−84	Media	−15	Police	−36
11	Civil Service	−86	Military	−19	Civil Service	−44
	Argentine n = 1102		Chilean n = 1500		Mexican n = 1464	

Source: Mark Jones, "A Comparative Study of Popular Confidence in Democratic Institutions in Argentina, Chile, and Mexico," paper prepared for the eighteenth Latin American Studies Association Congress, Los Angeles, 24–27 September 1992.

a. The confidence score is the sum of the percentage expressing "very much" or a "great deal" of confidence in an institution minus the percentage of those with "not very much" or "none at all" confidence in the institution.

TABLE 4.3
Demographic and Attitudinal Cleavages, 1991

	Significant Cleavages by Country		
Cleavages	Argentina	Chile	Mexico
Education	0	1	0
Age	1	1	0
Socioeconomic	0	1	1
Town	n.a.	0	4
Gender	0	3	1
Religiosity[a]	2	4	5
Ideology	2	3	5
Political Interest	0	4	1
Total	5	17	17

SOURCE: Mark Jones, "A Comparative Study of Popular Confidence in Democratic Institutions in Argentina, Chile, and Mexico," paper prepared for the eighteenth Latin American Studies Association Congress, Los Angeles, 24–27 September 1992.
a. Since the religion and religiosity variables are highly correlated and since the religion variable cleavage was only significant for the same institutions as was the more refined and generally more salient religiosity measure, only the latter variable is included in this portion of the analysis.

works may be explained in part by the fact that the legacy of the political stalemate of the 1950s and 1960s and the ensuing urban terrorism and military repression of the 1970s was a yearning for moderation.

Although highly individualistic in personal concerns, Argentines supported strong state involvement in both the economic and social spheres. The majority of the people polled in 1986 held the state responsible for providing full employment, price controls, rent controls, and cheap public services. (See table 4.4.) Half of those surveyed also regarded the state as the best institution to mediate social conflict. Such attitudes toward the state were positively correlated with socioeconomic status, with the lower class expressing its desire for greater state involvement than the middle and upper classes. Catterberg divided the lower class into two groups: the (structured) lower class, composed of salary and wage earners (blue-collar workers and clerks), and the unstructured, or marginal, lower class, made up of unskilled workers who find temporary employment in the informal sector of the economy.

These findings were not so surprising if one considers that since 1930 strong state intervention has been a dominant characteristic of Argentina, regardless of regime. Since the first Peronist administration, the lower class grew accustomed to expecting benefits from the state aimed at diminishing income inequalities across social sectors. Moreover, conflictive, individualistic values and state interventionism are, according to Catterberg, complementary, because the state is not per-

TABLE 4.4
Attitudes on Statism, by Socioeconomic Level (percentage)

| | | | | Working Class | |
Response and Statement	Total	Upper Class	Middle Class	Lower (structured)	Lower (marginal)
Agreement that the state must provide work to all who want to work	83	57	76	83	92
Disagreement that it is better if the state does not control prices	83	66	75	83	93
Agreement that the government should freeze rents	75	56	61	76	88
Disagreement that the state should provide moderately priced public services without worrying about possible losses	58	44	51	57	67
Agreement that the state solves social problems better than other institutions	49	45	41	49	57

SOURCE: Edgardo Catterberg, *Argentina Confronts Politics: Political Culture and Public Opinion in the Argentine Transition to Democracy* (Boulder: Lynne Rienner, 1991), p. 18.

ceived (nor does it behave) as an impartial actor promoting the public good but as an institution to be used to maintain or create benefits sanctioned by law.[31] In this sense, the state is expected to provide material goods that are the end of the individual pursuit of personal well-being. To reverse John F. Kennedy's thought: Ask not what you can do for your country but what your country can do for you. This is, in the end, the standard by which government is judged.

However, Mora y Araujo has contended that, slowly but steadily, the Argentine public has changed its perception about state intervention. While up to the mid-1980s few doubted that Argentines supported interventionist, corporatist, nationalist, and distributive policies, by the early 1990s their attitudes had come full circle, and they were endorsing growth-oriented policies based upon the initiative of the private sector, privatization policies, and greater links to the capitalist economies of North America and Western Europe.[32] (See figure 4.1.)

What brought about such a turnaround? In Mora y Araujo's view, the answer can be found in the exhaustion of the ISI development model pursued through state intervention after the Great Depression, which reached its height under Perón's first two terms. As noted in

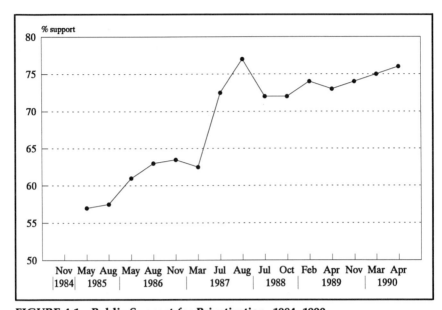

FIGURE 4.1   Public Support for Privatization, 1984–1990
SOURCE: Manuel Mora y Araujo, *Ensayo y Error* (Buenos Aires: Planeta, 1991) p. 73.

chapter 2 in the discussion of the motivations behind the free-market policies endorsed in Argentina and other major Latin America countries in the early 1990s, many people singled out state intervention as the cause of the huge fiscal deficits and high inflation. State enterprises were burdening the taxpayer with these problems while providing jobs and contracts for narrow political clienteles of the government. Public services were poor and plagued by continuous labor conflict. In the eyes of many frustrated citizens, state intervention, instead of creating a fairer society, had led to discriminating privileges, whose costs were dumped on to everyone else. By the second half of the 1980s people "wanted an economy capable of producing more, not distributing better; gradually they reoriented their preferences toward the first world, and were confident in the entrepreneurs as a reserve of credible and necessary leadership."[33] In short, people wanted less state intervention and union power and hoped that free-market economic policies, the only readily available alternative, could solve the problems of economic stagnation and inefficiency.

However, it remains to be seen if the dramatic attitude change portrayed by Mora y Araujo is a long-lasting behavioral trend or a transitory one. Did Argentines embrace the free-market economic model by default or out of conviction? Other opinion polls showed growing discontent with the privatization policy effort, which was a crucial test for the Menem administration's neoconservative effort to create a "new Argentina." Privatization reached its greatest popularity in October 1989, with approval ratings of 70.5 percent. However, by April 1991 support had declined to 53.9 percent, while opposition to privatization had doubled, climbing to 25.9 percent.[34] According to one opinion poll, the poor way in which the privatization of ENTel, the telephone company, and Aerolineas Argentinas had been carried out tarnished public perception of the policy effort. Equally important was the fact that three-quarters of those interviewed found out that, since its privatization, telephone service had not improved, and 14 percent actually believed it had worsened.[35]

What about attitudes toward the democratic system? Mora y Araujo comments that "the essential note of change in Argentina was a renewed democratic attitude in the traditionally undemocratic Argentines."[36] Time-series data collected by Catterberg between 1982 and 1988 also suggest a widespread and increasing agreement on government chosen through the democratic process and an equally strong disagreement with elitist politics.[37] However, while Argentines seem clearly in favor of basic forms of participatory democracy, once the questions shift to political tolerance of basic liberties, the picture changes substantially. Half of the population surveyed believe that democracy can be detrimental, that the majority is entitled to disregard minority rights, and that the government should control the press, slightly less than half feels that a one-party system is the best form of government. (See table 4.5). These findings confirm an earlier survey carried out by Natalio Botana right before the 1983 elections, in which 86 percent of respondents were in favor of democracy, but 84 percent were also supportive of a "strong government."[38] When the focus is on socioeconomic status, Catterberg contends that the consensus on tolerance and pluralistic values is greater among the upper and middle classes. Conversely, authoritarian values are associated with lower social status. (See table 4.6.) When education is used to control for socioeconomic status, pro-democratic attitudes are even stronger (yet table 4.7 shows that socioeconomic status and education may have independent effects).[39]

Catterberg also argues that people's dissatisfaction has a negative effect on their commitment to participatory democracy and political tolerance. Discontent with the country's overall situation had a greater impact than discontent with one's personal situation. As things got worse, so did public opinion on the viability of the political system.[40] How can we explain the fact there was more consensus on indicators of political participation than on indicators of tolerance and individual

TABLE 4.5
Attitudes on Libertarianism and Democracy, 1982–1988 (percentage)

Response and Statement	May 1982	May 1983	May 1984	April 1985	August 1985	April 1986	Sept. 1986	May 1988	June 1988
Disagreement that democracy is dangerous because it may bring about disorder and disorganization			67	67	65	67	63	54	52
Disagreement that majorities are entitled to deny the rights of minorities	58	63	81	54		51	50		
Disagreement that the government has the right to control the press	42	57	48		51	57	52		
Disagreement that the country would be better off with a one-party political system	58	64				67	59		60

SOURCE: Edgardo Catterberg, *Argentina Confronts Politics: Political Culture and Public Opinion in the Argentine Transition to Democracy* (Boulder: Lynne Rienner, 1991), p. 41.

TABLE 4.6
**Attitudes on Political Tolerance, Pluralism, and Authoritarianism, by
Socioeconomic Level (percentage)**

			Working Class	
Statement and Response	*Upper Class*	*Middle Class*	*Lower (structured)*	*Lower (marginal)*
The best political system is the one based upon periodical elections				
Democratic attitude	87	89	80	73
Antidemocratic attitude	11	7	11	16
Democracy is dangerous because it may bring about disorder and disorganization				
Democratic attitude	82	68	53	38
Antidemocratic attitude	15	29	43	54
The country would be better off with a one-party political system				
Democratic attitude	85	77	60	39
Antidemocratic attitude	13	20	32	49

SOURCE: Edgardo Catterberg, *Argentina Confronts Politics: Political Culture and Public Opinion in the Argentine Transition to Democracy* (Boulder: Lynne Rienner, 1991), p. 42.

freedom? The answer may be found in the coexistence of different and often contrasting political values held by a socioeconomic group following Charles Anderson's "living museum" model.[41] In this regard, Catterberg divides Argentines into four categories based upon degree of political participation and tolerance. "Pure types" are those both adhering to participation and tolerance (democratic) and rejecting them (authoritarian). "Mixed types" are those accepting participation but not tolerance (populist) or tolerance but not participation (elitist). Democrats corresponded in percentage terms to the total vote obtained by Alfonsín in 1983, while the populists percentage was only 5 percent below Luder's electoral result (see figure 4.2). Catterberg's results confirm, in large part, earlier findings by Mora y Araujo: although the latter used a somewhat different typology, he concluded that 35 percent of the population sampled were social democrat, 30 percent corporatist, 20 percent liberal, 10 percent traditional, and 5 percent leftist. Mora y Araujo's social democrats and liberals together (totaling 55 percent) are very close to their democratic counterparts in Catterberg's typology. Similarly corporatists are quite similar to populists.[42] Although neither study produced conclusive evidence of the sociological composition of Argentina, their findings can be taken as good approximations.

TABLE 4.7
Attitudes on Democracy, by Socioeconomic and Educational Levels (percentage)

			Working Class	
Statement and Response	Upper Class	Middle Class	Lower (structured)	Lower (marginal)
Agree that democracy is dangerous because it may bring about disorder and disorganization				
Primary school (grammar school)		47	35	42
Incomplete secondary		30	37	49
Complete secondary	30	33	31	39
Incomplete college education	16	18	15	25
Complete college education	12			
Agreement according to socioeconomic status	16	27	32	42
Agree that the country would be better off with a one-party political system				
Primary school (grammar school)		40	38	42
Incomplete secondary	25	39	34	49
Complete secondary	10	26	25	39
Incomplete college education	8	13	17	
Complete college education	5			
Agreement according to socioeconomic status	8	23	30	45

SOURCE: Edgardo Catterberg, *Argentina Confronts Politics: Political Culture and Public Opinion in the Argentine Transition to Democracy* (Boulder: Lynne Rienner, 1991), p. 43.
NOTE: Data collected in April 1988 in major urban centers.

If we break down Catterberg's typologies according to social class, the number of democrats increases monotonically with higher socioeconomic status, while the opposite is true for populism and authoritarianism. (See table 4.8.) If we divide the sample according to occupational level, the democratic type is prevalent among teachers, managers, students, and skilled workers, the populist type is predominant among unskilled workers, while housewives and retirees are evenly split. As Catterberg argues, an interesting contrast is the different beliefs of skilled versus unskilled workers.

When age enters into the analysis, Catterberg finds that younger individuals tend to be more democratic than older people, while the opposite is true for the populist typology. Interestingly, authoritarians are slightly more represented in the younger cohorts than in the oldest one (table 4.9). Taking these results together, Catterberg concludes that the Argentine political culture in the transition period was mixed, since political participation was more positively valued than political tolerance,

<table>
<tr><td colspan="3" align="center">**Participation**</td></tr>
</table>

	yes	**no**
yes	**Democrat** **52%**	**Elitist** **5%**
Tolerance		
no	**Populist** **35%**	**Authoritarian** **8%**

FIGURE 4.2   Ideological Typology, by Opinions on Participation and Tolerance

SOURCE: Edgardo Cattergerg, *Argentina Confronts Politics: Political Culture and Public Opinion in the Argentine Transition to Democracy* (Boulder: Lynee Rienner, 1991), p. 46.

TABLE 4.8
Typology of Attitudes Toward Political Regimes, by Socioeconomic Level (percentage)

Typology	Total	Upper Class	Middle Class	Working Class	
				Lower (structured)	Lower (marginal)
Democrat	52	78	66	51	36
Populist	35	11	11	37	46
Elitist	5	8	8	5	5
Authoritarian	8	3	3	7	13

SOURCE: Edgardo Catterberg, *Argentina Confronts Politics: Political Culture and Public Opinion in the Argentine Transition to Democracy* (Boulder: Lynne Rienner, 1991), p. 46.
    NOTE: Data collected in April 1988 in major urban centers.

TABLE 4.9
Typology of Attitudes Toward Political Regimes, by Age (percentage)

Typology	Total	Years of Age			
		18–24	*25–34*	*35–50*	*55 or older*
Democrat	52	54	52	53	49
Populist	35	31	33	35	42
Elitist	5	8	7	4	4
Authoritarian	8	7	8	8	5

SOURCE: Edgardo Catterberg, *Argentina Confronts Politics: Political Culture and Public Opinion in the Argentine Transition to Democracy* (Boulder: Lynne Rienner, 1991), p. 47.
NOTE: Data collected in April 1988 in major urban centers.

which declined as popular dissatisfaction increased. Participatory democracy is likely to be closely related to populism; in fact, direct participation mediated not by strong institutions but by charismatic leaders is a main feature of populist politics, which in Argentina found its expression in political movements like Yrigoyenism and, even more, in Peronism. Not by chance, it is among the lowest social strata, which were the core of Peronism, that we find the largest number of populists.

Catterberg underscores that the turn to democratic institutions, contrary to what has been argued, failed to lead to greater support for pluralist values. However, given the small time span covered, it is unwarranted to make any clear-cut generalization from such findings. While Catterberg hypothesizes that this may be due to bad economic conditions, an equally important explanation may be that political parties missed the opportunity to give credibility to democratic institutions.

What were the most pressing demands of the Argentine public after the return to democracy? For Catterberg, economic issues dominated people's concerns and demands, never scoring less than 54 percent of total responses between 1984 and 1988, with a peak of 73 percent in April 1985 when the country was entering a hyperinflation spiral (see table 4.10). Preoccupation with economic issues fluctuated depending on the inflationary trend.[43] When inflation surged, people's concern for economic issues was highest; during periods of relative price stability, people shifted their attention to other issues. Table 4.10 also indicates the secondary importance of social and political issues: according to Catterberg, an important discrepancy took place during this period. While the Alfonsín administration was emphasizing problems linked to the consolidation of democracy, the public continued to be concerned mainly with economic problems.[44] The government's incapacity to address these concerns had negative electoral repercussions later on. Mora y Araujo adds that the worsening fiscal crisis and the inflationary trend

TABLE 4.10
Opinion on the Country's Most Important Problems, 1984–1988 (percentage)

Problem	May 1984	April 1985	August 1985	April 1986	Sept. 1986	April 1987	June 1988
Inflation	24	44	24	16	21	18	23
Salary	10	12	14	24	23	27	16
Unemployment	12	11	18	16	14	14	10
Foreign debt	10	6	7	8	3	4	5
Total economic issues	56	73	63	64	61	63	54
Polarization of industry and commerce	10	5	12	8	7	4	8
Social problems, health, housing	16	10	14	14	14	11	11
Crime and violence	1	1		3	9	7	12
Education	3	4	5	6	6	6	8
Democratic stability	5	3	5	2	1	3	1
Human rights	2	1		1	1	1	1
Military relations				1	1	1	1
Other	7	3	1	1		4	4

Source: Edgardo Catterberg, *Argentina Confronts Politics: Political Culture and Public Opinion in the Argentine Transition to Democracy* (Boulder: Lynne Rienner, 1991), p. 26.

created a demand for austerity policies, which the Alfonsín government did not meet because it believed that austerity policies were unpopular.[45]

Catterberg contends that popular perceptions of the government's ability to solve the crisis deteriorated over time (see table 4.11), and that a decline in optimism, assumed to be related to people's perception of

TABLE 4.11
Opinion on Resolution of the Country's Economic Problems, 1984–1988 (percentage)

Response and Statement	May 1984	April 1985	August 1985	April 1986	Sept. 1986	June 1988
Agree that the government is solving economic problems	3	3	5	4	3	2
Agree that the government has the capacity but needs time	76	62	65	59	58	22
Agree that the government can't solve economic problems	10	18	14	21	20	44
Agree that neither this nor other governments can solve economic problems	9	14	13	14	16	26
Don't know	2	3	3	2	3	6

Source: Edgardo Catterberg, *Argentina Confronts Politics: Political Culture and Public Opinion in the Argentine Transition to Democracy* (Boulder: Lynne Rienner, 1991), p. 26.

TABLE 4.12
Perception of Personal and National Economic Situation, 1984–1988
(percentage)

Question and Response	May 1984	April 1985	August 1985	April 1986	Sept. 1986	April 1988	June 1988
How is your personal economic situation now compared to last year?							
Much better/a little better	31	18	27	22	24	10	10
The same	43	39	39	43	36	28	28
A little worse/much worse	26	42	33	34	40	61	62
Don't know		1	1	1		1	
What do you expect your personal economic situation to be in the next two years?							
Will improve much/a little	65	45	60	53	48	30	32
Will be the same	20	26	17	21	24	33	36
Will worsen much/a little	9	18	15	20	19	24	21
Don't know	6	11	8	6	9	13	11
What do you expect the country's economic situation to be in the next two years?							
Will improve much/a little	74	48	60	53	43	26	31
Will be the same	10	19	17	20	22	27	29
Will worsen much/a little	9	23	15	21	26	36	29
Don't know	7	10	8	6	9	11	11

SOURCE: Edgardo Catterberg, *Argentina Confronts Politics: Political Culture and Public Opinion in the Argentine Transition to Democracy* (Boulder: Lynne Rienner, 1991), p. 27, 28.

their own and the nation's well-being, corresponded to the deteriorating economy (table 4.12). In turn, declining optimism was closely associated with the perception that individual expectations, particularly economic ones, were not fulfilled. Since many Argentines held the government responsible for their own well-being, their frustrations ate into their support for the democratic system, and they ended up evaluating the previous authoritarian regime more positively. In 1988, almost 45 percent of those dissatisfied considered democracy dangerous, and 30 percent believed that the military government was more efficient than the civilian one.[46] By early 1991, the majority of people interviewed (64 percent) in the Federal District and metropolitan Buenos Aires no longer believed in the possibility of a military coup.[47] Moreover, 60 percent believed that only some of the military had participated in the violation of human rights, while only 26 percent still thought many or all had participated in the "dirty war." The survey concluded that people were demanding—although not in a clear way—policies toward the military emphasizing professional excellence, territorial security issues, and government control over the armed forces.

Before the 1983 elections, parties showed no intention of entering into a socioeconomic pact, nor was one made after Alfonsín was sworn in. Interestingly enough, in May 1984 most of the public favored collaboration between opposition parties and the government; however, by April 1987, the public mood had swung back in support of competition among parties. This rather dramatic switch partly explains why the confrontational Peronist campaign of 1985 ended in disaster, while in 1987 a more moderate but equally aggressive strategy led the PJ to victory. Catterberg interprets this change as a clear split between support for the president and for his party in government. In fact, about 68 percent of the people favoring Alfonsín in metropolitan Buenos Aires affirmed that it was plausible to support the president while voting for a party other than the UCR. In explaining such behavior, almost 50 percent of the people interviewed maintained that in so doing pluralism was strengthened (only 10 percent thought that other parties had better candidates.)[48]

On foreign policy, a 1991 survey shows that many people did not have a clear idea on the subject, or were simply uninformed or misinformed on key issues.[49] Yet the great majority of those with an opinion stressed pragmatisms like pursuing commercial ties with other countries (48 percent), luring foreign investments (18 percent), developing scientific and technological exchanges (13 percent), creating cultural ties (7 percent), and promoting tourism (7 percent); the remaining 7 percent had no opinion. Nationalism, although still supported by an important segment of the population, appeared to be declining and was replaced by a desire for closer ties with foreign countries, particularly in the First World (North America, Western Europe, and Japan) whose alliance would be economically advantageous. This scenario was quite different from the one detected in 1985. Some argued that the outbreak of the debt crisis in 1982 was going to create a new solidarity among Latin American countries and a reconsideration of relations between developed and developing nations. Alfonsín's foreign policy, as a matter of fact, explored such a possibility in the beginning. The president gave priority to ties with other Latin American and Third World countries and tried to implement a foreign policy independent of the Western and Soviet blocs. Survey data indicates that in 1985 over half of the respondents agreed that Argentina was better off having close ties with Latin America. (See table 4.13). However, by 1991, about 70 percent thought that priority had to be given to relations with the United States, Western Europe, and Japan.[50] Preferences for communist or nonaligned nations remained negligible during this period.

TABLE 4.13

Opinion on Countries with Which Argentina Should Strengthen Ties,
1985–1991 (percentage)

	Oct 1985	August 1987	April 1989	Sept. 1990	Dec. 1990	August 1991	Dec. 1991
United States, Western Europe, Japan	40	44	53	55	61	53	70
Latin America	42	36	22	23	20	25	15
USSR and communist countries	4	4	5	3	3	3	2
Third World/Nonaligned countries	3	4	3	1	2	2	1
Don't know	11	13	18	19	15	17	13

SOURCE: Manuel Mora y Araujo, Graciela Di Rado, and Paula Montoya, "La política exterior y la opinión pública argentina," Estudio Manuel Mora y Araujo, Noguera y Asociados, Buenos Aires, 1991.

How can these changes be explained? For one thing, in spite of a great deal of rhetoric, a cartel of debtor Latin American countries never materialized, as each government thought it was more convenient to deal with the IMF, the United States, and foreign banks on a one-on-one basis. A related factor may be the realization that, whether Argentines liked it or not, without the Western world's help the economic crisis had no solution, and no support could be expected from neighboring countries nor from the crumbling communist bloc. Indeed, Menem's foreign policy of pursuing stronger ties with the First World nations received an overwhelming 69 percent support. Public support was positively correlated with higher socioeconomic status. On specific issues, however, the administration's approval ratings varied. While 82 percent endorsed economic integration with Brazil, Uruguay, and Paraguay through

TABLE 4.14

Correlations Between Occupation and Voting in the Federal District,
1940 and 1946

	1940			1946		
Occupation	Peronist	Socialist	Radical	Peronist	Socialist	Radical
All workers	−.076	+.197	−.243	+.973	−.820	−.908
Industrial workers	−.268	+.276	−.340	−.898	−.705	−.966
Public service workers	−.004	−.006	−.196	+.920	−.853	−.802
All employees	+.104	−.174	+.353	−.653	+.571	+.692
Public employees	+.238	−.143	+.250	−.698	+.566	+.720
Professionals	+.316	−.215	+.226	−.869	+.810	+.918
Industrialists	−.262	+.064	−.032	−.095	+.082	−.036
Businessmen	−.217	+.163	+.272	−.515	+.430	+.435

SOURCE: Gino Germani, *La estructura social de la Argentina* (Buenos Aires: Raigal, 1955), pp. 253–55.

MERCOSUR, and 43 percent approved Argentina's decision to abandon the NAM (43 percent did not know what it was), only 38 percent favored negotiations over border disputes with Chile (36 percent was opposed and 26 percent showed no opinion), and an average of 64 percent disapproved of Argentina's involvement in the Gulf War.[51]

Voting Behavior from 1940 to 1973

Gino Germani's seminal work on voting behavior using aggregate data show a weak correlation between occupation and 1940 party vote in congressional elections in the Federal District, while a study by Pedro Huerta Palau showed no significant correlation between occupation and party vote in the 1935 elections in Córdoba.[52] However, the whole picture changed with the advent of Peronism. Strong correlations were found between occupation and party vote in the 1946 congressional elections in the Federal District (see table 4.14). According to Peter Snow, Peronists did extremely well in the working-class districts, whereas socialists and Radicals had their best performance in districts dominated by white-collar workers, members of the liberal professions, and businessmen (in order of importance); industrialists showed no correlation with any party.[53] Lars Schoultz challenged the Germani-Snow thesis, which postulates no significant class-oriented voting prior to 1943. Through a correlation analysis of the 1942 election in the Federal District, he showed that there were "fairly strong tendencies toward conservatism among professionals and toward laborism among blue collar workers."[54] The Peronist victory in the 1946 presidential election was ascribed to two factors: the vote of urban workers, which the Labor party had taken away from the socialists and the syndicalists, and the vote of the lower classes in the interior, whom Perón won over by including local conservative notables in his coalition.[55] A subsequent study, done during the 1962 election in Córdoba, showed similar results, although the correlation was not as strong.[56] The Peronists captured the majority of the votes in districts with a high concentration of workers or farmers but performed poorly in middle- and upper-class districts. Conversely, the UCRI and the UCRP did better in more affluent districts (the UCRI more than the UCRP).

Another finding of Schoultz's analysis was that "an area's rate of industrial growth and the size of its working-class population account for more than four-fifths of the variation in Peronist electoral behavior that can be attributed to socioeconomic variables." Finally, using Parson correlations between the Peronist vote and occupation for the 1946, 1951, 1957, 1960, 1962, 1965, and 1973 elections in 209 districts of the Federal District, Schoultz concluded that while blue-collar and unskilled workers voted disproportionately for Peronism, substantial segments of the middle class also did, although not as massively.[57] These results were eventually challenged because they did not take into account the fact that domestic servants and maids tended to live in the homes of their upper-class employers and vote in these districts. Presumably, these people were prone to vote for Peronism and thus biased the results. Once this problem was controlled for in upper-class districts, the conservatives received the great majority of their votes from the upper and upper-middle classes. The Peronist vote, on the other hand, was not confined to the working class, nor was the middle class the only group supporting the Radicals; they received nearly as many votes from upper-class and working-class districts. Thus "Argentine conservatism, between 1960 and 1973, was limited in appeal to the upper and upper-middle class, and . . . Peronism was largely, but certainly not exclusively, a movement of the working and lower-middle class. The Radicals, on the other hand, must be considered multi-class rather than merely representative of the middle class."[58]

Voting Behavior from 1983 to 1989

Polls taken immediately after the 1983 and 1989 presidential elections confirm the multiclass bases of Peronism and Radicalism. The samples were taken only in the Federal District and metropolitan Buenos Aires, which differ appreciably from the rest of the country. However, their findings are consistent with most of the other individual data analyses carried out at the time, as well as with the observations of journalists and pundits, and therefore can be considered useful indications of electoral trends. A substantial swing occurred in the class composition of the Radical vote between the two elections (see table 4.15). In 1983, Alfonsín gained most of the votes of the upper and middle classes. However, he made surprising advances among the lower structured working class, crucial for the UCR victory, in Catterberg's view. The Peronists kept their supremacy only among unskilled workers.

This was disputed by Mora y Araujo, who asserts that the overwhelming support of the upper and upper-middle classes, which traditionally had voted conservative, swung the election in Alfonsín's favor. He also attributes the Peronist loss of the lower-middle class vote to changes in the social composition of that class. Historically, the Peronist vote was concentrated in the less developed provinces of Argentina and in the working class suburbs of metropolitan Buenos Aires, Rosario, and other minor industrial cities.[59] The decrease in the work force in the industrial sector (see chapter 6), forced many people into self-employment; in Mora y Araujo's view, the self-employed were likely to have expectations typical of the middle class and, therefore, to feel more comfortable with the Radical candidate rather than with Luder. Finally, Mora y Araujo underscores the importance that new voters (the previ-

TABLE 4.15

**Votes for President, by Party and Socioeconomic Level, Federal
District and Metropolitan Buenos Aires, 1983 and 1989 (percentage)**

Social Class	Peronist	Radical
Upper class		
1983	20	71
1989	23	48
Middle class		
1983	25	67
1989	27	53
Lower class (structured)		
1983	38	53
1989	52	34
Lower class (marginal)		
1983	56	41
1989	72	20

SOURCE: Edgardo Catterberg, *Argentina Confronts Politics: Political Culture and Public Opinion in the Argentine Transition to Democracy* (Boulder: Lynne Rienner, 1991), p. 98.

ous elections were held in 1973) had in determining the electoral outcome: according to his data, about 34 percent of Alfonsín's total vote came from such new voters, 30 percent from traditional UCR supporters, 20 percent from conservative voters, 12 percent from Peronist defectors, and 4 percent from left-wingers.[60]

In sum, Mora y Araujo gives a lot of importance to conservative and new voter support and also differs from Catterberg on why parts of the lower class voted Radical. Discrepancies among their findings seem to arise from differences in sampling techniques and sociological definitions. Although the data do not warrant any definite conclusion on the specific impact of each social class in the 1983 electoral contest, there is little doubt that Alfonsín's victory took place for the reasons explained in previous chapters.[61] In 1989, the UCR candidate lost an average of 19 percent of the 1983 vote across social classes. Angeloz retained, among upper- and middle-class voters, a two-to-one advantage over Menem, who did not improve the Peronist's share of those social classes' vote by much. The key to Menem's victory seems to have been his ability to bring back to Peronism many of the structured lower class voters who had defected to Alfonsín. Therefore, the 1989 election appears to more closely fit the traditional class support of the UCR and the PJ. Both parties are multiclass, with Radical support being more dependent upon affluent social classes and Peronism upon the less affluent.

A breakdown by occupation shows some interesting turnarounds. (See table 4.16.) Many housewives, retirees, and the self-employed who had supported Alfonsín in 1983, switched to Peronism in 1989; unskilled

TABLE 4.16
Votes for President, by Party and Occupation, Federal District and
Metropolitan Buenos Aires, 1983 and 1989 (percentage)

Social Class	Peronist	Radical	Other
Housewives			
1983	37	58	5
1989	53	34	13
Retirees			
1983	42	52	6
1989	46	40	14
Students			
1983	19	61	20
1989	36	43	21
Unskilled workers			
1983	69	27	4
1989	73	17	10
Skilled Workers			
1983	45	47	8
1989	58	29	13
Clerks/salespeople			
1983	30	60	10
1989	40	42	18
Self-employed			
1983	43	50	7
1989	53	32	15
Managers			
1983	22	71	7
1989	24	58	18

SOURCE: Edgardo Catterberg, *Argentina Confronts Politics: Political Culture and Public Opinion in the Argentine Transition to Democracy* (Boulder: Lynne Rienner, 1991), p. 99.

workers remained heavily Peronist, while students and the managerial professions continued to back the Radicals, although to a lesser degree in 1989 than in 1983. The congressional vote of the 1985–1989 period shows a similar pattern. (See table 4.17.)

Other factors, too, are often cited as key indicators in shaping electoral choices. Party identification was one of the strongest variables in the 1985 and 1987 congressional elections (see table 4.18), although in Argentina, party identification is based more on family tradition and political socialization than on ideology. Ideological voting was absent among Radicals and had only a moderate impact among Peronists. (Justicialismo, or social justice, which many Peronists perceive as an ideology, is not considered so by most political theorists.) Therefore, for

TABLE 4.17
Votes for Congress, by Party and Socioeconomic Level, Federal
District and Metropolitan Buenos Aires 1985, 1987, and 1989 (percentage)

Social Class	Peronist	Radical
Upper class		
1985	12	47
1987	14	50
1989	28	41
Middle class		
1985	27	41
1987	23	55
1989	30	50
Lower-middle class		
1985	30	44
1987	48	37
1989	59	29
Working class		
1985	52	31
1987	67	23
1989	74	17

SOURCE: Edgardo Catterberg, *Argentina Confronts Politics: Political Culture and Public Opinion in the Argentine Transition to Democracy* (Boulder: Lynne Rienner, 1991), p. 98.

supporters of the two largest parties, ideology played little or no part in voting decisions. However, ideology appeared to be quite important for conservative (UCD) and leftist (Intransigent party) voters, although it underwent large fluctuations from year to year. A possible explanation for these fluctuations may be that the sample size was quite small and magnified results for the UCD and the PI, whose voters are substantially fewer than those of the PJ and the UCR. There was a strong tendency, particularly among small parties' voters, to favor the opposition in order to promote change and new alternatives.

For Radicals, voting as a means to support the president and his government was an important determinant in 1985 but not in 1987. The candidate's personality had only a moderate impact across parties. For the Peronists the impact was greater in 1985 than in 1987 because the renovators and the orthodox ran competing tickets in 1985. The relative importance of a candidate's personality can be ascribed to the nature of the election process in Argentina, where people are traditionally selected to run for Congress by party committees. Only in the 1980s did Peronist and minor parties begin to use primaries. Yet the seat does not belong to the candidate, but to the party, and constituency representation plays a small role. Taking all these things into account, it is quite logical for

TABLE 4.18
Reasons for Voting for a Candidate in Congressional Elections,
1985 and 1987 (percentage)

Reason	Radicals		Peronists			Intransigents		UCD	
	1985	1987	1985	1985	1987	1985	1987	1985	1987
Candidate personality	6	17	28	29	12	50	20	14	14
Party Identification	25	32	21	23	38				
Support for the president	36	16							
Agreement with governmental policies	27	12							
Social class identification/ ideology			20	11	11	9	36	45	29
Alternative of change			22	16	24	36	21	32	35
Vote against the government			8	8	8	5		9	4
Only or best option		15		12	6		16		14
Other answers/ Don't know	6	8	1	1	1		7		4

SOURCE: Edgardo Catterberg, *Los argentinos en frente a la política: cultura política y opinión pública en la tranisción argentina a la democracia* (Buenos Aires: Planeta, 1989), p. 129.
NOTE: In 1985 "orthodox" and "renewal" Peronist factions presented different lists.

voters to pay little attention to the candidate, as they well know that what counts at the congressional level is the party under whose banner the person runs. There was scant evidence of voting against the government; voting for a better option was a stronger indicator. In Catterberg's opinion, what mattered here was dissatisfaction over personal socioeconomic conditions, which induces people to look for a party that presents a good alternative to the present state of affairs. This contention is countered by other analysts, who argue that Angeloz's 1989 defeat was largely due to a protest vote against the outgoing Radical administration.[62]

Contrary to common wisdom, the congressional vote for the UCR was more related to agreement with government policies than to support for the president. In both 1985 and 1987, Radical voters supported the president more than they did the government (which can also be seen in presidential systems, like the United States and France). Unfortunately for the Radicals, only 55 percent of those supporting the president in 1985, and 59 percent in 1987, voted for the UCR candidates for Congress.[63] Conversely, 75 percent of those who positively evaluated the government in 1985, and 82 percent in 1987, voted Radical. In other words, presidential popularity did not translate into support for the UCR as much as the government's popularity did. As the latter plummeted, so did the Radicals' electoral fortunes. Figure 4.3 shows the trends of presidential and government evaluations and inflation. I

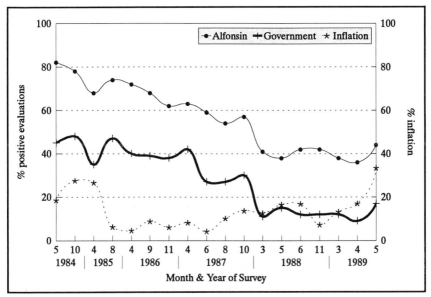

FIGURE 4.3   Catterberg's Measures of Inflation and Government Approval, 1984–1989

Source: Edgardo Catterberg, *Argentina Confronts Politics* (Boulder: Lynne Reinner, 1991) p. 91.

added to Catterberg's survey the inflation rate increase of the month be-fore the opinion poll was taken. I chose inflation because it is the eco-nomic factor whose monthly measurement is most reliable, and it is most commonly associated with the state of the economy by the public. There is a greater negative association between inflation and govern-ment evaluation than between inflation and presidential evaluation (a phenomenon common in the United States). In other words, as inflation increases, popular opinion of the government drops, and vice versa. This was especially obvious between May 1984 and March 1988. After that, the picture becomes blurred, and inflation ceases to be a good pre-dictor. In fact, the evaluation of Alfonsín improved with a surge in in-flation between April and May 1989. Mora y Araujo also investigated the relationship between inflation and the image of the government be-tween 1985 and 1990, thus extending the comparison into the Menem administration. (See figure 4.4.) According to him, government popu-larity during this period showed a −.60 correlation. What is puzzling about Mora y Araujo's surveys is that, contrary to Catterberg's data, there is not a clear relationship between inflation and government pop-ularity between June 1985 and March 1988. From that point on, how-ever, the relationship becomes very clear.

Other polls during the Menem administration concentrated on the popularity of the president and of the government's economic policies.

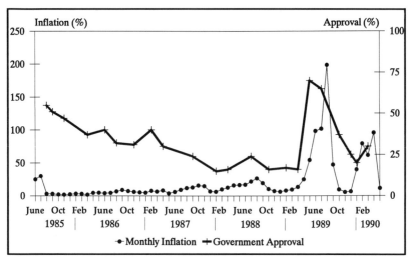

FIGURE 4.4 Mora y Araujo's Measures of Inflation and Government Approval, 1985–1990

Source: Manuel Mora y Araujo, *Ensayo y Error* (Buenos Aires: Planeta, 1991) p. 45.

Usually the results showed a great volatility of public response. The ups and downs of the president's popularity, according to many commentators, closely followed the economic situation but was also affected by the many scandals involving Menem's political associates and cabinet members. Thus, when the economy did well, presidential popularity was positively affected, but economics was by no means the only explanatory variable. What is interesting is that by April 1991 opinion polls taken in the Federal District show, for the first time, that the performance of the Minister of the Economy (Domingo Cavallo) was ranked higher than that of the president—in contrast to the trend under Alfonsín, during which the president always enjoyed greater popularity than his economy minister or his cabinet. Equally interesting was that 79 percent of the respondents (a few weeks after Cavallo launched his austerity plan) believed that the minister's stabilization effort could be jeopardized by the corruption and incompetence of administration leaders.[64] The Peronist victory in September 1991 was widely credited to Cavallo's successful economic policies. One exit poll showed that 63 percent of those voting Peronist in the congressional election for the Federal District cited economic stability as their primary motivation.[65] One possible explanation for Cavallo's high ratings, aside from his economic achievements, is that he was perceived as a man not involved in party politics (an academician by training, he had been elected in 1987 in his native Córdoba as an independent under the Peronist banner) nor was he involved in the corruption that was assumed to be part of party politics. Second, that he allowed Congress to enact economic reforms, instead of relying on executive orders as Menem had done, enhanced his reputation as a competent bureaucrat who abided by the rules of the democratic system.

Unfortunately, the small number of surveys and the uneven time intervals between them prevent us from reliably estimating through regression analysis the relationship between economic conditions and public evaluations of the president or government. A relationship seems to exist, but in all likelihood inflation per se does not explain the trend observed in figure 4.2. More control variables and data points are needed to make any generalization on the issue, since other noneconomic factors probably played a role. Judging from Mora y Araujo's data, the public's evaluation of the government does react to sudden swings of the inflation rate. On the other hand, when inflation fluctuates moderately, other issues may be more important.

What survey data in postauthoritarian Argentina seem to indicate, despite their many contradictions, is that democracy enjoyed the support of most sectors of society, particularly the young, the better educated, and the middle and upper classes. However, the ability of the politicians to solve the socioeconomic problems inherited from the military dictatorship disappointed many hopes. Thus, toward the end of the Alfonsín administration some authoritarian tendencies regained momentum. Many thought rather naively that democracy by itself would solve all problems, a perception encouraged by politicians of all beliefs, Alfonsín included. No wonder then that political parties fell into disrepute as they failed to deliver on their promises. Post-1983 Argentina is still a fragmented political culture, where democratic, populist, authoritarian, and elitist beliefs uneasily coexist. This in part explains such contradictory attitudes as strong support for participatory democracy but not for political tolerance and civil rights. However, by the end of the 1980s the deepening economic crisis seemed to have produced an important change, as many people, particularly the better educated and more affluent, supported structural reforms emphasizing free enterprise over state intervention and big government.

Equally important, Argentines have been able to overcome the socioeconomic cleavages that have plagued the country since 1983 and have resisted the temptation to use authoritarian means to solve their differences. This is indeed a positive step. Whether populist and authoritarian tendencies give away to democratic trends will largely depend on whether political parties and interest groups strengthen the role of democratic institutions by abiding by the rules. But "the low confidence expressed by Argentines in their national institutions, and particularly in their democratic institutions, is a source of deep anxiety to anyone concerned with the future of democracy in Argentina. [Argentines] appear . . . disenchanted."[66] If Argentines see their leaders as acting responsibly, they may come to believe in democracy and its institutions. Economic restructuring, despite its high social cost, may gain popularity. However, politicians and traditional elites will have to narrow their interests for the benefit of society as a whole, especially those sectors hardest hit by the current recession. After all, democracy means little to Argentines living in poverty and deprivation unless it is backed up by tangible benefits.

5

THE ARMED FORCES

THE POLITICIZATION of the armed forces is quite common in Latin America, but in Argentina it has become endemic. Since 1928 the country has experienced six major military coups and no democratically elected president has served a full term since 1952. Three factors—political, military, and external—account for this trend. Much has to do with the political system itself: "The failure of Argentina to develop an integrated society, the existence of unresolved regional, group, and ideological tensions, the inability to develop political organizations capable of cooperating with one another and of generating both the broad support and the effective leadership needed for stable government, these are the conditions that have encouraged military intervention."[1]

Samuel Huntington postulated that in the most advanced developing countries the failure of political institutions to keep pace with economic growth and mass mobilization triggers instability, and social groups then use force as a means of conflict resolution, leading to a "praetorian society" and "political decay."[2] In Argentina, military intervention has indeed coincided with political decay. At one point or another conservative, Radical, and Peronist leaders, when they saw the ballot box as ineffectual, knocked on the barracks doors for help in removing their enemies from power. The same can be said of entrepreneurial groups. Maintaining close links with high-ranking officers has long been important to politicians, union bosses, and entrepreneurs, not to mention Catholic bishops. In the Argentine political game, "the military was perceived as difficult—even unpredictable—partners in a complex and sometimes Byzantine game in which nothing could take place against or without them."[3]

Civilians soon found that the military (the term *military* refers here to the officer corps) was not content to be a mere instrument to further the interests of specific groups or parties. As time went on, officers began to express their corporate interests, which were often distinct from those of civil society. Far from being the party of the middle sectors or the oligarchy, the armed forces after 1930 represented a distributional coalition of their own or, as Argentines call it, the "military party." In turn, the military party could count on a civilian constituency among frustrated opposition politicians and business groups. This does not mean that the military acted as a monolith—quite the contrary. Like any other party, it had its own contending factions, which often lobbied parties and interest groups to prevail over their brothers in arms. However, by identifying its cause with that of the nation and pretending to be above parties, the military saw in the state the means to implement its political agenda on issues like "national sovereignty, security, the defense of territorial integrity, and international status."[4] "The army-state that has a margin of autonomy in relation to the upper-classes—specifically the dominant one—is marginally linked to all organized groups. This permits divergent sectoral interests to "aggregate" from an institutional perspective—that is, pursuit of professional objectives. Thus at times the army can impose on the system, in order better to defend it, the changes that appear to be necessary in the economic and social areas."[5]

It should also be noted that, while the armed forces and their vested interests were the primary benefactors of the coups that led to military-dominated governments, they were not the only ones, since such interventions led to substantial income transfers. During the 1943–1946 period, thanks to Perón's leadership within the military government, the working class secured a substantial increase in its share of the national income. However, this was more the exception than the rule. Most military administrations before and after Perón allowed some sectors of big capital (agricultural exporters, industrial entrepreneurs, financiers, and multinational corporations) to capture substantial windfalls of income transfers at the expense of salaried workers. Yet such transfers were often transitory and negatively affected other sectors, which learned that a military takeover did not automatically translate into material benefits.

Military involvement in politics is also a function of internal dynamics in the armed forces. During the late 1950s, increased military professionalism was said to be a key to keeping the military out of politics.[6] Nevertheless, in Argentina the greater professional skills acquired by the officer corps did not deter coups. Actually, in the name of professionalism the armed forces deposed presidents, withdrew from power, imposed vetoes, supported authoritarian regimes or civilian administrations elected under restricted political participation, and often fought each other. For instance, corporateness, one of the key components of professionalism, while strengthening collective identity has also downgraded democratic values. "For many officers, this sense of separate identity has been accompanied by an attitude of contempt for civilians, especially politicians. This was especially true of young officers commissioned in the 1930s and 1940s in an atmosphere charged with political and administrative corruption."[7]

This contradictory behavior can be partly explained by the fact that over time professionalism came to assume different meanings and was interpreted in many different ways within the officer corps, and disputes over the real meaning of professionalism have often created factionalism within their ranks. Moreover, ideological disputes have profoundly influenced the way some sectors of the officer corps interpret professionalism. At one point or another, liberal, fascist, corporatist, legalist, democratic, Catholic-nationlist, and technocratic ideologies were embraced by at least some sectors of the armed forces. On the other hand, factionalism has also been caused by disagreements over promotions and intraservice and interservice rivalries. This last factor accounts for the relative independence of the three armed services (within which the army plays the role of first among equals) and the relative weakness of the joint staff system, as proven by the poor performance during the war with the United Kingdom in 1982.

The last factor is foreign influence. The adoption of German military training as a model of army professionalism until World War II reinforced for some the army's antidemocratic nature.[8] After 1945, the United States replaced Germany as the most influential power in military thinking and should be credited for the Argentine military's emphasis on national security and anticommunist subversion. Not only were the armed forces permeated by foreign ideas, but they also tried to project Argentina as a regional power. At least until the first half of the twentieth century, nationalism was strong in an officer corps concerned about national greatness. Many high-ranking officers perceived Argentina as the natural leader of the Western Hemisphere—in direct competition, as odd as it may seem, with the United States. After Perón, such hegemonic projects were confined to South America, in an attempt to influence such small neighboring countries as Uruguay, Paraguay, and Bolivia. Consequently, disputes over regional supremacy ensued with the other major South American giant, Brazil. Border controversies with Chile almost ended in armed conflict. Conflict with the United Kingdom over the Falklands/Malvinas islands ended in a costly war. Such expansionistic designs translated into a military-controlled industrial conglomerate and arms and nuclear power production.

These three factors are closely related and have been treated separately only for reasons of simplicity. None of them alone explain the political behavior of the military, but they all have contributed at different points in time and in varying degrees to the military involvement in politics. Because of that, theorizing on the issue is problematic: In fact, "the political interventions of the armed forces and their increasing institutional autonomy produced . . . changes in the definition of their roles, their institutional objectives, and the doctrines that shaped their perception of threat. At the same time, as a product of this combination of factors, each branch took independent paths of institutional development, which led to duplication and overlapping in the fulfillment of tasks and the use of resources and created tremendous difficulties in order to prepare and execute coordinated actions."[9]

Nevertheless, as in many other Latin American countries, the greater the political polarization and the government's lack of legitimacy, the more likely the armed forces were to intervene. Broadly speaking, the military has played three roles in Argentine politics: (1) as an instrument of civilian power; (2) as a factor in governmental decisions; and (3) as an institution controlling the body politic.[10] Each role is further divided into subsets to explain variations on the theme. The first role was dominant in 1862–1930, 1932–1943, 1946–1955, 1963–1966, 1973–1976, and 1983–1992. During these periods the upper echelons of the military supported the regime, while remaining politically subordinated to it (even if minority groups unsuccessfully tried to rebel at different times). Within this pattern, in 1919–1930, 1932–1943, 1946–1955, 1963–1966, 1973–1976, 1983–1993 the military tried to safeguard its interests by acting as a pressure group. The second role, that of affecting government decisions, was dominant during the Frondizi administration in 1958–1962, when the military had de facto veto power. The third role, that of controlling politics, was played in 1930–1932, 1943–1946, 1955–1958, 1966–1970, 1970–1973, and 1976–1983. Within it, there are two subsets, the first made up of those regimes in which the military ruled as an institution and when most public offices were held by military officers as in 1962–1963, 1970–1973, and 1976–1983. The second subset comprises those regimes in which the armed forces were the most important supporting group of an authoritarian administration led by a former military man, as in 1930–1932, 1955–1958, and 1966–1970.[11]

The Early Development of the Armed Forces (1810–1930)

The Argentine military traces its origins to General San Martín's army, which liberated the southern cone from Spanish domination. However, the chaos that ensued after independence from Spain prevented the formation of a unified, professional military institution. Until 1862, regional caudillos controlled their own armies, whose core was composed of gaucho cavalry troops. As in other Latin American nations at the time, these armies were guided by amateur and self-proclaimed officers, tended to be relatively small, and were poorly equipped, trained, and disciplined. In the wake of the civil war, The Federal Government made a concerted effort to create a modern national army. A strong and disciplined military was considered a prerequisite for the creation of a modern nation-state. It was meant to weld the country together by preventing regional caudillos from rising up and by fostering the colonization of the pampas and Patagonia. To this end President Domingo Sarmiento created the Colegio Militar in 1869 and the Escuela Naval in 1872, which were charged, respectively, with training the officer corps of the army and navy. The armed forces were soon tested in the long and bloody war against Paraguay of 1865–1869. Later, under the leadership of General Julio Roca, the army embarked on the so-called Campaign of the Desert (1879–1883), which exterminated the last pampas Indians in order to open up new territories for agriculture. These two military ventures were quite successful and greatly enhanced the prestige of the armed forces.

In 1880, Roca became president and under him the military turned into a loyal defender of oligarchic rule. In fact, although some junior officers joined the Radicals in the uprisings of 1890, 1893, and 1905, the top echelons of the military establishment remained firmly behind PAN administrations until 1916. During his second term (1894–1904), Roca instructed General Pablo Richieri to reorganize the military to improve its professionalism. A German military mission was invited to help Richieri in his task. This event marked the beginning of German influence over the Argentine army, which lasted until World War II. The Superior War College (Escuela Superior de Guerra) for the training of general staff officers was created in 1900 and was patterned after its German equivalent. [12] A year later, the government established compulsory military service. The navy, on the other hand, fell at first under the influence of the British. At the turn of the century, a Royal Navy training mission was invited, and several ships were purchased from the United Kingdom. However, by the time World War I broke out, the United States had begun to replace Britain both as an arms supplier and as a training adviser. The move toward greater professionalization continued early in the twentieth century. To thwart presidential patronage over career patterns, new reforms were enforced in 1910. A qualification commission composed of high-ranking officers was put in charge of promotion based on merit.

The advent of the Radical administrations was marred by increasing civil-military feuds. The army appreciated the fact that Yrigoyen, despite heavy pressure from the United Kingdom, kept Argentina neutral in World War I and refused to break relations with Germany. However, on the domestic front many issues turned the military against the president, one of the most salient being Yrigoyen's attempt to politicize the armed forces. One instance of such an attempt was the president's effort to reward officers loyal to him. In 1923, Congress approved an executive bill that would have promoted those officers who had joined the Radical revolts and, as a consequence, had seen their career prospects torpedoed. The initiative was regarded as a direct attack on military autonomy and the professional standards set in 1910. A second instance came in the form of Yrigoyen's extensive use of the army to enforce his removal of recalcitrant Conservative governors and provincial legislatures. Many officers resented being downgraded to police duties and felt the military was being used to benefit Radical partisan interests.

By the early 1920s, whatever unity of purpose had held the officer corps together had vanished.[13] In 1921, several groups of disgruntled officers organized the Logia General San Martín, a secret organization whose goal was to reassert the autonomy of the military by ending politicization within its ranks. Nevertheless, as time went by, Logia members themselves became heavily involved in politics. One of their goals was the isolation of those officers who collaborated with Yrigoyen's patronage politics; another goal was to pressure the government to crack down on left-wing political parties and trade unions. In 1919, army and navy officers had been heavily involved in the Semana Trágica. Later the discovery that soldiers and noncommissioned officers (NCOs) had attempted to organize communist-style "soviets" convinced the military that the seeds of a Bolshevik revolution existed and had to be eradicated. Under President Alvear, many of the Logia's misgivings seemed to fade away, not only because the new administration accepted some of its demands for greater funding but also because some of its members came to occupy key institutional positions. The most important of these was given to General Augustín Justo, who was appointed to head the War Ministry.[14] In 1926, the Logia dissolved, but factionalism persisted and divided ex-logistas now in positions of strength, and Yrigoyenista officers whose fortunes had turned sour. The return of Yrigoyen to the presidency in 1928 again fueled old rivalries and added new strains. As the president resumed old patronage tricks, like meddling in promotions to strengthen his backers in the military, the loyalty of the officer corps eroded to the point of no return.

The Armed Forces Enter Politics (1930–1943)

Taking advantage of an unprecedented political opposition to Yrigoyen's ineffective and often arbitrary policies, the armed forces deposed the president. The event did not mark the politicization of the military, which had started much earlier; however, it created an important precedent as it broke the tradition of at least keeping a façade of political neutrality and noninterference in civilian affairs. From then on, "professional values tended to be subordinated to political issues, and what had once been regarded as beyond [the officers'] competence became matters of daily discussion."[15] This change of attitude constituted a watershed in Argentine politics. The growing belief in the armed forces that politicians were prone to corruption, partisanship, and mismanagement led them to conclude that only the military with its patriotic principles embodied the true national interest. Thus, democracy came to be perceived in many barracks as ineffective. Pushed to its extreme consequences, this line of reasoning almost by exclusion left the armed forces with an obligation to act whenever civilian regimes jeopardized the national interest; and of course the definition of what constituted the national interest was now an institutional prerogative of the military.

The coup was executed by only a small faction of the military. It was poorly organized and could count on the initial backing of only a few civilian groups. Among the participants of the coup there was a thirty-five-year-old captain, Juan Domingo Perón, who described the event as "an operetta uprising more fitting to some mini-republics of Central America."[16] Despite its poor organization and the fact that some opposition parties were not looking for a military solution, the coup succeeded. This gives an indication of the apathy and disillusionment generated by the Radicals' inability to strengthen democratic institutions. Yrigoyen fell not because the coup coalition was unstoppable but because nobody seemed to back his ineffective and corrupt administration.

The Revolution, as the military quickly dubbed the coup to give it some legitimacy, was not truly revolutionary. Its leader, former General José Uriburu, who shortly afterward became provisional president and who remained president for the next seventeen months, came from a well-known oligarchic family from Tucumán. An outspoken nationalist, Germanophile and charismatic leader, Uriburu in his first address to the nation envisioned the creation of an authoritarian state with the armed forces as a guardian of the constitution, thus placing them above the law. In the weeks following the Revolution, most opposition parties, interest groups, and even some unions gave their support to Uriburu. The Supreme Court reluctantly blessed the constitutionality of the new government after Uriburu threatened to dismiss it. Originally, the new president planned to amend the constitution. His goal was to put into effect the checks and balances among the judiciary, the legislature, and the presidency to avoid the recurrent abuses perpetrated by Yrigoyen. However, most important, vague proposals were given out for the creation of a functional system of representation wherein societal groups rather than parties would sit in Congress.[17] Such a scheme was reminiscent of the corporatist ideas previously expressed by Italian fascists and Spanish Catholic nationalists.

To what extent Uriburu wanted to carry out a European-style corporatist experiment is not clear, for the simple reason that, once his tentative plans for constitutional reform were revealed, support began to evaporate.[18] Resistance to Uriburu's reforms came not only from former conservative backers but also from the armed forces. Many officers voiced their concern that the Revolution, by involving the military in political squabbles, was tearing the institution apart and undermining its reputation. General Severo Toranzo attacked Uriburu: "Until 6 September 1930 we had an army that was idolized by the Argentines. Not one of the worst rulers had dared to use it as an instrument of oppression against the people. The army was quietly devoted to preparing itself for the defense of the sovereignty of the nation. You and your followers violated its discipline, corrupting it with bounties and sinecures and using it for the achievement of unethical objectives. Today the Argentine army is detested by the real people."[19]

While Toranzo's accusations can be regarded as partisan due to his Yrigoyenist past, this could not be said of Captain Perón, who later expressed his disappointment: "We all thought that the worst thing we could do was to enthrone a military dictatorship which would be opposed by the nation as a whole."[20] In the meantime, several unsuccessful pro-Yrigoyen military-civilian uprisings rose around the country, one led by General Toranzo himself. With the momentum shifting away from Uriburu, General Justo, who had garnered considerable support for his own plan among the military and conservative parties, forced Uriburu to call for new elections in 1932.[21] After Uriburu banned the Radical electoral participation prior to the elections, it was relatively easy for Justo to win the presidency through the endorsement of the three parties that would be the pillars of the Concordancia until 1943. Upon taking office, Justo, who had gained a reputation as an officer of high moral and professional standards, could count on the loyalty of the bulk of the military. With regard to the armed forces, his primary objective was to depoliticize it by emphasizing strictly professional and technical matters. This was accompanied by a rearmament campaign and new budgetary allocations to upgrade equipment, facilities, and salaries. Pro-Uriburu and Yrigoyenist officers were isolated and put in positions where they could do no harm, although the latter group attempted some coups. The armed forces' loyal support for the Concordancia continued under Justo's successor, President Roberto Ortiz.

Although suppressed, the politicization of the armed forces was not eradicated and began to manifest in the second half of the 1930s under nationalist themes. A growing number of officers—perhaps influenced by military expansion in Franco's Spain, Fascist Italy, and Nazi Germany—argued that Argentina had to fulfill its manifest destiny as a hemispheric power and, accordingly, the armed forces had to have a say in foreign policy issues. For these officers, the United States and Brazil, in different ways, posed a threat to Argentine ambitions for hemispheric domination. Probably responding to such concerns, in the late 1930s

Argentina refused President Franklin Roosevelt's request to join in a U.S.-led hemispheric security pact. The armed forces had long expressed their misgivings over the country's dependency on imports of strategic raw materials and industrial equipment; these misgivings were furthered in the 1930s when Argentina's vulnerability to fluctuations in the world economy became all too clear. For the military, such vulnerability posed a threat to Argentina's national security defined in geopolitical terms.

The remedy advocated was development of a heavy industry capable of making the country self-sufficient in strategic goods, ranging from steel to aircrafts. In 1922, General Enrique Mosconi had organized the first domestic petroleum company Yacimientos Petroliferos Fiscales, and in 1927 the army set up an airplane factory, Fábrica Militar de Aviones. To further explore the problems involved with industrial development, President Uriburu entrusted Lieutenant Colonel Manuel Savio with the creation of the Superior Technical School. The military then expanded its interests to include the manufacture of not only small arms, ammunition, and explosives but also pig iron, chemicals, steel, and electrical equipment. In 1941, these activities were brought together under the centralized control of a military-run conglomerate, the General Directorate of Military Manufactures (Dirección General de Fabricaciones Militares, or DGFM) under Savio's leadership. With the creation of the DGFM, the development of certain industrial sectors came under the exclusive jurisdiction of the armed forces, thus discouraging private investors from entering key economic activities. In the name of economic independence, military managers sheltered their companies from competition by establishing monopolies and import restrictions, thus behaving like a typical distributional coalition. Moreover, they administered their companies using criteria that disregarded cost-efficiency principles.[22]

The outbreak of World War II added another issue to old factional divisions as officers wondered whether Argentina should join the Allies or the Axis. In 1943, pro-Axis nationalist officers organized themselves into a secret lodge, the Grupo de Oficiales Unidos (GOU), in which Perón, now a colonel, came to play a dominant role. As with the Logia San Martín, the creation of the GOU coincided with a time of profound domestic political crisis. Both pro-Axis and pro-Allies officers were dissatisfied with the administration of President Ramón Castillo. The president resorted more and more to authoritarian measures, such as the right to intervene and to call a state of siege to evade congressional and provincial opposition; these were to be enforced by the military. As the administration became increasingly unpopular, so did the officers' uneasiness in carrying out its orders. As a new presidential election drew to a close, Castillo tried to enlist the support of the armed forces for his hand-picked candidate, Robustiano Patrón Costas, a wealthy sugarcane plantation owner from Tucumán. Many officers felt they were being used by the president for partisan purposes and were concerned over the prospect of a new round of fraudulent elections. Moreover, Patrón Costas's open support for the Allies clashed with the pro-Axis military factions.[23] By mid-1943 the majority of the officer corps, seeing no alternative to an institutional crisis triggered by a corrupt and illegitimate regime, had resolved that Castillo had to be deposed.

From Military Populism to Peronism (1943–1955)

On June 4, 1943, the president was ousted, and a few days later an all-military cabinet was created. Having failed the test of even restricted democracy, the military disbanded Congress and political parties. Thus for the first time the armed forces as an institution were ruling the country, occupying most of the key posts in government, public administration, and state companies. Nevertheless, there was a complete lack of agreement on what to do next. "The 1943 coup . . . ushered in a military oligarchy which lasted some one-and-a-half years. And here again is seen the push-pull towards and away from open supplantment of the civilian regime. On this occasion, unlike 1930, the army plotters—the G.O.U.—had no intention whatever of holding new elections. They unquestionably envisaged some sort of military oligarchy, though their precise plans are still obscure, and indeed it is very likely that they were both disunited and vague on anything but short-term objectives."[24]

By February 1944, GOU officers emerged from the internal squabbles as victors, forcing the president, General Pedro Ramírez, to step down in favor of the more sympathetic General Edelmiro Farrell, patron and friend of Colonel Perón. The GOU's nationalism served to emphasize the pro-Axis and authoritarian nature of the military regime of General Farrell. Plans for future elections were canceled, and the country embarked in a full-scale mobilization as if an armed conflict with Brazil were imminent. Many political parties that had welcomed the coup, including the Radicals, were now demanding the end of the state of siege and a return to democracy. They were joined by university students, journalists, business groups, and some trade unions. In response, the regime stepped up its repression, particularly targeting communist trade unions. The universities were also affected: many professors were fired, and the curricula were changed. At the same time, some populist measures were enacted to gain the support of the population: rural rents were cut by 20 percent, some price controls were imposed, apartment rents in Buenos Aires were frozen, tramway fares were reduced, and a number of foreign companies were taken over in the name of economic nationalism.[25]

While many GOU officers were eager to crack down on organized labor, Perón was not. Realizing the growing unpopularity of the regime, Perón determined to carry out his political plans by using his institutional powers. After traditional parties and business groups turned down his plan for a neoconservative alliance, Perón by mid-1944 drafted the support of labor leaders with whom he had established contacts in 1943. The details of Perón's rise to power are described in greater detail elsewhere (chapters 2 and 6), so there is no need here to reiterate them. What is important to note, as far as the armed forces were concerned, is that Perón dragged them into his populist agenda with little or no consultation. From mid-1944 on, the colonel and his initiatives foreshadowed the military regime, creating great concern among the officer corps—particularly the generals, who felt completely outmaneuvered. Moreover, the anti-Peronist sectors of the military were, as in the past, unnerved by what they perceived as Perón's manipulation of the institution for personal ends. Further, many officers found Perón's relationship with María Eva Duarte inappropriate for an army man due to her alleged turbulent past.

Strong opposition to Perón came also from the navy, which unlike the army was pro-Allies and entertained close ties with the British and U.S. navies. At the time, according to some analysts, the navy differed appreciably from the army in social background, a factor regarded as important in explaining Perón's different political outlook. Starting at the turn of the century, the army's officer corps began to be dominated by individuals from the middle class. Many immigrant families saw in the military a means of social mobility. By the 1940s, many junior officers had Italian, Spanish, German, and Irish last names; they did not belong to the traditional oligarchic families that had dominated the army since 1880. On the contrary, navy officers continued to come to a large extent "from the rural oligarchy and the wealthy urban families, and hence were hostile to any regime bent on upsetting the nation's basic institution. So unsympathetic was the navy to the GOU and its program, even in the very beginning, that the government after the 1943 revolution could find no high-ranking naval officer willing to accept the post of navy minister until March 1944. As early as February of 1944 the navy launched a conspiracy to oust the Farrell-Perón regime. In August and September of 1945, high-ranking navy men were demanding and petitioning Perón not to be allowed to assume the presidency and that the 'sovereignty of the people' be restored."[26] While there is no conclusive evidence that social background explained the navy's behavior, there is little doubt that most of its officers were aloof to Peronism. In the 1950s, they led the anti-Peronist cause. After the failure of the palace coup in October 1945, the armed forces resigned themselves to allowing free elections, and they returned to their barracks, reserving the right to intervene when circumstances required.

Although some in the army shared the navy's suspicion about Perón's intentions, the army accepted his election in 1946 and pledged its loyalty. Perón, promoted to the rank of general before Farrell left office, made continued efforts to retain military support. He purchased large quantities of weapons, expanded the military-industrial sector, and increased the salaries of officers to levels comparable with those of the United States.[27] Besides, a host of personal favors, sinecures, and perks were granted to officers sympathetic to the president.[28] In spite of rumors of military conspiracies, the president retained his grip on the armed forces until the early 1950s.

Several factors contributed to the first real effort by the military to depose Perón. While the officer corps tolerated many of Perón's abuses, like impeaching the Supreme Court, restricting freedom of the press, and intimidating the political opposition, many officers could not tolerate Perón's intention to run for a second term (allowed by the constitution approved in 1949) or his plan to have Evita as his running mate. The deteriorating economic situation and difficult diplomatic relations with the United States gave the impression that the administration was now more vulnerable than at any point in the past. A coup was launched in September 1951 by some army units, with the tactical support of air force and navy pilots, but its poor organization and the divisions among the plotters doomed it to failure. As a result, Perón purged the three armed services from the top down.

While such measures bought Perón some time, they also fueled even greater animosity in the officer corps. With the administration's popularity waning, the president stepped up his efforts to indoctrinate the military with justicialismo rhetoric and to turn it into another branch of Peronism. Like Yrigoyen, Perón resorted more and more to interfering in the promotion of officers; many were passed up for promotion to the advantage of Peronist loyalists. However, these moves rebounded against Perón, since they offended the professionalism of the armed forces and their institutional autonomy.[29] More threatening to the military's interests was Perón's talk about creating a workers militia, which (even though it never materialized) further undermined the president's support even among Peronist officers. Finally, Perón's reversal of several nationalist policies, his attack on the Catholic church, and his alleged relationships with high school girls alienated even military men who usually did not meddle in political matters. All these factors combined may explain why a coup attempt in 1955, although being supported by the bulk of navy and air force but only a minority of the army, in the end succeeded. Army loyalists outnumbered the rebels but probably found it difficult to defend a leader who had made a mockery of their ideals.

The Proscription of Peronism and the "Impossible Game" (1955–1966)

As we have seen, the 1930, 1943, and 1955 coups claimed to defend military professionalism and the polity from a corrupt civilian government. At every turn, however, the politicization of the armed forces reached a new high and so did the polarization of civil society on the basic issues of political participation and economic policy. In 1932, political polarization had led the military to endorse the electoral proscription of the Yrigoyen faction of the UCR. At the time of his ouster Perón, like Yrigoyen, still enjoyed substantial, although declining, popular support. The resilience of the Peronist legacy convinced the most hard-line sectors of the officer corps that Peronism had to be repressed. Between 1955 and 1966, Argentine society was split between Peronists and anti-Peronists. To thwart Perón's return, the military and important political and economic sectors of civil society excluded Peronism from the electoral arena.

However, there was a fundamental difference from the 1930s. Whereas during the Concordancia conservative politicians administered the proscription with the blessing of the armed forces, after 1955 the military was the ultimate arbiter on how the political game was to be played. The proscription of Peronism led to what has been called the "impossible game."[30] With Peronism capable of winning a plurality (35–40 percent) of the vote in an honest contest, its exclusion left the Radicals and a large number of weak conservative parties competing for office. The outcome was the creation of minority, unstable governments lacking the legitimacy to rule. To solve the legitimacy question, party politicians had two options. One was to make concessions to Peronist voters. The second was to put together a coalition of anti-Peronist forces that could attract a stable majority. Unfortunately, neither of these options was viable. Opting for the first was tantamount to inviting the military to nullify the election or to stage a coup. The second alternative was doomed to failure by the deep divisions in the anti-Peronist camp. The result was prolonged political instability, which grew worse over time. For their part, Perón and his followers by the mid-1960s saw in the political stalemate the opportunity to maximize their interests. By refusing to compromise, they hoped to so discredit the weak civilian governments that the military would see Perón's return as the only way out.

The initial attitude of the 1955 coup leader, former General Eduardo Lonardi, had been moderate; not wanting to alienate the Peronist constituency, he proclaimed there were to be neither victors nor van-quished. Also, most of Perón's social reforms were to be kept. However, for many military hard-liners Lonardi was too soft, and in a few weeks he was replaced by General Pedro Aramburu, a staunch anti-Peronist whose charismatic leadership could unite the armed forces. Wholesale purges, initiated under Lonardi were intensified to rid the military of Peronist sympathizers and affecting high-ranking officers as well as NCOs. The purges were extended to the civilian bureaucracy, unions, and state enterprises. In 1956, some military men loyal to Perón staged a countercoup. Aramburu crushed this revolt, but in an unusually harsh manner. Contrary to the established tradition that let losers save face through early retirement or dismissals, Aramburu ordered the ex-ecution of twenty-seven rebel officers, which widened the split between Peronists and anti-Peronists. If Peronist allegiance was, until 1955, likely to help an officer's career, after the coup anti-Peronist credentials be-came a prerequisite, thus fueling factionalism and weakening profes-sional standards.

> The armed forces became the reflection of the praetorian competition of the non-Peronist sectors of Argentine society. This situation, together with the frequent coup threats in support of sectoral demands, resulted in the severe factionalization of the armed forces. This factionalization, in turn, resulted in several internal *putsches*, the destruction of vertical patterns of authority, and the abrupt end of careers for numerous officers.[31]

Three major factions evolved among the officers in the politicization process that followed the coup. The *continuistas* believed that elections should be held but that they should lead to a government consistent with the anti-Peronist principles that had inspired the Liberating Rev-olution. The "fair play" group were those who would hand over power only to non-Peronist politicians. Last were the *quedantistas,* who favored a simple military dictatorship until Peronism was eradicated. By 1957, the fair play group, headed by Aramburu and the commanders of the armed forces, had prevailed, and elections were scheduled a year later. Contrary to this group's wishes, the candidate who had campaigned to reinstate the Peronists in the political arena, Arturo Frondizi, won the 1958 election.

Frondizi chose the first option postulated by the impossible game, but in so doing he alienated the armed forces, which were suspicious of his administration throughout his term in office. When, after a few months, Frondizi's overture to Peronism collapsed, he was forced to call upon the armed forces to enforce a state of siege designed to end a wave of strikes. His room for maneuvering was narrowed: from mid-1959 un-til Frondizi's removal from power in March 1962, the armed forces held a veto power over his decisions. A series of mini-crises followed, often involving aborted coup attempts by military hard-liners.[32] Frondizi then attempted to pit rival factions of the military against each other, making deals with rebellious officers and disciplining those who had tried to uphold the law. As a result, even officers committed to the rule of law became alienated; they perceived the president's attitude as suicidal and criminal.[33] Even more damaging to Frondizi was his ambiguity regarding Peronism, which angered anti-Peronist parties and, once the final showdown came, left him with no real base of support outside his UCRI.

> The ouster of Frondizi in 1962 was the culmination of a series of crises that reflected on the one hand internal rivalries and jealousies within the officer corps, and on the other, the deep distrust that the president's policies inspired among militant antiperonists in and out the uniform. Even though the ouster was carried out by the commanders-in-chief of the three military services, support for this decision was far from universal in the Army or Air Force. Indeed, had Frondizi been willing to risk a military confrontation, he would have found powerful Army units prepared to fight in defense of the constitutional order. His ouster was the work of a military faction temporarily in control of the Army, allied to an adamant and unified officer corps, and encouraged by powerful but limited sectors of the civilian community . . . the military's political intervention in March 1962 was not professionally responsible. It was an act of emotionalism, of anger and revenge; and it reflected the breakdown of professionalization, rather than its influence.[34]

In the aftermath of Frondizi's ouster, the deep split within the military came out in the open. Two military groups battled for supremacy, holding hostage the caretaker Guido administration which was hurriedly put together to fill the power vacuum following the coup. The *colorados*, or *golpistas*, were military hard-liners who had been instrumental in deposing Frondizi. They could be traced back to the continuistas of the mid-1950s. Colorado officers supported the reestablishment of the rule of law and democracy but believed that it could not be accomplished until Peronism was eradicated. Indeed the colorados insisted that Peronism was just a disguised form of communism and that only a prolonged military dictatorship could eliminate it and prepare the ground for "true democracy." The core support of the colorados came from the navy and important sectors of the infantry and army engineers. The colorados tended to be porteños, and economically speaking, they endorsed the conservative economic liberalism of pre-1930 Argentina.[35]

The *azules*, or legalists, on the other hand, had for the most part opposed the 1962 coup. They opposed Peronism but rejected the idea of a military dictatorship, contending that the politicization of the armed forces was tearing apart the military. Discipline and profesisonalism had seriously deteriorated, and direct military rule was likely to make things worse. The azules believed that the armed forces should end partisanship and factionalism—and the best way to do it was to return to the barracks and dedicate themselves to strictly professional matters, leaving political matters to civilians. The azules were endorsed by many political parties scared at the prospect of rule by the unpredictable colorados. The azules were mainly in the mechanized cavalry units, and tended to be from the provinces and to espouse economic nationalism and ISI geared to heavy industry and capital goods. Quite a few were staunch Catholics and sympathizers of the dictator of Spain, General Francisco Franco.[36] After two armed confrontations in September 1962 and April 1963, the azules finally prevailed and new elections were called. However, the azules, in violation of their pledge, excluded the Peronists in order to placate the colorados and promote internal reconciliation.

Between 1963 and 1966, under the leadership of General Juan Carlos Onganía, the armed forces experienced crucial changes. Internal discipline and the vertical structure of authority were reimposed. Moreover, military training was revamped to emphasize new strategies and techniques. Although the presidential election of 1963 was won by Illia, who had been close to the colorados in 1962, Onganía and the legalists renewed their commitment to an apolitical role for the military.[37] The consensus among the armed forces was that they stayed out of civilian affairs unless the political situation got out of control, in which case the officer corps reserved the right to intervene as guarantor of the constitution. Another important change was the increasing influence of the United States over the Argentine military, which had grown steadily over Perón's downfall. This did not stop with the purchase of equipment, but included visits by U.S. military missions to Argentina and the training of Argentine officers in the United States or at the School of the Americas or the Inter-American Air Force Academy in Panama. Like the military in other Latin American countries, the Argentine officer corps embraced the U.S. interpretation of the National Security Doctrine (DSN).[38]

Military concerns with national security issues were not at all new. We have seen that they were decisive in the creation of Argentine heavy industry under the control of the DGFM. Developed in Germany in the first quarter of the twentieth century by geopolitical thinkers, DNS theories were revised and updated in the 1950s by French and U.S. analysts. In point of fact, Argentine officers' views of the DSN were deeply influenced first by French military missions in the late 1950s and, later, by the U.S.-sponsored training programs in the early 1960s. The U.S. version of the doctrine emphasized that the military had to thwart both external aggression and internal subversion sponsored by Castro and the Soviet bloc. Because communist subversion was based on interlocking military, ideological, and economic strategies, the military response had to be equally diversified and encompassing.

Military preparedness focused not only on counterinsurgency but on socioeconomic issues, since communist infiltration was more likely to occur in situations of socioeconomic underdevelopment. As the head of the National Security Council (CONASE), General Guillermo Osiris Villegas, said, there could be no "security without development, nor development without security."[39] To the military, security and development were two faces of the same coin and were both part of its institutional task. "According to the national security conception, poor government management and the strangulation of development interacted to facilitate 'subversion.' Therefore, the underlying logic of the national security conception indicated that it was part of the 'specific duty' of the armed forces to eliminate these two 'authentic causes' of 'subversion.' "[40]

The DSN provoked profound changes in the armed forces because it meant a new, more sophisticated, and encompassing way to perceive military professionalism. The internal dynamics set in motion by this new professionalism provided the ideological grounds to justify military intervention and the organizational skills to carry it out.[41] The new professionalism explained not only the evolution of military intervention in Latin America in the 1960s but also the timing of the coups. The armed forces began to ascribe to themselves political prerogatives far greater than in the past. They also believed that their organizational capacity and their socioeconomic training better qualified them than civilians to solve the development problem. As the armed forces' corporate interests expanded so did their stake in the political game. However, the DNS, while widely accepted, was not a monolithic doctrine. Many of its tenets allowed different interpretations, and its implementation was heavily contingent upon the circumstances of the moment.[42] The difference between the Onganía regime and the Proceso can be partly interpreted in this vein. Whereas the first attempted, although clumsily, to reshape the political system and promote economic development, the second emphasized counterinsurgency and the dismantling of inefficient sectors of the economy. (Nonetheless, after the debacle of the last military regime, the DSN lost most of its appeal and credibility in the armed forces; and little has been heard of it since.)[43]

The DSN provided yet another justification for the 1966 coup. For a time legalist officers had tried to give the weak Illia administration a chance; many were sympathetic to Vandor's effort to create Peronism without Perón. However, when Vandor's candidate lost to Perón's in the local Mendoza election, many legalist officers lost faith in Vandor's project. The event played into the hands of military hard-liners, who argued that, with the 1967 presidential election nearing and with no prospect of beating Perón in an honest electoral contest, the only option to save the country from "populist authoritarianism" was to dislodge Illia beforehand. A second factor leading to the coup was President Illia's interference in military affairs. One by one he forced into retirement the azul-dominated upper echelon of the three armed services, the latest casualty being Onganía, who was cashiered in 1965. During the same year, the president reinstated sixty-four colorado officers who had been retired after losing the battle with the azules in 1963. As with Frondizi, Illia's manipulation of military affairs and his fueling of military factionalism was regarded by the legalists as a slap in the face. The inability of the government to tackle the economic crisis and its unwillingness to get tough with unions increased the lobbying by opposition parties, economic interest groups, and even many unions to convince the armed forces to step in.

From the Argentine Revolution to the Peronist Return (1966–1976)

In June 1966, the commanders in chief of the armed forces, to the surprise of no one, deposed President Illia and issued the following statement: "Argentina has completed a historic cycle. In the future, no one will be able to excuse his aberrancy by appealing to the legacy of some anonymous past which [once] existed. Our political and institutional resources have been exhausted. The time has come to live to our fullest capacity and to create a new nation for ourselves and for our prosperity. The future will be the inexorable result of the common efforts of all of today's Argentines. The Armed forces have been the instrument of the Argentine Revolution and because of that our celebration is filled with a sense of history and responsibility."[44]

Like its predecessors of 1930, 1943, and 1955, the military-sponsored Argentine Revolution of 1966 was not truly revolutionary. Once again Congress was closed, parties disbanded, universities purged, governors removed, the Supreme Court suppressed, and civil liberties suspended. What was different from the past was the insulation of the decision-making process ensuing from the belief that even limited democracy was not viable in Argentina. From then on, authoritarian rule was imposed, although there was no agreement on how. To keep its internal cohesion and avoid the negative effects of politicization on the military, the commanders in chief asked Onganía to come out of retirement and solve the puzzle for them.

Onganía did not establish a military regime as has often been suggested, but an authoritarian one with the backing of the armed forces.

In fact, Onganía made clear to the military commanders that if he had to be president he was going to be the sole person in charge and the armed forces would stay out of politics.[45] Onganía thought that, had the military cogoverned, the old factional splits would multiply—with predictable consequences. He also probably believed that only through the centralization of the decision-making process could his brand of authoritarianism succeed. Perhaps caught unprepared, military leaders initially accepted the deal. The early days of the Onganía regime were uncertain, as Catholic nationalists attempted, with no success, to promote corporatist institutional arrangements as a viable alternative to the "evils" of "corrupt and decadent" democratic institutions. It was only after Adalbert Krieger Vasena was appointed to head the Ministry of the Economy that the regime began to show some direction, although contradictions persisted within the cabinet, dividing nationalist-oriented ministers from Krieger Vasena and the supporters of economic liberalism.

A few theses were advanced to explain the 1966 coup as well as similar events in the rest of Latin America. José Nun, for instance, contended that the inability of the middle class to replace the oligarchy as the dominant social sector and its unwillingness to forge an alliance with the working class led it to lobby the military, whose ranks were now overwhelming middle class in background, to defend its interests. Thus, from being the guardian of oligarchic rule in the eighteenth century, the armed forces had become the right arm of the middle sectors. His thesis is that "in Latin America . . . it is the armed forces that assume the responsibility of protecting the middle class. It was with their support that the middle class achieved, at the beginning of this century, political recognition from the oligarchy, it was with their protection that it later consolidated itself in power, and now it is with their intervention that it seeks to ward off the threat posed by the popular sectors that it is incapable of leading."[46]

Similarities between Onganía's government and the Brazilian military dictatorship that began in 1964 led Guillermo O'Donnell to an intriguing, more sophisticated explanation of a new type of military intervention (partially based on Huntington's thesis, discussed at the beginning of this chapter). According to O'Donnell's thesis, the military did not toss out civilian presidents to benefit the middle class but to create permanent, authoritarian, development-minded regimes. The exhaustion of the easy phase of the industrialization process brought with it a phase of industrial deepening, marked by a shift from consumer goods to capital goods production, resulting in political stalemate. The deepening process called for an economic restructuring based upon efficiency and increased productivity, that penalized the middle and working classes, who had previously benefited from populist policies. The refusal of these sectors to renounce their demands for political power and consumer goods caused polarization in the political arena. This, for O'Donnell, led the "propertied classes," increasingly impatient with the "incompetent" policies of the populist administrations, to join the military and exclude the popular sector. This created a new ruling coalition of upper bourgeoisie, development-minded officers, and technocrats devoted to a "technical" and "rational" approach to problem solving (in contrast to the "political" style adopted by populist governments) and to economic stability. Although the validity of Nun and O'Donnell's theses have been questioned on a number of counts, their merit was to point out that the modernization process in advanced developing countries was not associated with greater democracy, (as argued by modernization theorists) but rather with a new type of regime which O'Donnell labeled bureaucratic-authoritarian.[47]

The Onganía administration quickly silenced its critics, without too much violence. Unlike other authoritarian experiments, the abolition of party activity, and most political activity for that matter, weakened the ability of societal groups to lobby the government. Business interest groups and unions were also kept at bay and dealt with in an ad hoc manner. With traditional channels of communication virtually closed, societal groups found it difficult to mount opposition to a government that many of them had welcomed just a year before. In 1967, the Law of National Security, inspired by the DSN, made punishable practically any crime perpetrated against the state. At the same time, the president substantially strengthened executive authority. The office of the Presidencia de la Nación was given the status of a superbureau, overseeing and, in theory, coordinating all ministries and departments.[48]

The insulation of policy making made relations between the military and Onganía increasingly difficult. With Onganía in charge after the coup and without a specified role for the armed forces, things became confused. The commanders of the three armed services thought that the president should act in consultation with them, as he was "their" representative. Onganía, on the contrary, insisted that they had given him a blank check and that the military's role was merely supporting. The president tried to minimize the role of the CONASE and its complementary agency, the National Development Council (CONADE), created in 1964 by Illia to make national policy for economic development. Nationalist officers regarded both CONASE and CONADE as essential to the promotion of their model of development, which often clashed with Krieger Vasena's. The nationalists were concerned that Krieger Vasena's open-door policy to foreign investments was detrimental to domestic manufacturers and to the DGFM. Moreover, they were more willing than Onganía to cooperate with the trade unions to avoid the radicalization of the working class. The liberals were, on the other hand, sympathetic to Krieger Vasena's economic project but were critical of the corporatist tendencies of other ministers. Eventually, Onganía replaced the leader of this faction, army commander General Julio Alsogaray, with General Alejandro Lanusse. The president was determined to eliminate all high-ranking officers who were potential leaders for factional division; he succeeded in this task as long economic stability and law and order were maintained.[49] However, the Cordobazo gave the military the occasion it had been looking for. The deterioration of the economic situation coupled with growing violence destroyed the very conditions that had enabled Onganía to hold off the military's intrusion. In 1970, Lanusse and his navy and air force colleagues deposed the president.[50]

Onganía's departure marked the beginning of the end for the Argentine Revolution. Suspicious of Lanusse's ambitions, the navy and air force convinced the army to select as next president an unknown intelligence officer stationed in Washington, D.C., as military attaché, General Roberto Levingston. With no base of support of his own, it was reasoned that Levingston would merely be a spokesman for the armed forces, while the commanders of the three services would try to agree on what to do next. Surprisingly, president Levingston began to act independently, trying to create his own constituency to consolidate his hold on power. The result of this defiant attitude ended in another palace coup, ousting Levingston after only eight months in office. In 1971, conditions were ripe for General Lanusse to assume the presidency in the name of the armed forces. He did so in the midst of a social crisis compounded by guerrilla warfare and public unrest. To show his conciliatory nature, Lanusse eased most of the restrictions on political activity imposed by Onganía. At the same time, he called upon the traditional political parties and unions to endorse his GAN in order to keep the country from falling into anarchy (see chapter 2). Nevertheless, Lanusse's hopes that the GAN could develop into a multiparty conservative alliance backing his presidential ambitions in an honest electoral contest were soon frustrated. He then rallied enough military support to call new presidential elections with the participation of the Peronists (but not Perón, who was barred from running due to some residency gimmick). By ending the proscription of Peronism, Lanusse aimed at isolating the revolutionary left.

The eventual return of Perón to the presidency, after the brief parenthesis of the Cámpora administration, was in the end accepted by most of the officer corps. By that time, the military seemed to recognize that the real enemy was the left-wing guerrillas and therefore that old divisions should be set aside in the name of that common cause. Until mid-1974, the armed forces made an effort to steer away from political interference and gave the Peronist administration a fair chance to tackle the growing socioeconomic problems. Unfortunately, Perón's death precipitated the escalation of terrorist violence and economic instability. In the fall of 1975, with President Isabel Perón taking a leave of absence, acting President Italo Luder issued a decree giving the military a blank check to combat subversion. In the meantime, preparations for the coup were in full swing. Although as army commander, General Jorge Videla believed in pure professionalism and opposed military intervention, the incompetence of the Isabel Perón administration drove the three armed services to agree that the military had to save the country from chaos. It was now only a question of time. The armed forces waited until March 1976, when most sectors of society were begging them to restore law and order. They did, and in a way almost no one anticipated.[51]

The Proceso (1976–1983)

Upon returning to power in 1976, the armed forces wanted to avoid the mistakes of the Onganía experiment. No one would be left in sole control of the decision-making process. The military as an institution would rule, paying lip service to the demands of civil society. The ruling junta, composed of army, navy, and air force commanders in chief, would be responsive only to the high commands of the three armed services and bureaucratic organizations like the Military Legislative Council. Collegiality was to be paramount, and no decisions were to be made unless they were compatible with the interests of each armed service.[52] This arrangement was devised to diffuse potential cleavages among the three arms. Accordingly, the spoils of government were divided in an equal manner. This process has been called the feudalization of the state.[53] The army, the navy, and the air force formalized their status as independent distributional coalitions, establishing the boundaries of their respective spheres of influence, which were to be supervised by, and dependent upon, the commander in chief of each armed service. As a consequence, both active duty and retired officers began to colonize key posts in the state (ministries, provinces, municipalities) and in public corporations and independent agencies. This, in turn, imposed a decentralized and parallel chain of command upon the existing civilian structure and made coordination among the branches of government and the rational use of scarce resources difficult.

To fight subversion, the country was divided into zones, with each of the three armed services in control of a zone. The ideological-military threat posed by left-wing guerrillas explains in part the harshness of this military control compared to the Onganía period, when this threat was basically absent. However, this decentralized way of fighting terrorism led to intelligence, police, and military units pursuing their objectives in competition with each other. The operational autonomy that many of these units acquired led to all kinds of abuses. Moreover, the inability or unwillingness of the junta to regain control of the situation eroded the military chain of command due to institutional autonomy, multiple loyalties not always linked to military hierarchy, and corruption.[54] The anarchy that ensued was even acknowledged by Minister of Interior, General Albano Harguindeguy, who stated in a public speech in May 1978 that "this way of behaving produced distortions: the total and generalized disregard for the rule of law; the power of the state was turned in some cases into violence exercised by groups out of control. The lack of restrictions over such a violence created an environment conducive to ethical abuses."[55]

Human rights organizations have seen in such pronouncements a way for the top echelons of the military to place the responsibility for the atrocities of the "dirty war" onto their subordinates. In their view, the top echelons were responsible for giving the orders, even though field commanders had ample liberty in selecting the means to carry them out. A more conservative view sees Videla as a moderate too busy keeping the regime united in the face of squabbles within the junta, intraservice rivalries, controversial economic policies, the border dispute with Chile, outside pressure to end human rights violations, and the coup attempt of General Luciano Benjamin Menéndez, to keep antisubversion forces in check.[56] No matter what interpretation one accepts, the end results were the same: the repression's abuses created a deep aversion in most of civil society against the military, which would have long-lasting effects; and the military's internal discipline and cohesiveness deteriorated sharply, particularly after Videla's retirement.

Up until Videla's retirement, the military was divided into three main factions. Videla's group, the moderating force, was the largest. It supported the economic policies of Martínez de Hoz but rejected most of his plans for the privatization of money-losing state enterprises not only within DGFM but also others that military men had come to control after the coup. The second faction was led by Admiral Emilio Massera, an open supporter of economic nationalism. His aim was to forge a populist alliance between the armed forces and the labor movement to repel the communist threat. (In fact, Massera was one of the masterminds behind the "dirty war.") Allegedly, his long-term plan was to gather support from sympathetic civilian groups in order to run as a neoconservative when the regime called elections. The third faction was headed by Generals Luciano Menéndez and Carlos Suárez Masón, direct heirs of the colorados of the 1960s. Bitterly anti-Peronist, they were for an endless military rule that could annihilate Peronist union leadership, the Catholic left, and Marxists.[57]

During the Proceso, the armed forces increased their military capability, as the arms race with Chile and Brazil grew in intensity. Although feuds with the Carter administration over human rights violations had led to the suspension in 1977 of the U.S. military aid agreement, Argentine officers coped. By then, the DGFM was capable of producing, thanks to European technology and licenses, part of the needed military equipment. The rest was imported from France (Mirage fighter jets, Exocet missiles, etc.), West Germany, Italy, the United Kingdom, Spain, and Israel.[58] As during the other period when the armed forces had ruled directly (1943–1946), the military budget increased to record levels. In terms of per capita GDP, each Argentine paid $125 for his/her military budget, while each Brazilian contributed only $12.5. In 1980, the Argentine armed forces reached a strength of 175,000 men, compared to 273,000 for Brazil, 92,000 for Chile, and 29,700 for Uruguay.[59]

In 1981, Videla's successor and strongest ally, infantry General Roberto Viola, was unable to command the junta and least of all army commander in chief General Leopoldo Galtieri, who, coming from the cavalry, had no service ties with the new president. Galtieri's successful coup against Viola only nine months after the latter had taken office testified to the profound divisions within the armed forces. Finally, the debacle of the Falklands/Malvinas war not only symbolized the death of the military regime but made public the two main internal cleavages that were tearing that institution apart. The horizontal cleavage (intraservice) became clear when the navy and air force withdrew from the ruling junta and let it be known that from that time on the army would bear the responsibility for the regime. The vertical cleavage was between generals, admirals, and brigadiers on one side and middle-ranking and junior officers on the other.[60] This was in part the result of the feudalization and decentralization process described above, but other factors had come into play by the time the Proceso drew to a close.

First, the officer corps became aware of the fact that the defeat with Britain had a lot to do with the poor management of the campaign by their superiors. Consistent with the feudalization approach, the army, navy, and air force fought three separate wars against the British. For example, the navy, which had drawn up the invasion plans, kept all its units secure in Argentine ports once its main battleship was sunk at the beginning of the hostilities. Moreover, the emphasis on internal security had made each armed service quite unprepared to fight an external enemy. British officers later acknowledged that had the Argentine armed forces had an overall strategy to rebuff the British army's attack from its start, they might have succeeded.[61] On the contrary, field commanders had the responsibility of taking the initiative due to the ineptness of those at headquarters in Buenos Aires. In 1983, a military commission was appointed to investigate the causes of the defeat. It was chaired by General Benjamin Rattenbach. The commission concluded that the war had been poorly planned and carried out and General Leopoldo Galtieri and Admiral Jorge Anaya, along with fourteen other officers, were directly responsible for the defeat. For some such a debacle could also be related to the DSN: "the Argentine military, since it had organized itself to dominate internal enemies, was completely unprepared to fight a major international war."[62] Regardless of the causes, Falklands/Malvinas veterans were angry at their superiors for abandoning them.

Second, to many officers who in 1976 truly believed in the superior capacity of the military to solve the country's problems, the political failure of the Proceso was as embarrassing as the military defeat. The overlapping of political and military power fostered widespread corruption, particularly among senior officers, which added to the frustration of the junior officers. Third, the failure of the military administration to negotiate its exit from power in return for retaining traditional military prerogatives and judicial immunity for its members increased tension between seniors and their subordinates in the officer corps. Defeated militarily and with a bankrupt record both in political and economic terms, the armed forces came out of the Proceso with their morale and internal unity shattered. Under strong civilian pressure, they had no choice but to quit unconditionally, hoping that would be enough to placate an outraged population.

Military Resistance to Civilian Supremacy (1984–1993)

Unfortunately for the military, the winner of the 1983 election was the very candidate who had called for the prosecution of those military officers (as well as civilian terrorists) guilty of human rights violations and for civilian supremacy. Civilian supremacy is "the armed forces' acceptance of a government's definition of defense goals and means, and of the appropriate areas of military responsibilities. This means the ability of acivilian, democratically-elected government to affect the size, recruitment, organization, composition, training, budget, equipment, deployment and mission of the armed forces. This definition assumes thatthe military does not participate in a sphere deemed as civilian; rather, it emphasizes an active presence of civilians in the military and defense spheres."[63]

The armed forces were in complete disarray and unable to mount strong opposition to civilian rule. Sectors of the officer corps were resigned to being subordinated to civilian authority. Among the civilian presidents of the past three decades, Alfonsín was in the best position to impose such civilian supremacy over the military. For one thing, he could count on a clear popular mandate. Many Argentines had voted for him precisely because of his stand on military and human rights issues. Furthermore, his proposal was supported by left-wing parties, some Peronists, and foreign governments and organizations.

Alfonsín focused on three major objectives: bringing to justice those military officers guilty of human rights violations, reducing the armed forces prerogatives, and cutting the military budget. As for the first objective, a few days after taking office, Alfonsín sent to Congress a number of bills dealing with this military issue. The Protection of the Constitutional Order Law sanctioned severe prison terms for those attempting to overthrow the democratic regime and for public officials collaborating with them. It also eliminated the death penalty imposed by the Proceso.[64] The Law of National Pacification, which the military passed before withdrawing from power to protect them from punishment for crimes committed during the Proceso, was repealed. Finally, an amendment to the code of military justice was submitted to the Congress. Its main tenets were that (1) the Supreme Council of the Armed Forces (CSFA), made up of retired high-ranking officers, would be in charge of investigating crimes ascribed to members of the armed forces (and intelligence and policy personnel under military jurisdiction) during the Proceso, in violation of the old code of military justice; (2) the attorney general would act independently on behalf of the government unless otherwise indicated by the executive branch or the defense minister; (3) state prosecutors as well as defendants would be allowed to appeal the CSFA's rulings before the appropriate federal court; (4) after six months from the beginning of a prosecution, the CSFA would notify the federal court if no verdict had been reached so the court could take over the case if it was determined there had been negligence or undue delay; and (5) those who acted under their superiors' orders would be exonerated except in those cases when the crime was of an atrocious or unusual nature.[65]

Moreover, Alfonsín appointed the CONADEP, whose task was to determine how many people had disappeared or been killed during the "dirty war." After months of public hearings and a thorough investigation, in September 1984, the commission reported to the president that as many as 8,690 people had disappeared during the repression years. By having military courts take care of the trials and nonpartisan body like the CONADEP establishing the facts, Alfonsín hoped to reassure the officer corps of the fairness of the procedures and to convince them that the administration was not seeking all-out confrontation. Moreover, both the president and Defense Minister Raúl Borrás explicitly stated that the amendments to the military justice code were specifically designed to discriminate between the officers who gave the orders or committed the abuses and those who simply followed their superiors' commands.[66] In other words, Alfonsín's original goal was to try a relatively small number of high-ranking officers, so that verdicts could be quickly reached and the issue closed. In early January 1984 the CSFA began investigating the nine officers who had been members of the three juntas that had ruled during the Proceso.[67]

As for the limitation of the armed forces' prerogatives, the government reorganized the Defense Ministry and put it back under civilian control (as it had been under Frondizi, Illia, and Perón in 1973). The authority of the Defense Ministry over the three branches of the armed forces was enhanced, reversing the decentralization that had taken place during the Proceso. First, the gendarmerie and prefectures, previously under the control of army and navy, respectively, were made dependent upon the Defense Ministry. Second, the Defense Ministry was given control of the DGFM and the COVIARA (Cooperative of Sales for the Navy), which made up the vast military-controlled industrial complex.[68] The once powerful post of commander in chief was eliminated and its functions divided among several offices. The president was now the supreme commander of the armed forces, whose authority could be delegated to the defense minister. The latter, in consultation with the president, would make all major decisions on military matters, from officers' promotions to military strategy. Subordinate to the defense minister were two new levels: chief of the joint general staff, who would function as the minister's closest adviser, and a chief of staff for each of the three services. The intelligence services were purged of most of their military personnel and made dependent upon the executive branch. Finally, the Law of National Defense, approved by Congress in November 1987, disappointed the expectations of the military. It failed to define a clear mission for the armed forces in terms of external and internal threats or to set up a timetable or new guidelines for their reprofessionalization. Although these were in the original plan, they were never carried out.[69] Therefore, while old prerogatives were taken away or limited as had never happened before in Latin America, no new ones were given in return to compensate for the losses.

The third objective, cutting the military budget—although also justified by the economic crisis—was really part of the overall policy to weaken the armed forces. Table 5.1 shows the percentage of GDP allocated to the military between 1970 and 1992.[70]

From an average of 3.9 percent during the Proceso, the military budget shrank to 2.5 percent in the first five years of the Alfonsín administration. Moreover, once we take inflation into account, the 1988 budget shrank to 1.8 percent in real terms.[71] Also, the Defense Ministry's share of the military budget increased from 26 percent in 1980 to 33 percent in 1988, while the three services saw theirs dropping from 74 percent to 67 percent.[72] The army's average share of the services' budget was 39 percent during the Proceso, but it declined to 34 percent under Alfonsín, while the navy and air force experienced the opposite trend. (See table 5.2.)

Taking all these factors into account, it is clear that the armed forces, but particularly the army, experienced a severe monetary squeeze with the restoration of democracy. The budget cuts profoundly affected the internal organization of the army, which from a total force of 119,964

TABLE 5.1
Military Expenditures as Percentage of GDP, 1970–1992

Year	% of GDP	Year	% of GDP
1970	2.5	1982	4.2
1971	2.2	1983	4.2
1972	2.1	1984	2.8
1973	2.3	1985	2.4
1974	2.4	1986	2.5
1975	2.9	1987	2.5
1976	3.3	1988	2.4
1977	2.9	1989	2.4
1978	3.8	1990	1.8
1980	4.3	1991	1.7
1981	4.7	1992	1.0

Source: United Nations Institute for Disarmament Research: *National Security Concepts And States: Argentina*, (Geneva: United Nations, 1992), p. 54. Figures for the 1989–1992 period were provided by the Centro Estudios Unión para la Nueva Mayoría.

men in 1983 declined to 76,589, a net loss of 36 percent. The hardest hit was the enlisted force (–54 percent), followed by cadets (–47 percent), civilian personnel (–11 percent), and NCOs (–9 percent). Salaries dropped to historic low levels (in 1988 they were only half of what they were in 1983); according to some sources, 70 percent of lower ranking officers and 90 percent of NCOs in the largest urban centers were forced to hold a second job in defiance of the military code.[73] By the same token, while the air force and navy were allowed to replace equipment lost in the Falklands/Malvinas conflict, army equipment fell apart for lack of spare parts. Army training standards for new recruits dropped significantly due to lack of uniforms and ammunition.

Unfortunately, Alfonsín's strategy to end the military trials in a short period of time so he could proceed with national reconciliation was frustrated by unexpected events. The first was the CSFA's decision in September 1984 to drop the most serious charges against members of the military juntas, which in practice legitimized the measures adopted by the Proceso to fight terrorism. The decision reflected a growing feeling among the armed forces, and in particular the army, that instead of being attacked the military should be praised for the elimination of terrorism, which, in their view, made the return to democracy possible. Therefore, in spite of vertical and horizontal splits, the vindication of the "dirty war" began to be the single most important issue uniting the officer corps, regardless of rank or service.

At this juncture, the government was left with no option but to rely on the civilian legal system to accomplish the task. Following the provisions of the new military justice code, the Federal Appeals Court of

TABLE 5.2
Army, Navy, and Air Force's Shares of the Armed Forces' Budget,
1970–1988 (percentage)

Year	Army	Navy	Air Force
1970	43	33	23
1971	42	34	24
1972	41	33	26
1973	41	33	26
1974	41	33	26
1975	40	36	24
1976	39	37	24
1977	42	33	25
1978	39	36	25
1979	40	38	22
1980	39	37	24
1981	40	35	25
1982	37	36	26
1983	37	37	26
1984	36	38	26
1985	31	44	30
1986	35	38	27
1987	34	39	26
1988	33	40	27
1976–83	39.1	36.1	24.6
1984–88	33.8	39.8	27.2

SOURCE: Rosendo Fraga: *La Cuestión Militar, 1987–1989* (Buenos Aires: Centro Estudios Unión para la Nueva Mayoría, 1989), p. 167.

Buenos Aires took over the trials of junta members and other courts began a score of legal investigations of junior officers. For a time, the military establishment (generals, admirals, and air force brigadiers) was able to convince their subordinates to be patient. Although, like their junior colleagues, they opposed the trials, they also believed that it was in the best interest of the armed forces to comply with the democratic regime's policy of military subordination and that it was possible for the officers under investigation to win their trials.[74] Nonetheless, junior officers grew more restless as the mass media (part of which was controlled by the government) stepped up their denunciations of military crimes, human rights groups intensified their attacks and law suits, and Radical congressmen publicly blasted the armed forces. As the trials increased in number so did the bombings and intimidations of judges, allegedly organized by off-duty military and police officers. By late October 1985 the government declared a stage of siege. The following December, a federal court passed a verdict on the junta leaders, an unprecedented event in Latin America. General Videla and Admiral

Massera were sentenced to life imprisonment, General Viola received seventeen years, Admiral Armando Lambruschini eight years, Brigadier Orlando Agosti four and a half, while General Galtieri, Brigadiers Jorge Lami Dozo and Omar Graffigna, and Admiral Anaya were acquitted. The latter three were subsequently tried and convicted for the mismanagement of the Falklands/Malvinas war.

Contrary to the administration's expectations, these sentences failed to calm the situation. Alfonsín was caught between two contending needs: on the one hand, he had to put an end to the trials if he wanted to avert a military reaction; on the other hand, his pledge to respect the independence of the judiciary and the freedom of expression of the mass media and human rights groups prevented him from acting unilaterally. Between November 1985 and the end of 1986 Alfonsín and the minister of defense lobbied the Supreme Court for a definition of *due obedience* consistent with that in the new military code. At the end of December, despite some opposition from UCR and PJ representatives of the Renovation faction, Congress passed the Full Stop Law.[75] The law set up a sixty-day limit on indictments for human rights crimes. Again, contrary to the administration's predictions, instead of putting the issue to rest, the law spurred a new wave of legal activity. Many federal judges, feeling that the executive was bypassing the law, defied the government and feverishly set up as many prosecutions as possible before the time period expired.[76] Although the Full Stop Law decreased the number of officers on trial from about 1,100 to 450, many of those left were the very ones the law aimed to shelter, the junior officers.

Military reaction to these last events came quickly. During Easter Week 1987, about 150 men led by Lt. Col. Aldo Rico, a Falklands/Malvinas veteran, staged a mutiny against the army leadership by holding out in a military base in the outskirts of Buenos Aires. The rebels, later labeled carapintadas for the commando-like camouflage paint on their faces, would soon gain national prominence and become a major political actor in the next few years. Most carapintadas came from the ranks of infantry junior officers and NCOs, especially those in commando units (Rico was a commando officer). Because of their combat expertise, they considered themselves the true "professionals" of the army, as opposed to the detested bureaucrats identified with their senior commanders who had stayed behind desks during the Falklands/Malvinas war and later had "sold" them to the civilian administration. Aside from their claim to be the heirs of the old nationalistic faction of the army, their ideological stance early on was unclear. "The only conviction that the rebels had as yet expressed was their belief in the legitimacy of the military's actions during the internal war and the illegitimacy of the government's attack on the armed forces, and their perception that their military superiors had failed in their obligation to defend them."[77]

Accordingly, the carapintadas made a number of specific demands for their return to the barracks: (1) the retirement of the army chief of staff and his collaborators, (2) the end of all trials involving military officers, (3) the end of media attacks on the armed forces, (4) the enhancement of professional standards, and (5) amnesty for the mutineers. The rebellion made it clear that the military chain of command had, for all intents and purposes, been broken. Although Alfonsín could still count on the navy, air force, and army establishments, support for carapintada demands was widespread among junior officers, and loyalist troops refused to move against them. For their part, the carapintadas adroitly argued that their rebellion was not against the constitutional order, which they claimed to respect, but against their superiors, who had failed to protect the interests of the armed forces, particularly of their subordinates, in order to comply for their own sakes, with the administration's policies.

At this juncture, the civilian population took to the streets to show their support for democracy. After four days, the holdout ended. Despite Alfonsín's denials, concessions were made, most notably, the retirement of the army chief of staff and a score of other generals.[78] Moreover, the following May, Congress approved the long-debated Due Obedience Law which dropped charges against all officers below the rank of colonel, leaving only twenty people or so on trial.[79] In January, 1988, Rico and 350 carapintadas staged a second mutiny at Monte Caseros, north of Buenos Aires. Rico asked for the retirement of the new chief of staff of the army, General José Caridi, and repeated the demands of a few months before. However, after five days, the carapintadas surrendered. Being far from the capital city, the rebels failed to gain the support of major army units. Moreover, most officers believed the uprising had more to do with Rico's and his cronies' personal ambitions than with institutional demands and saw no reason to put their careers in jeopardy.[80] As a matter of fact, the army establishment disciplined the rebels and froze their promotions.

The worst crisis came in December 1988, when about 500 troops took control of Villa Martelli (a military base in the western suburbs of Buenos Aires). Colonel Mohamed Alí Seineldín, a former commando officer passed up for promotion, replaced Rico (who was in jail) as the carapintada leader. Seineldín was a strong nationalist and conservative Catholic who had gained a following among junior officers he had trained in commando techniques. However, his maverick behavior had alienated the military establishment, which dispatched him to Panama (where he allegedly helped organize General Manuel Noriega's infamous dignity battalions). Although some analysts regarded the Villa Martelli uprising as the natural extension of the previous two mutinies, Seineldín had more ambitious goals in mind. In fact, the demand for the end of all military trials at a time when only twenty officers (all retired) were still facing charges had lost importance as an issue.[81] Besides asking for further reshuffling of the army high command and a bigger defense budget, Seineldín asked the government to publicly vindicate the "dirty war" and to grant amnesty to those who had participated in the mutinies. The stalemate continued for eight days, after which the carapintadas finally laid down their arms. Alfonsín refused to capitulate on the "dirty war" issue, but despite government denials, concessions were made again. In the weeks that followed, only Seineldín and another officer who had refused to surrender were jailed. Salaries were raised and so were budget expenditures for the military. Finally, Caridi stepped down as army chief of staff.[82]

The left-wing terrorist attack against the La Tablada military base in January 1989 was used by the carapintadas, as well as by right-wing political groups, to support the claim that the Marxist threat was still alive and well. Moreover, they said that the administration's attempt to establish civilian supremacy was part of a strategy to pave the way for a communist takeover.[83] As the Alfonsín administration drew to a close, Seineldín and Rico became more and more outspoken against the army leadership and the president, whom they saw as their archenemy. Their attention began to shift from military to electoral issues, and by early 1989 they were actively campaigning in favor of Menem's presidential bid.[84] This was due in part to their overt confrontation with the Radicals. Besides, Menem's nationalism appealed to the carapintadas. However it was Menem's hint of appointing Seineldín as army chief of staff, once he had been elected, that drove them into his camp.[85]

Once in office, Menem adopted a strategy fundamentally different from Alfonsín's, who was obliged by his electoral promises to prosecute human rights violations and to behave according to the moral principles he had campaigned for in 1983. Menem's first step was to settle the military issue as quickly as possible regardless of the means. He was thus willing to pardon those who had been responsible for human rights violations and for the more recent mutinies in return for the military's obedience to the civilian executive.[86] His second step consisted of gaining control over the military by playing rival factions against one another. This meant the destruction of the dangerous carapintadas, whom he had used for his presidential bid. His advantage over some of his predecessors who had unsuccessfully tried the same approach was that the armed forces were debilitated and were thoroughly discredited in civil society. The third and final step was the emasculation of the military as a distributional coalition by eliminating its socioeconomic clout through the privatization of the DGFM industrial conglomerate.

Some of Menem's first decisions appealed to the carapintadas. General Isidro Cáceres, one of the very few high-ranking officers who had their trust and who had negotiated their surrender in the last munity, was named army chief of staff, while many generals they did not like were sacked. At the same time, the appointments of Italo Luder as defense minister and Humberto Romero as defense secretary (the second highest civil servant in the Defense Ministry), two men who had shown sympathy to some of their early pleas, were also to their liking (Romero was a personal friend of some carapintada leaders.) Finally, Menem's decision in early October 1989 to grant sweeping presidential pardons to 277 people, including Seineldín and other carapintadas, was received very favorably. However, the honeymoon soon came to an end. Although Cáceres accepted the president's initiative to drop the charges by civilian courts against the carapintadas, he obtained Menem's permission to subject the rebels to military sanctions. Cáceres was in fact determined to reestablish internal discipline and was no longer willing to tolerate the maverick attitude of Seineldín and Rico.[87]

Thus, disciplinary measures were enacted a few weeks after the pardons, forcing Seineldín into retirement, while Rico was dropped from the army altogether. Menem's close collaboration with his army chief of staff left Luder out of all major decisions. Under the circumstances, Luder had no option but to resign. As the carapintada discourse became more politicized and Seineldín's and Rico's ambitions more obvious, their support within the officer corps diminished appreciably. By early 1990, Seineldín and Rico, both out of the army and with little prospect of making new inroads among the officer corps, brought their message directly to the people. They portrayed themselves as military populists, like Perón, using old-fashioned slogans like God, Country, and Social Justice, and toured Argentina's shantytowns, whose state of deprivation was a fertile ground for proselytes. Besides playing the political card, the carapintadas, believing that Menem had betrayed them, kept working within the armed forces for a military solution to their grievances. In September 1990, the State Intelligence Agency (Secretaría de Informaciones del Estado, or SIDE) uncovered a carapintada plot to topple the government.[88]

The following December, just two days before President George Bush's visit to Argentina, the carapintadas staged a coup attempt. By this time, however, the tide had turned against the rebels. Menem did not, as in the three previous uprisings, accept their offer of negotiations and ordered loyal troops to crush them. The clash that ensued was the bloodiest armed confrontation among military factions since the 1962–1963 infighting between the azules and the colorados. The uprising was over in less than twenty-four hours, leaving thirteen people dead (including five civilians) and fifty-five injured. The determination of the loyalists' response was perhaps due to the killing of two of their officers, which broke the unspoken rule that coups must be confined to a show of force rather than its actual use.[89] Moreover, by then many loyal officers had concluded that the carapintadas discredited the military and that the role played by NCOs among the rebels seriously undermined their authority and the chain of command. In fact, only 5 percent of those who joined the coup attempt were commissioned officers, while the rest were primarily NCOs, which marked a change in the carapintada makeup and leadership.[90]

President Menem came out of the events greatly strengthened. His firm handling of the situation brought overwhelming praise from all political sectors and from Bush, who made a point of keeping his visit to Buenos Aires on schedule to show his support for the young Argentine democracy. Enhanced in their positions were army chief of staff General Martín Bonnet (who had replaced Cáceres after the latter's death a few months before) and loyal members of the armed forces, who could claim to be the true professionals. The coup signified the political end of the carapintadas. Seineldín and six other officers were sentenced to life terms by the Supreme Council of the Armed Forces; smaller jail terms were given to six other officers.[91] That the military courts acted quickly and sentenced the coup leaders to stiff sentences was an important step toward the democratization of the armed forces.

Strengthened by the triumph, Menem quickly set out to remove the last obstacle to national reconciliation, pardoning the few people still serving jail terms for human rights violations. This included eleven members of the Proceso (i.e., former Presidents Jorge Videla and Roberto Viola) and montonero leader Mario Firmenich. The pardons met with strong public opposition (70 percent of people interviewed opposed them) and were denounced by most parties, religious leaders, union representatives, and human rights organizations. On 31 December, in spite of the fact that many porteños had left Buenos Aires for their summer vacations, 60,000 people showed up in front of the presidential palace to denounce the pardons.[92]

Throughout 1991, Menem continued to consolidate his authority over the military, redefining the rules of the game to his advantage. The severe CSFA sentences on the leaders of the last carapintadas rebellion showed that the army high command agreed with the president that disobedience would no longer be tolerated.[93] An indication of how times had changed came when, in late September 1991, the Defense Ministry announced plans to streamline the state-owned military industrial complex, controlled by the DGFM.

As we saw earlier, the DGFM allowed the military to be self-sufficient in the production of some strategic arms and capital goods. All three armed services had established industrial complexes, but things did not stop there. The navy for instance gained control of the National Atomic Energy Commission, and by 1974 Argentina had built its first power reactor (Atucha I) and proceeded to the construction of another, Atucha II, thanks to German technology. In 1983 the navy announced that it was capable of enriching uranium, the first step toward manufacturing a nuclear bomb. DGFM industries also produced light tanks, destroyers, submarines, civilian aircraft, jet fighters, machine guns, engines, and middle-range ballistic missiles. It was also engaged in companies ranging from shipyards to steel, and railway car manufacturing. Most of these companies were a drain on the national budget, with their tax breaks and government subsidies, and they operated at huge deficits with little concern for efficiency. Often, the army, navy, and air force managed industries in direct competition with one another, creating a useless duplication of industrial activities. As we saw earlier, the attempt of Economy Minister José Martínez de Hoz to privatize some of them failed due to the opposition of the armed services: free-market economics was good business as long as it did not touch the military's vested interests. DGFM companies were also used, like many other state corporations, to employ retired officers as members of executive boards, managers, and consultants.

In 1990, DGFM assets were estimated to be at $5.6 billion, with annual sales of $1.3 billion, and a total employment of 40,000 people.[94] Yet by 1991, with a cumulative deficit of $700 million, the DGFM was the largest drain on the federal budget.[95] Menem and his Economy Minister Domingo Cavallo made the DGFM a main target of the administration's privatization policy. In November 1991 plans were announced to sell the twenty-seven DGFM companies by the end of 1992.[96] The government also announced the sale of army, navy, and air force bases and properties, including the Campo de Mayo army base outside Buenos Aires, the site of the most important coups in the country's modern history. Through such sales, the air force—which had recorded a deficit of $22 million in 1990—showed a surplus of $4 million in 1991.[97] The military establishment grudgingly accepted such sales, which in the past would have triggered a major crisis, partly because the government promised to use some of the money from these privatizations to increase officers' salaries and upgrade equipment. By 1993, the only salient issue of contention between the military and Menem was the armed forces' budget, which had fallen to an all-time low (see table 5.1).

Political Changes and Military Responses

The events described above point to an evolutionary trend. Initially, the government was able to impose its authority on the military, but as the original strategy ran into trouble so did Alfonsín's mastery of events. With the transfer of the military trials to civilian courts and, even more, with the first military mutiny in 1987, the administration found itself increasingly on the defensive. Over time the mutinies reached a crescendo in terms of duration, the number of people involved, and the boldness of their demands. By the time Alfonsín left office, the armed forces had regained the initiative. They imposed many of their demands, both in terms of bread and butter issues (greater budge allocations) and institutional prerogatives (their status as an institution above the rule of law). Alfonsín's double objective of inducing self-criticism by the armed forces and of having them purge those who committed crimes or who were antidemocratic failed. In fact, not only did the armed forces not apologize, but senior officers who tried to carry out the president's objectives were forced out. Some contend that Alfonsín's approach was naïve: "To purge itself, the military had in some way, however, faintheartedly, to acknowledge the illegitimacy of the actions taken institutionally during the Process [Proceso]. To expect the military to make such an acknowledgment at the beginning of 1984 was unrealistic."[98]

Experts on Argentine military affairs generally agree that in the end Alfonsín achieved only limited civilian supremacy over the armed forces. Rosendo Fraga simply stated that such a policy based on the northern European model does not fit Argentine reality and is unlikely to work.[99] Andrés Fontana, Deborah Norden, and David Pion-Berlin stressed in their writings that the lack of attention to those aspects linked to the military's reprofessionalization (enhancement of technical and professional standards) and mission (a role in both internal and external security), two themes extremely important to the officer corps, was Alfonsín's biggest mistake. The military in Latin America "are happiest when they have a clear mission, one that makes them feel important and causes them to be appreciated by their compatriots."[100] Clearly, this did not take place in Argentina. "By denying that the nation faced any credible threats, the government pulled the rug out from under its own reforms, because it left the military in a state of intellectual paralysis—without the strategic underpinnings necessary to orient the reorganization process."[101] Fontana, acknowledged that the lack of civilian experience in crafting and managing a military policy aimed at civilian control of the military had a lot to do with some of the mistakes.[102] The high turnover of defense ministers (the first two, Raúl Borras and Roque Carranza, died in office, while the third, Germán López, left the administration in 1986) made policy continuity more difficult. Furthermore, the military trials began to slip out of government control in late 1984 and to acquire a dynamic of their own, which made things even more complicated. The different judicial means used prolonged the trials. As trials dragged on, so did the mass media's attacks, which led many military officers to conclude that they were the target of a well-orchestrated attempt by the government to destroy the armed forces as an institution. For its part, the Alfonsín administration behaved in an ambiguous manner, which reinforced the officers' misgivings. In fact, while the president tried to reassure the officer corps that plans were being made to safeguard their prestige and institutional interests, Radical leaders in Congress and the government-controlled media were attacking them at every turn. Thus, while Alfonsín's original intentions were quite sound, strategically and tactically he often showed poor judgment and tended to overwhelm the armed forces with measures that bewildered them and left them in a professionally moribund state.[103] "(1) The policy of legal prosecutions that characterized the first stage of the Argentine transition was not designed by the executive power but was the consequence of the articulation of related strategies implemented by those actors involved [government, human right groups, the judiciary, parties, the military]; and (2) the direction taken by this process did not respond to the general objectives of any of the actors involved in the political fight tied to the violation of human rights."[104]

In spite of these disappointments, Alfonsín's policies delimited military prerogatives in some areas. The strengthening of the Defense Ministry's authority over the three armed services was a major accomplishment. It set an important precedent in establishing civilian control over the budget and the internal organization of the armed forces. The transfer of most military-controlled industrial complexes and the nuclear energy agency to the civilian bureaucracy was another important step in diminishing the military's stake in economic development. The problem, according to some, is that Alfonsín's military policy alienated the armed forces and triggered their repoliticization.[105] This, however, would imply that upon returning to the barracks the military withdrew from politics. Yet the low profile assumed by the military in the first three years of the Alfonsín's administration does not mean that they had suddenly become democrats or apolitical actors. The mutinies are a case in point. Although Rico and Seineldín presented their rebellions as merely internal affairs of the army, directed not against the government but against their superiors, they are not very convincing. In the end, the objective was to change a specific government policy by removing the military allies of the president, and that is politics at its best. The development of the carapintadas into a Peronist ally first and an amorphous military-populist movement later suggests that at least their leaders had a clear political agenda, if not from the start, shortly thereafter.

Just as the armed forces gained important concessions from Alfonsín, under Menem the same trend continued. First Cáceres and later Bonnet successfully used the carapintada issue to obtain greater budget increases and to strengthen their grip on the army's internal affairs to fend off the threat posed by Seineldín and Rico. The defeat of the carapintadas in December 1990 marked a success for the "official army" that Cáceres and Bonnet claimed to represent (as opposed to the unofficial army of the rebels).[106] In the process, the army paid dearly. The vertical split within the officer corps posed a problem for the legitimacy of the army's establishment. In addition, the high turnover of senior officers increased uncertainty and weakened the army in terms of both internal cohesion and operational efficiency. During Alfonsín's tenure there were five army chiefs of staff, compared to two for the air force and one for the navy. The same applies to other high posts in the three armed services, although not in the same proportions.[107] Interestingly enough, the turmoil caused by the mutinies came primarily from the army's ranks. Both the navy and air force kept a low profile. Their good relations with the Alfonsín administration (particularly the air force) translated into greater budget allocations. It may not be a coincidence that only a few air force officers were implicated in the mutinies. Eventually, the air force put down the December 1990 coup by threatening to bomb the carapintadas. Internal discipline was not broken in the navy and air force to the extent it was in the army, and both branches have fared better under Alfonsín. Moreover, the air force and navy distanced themselves from the army after the Falklands/Malvinas war, and their chiefs of staff publicly supported the democratic regime. They began retraining their middle-ranking officers in civilian universities to show their relation to society as a whole. Last, as pointed out by Carlos Acuña and Catalina Smulovitz, the fact that officers were made accountable to civilian law and the embarrassment and internal divisions caused by public trials were a severe blow to the prestige of the armed forces.[108] Thus, in spite of the pardons, the menace of public trials (and their expected costs) in the end induced the armed forces to compromise with Menem and to subordinate themselves to the executive branch.

As for Menem, his divide-and-rule strategy was successful in the first four years of his administration. Besides the pardons, several measures were adopted to please the armed forces: (1) the navy was given jurisdiction over the coast guard, while the air force took away from the border guard control of the country's airports; (2) the navy and army participated in the U.N.-sponsored peacekeeping efforts in Iraq and Yugoslavia, respectively; (3) a new Domestic Security Law was approved by the Senate, amending Alfonsín's Defense Law and providing for the Ministry of the Interior to use the armed forces "under exceptional circumstances" in cases of serious domestic unrest; (4) the government secured a cooperation agreement with the United States for the supply of new ships and transport airplanes during the visit of Defense Secretary Richard Cheney in February 1992; and (5) pay hikes were granted.[109]

On the other hand, the president not only began the privatization of the DGFM, he also announced plans to cut the 76,000-man armed forces by an additional 30 percent.[110] This restructuring led to the elimination of the Fourth Army Corps, whose units joined either the Third or the

Fifth Army Corps. A more important indication of how the balance of power between civilian and military had tilted was the resignation of army chief of staff Bonnet in October 1991, when the president backed the Defense Ministry's decision to interfere in the promotions of the army. In the past, this event could have triggered a major crisis—but not this time. Finally, the armed forces were forced to accept the scrapping of the Condor II missile, allegedly under U.S. pressure.[111]

Were the carapintada mutinies aimed at defending their institutional prerogatives or were they disguised coup attempts? Some contend that the first three mutinies were not and that they can be regarded as "strikes"; others believe that a coup was the real intention.[112] Although there is no clear-cut evidence that the rebels intended to overthrow the government, there is little doubt that authoritarianism is alive and strong in many quarters of the armed forces. Whether such authoritarianism and disregard for the rule of law will lead to another military takeover is a matter of conjecture. Several factors, however, suggest that this is unlikely, at least in the short run.

First, Menem's pardons have defused the crucial point of tension, as only a handful of carapintada officers are now serving jail terms. Second, there seems to be enough agreement within the officer corps that continued politicization is detrimental to the military and that their attention should turn to more professional matters. Although funds are scarce and morale is low, and although Menem has still to define a clear mission for the armed forces, top echelons of the military appear willing to collaborate with the government's reform program. The new army chief of staff, General Martín Balza, upon replacing Bonnet, declared, "The [army's] essential mission . . . is to contribute to the achievement of the political objectives set forth by the government, guaranteeing that it has the freedom to make decisions in this regard."[113] As long as this approach is dominant, it is unlikely that a strong coup coalition can emerge. Coups are successful when economic conditions are very unstable and the ruling government encounters strong opposition, and none of these conditions were present in 1993. Third, the failure of the Proceso will be a powerful deterrent for some time, as many officers realize that much more is to be gained from pressuring a civilian government than ruling directly. Fourth, the democratic system still enjoys the support of most of the population and of those economic and political groups that in the past have supported military takeovers. This is due not so much to what civilian politicians have accomplished as to what the military have destroyed. Fifth, Rico's electoral success in the 1991 midterm election, when his populist movement (MODIN) captured 10 percent of the popular vote in the Buenos Aires province and three seats in the Chamber of Deputies, seemed to convince many former carapintadas and their followers that political means serve their goals better than military means. Sixth and last, the United States, the European Economic Community, the international lending agencies, and foreign businesses strongly support the democratic system. Although foreign opinion is not sufficient to prevent a coup, it is likely to make an irresolute coup coalition think twice.[114]

This does not mean that from now on the military will refrain from intervening. In 1987 an observer pointly underscored that, "from a democratic viewpoint, the good news is that as governors the armed forces are thoroughly discredited. The bad news is that the armed forces are thoroughly unrepentant."[115] This lack of remorse for the atrocities committed during the Proceso troubles many, even though in recent times the armed forces have lessened their appeals for a "vindication" of the "dirty war." However, should economic conditions deteriorate, social unrest could lead to the power vacuum that triggered the 1976 coup. Under such conditions, elements like the carapintadas could attempt a coup. The failed coup in Venezuela of early 1992 is a good indication that in severe socioeconomic distress even an apolitical military can be tempted to intervene if it perceives that large sectors of society would be supportive.[116] Nonetheless, as long as a left-wing subversive threat does not exist and the opposition stays within the democratic rules of the game, the military will be very reluctant to step in.

The *Buenos Aires Herald,* an English-language daily that continued to denounce the military repression even during the darkest days of the Proceso, gave a sad but realistic analysis of civil-military relations:

> In purely political terms most of the grievances existing then [during the Holy Week rebellion of 1987] have been since superseded by other events which have reduced them to little more than academic points of principle. Today there is no major "military" problem as such and, against 60 years of continuous unrest, this is in itself a remarkable achievement in its own right. Much has been sacrificed to obtain this apparent peace, with most of the country's basic institutions paying a high price for their pains. The reputation and credibility of the Executive, Legislative and Judicial powers have all been badly undermined in the name of a conciliatory policy toward the military rebels of no legal, ethical or moral content. While it is debatable whether history will confirm the wisdom of this policy or prove it wrong, there can be no doubt that today the relationship between the government and the Armed Forces has rarely been so good, and in the difficult times we live this could be seen as one reason to feel moderately optimistic about the future.[117]

6

THE LABOR MOVEMENT

ARGENTINE UNIONISM has been undoubtedly the strongest in Latin America. In many ways, its strength and bargaining power make it comparable to some of the most powerful union movements in Western Europe. Many factors make Argentine unionism important in national politics, among them its size and organizational skills. According to one source, in 1986 union membership was about 3.9 million strong, although it is likely that, due to the deep recession since then, the number of unionized people is today below the 3 million mark.[1] Nevertheless, in the 1980s the proportion of unionized wage earners (56 percent of total) remained second only to Scandinavian countries and Belgium and ahead of the United States, the United Kingdom, France, and Italy. (See table 6.1.) Unionization encompasses both blue-collar and white-collar employees and is particularly strong in the old industrial belt of metropolitan Buenos Aires and in the cities of Rosario, Santa Fe, and Córdoba; it is much weaker in rural areas.[2] In 1989, the retail clerks, metal workers, construction workers, and bank employees unions had over 150,000 members each, and several others had over 100,000. (See table 6.2.)

Another factor accounting for the unions' strength is their financial assets. After Perón's labor reform of the mid-1940s, 1 percent of the salary of all employees, both union and nonunion, was deposited in the national union's bank account; an additional 3.5 percent was paid by the employer. These contributions were used to fund union-run social services (*obras sociales*) like health care, recreational facilities (movie theaters, libraries, resort hotels, sport centers), food stamps, pharmacies, and training schools. In 1976, it was estimated that these social services covered 17.5 million people, out of a population of 27 million. The economic clout of some unions even extends to the ownership of banks and insurance companies.[3] In 1980, the net value of union assets was estimated at $2 billion.[4]

TABLE 6.1
Union Membership, by Country

Country	Union Membership	*Percentage of Employed Labor Force in Unions*
Argentina	3,972,000	59
Belgium	2,641,000	70
Denmark	1,588,000	64
France	5,550,000	26
West Germany	9,400,000	37
Ireland	671,000	58
Italy	7,148,000	35
Netherlands	1,459,000	31
United Kingdom	12,250,000	50
United States	22,463,000	23

SOURCE: James McGuire, "The Causes of Strikes in Alfonsín's Argentina, 1983–1989: New Ideas, New data, and a Quantitative Analysis," paper prepared for the American Political Science Association Meeting, San Francisco, 31 August to 2 September 1990, p. 6a.

However, the most important feature of Argentine unionism remains its politicization. In fact, unlike their U.S. counterparts, Argentine unions have formally affiliated with political parties. On occasion, they have sought to represent particular social groups politically, in direct competition with parties. Politicization of the labor movement is common in Europe, but the Argentine case differs significantly from its European counterparts at least in one respect. Whereas in Europe politicization occurred over many decades in which labor gained its status through long struggles with capital and the state, the political status of Argentine unions was a result of gifts from the state granted by a charismatic leader, Juan Domingo Perón. Equally important is that Argentine unionism has since been extremely resistant to efforts by civilian and military governments to depoliticize it.

After World War II, Argentine union leaders imposed themselves on management in order to solve labor disputes. They also demanded that government, political parties, and the military consult them on all major political questions, not only labor relations issues. Consequently, the leader of the CGT, as well as the leaders of the largest unions, carry tremendous political weight, which enables them to deal with politicians on an equal basis. Thus, the economic and political importance of the union movement has made it one of the country's most powerful distributional coalitions.

The history of the Argentine labor movement has been characterized by continuous struggle. Governments have used repression, co-optation, or bargaining (or a combination of all of the above) to diminish the unions' autonomy and political clout. For their part, union leaders have

TABLE 6.2
Claimed Membership of Major Unions, 1963–1989

Union	1963	1973	1984	1989
UOM (metalworkers)	219,000	270,000	287,000	130,000
CGEC (retail workers)	200,000	170,000	260,000	408,000
UOCRA (construction)	95,000	260,000	110,000	101,000
SMATA (auto workers)		121,000	54,000	53,976
AOT (textile workers)	150,000	110,000	74,000	73,646
FGPIC (meat packers)	55,000	65,000	70,000	37,667
FONIVA (clothing workers)		60,000	37,000	
SUPE (oil workers)	30,000	45,000	45,000	25,588
UTG (food workers)	36,800	30,000	40,000	
UNPC (state workers)	190,00	180,000	133,000	133,188
UF (railway workers)	222,978	168,000	142,000	143,304
AB (bank employees)	65,000	84,000	186,000	156,080
ATE (state workers)	150,000	70,000	80,000	85,927
UOEM (Buenos Aires municipal workers)	55,000	70,000	65,000	60,400
UTA (transport workers)	50,000	60,000	50,000	56,214
UTGRA (restaurant workers)	60,000	55,000	80,000	85,481
FATLyF (light & power workers)	41,250	53,000	58,000	69,952
FATSA (health workers)	38,000	42,000	98,000	170,9000
FOETRA (telephone workers)	28,000	40,000	40,000	39,650e
FOYECT (postal workers)		35,000	40,000	31,500

SOURCE: Paul Lewis, *The Crisis of Argentine Capitalism* (Chapel Hill: University of North Carolina, 1990), p. 413 based on Rubén Rotondaro, *Realidad y cambio en el sindicalismo* (Buenos Aires: Editorial Pleamar, 1971), pp. 371–72; Edward Epstein, ed., *Labor Autonomy and the State in Latin America* (Boston: Unwin Hyman, 1989), p. 31, based on Alvaro Abós, *Los sindicatos argentinos: Cuadro de situación* (Buenos Aires: CEPN, 1985), p. 78; James McGuire, "Union Factionalism and Democratic Consolidation in Alfonsín's Argentina, 1983–1989," paper prepared for the Midwest Political Science Association Meeting, Chicago, 5–7 April 1990, p. 34; David Decker, *The Political, Economic, and Labor Climate in Argentina* (Philadelphia: Industrial Research Unit, Wharton School, University of Pennsylvania Press, 1983), p. 84; and *Clarín*, 12 October, 1989.

been deeply divided on how to respond to such government strategies and on what kind of political role the labor movement should play. Union collaboration in government plans was greatest under Perón, as his administrations were assumed to favor labor. Conversely, union opposition has been greatest under Conservative, Radical, and authoritarian administrations. In this chapter the focus is on the evolution of the labor movement, the dynamics of its internal divisions, its vested interests, its repeated attempts to acquire a privileged status within the state, and most recently, its effort to resist government policies aimed at emasculating its political and economic bargaining power.

The Early Development of Unionism (1872–1943)

Argentine unionism has historically been plagued by internal divisions, struggles, and rancor.[5] Its start coincided with the arrival during the last quarter of the nineteenth century of European immigrants, who brought with them socialist, Marxist, and anarchist ideologies popular in those days on the old continent. The unionization process went hand in hand with that of urbanization and industrialization. Between 1894 and 1914, employment in manufacturing rose from 100,000 to 400,000.[6] Growth was centered in Buenos Aires and, to a lesser extent, in Rosario, Córdoba, and Santa Fe. The first true union organization, the Printing Trade Workers Union (Unión Tipográfica), was founded in 1872.[7] However, the union movement did not really grow until the turn of the century. Between the 1880s and the early 1940s three main groups battled for the leadership of the labor sector: socialists, anarchists, and syndicalists.

Unlike Conservatives and Radicals, who ignored the working class, the Argentine Socialist Party (PSA), since its creation in 1894, incorporated labor demands in its political platform. Indeed, workers quickly became the PSA's core constituency. Argentine socialists were more moderate than their European counterparts of the time. Their aim was to push labor reforms through Congress and to create a European-style parliamentary democracy. While the Radicals shunned immigrants (the Radical revolts of the turn of the century had meaningless working class support), the socialists actively sought them, hoping to convince them to acquire citizenship and eventually vote for the PSA. At the same time, the socialists strongly supported the free-market, export-led economic model imposed by the Conservatives. They believed that an economic environment conducive to foreign investments would create jobs and bring in better technology. Following the same reasoning, they opposed protectionism, which they regarded as detrimental to consumers' interests. Despite their small congressional representation (before 1912 they had only one seat in the Chamber of Deputies) socialist advocacy of labor reform resulted in some minor labor legislation, including the regulation of woman and child work, compulsory rest on Sundays, and the creation of the National Labor Department in 1904 (which confined itself to gathering statistics and information about labor conditions). Yet the socialists' moderation and their effort to work within a system that many union leaders thought rotten prevented them from gaining control of most unions. Their appeal was confined to skilled workers, like the locomotive drivers and stokers of the La Fraternidad, who had high status in the labor movement. A closely related factor undermining the socialists was the widespread popular perception, adroitly exploited by their anarchist and syndicalist rivals, of being a party of middle-class intellectuals.[8]

The anarchists became the strongest group between the 1890s and World War I. Many of their leaders were European immigrants from Germany, Italy, and Spain. Whereas the socialists campaigned on a fairly sophisticated platform, the anarchists, most of whom were semiliterate, had a much simpler, more radical stance. The simplicity of their ideas and their rank-and-file leadership brought the anarchists closer to their fellow immigrants. Another significant difference from socialists was that anarchists rejected the use of parties and Congress to press their demands. Their main tool of political action was the "revolutionary general strike," which was often accompanied by violence, sabotage, and even assassination.[9] Argentine anarchists were more moderate than their European and North American counterparts, although they did adhere to the principle of anarchic communism.[10]

By the turn of the century the anarchist movement had gained a substantial following, making it one of the largest in the world. Their strength was greatest in small manufacturing (the bulk of the industrial sector) and service companies.[11] In 1894, anarchist and socialist unions joined forces in an umbrella organization named the Argentine Workers Federation (Federación Obrera Argentina, or FOA). However, squabbles between the two groups over tactics and the use of general strikes led to the FOA's demise. In 1904, the anarchists organized the Argentine Regional Workers Federation (Federación Obrera Regional Argentina, or FORA), whose membership was over four times larger than the Socialist General Workers Union (Unión General de Trabajadores, or UGT). Between 1902 and 1910, Argentina was shaken by a wave of anarchist-led general strikes.[12] The Conservative administrations' response was ever greater repression. They called a state of siege, and Congress passed legislation to purge the anarchist leadership. The Residency Law (1902) allowed the government to deport foreign union activists (who were of course dominant among anarchists), while the Social Defense Law (1910) sanctioned the crackdown of any union activity regarded as subversive, thus affecting both immigrant and Argentine-born workers.[13]

The year 1910 marked the pinnacle of the anarchist militancy. From then on a new group, the syndicalists, slowly replaced the anarchists within the labor movement. Starting as a left-wing splinter group of the Socialist party in 1906, the syndicalists placed themselves between the anarchists and the socialists. Like the anarchists, the syndicalists supported the notion of the class struggle of the proletariat and regarded the socialists' mild reformism as futile. On the other hand, they rejected the anarchists' indiscriminate use of general strikes, because in the end they only triggered greater repression. The syndicalists became more pragmatic as time went on, focusing their demands on bread-and-butter issues rather than ideology. They also remained aloof from political parties, as they believed that only the union could effectively bring about the "redemption of the working class" and establish a "new society."[14] Other factors differentiated the syndicalists from the other two groups.

Unlike the anarchists, their leadership was young and usually Argentine (as were their followers). Moreover, they gained positions of prominence in larger industrial companies, usually associated with more sophisticated kinds of production and employing more skillful workers. In 1906, the syndicalists succeeded in taking control of the UGT, which in 1908 became the Argentine Regional Workers' Confederation (Confederación Obrera Regional Argentina, or CORA).

After 1910, strike activity diminished substantially. The decreased militancy of the union movement coincided with the rising fortunes of the syndicalists, who, in 1914, joined the FORA. A year later, they gained control of the FORA and passed a motion calling for the abandonment of the federation's commitment to anarchic communism. In retaliation, the anarchists walked out and organized a rival FORA.[15] These internecine battles, first between socialists and anarchists and later between anarchists and syndicalists, were counterproductive. They prevented the labor movement from enhancing its bargaining power vis-à-vis the government and capital, and they undermined the possibility of creating a party link. Whereas the socialists had a clear program toward this end, they lacked appreciable working class support; and whereas the anarchists and syndicalists had a substantial following, they were uninterested in party politics.

If Conservative administrations had regarded the labor movement as detrimental to the regime's stability and wasted no time in repressing it, once in power the Radicals, who had little working class support in 1916, were ambivalent toward labor.[16] In the first three years of his administration, Yrigoyen seemed to be sympathetic to labor demands. From 1916 to 1919, partly as a consequence of the deteriorating purchasing power of wages brought about by prolonged inflation, a new wave of strikes hit Argentina.[17] To prevent the Socialist party from exploiting the situation, Yrigoyen expressed his sympathy for the "just cause" of the unions, particularly syndicalist unions. The president not only tolerated the strikes but his administration arbitrated disputes upholding the demands of the railworkers union and those of the longshoremen of Buenos Aires. In addition, Yrigoyen restrained the use of police action to break strikes. Foreign and domestic capital grew increasingly restless under Yrigoyen and denounced his attitude toward labor. Waiving the threat of the repetition of the Russian Revolution, rural and industrial interests joined forces and counterattacked, organizing vigilante units to crush strikers.

In January 1919, one of these organizations, the Argentine Patriotic League, made up of right-wing, anti-Semitic members of the upper and middle classes and off-duty military officers, went on a rampage. With the government no longer controlling the situation, the League gained the active collaboration of army, the navy, and business circles. It terrorized and killed workers and, worse, falsely accused Russian Jews of being communist organizers. The Tragic Week, as the events came to be known, virtually ended Yrigoyen's prolabor policy. Business elites and the military, through the League, gave the president a clear signal that labor concessions threatened the status quo and were not tolerable. Intimidation and bloodshed continued for some time, as the army put down strikes in the Patagonian region in 1921 and 1922.[18] For the remainder of the 1920s, organized labor kept a low profile. Finally, a few weeks after the 1930 coup, socialists and syndicalists set aside their differences momentarily and created the CGT, which would dominate the labor movement ever after, although it split into rival factions in 1935, 1943, 1968, 1982, 1989, and 1992.[19]

The union movement became passive when Yrigoyen was deposed. Initially, the CGT leadership reasoned that working class interests were best served by sticking to pure union issues. By adopting this approach, they believed they could remain independent of political parties. Further, the repressive posture of the administrations of the 1930s kept labor in check and discouraged strikes. Notwithstanding their goal of preserving union autonomy, some union leaders resorted to lobbying Congress to enact some moderate social legislation. This strategy was encouraged by the fact that in 1932 the ban against personalist Radicals had allowed the Socialist party to gain over 28 percent of the seats in the Chamber of Deputies. The socialist congressional delegation was instrumental in passing prolabor legislation during the Justo administration, such as half-day work on Saturdays, severance pay, vacations, and advance notice of layoffs. To be sure, much of this legislation was rarely enforced, but still it constituted a positive departure from the past.[20] Coincidentally, it was at this time that the socialists gained power in the CGT, relegating the syndicalists to a secondary role.

A third group that emerged in the early 1930s was the communists, who began to replace the anarchists as the labor movement's left wing. Since most existing unions were firmly in the control of socialists or syndicalists, the communists devoted themselves to the unionization of workers in the new import substitution industrial sector that had emerged during the Great Depression. Although small in number, the communists accounted for most CGT membership growth between the late 1930s and early 1940s. The ranks of unionized workers rose from nearly 370,000 in 1936 to almost 450,000 in 1941.[21] The communists also actively campaigned to create a common labor front against the threat of fascism and nazism and actively endorsed the Allies' war effort.[22]

In 1942, the CGT split again. Its moderate wing, the CGT-1, was composed of older socialist and syndicalist union leaders in the transport and service sectors who adamantly opposed communism. Communist unions in the new industries and some defecting socialists formed the

CGT-2. Unlike the previous decade, union disagreements were not so much on whether political involvement was advisable but on what form it should take.[23]

Perón and the Incorporation of Labor into the Political Arena

The political scenario just described was propitious "for forging new institutional relationships between labor and the state at the same time that a large number of labor's demands were yet to be met."[24] Besides the changing attitude of unions, a factor of crucial importance was the demographic and social changes that had taken place in the 1930s. In the wake of the Great Depression, a large number of people abandoned the Argentine countryside and flocked to the cities in search of a better life. One estimate is that between 1943 and 1947 one of five rural people left for the cities.[25] As a consequence, while at the turn of the century the bulk of the workers of metropolitan Buenos Aires was foreign-born, by 1947 three-fourths of them were migrants from the interior.[26] The key point here is that these recent arrivals, unlike their predecessors, were citizens and could vote.

Another factor was that, although in the early 1940s Argentine unionism was the largest in Latin America, it still excluded the bulk of urban and rural workers. Most of its membership was concentrated in metropolitan Buenos Aires and in a few sectors like services and transport, within which railway unions like La Fraternidad and the Unión Ferroviaria were dominant.[27] In contrast, only a fraction of the manufacturing sector was organized.

Finally, the working and living conditions of most wage laborers were "tragic."[28] As noted in chapter 2, Colonel Perón was one of the few officers who realized the explosive potential of the situation if the communists exploited it. Allegedly, shortly after assuming the post of head of the Labor Secretariat, Perón read a report by a chief officer of the secretariat, José Figuerola, and became aware of the miserable living conditions of the working class.[29] Perón tried to explain to big business his approach to the working class problem: "In the working sector we would like to achieve a professional organization akin to that of England's trade unions. In that fashion we could efficiently contain the Communist menace and create conscientious organizations which, through collective bargaining, would establish the bases for the relations between capital and labour in each line of activity. At the same time, the study and adoption of fair wages will raise the living standards of our working classes and transform them into consumers of our own production."[30]

As neither business distributional coalitions nor the Radicals backed his neoconservative project to thwart a communist takeover, Perón moved to gain control of the labor movement on his own. From 1943 until his election in February 1946, he devoted much of his energy to luring unions into his fold, a decision that marked a turning point in Argentine history. Up to 1943 organized labor had been relatively secondary in the country's politics. In a few months, Perón had brought it to the political center stage, where it remains today. The working class acquired a social status, an economic well-being, and a political clout unprecedented in Latin America. Perón achieved this by using the powers of his several official positions in the military administration of General Edelmiro Farrell. He met with union leaders in the Labor Secretariat and the War Ministry to "find out how the workers were going to cooperate with the government."[31]

Perón's strategy to co-opt union leaders consisted of favorable legislation, economic benefits, and special privileges for those who followed him and repression of those who did not. The public began to notice this previously obscure colonel. Perón first began to enforce existing labor legislation, which had been largely ignored. He also made the Labor Secretariat (which later was upgraded to the Ministry of Labor and Social Welfare) the nation's collective bargaining agency.[32] Often Perón personally arbitrated contract disputes, usually siding with the workers. He even urged union leaders to strike, giving them to understand that he would force their demands on management. Of course, Perón ensured that such actions would receive wide publicity through his skillful manipulation of the media. In addition, between 1944 and 1945, Perón issued a barrage of decrees that went well beyond the unions' rosiest expectations. As a result, labor-management relations changed overnight. Some of these provisions created

- The Statute of Rural Worker granting basic rights and regulating pay scales and working conditions for rural laborers and tenant farmers (Law 28.169)
- Labor courts (Law 32.347)
- Minimum wage, unemployment compensation, and a Christmas bonus equivalent to a month's extra pay (Law 33.302/45)
- Paid vacations of up to two weeks (Law 1740/45)
- Inspection committees to ensure the execution of collective bargaining agreements
- A state-run National Employment Agency (Law 13.591/49)
- A National Social Security Agency providing retirement benefits for employees, the self-employed, and professionals (Law 29.176)[33]

All these reforms met longstanding union demands, but they were achieved not through a struggle with capital, as happened in Europe and North America, but were gifts granted from above by a paternalistic caudillo, who instead of repressing the working class as his predecessors had, showed, at least from the masses' viewpoint, compassion and understanding. This sense of pleasant surprise is exemplified by the comments of a contemporary metalworker: "In 1944 we began to notice incredible things in our union work: labor laws not enforced before were now being enforced; there was no need to resort to the courts to obtain vacations; other labor provisions, such as the recognition of plant delegates, guaranties that they would not be dismissed, and so on, were immediately and strictly enforced. The nature of the internal relations between the employers and the personnel of the plants had changed completely. . . . The employers were as disconcerted as the workers were. The Secretariat of Labor and Welfare had become a factor in the organizational development and support of the working class."[34]

However, no matter how good Perón was to the working class, he was still a caudillo and, as such, demanded compliance. In practice, this meant relinquishing what union leaders had fought for since the beginning of the labor movement: political autonomy. Favorable government arbitration of contracts became dependent upon acceptance of Perón's authority. What could not be obtained through patronage was obtained through authoritarian measures. In January 1945, the government made strikes called without government permission illegal. The following October, Perón consolidated his control over labor by issuing the Law of Professional Associations. This legislation ruled that there could be only one union per industry or economic sector (*sindicato unico*) and that only unions with official government authorization to represent a sector's workers (*personeria gremial* status) could sign a valid collective bargaining contract (which had to be done through the Labor Secretariat).[35]

Personeria gremial status was not granted to the union with the largest membership but to the one the government regarded as most "representative."[36] Thus, if a union resisted Perón's authority, the government would simply deprive it of its personeria gremial status and confer this status on a union in the same industry or sector that was willing to cooperate. Many communist and socialist union leaders who tried to preserve their autonomy were ousted following this scheme. The rank and file helped the purging process, since it was now clear to them that the real benefactor of the working class was not union leaders but Juan Domingo Perón. When union representatives failed to follow *el líder*, as the masses quickly dubbed Perón, many of their fellow workers deserted them.[37] El líder not only encouraged the growth of older industrial unions but unionized the large mass of workers still unorganized. In 1943, there were about twenty-two unions nationwide. In 1953 there were sixty new ones. Consequently, union membership jumped from 450,000 in 1941 to 2.3 million in 1954.[38]

Much has been written about the makeup of Perón's working-class support. Some scholars contended that the recent migrants from the interior were culturally and psychologically inclined to forge a charismatic bond with the new caudillo. "These migrants had left economic circumstances which had become intolerable, but they also left behind what earlier had been a degree of security and a sense of personal identity. Neither was available in their new urban environment. And the migrants from the countryside, accustomed to a patron-client relationship, were perhaps especially willing, if not eager to accept proxy control."[39] Other scholars rejected this hypothesis, arguing that the vote of union workers was more statistically significant than that of recent migrants in the 1946 election. Still others found only slight differences between the backgrounds of migrants and union workers.[40] Neither hypothesis is conclusively proved, and some of these works have been flawed by inferential fallacies. In the end, "both the migrants and organized workers were important in Perón's electoral coalition, though obviously at key points in Perón's rise to power it was the organizational capacity of the union movement that was crucial in massive support demonstrations."[41]

In fact, the CGT's call for a general strike and mass demonstrations on 17 October 1945 forced the military officers, who had arrested Perón few days earlier, to release him.[42] The officers opposed both Perón's use of the government to build personal support and the politicization of the labor movement. Some were eager to leave government and return to the barracks. Later, the newly created Labor party nominated Perón for president.[43]

After Perón became president, few additional labor laws were passed, and these were enacted by the Peronist-controlled Congress. The constitution of 1949 (repealed in 1956) incorporated many decrees previously enacted and added unemployment compensation, an eight-hour workday, and a forty-eight-hour workweek. Unions were also given constitutional status and were allowed, for the first time, to participate as a corporate interest in politics. A bill for the Rights of the Worker was also passed, which however noticeably omitted the right to strike. Besides these legal accomplishments, the president made sure that the economic well-being of the working class improved. Although inflation rose after 1946, wages rose even faster. In 1948 real wages for unskilled workers were 37 percent higher than in 1943; the real wages of skilled workers went up by 24 percent during the same period.[44] As a result, the share of wages in terms of national income rose from 38 percent in 1935–1936 to 46 percent by 1953–1955; the government provided accident and sickness insurance and retirement programs; and the number of people covered by the social security program increased from 500,000 in 1943 to 5 million in 1951.[45]

As the well-being of wage and salary earners was enhanced, so was the power of their unions, thanks to state protection and guidance. At the same time, Perón put unions on solid economic footing. Through the checkoff system for union dues and the administration of social welfare programs, unions began to control large economic resources. Unions also became bureaucratized, and union leaders began to act more like government officials than representatives of the rank and file.[46] Several such leaders were handsomely rewarded by Perón: some were appointed to his cabinet, others became governors, congressmen, chairmen of state corporations and agencies, and mayors. With political influence also came personal wealth, as union leaders not only received fat paychecks but controlled large state funds, which they often could spend in a discretionary manner. Furthermore, in 1950 legislation was passed enabling the CGT, by then dominated by Peronists, to "intervene" (that is, having its bureaucrats taking over the administration of the union) recalcitrant unions by replacing their leadership with CGT bureaucrats. This legislation also enabled Perón to repress strikes by declaring them illegal, something which he was not too fond of when called without his assent.[47] Through the manipulation of the personeria gremial first, and CGT intervention later, Perón purged, one by one, independent union leaders.[48]

Perón put the last touch on government control over collective bargaining by enacting a law in 1953 that allowed the government to make collective bargaining agreements valid nationwide, regulated working conditions and wages, established state compulsory arbitration if capital and labor failed to reach an agreement, and penalized parties that failed to comply with state-supervised contracts.[49] The law gave unions unprecedented bargaining power and de facto monopoly over the regulation of the labor market in a country quickly approaching full employment. It was at this time that the labor movement gained most of the features that made it a key distributional coalition. With collective bargaining and labor legislation biased in their favor, unions could demand job protection and wage hikes regardless of productivity and efficiency. Entrepreneurs gave in to these demands, since they operated a heavily protected economy and received a host of government incentives in the form of subsidized credit and tax breaks. They simply passed both labor and production costs on to consumers. This tradeoff led to collusion between labor and management, and as a result, prices and wages were kept artificially high, discouraging both investments and productivity. The loser was of course the citizen, both as consumer and taxpayer.[50] Although the 1953 law was modified by later governments, many of its basic tenets remained in place until the early 1990s.

Besides conferring material benefits, Perón manipulated workers by reminding them of his social justice policies. He constantly referred to his administration as the government "of the people." As time went on, his wife, Evita, became the principal agent of this indoctrination campaign. A very effective public speaker, Evita broadened popular support for her husband, among not only unionized workers but the poor, by dispensing favors through her own charitable foundation. Moreover, Perón boosted Argentine nationalism through the nationalization of foreign-owned enterprises (mainly British and German) and by speeding up the ISI. Such initiatives, coupled with diplomatic efforts to promote Argentina as a regional power, were aimed at portraying Perón as the ultimate defender of economic independence from the United States and Western Europe.

The price for all this was the complete subservience of the labor movement to Juan Domingo Perón. First, Perón destroyed the Labor party, whose leaders, even though loyal to him, were determined to be independent of the government. The Labor party had been created a week after the 17 October rally by union leaders like Luis Gay (telephone workers) and Cipriano Reyes (meat packers).[51] In May 1946, Perón announced that the three political parties that had supported his presidential candidacy (the Labor party, the Renewal Committee of the UCR, and those pro-Perón conservative splinter groups organized in the Independent Centers) would unite into the Single Party of the Revolution (renamed Peronist party in 1947). Most laborites went along with the reorganization plan. Gay, Reyes, and a few others tried to keep the Labor party alive. Perón, however, refused to allow any organization to compete with him for the allegiance of the workers, and thus the Labor party was banned shortly before the 1948 congressional elections.

Having dissolved the Labor party and purged most communist and socialist unions, el líder was left with nearly total control of the labor movement.[52] The CGT became a docile instrument of the administration's policies, and its leadership was filled with personal friends of the president. In 1950, the CGT's statute was changed to make it completely subordinated to Perón. In 1951, the CGT was the main factor in mobilizing electoral support for Perón's reelection. A year later, it docilely accepted Perón's request for a two-year wage freeze to meet the unfolding economic crisis. The president continued to receive the overwhelming support of the working class, drawing upon his political capital built up during the golden years of redistributive policies (1946–1948). However, the initial enthusiasm was no longer there. The burden of the austerity policies did not fall upon union leaders, who now enjoyed an enviable social status and salaries, but on the rank and file. During the 1949–1955 period, the real income of industrial workers averaged a 28 percent decline.[53] With the regime having consolidated itself, union meetings and worker participation in union affairs were discouraged, as were strikes.[54] Nonetheless, wildcat strikes did occur to protest contracts signed by bureaucratized leaders without consulting workers.[55] Moreover, Evita died in 1952, and Perón thus lost the one person creating an emotional bond between him and the masses. By the time Perón was overthrown, much of the nationalistic rhetoric had also faded. Economic difficulties had forced the president to invite previously vilified foreign companies to invest in the country under more favorable terms.

The Proscription of Peronism (1955–1966)

With Perón's overthrow, organized labor received a severe blow, from which it only momentarily recovered during the brief interlude of the third Peronist administration (1973–1976). From being the privileged ally of the state, the labor movement was confronted with administrations that wanted to severely restrict its autonomy. Perón had curtailed union autonomy through co-optation. His successors, tried to depoliticize (that is, to end the Peronist hegemony within the labor leadership) and emasculate union bargaining power vis-à-vis government and business. Three main strategies were used to achieve this end: repression, bargaining, and co-optation.[56] The first strategy became identified with authoritarian regimes (1955–1958, 1966–1973, 1976–1983) and consisted of eliminating or restricting the right to strike, suspending union rights to negotiate collective bargaining agreements, imprisoning union activists, intervening in the affairs of defiant unions, and pitting rival union factions against each other. The second strategy was used by minority Radical governments (1958–1962, 1963–1966), whose legitimacy was in dispute due to the ban on Peronist electoral participation. This strategy used government-supervised collective bargaining agreements to keep unions in line and to force compliance with the administration's economic policy. The third strategy was resumed by Héctor Cámpora and Juan Perón in 1973. It postulated the creation of a government-sponsored social pact according to which labor and capital restrained their demands in return for active involvement in the decision-making process.

Disagreement over the best response to such strategies (particularly by non-Peronist governments) has divided the labor movement ever since.[57] The paramount concerns of many unionists were to keep collective bargaining free from government interference and to retain control of their unions. In other words, to avoid government intervention. For diehard Peronist union leaders whose power and authoritarian methods had turned them into real bosses, "Peronism had given . . . them a taste for power and it remained the shortest route to regaining it."[58] Thus, any solution that fell short of a return to the good old days was unacceptable.

On the other hand, although Perón's authority remained unquestionable, his exile made it possible for maverick union leaders inclined to compromise, like Augusto Vandor, to gain leadership over parts of the movement. So-called pragmatic leaders had no difficulty in cooperating with authoritarian governments; after all, many had acquired their positions through Perón's authoritarian measures and were willing to make a deal as long as they could retain control of their unions. There were three groups of leaders, "those who sought accommodation with governments judged too dangerous to attack, those who urged strikes or other forms of collective action as the only means to preserve existing union gains, and those between the extremes who tried to negotiate for themselves a limited autonomy based on a combination of threats and potential cooperation."[59]

Strikes or the simple threat of strikes proved most effective under weak Radical governments. General strikes, in particular, had the effect of bringing all economic activities to a halt. Ministrikes, production slowdowns, and even sabotage of equipment were additional means to the same end. Strikes assumed a crucial importance for the simple fact that in Argentina the supply of labor was scarce and a large majority of the working force was unionized. These conditions enhanced union leaders' bargaining power vis-à-vis government and management. Besides strikes, the lobbying of government officials and agencies constituted an alternative approach. In a country where Congress was often either ignored by civilian presidents or closed down by authoritarian ones, exercising direct pressure on the presidency and key government officials was an important option. Finally, the labor movement used the ballot box to demonstrate its political muscle. Even during the proscription of Peronism, the labor movement played a crucial role in Frondizi's election in 1958 and in the 1962 and 1965 midterm elections, when they backed neo-Peronist candidates.

Disagreement within the labor movement was not confined to response strategies but also arose over ideological stance, personal rivalries, and cleavages within the Peronist movement.[60] Ideological confusion arose from the very nature of the Peronist phenomenon. Perón was never concerned with ideological matters; his justicialismo, or social justice, was as appealing as it was elusive. It claimed to be guided by "Christian and humanist" principles, to be neither capitalist nor socialist, although it aspired to synthesize the best "attributes [of] collectivism and individualism, idealism and materialism."[61] Perón was essentially a pragmatist, who "would never sacrifice practicality on the altar of ideological coherence."[62] Justicialismo was his catchall term, which people could interpret as they would. Marxists, Christian Democrats, and neofascists could all sympathize with justicialismo, and of course Perón avoided any clarification; the confusion that arose from this ambiguity made it possible for both left-wing and right-wing groups to claim to be true representatives of Peronism. Although Perón was indeed a conservative and most of the trade union leaders were adamantly anticommunist, Peronist youth groups and some trade unionists between the late 1960s and early 1970s were decidedly leftist. Such contradictions collided in 1973, as Peronist factions fought each other for control of the government.

Cleavages over party politics constituted an additional source of tension. Due to the long ban on the Peronist party, unionists acted as the representative of both labor and the Peronist movement as a whole. However, with the legalization of the party in 1973–1976 and again in 1983, the union leaders of the Peronist "62 organizations" tried to establish their dominance over the party. Other labor factions were more willing to subordinate themselves to party politicians or were not interested in the party at all, preferring to bypass the party and deal with government and other interest groups directly.[63]

Finally, rivalries among labor leaders were another major source of labor rift. This was partly due to the bureaucratization process of the first two Peronist administrations. Many union leaders became influential power brokers and were often busier playing politics with the government and other interest groups than listening to rank-and-file demands. On top of that, their ability to manipulate union elections allowed many leaders to lead their unions for extended periods of time. Between 1958 and 1969, Vandor, the leader of the powerful UOM and the "62 organizations" tried to take over the leadership of labor by acting independently of Perón.[64] This, of course sparked the opposition—first of loyalists like José Alonso of the clothing workers and later of leftists like Raimundo Ongaro of the graphic workers. In the 1980s, CGT General Secretary Saúl Ubaldini, UOM's Lorenzo Miguel, and Jorge Triaca, leader of the Commission of Management and Labor (Comisión Gestión y Trabajo, or CGyT) and later of the Group of 15, competed against each other, thus preventing any one of them from becoming dominant.

Keeping these cleavages in mind, we will now examine the chronology of labor factionalism from 1955 to 1966. A couple of months after Perón's ouster, the labor movement became the principal target of the Aramburu administration's full-scale attempt to de-Peronize Argentine society. To this end, Aramburu outlawed union participation in politics, jailed Peronist union leaders, put military officers in charge of the CGT, and limited the right to strike. Aramburu also encouraged "democratic" leadership (that is, non-Peronist) in Peronist-dominated unions.[65] In 1957, Aramburu convened union delegates in a congress whose explicit aim was to return the CGT to non-Peronist union leaders. However, much to the disappointment of the government, a majority of the delegates were Peronist.[66] Some older unions returned to communist, socialist, Radical, and anarchist control. As a consequence of the squabbles, the congress was suspended and the "normalization" (that is, the return to a legally elected union leadership) of the CGT was postponed.[67] The political sectors that emerged in the aborted congress soon came to be referred to by the number of unions they controlled in 1956. The Peronists were grouped in the "62," the Communists in the "19," and the noncommunist, anti-Peronist in the "32." This latter group, referring itself as the "democratic unions," had supported the 1955 coup. In 1958, some unions in the "62" and the "32" abandoned them to form the Independents.

Under Arturo Frondizi, government strategy switched from confrontation to bargaining, at least initially. As part of the electoral deal made with Perón in 1958, Frondizi had Congress pass legislation (1) establishing a new labor law favoring a Peronist takeover of most unions, (2) recalling legislation that banned Peronist political activity and restricted the right to strike, and (3) conferring amnesty for political crimes. However, the ban on the Peronist party and on Perón's return to Argentina remained, and the "normalization" of the CGT was postponed to avert a military reaction. These actions only strengthened Peronist influence over the labor movement—at the expense mostly of the communists, who were left in control of only a dozen unions. The Group of 32 almost disappeared, with many of its former unions joining the Independents. The Independents came to comprise mostly white-collar unions in the service sector, whereas the Peronist "62" had its stronghold in the industrial sector. In making these concessions to Peronist unionism, Frondizi was not merely respecting his electoral deal. Equally important was his hope of making the labor movement more representative (given that despite the repression years the rank and file had remained heavily Peronist) and more responsible. That is, labor would restrain its wage demands and collaborate with the administration.

When the strategy collapsed and strikes broke out, Frondizi resorted to carrot-and-stick tactics. He did not hesitate to use the state of siege and imprisonment of union activists to brake union unrest. However, he refrained from abolishing the just-reinstated labor law from which Peronist unionism had regained its political leverage, hoping that such a sign would induce unions to bargain. Particularly after 1959, the president pursued his integrationist policy unevenly (see chapter 2), talking to labor when necessary and trying to conquer it when possible.[68]

In January 1963, following Frondizi's overthrow, the CGT held its second national convention since 1955. The two main groups at the time, the "62" and the Independents, agreed to equally divide the seats of the CGT governing body and to leave out the communists, by now reduced to a handful of unions. In the final analysis, the Peronists got the best part of the deal. They outmaneuvered the Independents and elected a leader of the "62," José Alonso, as the CGT's new general secretary. Having prevailed over the Independents, the "62" began to experience factionalism in its own ranks. About this time, Vandor began to gather the moderate unions around him in order to challenge Perón's leadership within the Peronist movement. To counter Vandor's plans, Alonso took on the leadership of Perón's backers, the so-called orthodox, or Alonsistas. The Alonsistas, on orders from Perón, adopted a confrontational approach to the Guido and Illia administrations, usually in the form of violent strikes. Vandor, on the other hand, was more likely to compromise to avoid renewed government intervention in the CGT.

Illia's expansionary economic policies, coupled with the termination of Frondizi's IMF agreement and oil concessions to foreign corporations, initially seemed likely to gain union support. Moreover, the president allowed substantial wage increases, since workers' purchasing power had deteriorated during Frondizi's austerity program. Illia's strategy had two main objectives. "First, he hoped that the opportunity for normal electoral participation would encourage the Peronists to abandon the massive use of strikes and other disruptive tactics, leading them instead to work within the existing political framework. Second, he tried to weaken the Peronists politically and to convince workers that his own UCRP was a more effective vehicle for achieving their political aspirations."[69]

Disagreement soon arose on how to respond to Illia's challenge, pitting Vandor against the orthodox factions. In May 1964, the Peronist-dominated CGT called for a Battle Plan to protest against Illia's economic policies and his failure to lift all restrictions on Peronist electoral participation. A wave of general strikes and factory occupations followed, seriously disrupting economic activity from May to June. The Independents participated in the early stages of the Battle Plan, but they subsequently abandoned it because they thought it was becoming too partisan (that is, pro-Peronist rather than prolabor). In the aftermath, the Independents withdrew from the CGT, leaving the two factions of the "62" to fight for control of the organization.

In February 1966, Vandor finally prevailed and engineered Alonso's removal from the position of general secretary of the CGT. Although Alonso was eventually replaced by Francisco Prado of the light and power workers union, the real power in the CGT was now Vandor. In response, the Alonso and orthodox faction of the "62" created an alternative organization, the 62 *de pie.* Eventually, the defecting unions rejoined the CGT but refused to take part in its leadership.[70]

From Authoritarian Rule to Peronism and
Back to Dictatorship (1966–1983)

On the eve of the 1966 coup, the Peronists despite their rivalries controlled about 70 percent of the labor movement. The rest was shared by communists and Independents.[71] Shortly after Onganía seized power in 1966, the CGT suffered another crisis. The source of the conflict originated over the best response to adopt toward the Onganía regime despite the fact that both Alonso and Vandor had been instrumental in triggering the coup and welcomed it. At its inception, nationalist members of the Onganía administration tried to work out a deal with Alonso to divide and rule union power. For his part, Alonso hoped to convince Onganía to give unionism an active role in the new administration. The deal was short-lived, partly because a cabinet reshuffle eliminated most of the nationalists in December 1966 and partly because Vandor actively undermined it. In fact, Vandor launched a general strike that month.

The success of the strike induced Vandor to convince the CGT to organize the Action Plan (Plan de Acción), which resembled the earlier Battle Plan. The aim of the Action Plan was twofold. On the one hand, it aimed at forcing government concessions on wages and on the general content of economic policy; on the other hand, it tried to permanently defeat Alonso while keeping in check the most militant sectors of left-wing unionism. Onganía responded to the initiative with a series of repressive measures. After the strike of 1 March 1967, the government stripped six major unions of their personería gremial status and froze their bank accounts. The consequences were obvious: these unions could no longer represent their workers in collective bargaining negotiations and lost enormous amounts of funds, since employers were no longer obliged to deduct workers' dues and transfer them into union welfare funds. The CGT and Vandor were left with no option but to call off the Action Plan. The aborted plan was a total defeat for labor. The government now demanded the abandonment of union militancy and gave no clear guarantees in return.

Those unions in favor of at least a degree of cooperation with the government, led by Juan José Taccone (light and power workers) and Rogelio Coria (construction workers), created what was referred to as the participationist CGT. A second group was made up of Vandor's followers; it tried to keep its Peronist identity but was willing to compromise with the new regime on occasion. A third group, the oppositionist CGT, was represented by unions determined to oppose Onganía. Its leader was Raimundo Ongaro. Of the three, only the participationist CGT was officially recognized by the government, although informal talks were held with Vandor as well.[72]

In 1967, the government intervened in several oppositionist unions and arrested many of their leaders. Strikes and union political involvement were made illegal. Recalcitrant unions were stripped of their personería gremial status, and their financial and real estate assets were seized by the government.[73] Nonetheless, Onganía refrained from the harsh repression adopted by Aramburu in 1955.[74] He tried to find a working relationship with Vandor and with those participationists willing to make deals, while repressing the rest. However, in June 1969 Vandor was assassinated. A unionist whose loyalty was to the workers rather than to Perón, Vandor had been the dominant figure in the country's labor movement since the late 1950s. While he had harassed authoritarian and Radical administrations alike, his main intent had been to protect the interests of rank-and-file members and to reincorporate politically a Peronist constituency acceptable to anti-Peronist forces. His death left the Vandoristas leaderless and the participationist CGT virtually isolated, as Ongaro boycotted any compromise with the government and torpedoed the reunification of the CGT.[75] Shortly after Vandor's assassination, Onganía intervened in the CGT, something he had tried to avoid before in order to keep a communication channel with labor open.

Internal squabbles continued to plague unionism until 1973, when Perón reunited most of the labor movement behind Cámpora's election bid. While in exile, Perón supported the left-wing faction of Peronist unionism as an additional means to thwart Vandor's ambitions. After Vandor's death, Perón continued to use the leftwing unionists who had emerged out of the Cordobazo, as well as the montoneros, to create political instability in order to accelerate his return. Once Perón was back in power, left-wing unionism was his enemy once more, just as it had been until 1955, and it was purged.

The Peronist victory in the 1973 election put labor back in the center of the decision-making process. Through Cámpora's and Perón's mediation, the CGT and the CGE agreed to a social pact supervised by the government. The pact called for a four-year stabilization program to fight inflation. It consisted of a first period (two years), during which labor would voluntarily refrain from asking for wage increases, in exchange for redistributive measures favoring wage earners to be implemented in the second period—when it was hoped prices would have stabilized. To thwart rank-and-file demands for higher wages, which would jeopardize the pact, Perón strengthened conservative union bosses' control over labor by extending their terms of office and enhancing their authority over the workers.[76] One of the measures adopted to this end was the reintroduction of the CGT's right to "intervene" in recalcitrant unions, a provision that was used to purge many left-wing and non-Peronist unionists and to curtail the right to strike.[77]

However, the situation quickly began to unravel, and the social pact collapsed soon after Perón's death in 1974. In mid-1975, with the ousting of the ultraconservative Peronist faction headed by Minister of Social Welfare José López Rega, which had gained prominence after Perón's death, the "62" leader Lorenzo Miguel became the gray eminence behind the Isabel Perón administration. Taking advantage of Isabel's weakness, Miguel not only gained large (although ephemeral, as hyperinflation wiped them out) wage increases but also established the "62" as the dominant force over both labor and the Justicialist party. The "8" and the antiverticalistas, two splinter groups of the "62" that opposed Miguel, tried to undermine his leadership, but to no avail.[78] It would take the military to end Miguel's hegemony. Right after the 1976 coup, the "62" was outlawed and Miguel was jailed and later confined to house arrest. Many more were less fortunate. The security forces made union leaders and the rank and file the prime targets of their repressive strategy in order to destroy the only distributional coalition that could stand in the way of the armed forces' plans for economic and political restructuring. Over 300 labor leaders were arrested; others went into exile. Thirty percent of the 8,690 people who disappeared during the dictatorship were union members.

The armed forces' intervention that initiated the Proceso was aimed at drastically reducing union power. Besides taking care of Miguel and the "62," the military quickly enacted a number of repressive measures. The CGT and more than thirty of the nation's largest unions were taken over and their financial assets put under military control. Collective bargaining was revoked, the right to strike was suspended, and those unions spared from intervention were forbidden to engage in political activity. The military establishment's long-term goal was to clear labor of its "subversive" elements and turn it, once it had been "domesticated," into a docile support group for the new regime.[79] Union leaders who had not actively participated in the coup saw it as a "lesser evil" than complete chaos. As a matter of fact, unions that were not taken over (for the most part medium- and small-sized unions) began a series of meetings with the junta and other high-ranking officers in the weeks following the coup, hoping to find a working relationship with the new authorities. These leaders were willing to collaborate in spite of the arrests and kidnappings of many of their colleagues for several reasons. First, some Peronist leaders who had survived the purge had opposed Miguel and Isabel Perón and saw in their demotion an opportunity to gain more leverage within labor. Second, some Peronist groups that had collaborated with Onganía in 1966 were willing to subordinate themselves to the new military design. Third, UCR-affiliated or nonaligned leaders were trying to keep control of their unions. In sum, political survival was the name of the game.

For its part, the military establishment was hardly united on the best strategy to adopt with regard to these surviving unions. Some, like Interior Minister General Horacio Liendo and junta member Admiral Emilio Massera, believed that labor should be co-opted to support the government, while Third Army Corps chief General Luciano Menéndez and General Carlos Suárez Masón were for all-out annihilation.[80] Such division bought union leaders precious time to reorganize. After all, military officers and labor bosses shared a common concern: keeping left-wing elements from making inroads among workers. In fact, after the Cordobazo in 1969, the Peronist youth movement, the montoneros, and the Trotskyite ERP, had began to infiltrate the rank and file to spread their contending visions of class struggle and socialist revolution and to attack the labor bureaucracy for being an ally of capitalism.[81] In the end, the military moderates prevailed, reasoning that leaving unionists willing to collaborate in place was the best way to thwart Marxism. After all, as the Onganía experience had proven, labor could be a useful interlocutor.[82]

Between 1976 and early 1982, the main strategy "was one of mixed efforts by the labor leadership to engage in dialogue, cooperate, and collaborate with the dictatorship while simultaneously criticizing the economic policies and trying to resist the Proceso's project."[83] Labor leaders found themselves walking the razor's edge. On the one hand, they were under pressure to comply with the new economic policies. On the other hand, they had to deal with strong rank-and-file demands to maintain wage levels and union privileges. The divisions that arose from such a strategy, personal rivalries aside, rested on how to cooperate and to what extent cooperation had to be pursued. In March 1977, twenty-five unions, five of which had been taken over, formed the Group of 25, which would attempt to increase their bargaining power vis-à-vis the government. In November 1977 the country was shaken by a wave of rank-and-file strikes, which forced the government to make wage concessions and to recognize that negotiation with the union leadership was necessary to keep workers' demands in line. In April 1978, a moderate group within the Group of 25 seceded and formed the Management and Labor Committee (Comisión Gestión y Trabajo or CGyT), which was led by, among others, Jorge Triaca of the plastic workers.[84]

The Group of 25 wanted to preserve its Peronist identity. The CGyT, on the other hand, while still claiming allegiance to Peronism, contended that the old populist tactics advocated by the Group of 25 were ineffective to achieve social justice and proposed a more pragmatic unionism. A further source of division between the two stemmed from the fact that the goal of the Group of 25 was to gain concessions by making tactical alliances with the church, business groups, and nationalist officers, while avoiding hostile behavior. The CGyT, on the other hand, claimed that the old populist model was useless and that workers were best served by collaborating with the capital accumulation policies of the Proceso.[85] In June, another moderate dissenting group left the Group of 25 and joined the CGyT, which led to the creation of the National Commission of Labor (Comisión Nacional de Trabajo, or CNT).

Splits and regroupings continued to weaken labor's bargaining position, which suffered another blow when, in November 1979, the military enacted a new law of professional associations. The new legislation not only incorporated many of the measures adopted in 1976 but formally dissolved the CGT; the Ministry of Labor was given greater authority to intervene in union matters, and the administration of welfare funds and services, which provided labor with great economic power, was taken over by military officers.[86] The military's objective was the regimentation and emasculation of labor unions so that they would be strong enough to discipline the rank and file but too weak to articulate political demands.[87]

Between 1979 and 1982 quarrels between labor moderates and hardliners grew. Within the Group of 25, Saúl Ubaldini (a little-known leader from the small beer workers union) took the lead of the most combative union sectors. He was instrumental in organizing a general strike in 1979 (the first since 1976) and again in 1981 and 1982, despite harsh government repression. He also became a prominent figure in the new (but still illegal) CGT (which later would take the name CGT-Brasil and, subsequently, CGT–Republica Argentina), organized in November 1980. Ubaldini made negotiations with the government dependent upon political concessions.

Triaca's CNT and other minor groups that had maintained close ties with military leaders resented Ubaldini's aggressive stand and organized a rival CGT, which took the name of CGT-Azopardo.[88] Miguel, who had been released from prison in 1980, gave his support to Ubaldini and the CGT-Brasil. Although Miguel, like Triaca, was a conservative who favored compromise with the military and emphasized bread-and-butter issues over ideology, he feared that Triaca could become too powerful. He did not regard Ubaldini, who had no power base of his own, a threat and probably believed he could use him to accomplish his own plans against Triaca. Adding to the confusion was the fact that minority groups within many unions joined either the CGT-Brasil or the CGT-Azopardo, depending on which organization the official leadership had adhered to. For instance, twenty-six UOM locals that opposed Miguel joined the CGT-Azopardo. This constant swinging of subgroups made it difficult at the time to assess the relative strength of the two organizations and to pinpoint who was with whom.

Although the military had kept labor in check until 1981, things began to unravel after General Videla left office in March. Union aggressiveness and influence increased progressively with the deterioration of the Proceso. During the brief interval of the Falklands/Malvinas war, the regime gained some breathing room. In the wave of nationalism that swept the country in those days, union leaders found themselves in the odd situation of supporting the regime's action both at home and abroad.[89] Some union leaders traveled to North America and Europe to justify to foreigners the military conflict; in return, jailed CGT members were freed. However, the honeymoon lasted only a matter of weeks. As soon as the war with Britain was lost, all labor factions united to demand the armed forces' withdrawal from power and the return to constitutional democracy.

In the months preceding the 1983 presidential election most of the contending labor factions momentarily set aside their differences. It was at this time that Miguel and the "62" rose from the ashes, took control of the Peronist campaign, and selected congressional candidates through a series of under-the-table deals with labor leaders and party bosses. However, the unexpected Radical victory that followed shattered Miguel's hegemonic plans and the tenuous alliance he had put together. Pollsters and political analysts ascribed the defeat to, among other things, the collaboration of many Peronist labor bosses with the military regime and their tarnished democratic credentials. Indeed, the CGT leadership was the first to admit that the establishment of Peronist "social justice" was all that mattered. In their view, real democracy was accomplished only when the working class enjoyed a decent standard of living. Without this, democratic freedoms counted for little.

Labor and the Democratic Consolidation (1984–1993)

During the new democratic regime, both Radical and Peronist administrations, as in many other Latin America countries, were forced to implement recessionary policies to remedy the high inflation, huge fiscal deficit, and foreign debt inherited from the military. Such policies led to greater government intervention in labor-management relations. In fact, the anti-inflationary policies hinged upon control of variables like wages, which inevitably translated into a deterioration of workers' purchasing power. This control was to be achieved by government intervention in collective bargaining negotiations, where the government would prevent unions and management from agreeing on wage increases not in line with the government's macroeconomic goals. Of course, the labor movement resisted these attempts to limit its ability to negotiate and repeatedly clashed with both Alfonsín and Menem.

Alfonsín's strategy followed the bargaining pattern of his Radical predecessors. He first tried to undermine the control of Peronist bosses over the union movement through a bill introduced in Congress by Minister of Labor Antonio Mucci (see chapter 2). When this attempt failed, he tried to gain concessions from the unions by withholding legislation on collective bargaining, on a possible social pact, and on the legal status of the CGT and many unions. Further, the precarious status of both the leadership and the internal organization of some unions weakened labor vis-à-vis government. Although half of the officially recognized unions (54 percent) had escaped the military intervention and nearly a third (28 percent) had elected delegates prior to the return to democracy, others were either still under government supervision (8 percent) or were being internally challenged by rival groups because their leaders had been selected by the military (10 percent).[90] The importance of this odd situation was that most of the largest unions fell into the latter 18 percent.

During the Alfonsín government, the crisis of the Peronist movement deeply affected the labor movement as well. Peronist unions, comprising most of the large politically influential unions in the country, broke into four rival factions. The fact that each faction had roughly equal strength prevented the emergence of a unified leadership, fueling instability and suspicion and also depriving the Radical administration of a reliable interlocutor. Collaboration with the administration was a main source of controversy among Peronist labor leaders, in addition to personal, ideological, and party issues.[91]

The Group of 25 was a homogeneous group and suffered few defections (see table 6.3). It was characterized by service sector unions and was headed by relatively young leaders.[92] Its close relationship with the Renovation sector of the PJ allowed it to make demands on the government.[93] Its goal was to promote a more modern type of unionism aimed at strengthening political institutions as channels of interest mediation. As a consequence, its attitude toward the Alfonsín administration was like that of the renovators; when the renovators supported the government on the military trials, the divorce law, the treaty with Chile, and the military uprisings, they did the same. Conversely, they attacked Alfonsín for refusing a moratorium on the external debt. The group was also closer than others to the demands of the rank and file. It emphasized themes like class consciousness and the protection of workers' rights and job security, and it often took an aggressive stance toward capital-labor relations.[94]

The "62" represented traditional Peronist unionism. Although it was weakened by numerous defections, Miguel retained considerable influence by positioning his faction between the Group of 25 and Ubaldini on the left and the Group of 15 on the right.[95] In other words, he acted as a balancer in a multiple-actor game, thus making sure no one would acquire enough power to upset the balance. Accordingly, he endorsed Ubaldini's combative style to force government concessions and to

TABLE 6.3
Union Factions, 1983–1986

Faction	Unions		Membership	Leader	Faction Union Belonged to in 1983	Faction Union Belonged to in 1986
"15"			760,469			
	FATSA	Health Workers	170,900	West Ocampo	CGyt	62
	AB	Bank Employees	156,080	Zanola	62	Ubaldini
	UTGRA	Restaurant	85,481	Barrionuevo	62	62
	AOT	Textile Workers	73,646	Giménez	CGyT	Ubaldini
	FATLyF	Light and Power	69,952	Alderete	CGyT	Ubaldini
	UTA	Bus Drivers	56,214	Palacios	62	Ubaldini
	SMATA	Auto Workers	53,976	Rodríguez	25	25
	FGPIC	Meatpackers	37,667	Romero	62	62
	SUPE	Oil Workers	25,588	Ibáñez	62	62
	UOEP	Plastic Workers	17,975	Triaca	CGyT	62
	SOIVA	Glass Workers	13,000	Millán	Independent	Independent
"25"			764,729			
	CGEC	Retail Workers	408,000	Andreoni	62	25
	UF	Railway Workers	143,304	Pedraza	25	25
	ATE	State Workers	85,927	DeGennaro	62	25
	FNTCOTAC	Truckers	38,964	Pérez	25	25
	FATF	Pharmacists	28,112	Mujica	25	25
	FNCT	Taxi Drivers	24,000	García	25	25
	AOMA	Miners	19,057	Cabrera	25	25
	SOC	Rubber Workers	12,189	Borda	25	25
	SAON	Naval Workers	3,117	Castillo	25	25
	SUETRA	Tobacco Workers	2,059	Digón	25	25

Faction	Unions		Membership	Leader	Faction Union Belonged to in 1983	Faction Union Belonged to in 1986
"62"			268,656			
	UOM	Metalworkers	267,000	Miguel	62	62
	URGA	Silo Workers	1,656	Ponce	62	62
Ubaldini			500,985			
	UOCRA	Construction	186,614	Farías	62	Ubaldini
	FTIA	Food Packiging	148,703	Morán	62	62
	UPCN	Civil Service	133,188	Candore	CGyT	Ubaldini
	FENTOS	Water Workers	18,930	Lingeri	62	Ubaldini
	FONOPP	Hairstylists	7,550	Hernández		
	FOCARA	Beer Workers	6,000	Ubaldini	25	Ubaldini

SOURCE: James McGuire, "Union Factionalism and Democratic Consolidation in Alfonsín's Argentina, 1983–1989," paper prepared for the Midwest Political Association Meeting, Chicago, 5–7 April 1990, p. 31.

isolate Triaca. When Ubaldini obtained sole control of the CGT in 1986, Miguel formed an alliance with Triaca, fearing that Ubaldini's militancy could be ultimately detrimental for negotiations with the government and could gain him too great a following among the rank and file. Finally, when Triaca's Group of 15 got control of the Ministry of Labor in 1986 and again in 1989, Miguel helped the much weakened Ubaldini.[96] Politically, the long-range goal of the leaders of the "62" remained the establishment of a labor-dominated (or better, Miguel-dominated) Justicialist party as a means to achieve the ultimate prize: the control of government and its resources as during 1973–1976.[97] Unlike the Group of 25, the "62" belonged to the right-wing, or orthodox, sector of the Peronist movement. It opposed the divorce law and both communism and social democracy, but it kept a low profile on human rights (its congressional representatives' abstention made possible the passage of the Due Obedience Law) and sympathized with some of the carapintada demands of 1987 and 1988.[98]

Ubaldinismo was the faction around Ubaldini that began in the early 1980s. Ubaldini was a maverick, aggressive union leader, who in spite of his allegiance to Peronism often acted and talked like the old syndicalists. Ubaldini made the general strike the main tool to force the government. His political discourse transcended union interests to include the interests of retirees and the growing number of poor, an approach that gained him considerable support both among the rank and file and the needy.[99] In this sense, he was the quintessential populist labor leader. Although Ubaldini adopted a vaguely leftist rhetoric, he used above all his own personal charisma.[100] By the same token, he downplayed, unlike the Group of 25 and the "62," the role of the PJ, since one of his primary goals was the preservation of labor's and his own independence from government and party interference.

Having no power base of his own, Ubaldini saw in the CGT the vehicle that could help him fulfill his ambitions. Although he soon gained the reputation of being hot-blooded and averse to negotiation, Ubaldini worked his way to the top. In the early 1980s, with Miguel's support, he became a leader of the CGT-Brasil and later of the CGT–Republica Argentina. In 1984 he and Triaca reunited the CGT, sharing its leadership with two other general secretaries.[101] When the Alfonsín administration allowed unions to regain control of CGT (which had been taken over by the military in 1976), delegates to the 1986 CGT "normalizing" congress elected Ubaldini sole general secretary. Throughout his tenure, Ubaldini used the CGT to foster his own political agenda, which was invariably antagonistic and often blindly opposed to the Radical government. To this end, he established close ties with both the Catholic church and business groups to broaden the opposition to Alfonsín's economic policies. Ubaldini refrained from joining either the renovators or the ortho-dox factions of the PJ, preferring to negotiate with them independently.

The Group of 15 was the newest Peronist labor faction (see table 6.3). It was a highly heterogeneous group of pragmatic unionists who once belonged to the "62," the Ubaldinismo, and the CGyT, which Triaca disbanded in 1985. On most issues, it was diametrically opposed to the Group of 25.[102] It was against the debt moratorium and the divorce law, favored U.S. intervention in Central America, sympathized with the carapintadas, and was ambivalent about human rights violations. It emerged in 1987 partly as a result of some moderate leaders' dissatis-faction with Ubaldini's and the Group of 25's strategies, which, despite their aggressiveness against the government, led to few tangible results. Leaders of the Group of 15 were more interested in finding a political solution to socioeconomic problems with the administration.[103] In a sense, the Group of 15 shared the pragmatic and collaborative approach of the participationists of the 1960s and the CGyT of the Proceso, and in fact many of its founding leaders, notably Triaca, were former CGyT af-filiates. The Group of 15 looked to establish a special relationship with the state, as it knew all too well that only control of government levers could accomplish anything. Therefore, unlike the Group of 25 and the "62," the Group of 15 played down the importance of the PJ in articu-lating labor interests.[104] Alfonsín, whose stabilization policies were fall-ing apart by early 1987, saw an agreement with the Group of 15 as an occasion to divide and conquer the Peronist movement and buy some time. It could both weaken Ubaldini and the Group of 25 within labor and deepen the split between the up-and-coming renovators and the or-thodox factions within the PJ, as many Group of 15 leaders were close to the latter.[105]

In April 1987, the Alfonsín administration gave the Group of 15 gen-erous wage increases, above the government's guidelines. Moreover, one of its prominent leaders, Carlos Alderete of the light and power workers, was put in charge of the Ministry of Labor, and the govern-ment pledged to pass new labor legislation, replacing the 1979 Law of Professional Associations and reestablishing collective bargaining provisions. In return, the Group of 15 which at the time was numeri-cally the strongest faction of all, made sure that labor unrest would be minimal.[106] However, the Alfonsín-Group of 15 alliance lasted only six months. In fact, the unwillingness of Minister of the Economy Juan Sourrouille to involve Alderete in the definition of economic policy, par-ticularly on matters such as wage indexing, relative prices, and taxes, created tensions within the cabinet. The administration also kept post-poning the new bill regulating collective bargaining.[107] With the Radical defeat in the September 1987 congressional elections, the Group of 15 reasoned that Alfonsín's capacity to deliver had become minimal and any further association with the administration was counterproductive. In September, Alderete resigned, thus ending the brief alliance.

From September 1987 until May 1989 relations between government and unions remained tense. In 1988, Alfonsín and the Peronist leadership, headed by Buenos Aires Governor Antonio Cafiero, worked out a compromise that enabled Congress to pass the new laws regarding professional associations and collective bargaining. The new legislation was favorable to labor and allowed unrestricted free collective bargaining. It represented a sound defeat for Sourrouille and his economic team because the two laws curbed the Ministry of the Economy's ability to control prices and salaries, two of the major policy tools adopted during the Austral Plan. From then on, labor and capital could freely negotiate wage increases thus severely limiting Sourrouille's margin of maneuver. Notwithstanding these concessions, CGT militancy remained unabated until a few weeks before the 1989 presidential elections, when Menem asked a reluctant Ubaldini to stop further labor conflicts to avoid alienating middle-class voters.

The Peronist primary elections of 1988 saw CGT factions positioning themselves in different ways. From the start, the Group of 25 endorsed the renovator candidate, Cafiero, whereas the Group of 15 supported Menem. While the Group of 25's decision was consistent with its past behavior, the Group of 15's decision was more a matter of survival.[108] After breaking with Alfonsín, the 15 found itself estranged from both the PJ and the CGT. Therefore, Menem might give it an opportunity to rejoin mainstream Peronism and to be directly involved in government decision making. Ubaldini avoided taking sides, while Miguel threw his support to Menem, who promised labor greater political influence in his administration than Cafiero did. Once Menem gained the PJ's nomination, all four Peronist labor factions backed him; however, it was the Group of 15 that took the lead in organizing and funding his presidential campaign. Once in office, Menem rewarded the Group of 15 by naming Triaca minister of labor. In addition, the president named his closest ally within the Group of 15, Luis Barrionuevo of the hotel and restaurant workers, to head the ANSSAL (Administración Nacional del Seguro de Salud, or National Administration of Health Insurance), the powerful government agency in charge of allocating funds for health and pension plans administered by each union.[109] Barrionuevo readily gave subsidies to the labor-run welfare programs of Menemista unions, while ignoring Ubaldini's followers.

Menem's overture to labor ended shortly after his inauguration. Peronist unionism had jumped on Menem's bandwagon on the assumption that, once elected, he would forge a social pact as promised and that labor would play a major role in it. Not only did the social pact fail to materialize, but Menem adopted a strategy clearly aimed at destroying union political and economic power. From 1989 to 1992 the president used co-optation but in an entirely different way. Under Perón, co-optation was used to increase union members' socioeconomic status in return for decreased autonomy. Under Menem, co-optation meant labor support for the government's restructuring program. It also entailed the unions' acceptance of a dependent role in return for selective incentives benefiting those unions willing to cooperate and repression for those that did not. While this strategy may look similar to those employed by authoritarian regimes, the crucial difference was that Menem could claim to be the legitimate leader of Peronism. If the union bosses were true Peronists, they had to follow the new líder. This was the trap in which the union establishment found itself. Co-optation was demanded to avoid even greater damage.

Understandably, Menem's shock therapy treatment for hyperinflation was hardly what the union leadership had hoped for. Instead of giving wage earners the promised wage hike, or *salariazo*, Menem's economic policies aimed at restoring a free-market economy through privatizating state corporations, cutting state subsidies for domestic enterprises, reducing public employment, and opening the economy to foreign competition. In May 1990, the president sent to Congress a legislative proposal aimed at restricting the right to strike by public service unions. When legislators refused to approve the bill, Menem issued an executive order in October to attain the same end, thus bypassing Congress.[110] The unexpected alliance forged by Menem with conservative political groups and business distributional coalitions shattered the labor movement's hope for a social pact and for labor leaders' involvement in economic policy making. Although under Perón state interventionism had reached its peak, Menem, claiming to follow el líder's teachings, promised to go down in history as the state-shrinking president. Menem asked for labor compliance with his policies and more belt tightening. Triaca went so far as to propose a two-year strike freeze to create a favorable business environment and to attract investors. To union leaders who thought before May 1989 that Menem would usher in a new era of prolabor government, the announcement of the stabilization package the following July must have been a nightmare. In sum, Menem wanted to use labor as much as labor wanted to use Menem, the only difference being that Menem gained the upper hand, at least for the time being.

Bewildered and angered, many union leaders accused the president of betraying Perón's ideals, with Ubaldini publicly warning he would not waste any time by calling a general strike. However, Menem appears to have been not so different from Perón. El líder never liked strikes against his policies, nor did he like independent unionism; as a matter of fact he repressed it.[111] Perón asked workers for a two-year wage freeze and abstention from strikes upon implementing the 1952 economic emergency plan. The most crucial difference between the two men was that Perón in early 1952 could still draw the workers' support due to the distributive policies of his early years in office; in 1989 Menem took over a bankrupt country and had nothing to give in return for sacrifices.

Menem knew quite well that, although divided, labor had the potential to torpedo any stabilization plan. Therefore, he moved to remove the main source of opposition to his policies, namely Ubaldini. When the CGT leader turned down his offer of either an ambassadorial post in Europe or the Argentine seat in the International Labor Organization in Geneva, Menem proceeded to undercut Ubaldini's power base. With the support of Triaca and Barrionuevo, Menem put together a pro-administration labor group made up largely of unions in the Group of 15 but also including defectors from the other three CGT factions. This group took the name of the Union Liaison Board (Mesa de Enlace Sindical). In October 1989, a special CGT congress was convened to elect a new executive committee. In a preliminary vote for the congress's governing board, Guerino Andreoni of the shop workers (a member of the "25" and a former deputy of Ubaldini) led the pro-Menem group and defeated Ubaldini by obtaining the votes of 940 of the 1,635 union delegates present.[112] Ubaldini, claiming that the election had been rigged, walked out of the congress, along with many supporters, thus splitting the CGT after only five years of united leadership. Andreoni's victory did not necessarily mean a victory for Menem. Ubaldini, with the backing of Miguel's UOM and other important unions, refused to relinquish his post. As a result, two CGTs arose from the congress: the CGT-Azopardo, loyal to Ubaldini, and the CGT–San Martín, headed by Andreoni.

The split followed no clear-cut division. This scrambling may have been the result of the lack of a clear winner, which forced many union bosses during 1989 and 1990 to shift from one CGT to the other, depending on the circumstances of the moment. Although Andreoni had nominally won, he still faced substantial opposition. Conversely, Ubaldini was unable or unwilling to call a general strike against the Peronist administration in spite of his repeated warnings in this direction. In the months that followed, the unions in the state sector, threatened by Menem's privatization policies and cutbacks in public employment, supported Ubaldini, whereas private sector unions, as long as they received substantial wage increases and preferential treatment from the government, accepted the president's policies. This was true of Miguel, who in December 1990 traded his support of privatization for a hefty wage hike for his metalworkers and additional funds from Barrionuevo's ANSSAL (Barrionuevo resigned shortly afterward amid allegations of corruption).

Miguel's defection greatly weakened Ubaldini, as it became clear to unionists that support for Ubaldini meant substantial economic losses and political isolation. As a result, by early 1991 Ubaldini was left primarily with large but economically weak government workers' unions, representing only around one quarter of unionized workers.[113] Miguel, in the meantime, had positioned himself in the center of the labor movement, as the balancer between contending factions. He was joined by an increasing number of union leaders who found it advantageous to leave either CGT sector and bargain directly with the government. In July 1991, Miguel convinced the estranged Barrionuevo and Ubaldini to form an alliance to revive the "62" in order to unite Peronist unionism against the administration's policies. As in the past, what convinced these union leaders (Barrionuevo-Ubaldini-Miguel, or BUM) to set their differences momentarily aside was a short-term goal, namely, to kill a bill the government was to introduce in Congress that would allow employers to fire without severance pay. More generally, BUM expressed the frustration and anger of Peronist union bosses for having been left out of the decision-making process. As Barrionuevo put it, "we labor leaders have given him [Menem] a blank check, but now the cutbacks by the technocrats and the requests for money to fire workers are going to stop."[114]

Yet BUM did not last long. Shunned by the CGT–San Martín, which continued to support Menem, the three union bosses split again as the September 1991 midterm election came to a close. All three ended up supporting or heading (in the case of Ubaldini) tickets in direct competition with official Peronist candidates sponsored by Menem, and all three suffered burning defeats. The defeat was particularly embarrassing for Ubaldini, whose bid for the governorship of Buenos Aires received only 2.3 percent of the vote.

Menem's strategy to control labor, although not completely successful, had pushed recalcitrant unions into a corner by the end of 1991. This was particularly true of the public sector where the president used the compulsory arbitration spelled out by the antistrike executive order to force unions to accept wage settlements. He also resorted to stripping the personeria gremial status of striking unions, which made any strike action automatically illegal. Striking workers of the telephone, railway, and oil companies were fired; some of these dismissals were eventually revoked, but only after the unions had capitulated on many of their demands. Equally significant was the fact that many labor leaders, while expressing support for the fired workers, stopped short of criticizing the government, with the clear intention of avoiding a new confrontation with Menem. In the aftermath of the 1991 elections, sensing that opinion was shifting in favor of the administration's policies, Minister of the Economy Domingo Cavallo declared illegal "strikes called to oppose political decisions and which have nothing to do with real labor concerns."[115] This was an unprecedented attack on union autonomy.

The 1991 electoral results were interpreted as a public endorsement of the government's economic reform policy. The victory of Menem-backed candidates further strengthened his legitimacy within the Peronist movement. Taking advantage of this situation, the president launched a new offensive against labor autonomy. Its objective was to strip the labor movement of many privileges obtained under Perón that had made it such a dominant distributional coalition. Menem's measures were (1) reducing the labor movement's wealth by cutting the number of union-managed welfare benefits funds and replacing them with privately managed health and retirement funds; (2) decentralizing union power by allowing factory leaders to negotiate agreements; (3) democratizing union elections to deestablish labor bosses; and (4) giving management greater freedom in dealing with labor costs and employment issues. The legislative measures were as follows:

1. Executive Order Presidential decree 1334 amending the Law of Professional Associations made wage hikes contingent upon increases in productivity.

2. An Employment Reform Law, aimed at making the labor market flexible, legalized the position of 2.5 million workers lacking welfare benefits. It allowed companies to hire part-time workers and to set severance pay ceilings of three months pay per year of service. As part-time workers were not required to be unionized, the law was a severe blow to labor and strengthened the bargaining positions of management.[116]

3. As part of the deregulation decree, the government, ironically, gained control over the employers' and workers' contributions to social benefits (obras sociales) funds (worth $260 million a year). These contributions, previously deposited directly into union bank accounts, were now paid to the Ministry of Labor. Unemployment and family subsidy funds, which yielded millions of dollars to unions, were dissolved as well and consolidated with social security funds into one account.[117]

4. A Workers Compensation Law limited to $55,000 a worker's indemnity (at a time when expenses for a family of four were estimated at $1,200 monthly). The law was clearly in favor of management as it reduced labor costs.

5. In December 1991 an executive bill was sent to Congress aimed at privatizing pension funds, and in January 1992 plans were announced to eliminate the PAMI (the comprehensive medical assistance plan) and ANSSAL. The Menem administration justified these initiatives by the fact that the social security system was virtually bankrupt and owed an estimated $7 billion to pensioners. The government system replaced

obligatory payments into union welfare funds with a nonobligatory scheme, according to which workers could stay with union pension plans or opt for privately run plans. These bills struck at the heart of union power, as it jeopardized the economic base upon which unions had thrived since Perón's reforms of the 1940s.

6. The administration also sent new bills to Congress reforming labor relations and the law of professional associations. The bills were similar in scope to the proposal tried by Labor Minister Mucci in 1984. They allowed the creation of alternative umbrella organizations to the CGT. They democratized union elections by making it easier for the rank and file to compete with incumbent leaders. They also made possible company unionism and collective bargaining at the local rather than national level and replaced compulsory arbitration with mediation.

In March 1992, as a reaction to these measures, the CGT reunited again—after thirty months of disputes. However, the new CGT was far from representing a united front. Its leadership was divided among five general secretaries, who did not represent the whole labor movement nor were they the real power brokers within it. In fact, large and militant unions like those of state workers (the ATE) and teachers (the CTERA) stayed out and later created a rival organization, the Confederation of Argentine Workers (CTA). The new power arrangement was virtually an alliance between the old CGT-San Martín and Miguel's UOM, which excluded the left, Barrionuevo, and for the first time, Ubaldini.[118] The new CGT seemed to accept Menem's principle that Ubaldini's conflictive approach worked only under authoritarian or weak civilian governments and that labor had to be more "responsible." Indeed, afterward, CGT leaders, afraid of being excluded from major government decision making, were willing to accept pay raises based on productivity increases (Law 1334) in return for union control over welfare funds and for free collective bargaining. Self-restraint on pay hikes, which would have been unacceptable to the rank and file during the Alfonsín administration, indicates how much the bargaining power of the labor movement had deteriorated under the Peronist president.

In 1992, facing the competition of the CNT to retain the loyalty of a work force increasingly dissatisfied with the government's antilabor policy, the CGT began to criticize Cavallo openly. In November it launched the first general strike against the Peronist administration. In addition to a minimum wage hike, the CGT demanded that the government abandon the proposed labor bill aimed at decentralizing collective bargaining and restricting workers' rights, thus further limiting labor's political clout.

Menem rejected the CGT demands, but in early 1993 Cavallo concluded an agreement with both labor and big business. In fact, although labor's power has been substantially curtailed, the unions, with eighteen of their members in the Peronist delegation to Congress, could still block a number of government-sponsored bills that Menem needed to have approved. To overcome the labor leaders' resistance, Cavallo proposed that unions be allowed to administer pension funds under the new social security reform. This translated into an estimated $3 billion business, which for many Argentine union bosses, notorious for manipulating the health care funds they control, was too much to resist.

Thus, whereas labor had gained considerable momentum during the last three years of the Alfonsín administration, internal divisions notwithstanding, the return to power of the Peronists severely restricted labor's autonomy and bargaining strength. Alfonsín aptly described the dramatic changes that had occurred within the union movement since Menem took office when he said: "If I had taken the steps Menem has I would have been hanged. But there is a recession coming. Keeping a job will be a bigger issue than increasing one's wage."[119]

Government-labor relations under Alfonsín were exacerbated by the government's unwillingness to involve labor in the drafting of economic policy, by the high rates of inflation, which under the Radical administration eroded real wages by 56 percent, and by the hostile behavior of Ubaldini, who preferred strikes to negotiation. Between January 1984 and 1989, Ubaldini called thirteen general strikes, which, however, did not change the government's course but only disrupted economic activity. "Strike activity increased only in the public administration; in the rest of the economy . . . workers were fearful of losing their jobs to strike action. . . . While public administration accounted for just 37.5% of worker-days lost in 1984, it constituted more than 60% for 1985–87 and more than 80% of all worker-days lost in 1988–89."[120] Public employees were more strike-prone than employees in the private sector for two reasons. First, before Menem's antistrike executive order of 1990, job security in the public sector was assured, and unless the walkout was declared illegal by the government, workers were paid while on strike. Second, between 1983 and 1989 real wages in the public administration fell 40 percent, while wages in state corporations (−20 percent), retail (−25 percent), and manufacturing (−18 percent) suffered small losses; while bank employees' wages remained unchanged. (See table 6.4.)

Structural Changes and the Future Prospects of Unionism

The composition of the labor movement (table 6.2) has varied over time, and so has its political strength. Argentine unionism has been traditionally dominated by industrial unions, particularly in the early 1960s when the ISI process reached its peak. However, with the economy go-

TABLE 6.4
Real Wages, by Sector, 1984–1989
(1983 = 100)

Sector	1984	1985	1986	1987	1988	1989
Public administration[a]	104.5	71.6	72.9	76.3	75.9	60.6
Retail[b]	121.5	108.6	96.6	89.5	81.9	75.7
State enterprises[b]	103.3	91.3	97.8	92.2	91.2	80.5
Manufacturing[c]	125.9	108.7	108.3	98.1	94.0	82.3
Banks[b]	113.1	103.4	115.8	110.4	99.3	99.5

SOURCE: Charles Blake, "The Rise and Fall of Saúl Ubaldini: Peronism at a Crossroads," p. 28, paper prepared for the Midwest Political Science Association Meeting, Chicago, 18–20 April 1991, p. 28.
a. Wages are for category 10.
b. Wages are an average of all workers.
c. Wages are an average of skilled and semiskilled workers.

ing from the lethargy of the 1970s to the depressed conditions of the late 1980s, the structure of Argentine employment was changed dramatically. Jobs in manufacturing declined by 39.4 percent during the 1974–1983 period and by an additional 5.2 percent between 1983 and 1988.[121] This drop was partially compensated for by an increase in employment in the service sector (including self-employment), a trend mirrored in union membership. Between 1973 and 1989, manufacturing and construction unions, once the backbone of Peronist labor support, suffered a sharp decline in members. Service sector unions grew during this period. Union leaders who organized the service sector, like Andreoni and Ubaldini, gained in influence over labor, forcing the once-powerful manufacturing union leaders, like Miguel and Triaca, to deal with them and to reconsider the equilibrium of forces within the movement.

The point is that service unions are less likely to be Peronist than manufacturing unions. Of course, the self-employed, who are growing in number, escape unionization altogether. According to one source, self-employment in 1990 reached almost five million, close to 40 percent of the economically active population.[122] Futhermore, recession is a potent deterrent to labor mobilization, because many workers are afraid that striking may lose them their jobs—the government's 1990–1991 breaking of strikes by telephone workers, oil workers, and metalworkers protesting the privatization of their companies are a case in point. In April 1992, the government stepped up its antistrike activity. When rank-and-file engineers of La Fraternidad went on a wildcat strike, the government shut down operations completely. Further, the public is less willing to tolerate strikes than it once was. Government employees (whose salaries and jobs were prime targets of the Alfonsín and Menem administrations' attempts to trim the budget deficit) have found themselves isolated during salary disputes, an indication that the public mood is changing.[123]

A trend surfacing in the 1980s was increased competition in union elections. In the past, partly because of government apathy or outright complicity, incumbents manipulated elections to keep control of their unions and the economic power that came with it. Incumbents staged the elections, chose voting procedures, established eligibility rules, selected the committee that counted votes, and at times resorted to physical intimidation.[124] Stricter government supervision during the Alfonsín administration and rank-and-file disenchantment with incumbents, often seen as corrupt and too far removed from workers, has made possible the ouster of some bosses. Although a number of challengers were non-Peronists, most of them were from rival Peronist factions.

In 1993, the labor movement was very much in disrepute, weaker, smaller, and politically more heterogeneous than in 1983. Despite Ubaldini's attempt to revitalize the CGT in the 1980s, it could not deliver individual union compliance, which impaired its ability to negotiate with government or management. Often the real power lay with individual unions (e.g., the UOM) or factions within the CGT, all of which dealt separately with government and business. These negotiations occasionally paid off for these groups in the short term, both in economic rewards and in thwarting rivals, but in the long term, they undercut the CGT and therefore labor as a whole. Even Ubaldini stopped short of a complete break with Menem because he could count on the support of only a small and heterogeneous group in the CGT.[125]

It may be argued that the CGT's divisions are a repetition of a historic pattern. The umbrella organization has generally been either under the government's thumb or badly divided.[126] Even during its golden period (1946–1955), when through the right of intervention it kept a close grip on labor, the CGT had to submit to Perón's tutelage. However, unless its internal splits are resolved, it is unlikely that the CGT or labor in general can defend itself from government efforts to divide and conquer. Between 1955 and 1973 labor's political strategy was aimed at Perón's return, but since Perón's death, the union movement has suffered from an identity crisis, reacting to government initiatives instead of creating its own agenda. Thus labor's future rests as much on its capacity to solve its internal contradictions as on its relationship with the Menem administration and the state.

The labor movement gained prominence only when the state, through Perón, became its patron. Unionism thrived as long as the state treated labor as a privileged partner. The opposite is true today, not only in Argentina but throughout Latin America. The economic restructuring imposed by the debt crisis triggered market-oriented policies, and organized labor has been their main casualty. Oddly, in the name of economic freedom and deregulation, South American governments have limited the unions' rights to collective bargaining and the right to strike. Unlike North America and many European countries in which the state limits itself to setting basic regulations, in Argentina and Latin America the state has claimed for itself a strong role. In fact, it acts as legislator, regulator, enforcer, and arbiter of all aspects of labor relations. Thus the state can affect the internal organization and functioning of unions. Governments can rule on the legality of union organizations, regulate their electoral procedures, and limit their activity. In the heyday of Peronism, unions did not challenge these powers because they were used to their benefit. Today, the same powers are used against unions, putting labor leaders in a difficult situation. Whereas during authoritarian or non-Peronist administrations the labor movement resisted government attacks by forging alliances with opposition groups, today labor is virtually isolated. Moreover, the threat comes from within the very political movement that made unions such prominent distributional coalitions.

If Menem maintains his neoconservative economic stance, the union movement will have to decide between subordinating itself to his agenda and reconsidering its longstanding Peronist affiliation. In 1993, labor appeared resigned to the president's privatization plans. The second option, of course, has long been the hope of the Argentine left, which considers Peronism a conservative movement aimed at controlling the working class. Although there are signs that a debate between these two options is occurring among the rank and file, it would take a major change for this to happen among the current, predominantly Peronist, labor leadership.[127] Another solution is to create a true, independent, labor party.[128] A more likely outcome is that those willing to collaborate with Menem will do so and those unwilling to collaborate will remain loyal to their social justice ideals and continue to charge Menem with betraying the movement, as the creation of the CTA in 1992 seemed to indicate. Yet this division will further weaken the labor movement in the long run.

The unions' role has been ambivalent during the transition process. Some union leaders bargained with the military, while others helped speed its withdrawal. Some strongly supported the military trials and Alfonsín during the carapintada mutinies (Ubaldinistas and the Group of 25), while others played down the Proceso's repression (Triaca) and sympathized with some carapintada demands (the "62" and the "15"). Some emphasized the role of the PJ in representing labor demands (the "25" and the "15"), while others preferred to affect socioeconomic policy through strikes (Ubaldini) or under-the-table deals (Triaca). In general, though, the common feature of Argentine unionism has been to subordinate the interests of the rank and file to the political ambitions of their leaders.

Labor can best serve the consolidation of democracy by channeling its demands through political institutions like parties, the legislature, and elections. Hostile behavior simply discourages investment.[129] Although mass rallies provide outlets for the frustrations of the rank and file who see no other solution to a crisis and whose protests could otherwise take more dangerous forms (as the terrorist phenomenon of the early 1970s testifies), in the long run, filling up town squares with protesters is not the way to success. More structured ways of solving problems are more predictable and reliable. However, it is doubtful whether such a trend will occur in the near future. Menem, Ubaldini, Triaca, and Barrionuevo are all uninterested in institution building; their ultimate goal is to create a new form of populism that does not impose formal limits on their power and freedom of action.

7

AGRICULTURAL DISTRIBUTIONAL COALITIONS

ARGENTINA'S HISTORY has been profoundly influenced by the development of its agriculture. As we saw in chapter 2, exports of beef and grain brought the country spectacular economic growth between 1880 and 1930. Agricultural and agrindustrial production accounted for 70–80 percent of export earnings.[1] As a consequence, the sector's dominant interest group during that period, the Argentine Rural Society (SRA), acquired enormous economic power and political clout, as many of its members went on to become presidents of the republic and to staff the most important ministries. Because of this political influence and its ability to defend its economic rents, the SRA became the country's most important distributional coalition.

The SRA's hegemony came to an end in the mid 1940s, when manufacturing replaced agriculture as the main contributor to the nation's GDP and Peronism removed the landowning elite from power. The agricultural sector continued to take a back seat in the priorities of most of the administrations that followed after Perón's downfall in 1955, as they perceived Argentina's future as resting upon the promotion of ISI. Agricultural interest groups were never again able to gain the same kind of access to economic policy making which they once enjoyed. To make matters worse, the rural sector was forced to finance state-led industrialization through various direct and indirect government taxes. Frustrated by such policies and by the lack of responsiveness by Peronist and Radical administrations to their needs, most rural distributional coalitions began to look to the military to help them achieve their goals.

These agricultural coalitions became part of the so-called military party, encouraging military coups and supporting military governments. Members of these coalitions were appointed to key ministerial posts and agreed more with the political views of governments produced by coups than with those preceded by honest elections. However, military regimes almost invariably disappointed them: once in power, these regimes did not so readily favor the rural sector, as they adopted an arbitrary decision-making style that insulated them from external lobbying.

The rural sector today does not speak with a unanimous voice, as it did early in the twentieth century through the SRA. New interest groups have developed that testify to the diversity of agricultural interests stemming from the nature of rural production, the markets targeted, the size of landholdings, and political views. These groups have often disagreed, but on occasion have united against industrial, commercial, and financial distributional coalitions over the division of income shares. At the same time, most agricultural interest groups have consistently resisted government attempts to jeopardize their interests in areas like land taxation, export tariffs, and price controls. The rural sector's representatives no longer enjoy the prestige and political hegemony they once did, but they remain a crucial element in the Argentine political economy, as witnessed by the fact that although agricultural production and its industrial derivates accounted for only 14 percent of the nation's GDP in 1991, they still comprised 68 percent of Argentina's total exports.[2] Because of this economic leverage, agricultural distributional coalitions continue to play a paramount role in the country's political life. The evolution of the forms and content of their political involvement is the subject of this chapter.

The Early Development of
Rural Groups (1866–1943)

The first rural association of the country was the Sociedad de Laboradores y Hacendados, which lasted from 1819 to 1857. Its last president, José Martínez de Hoz, one of the most important Argentine landowners, eventually became the president of the SRA, founded in his Buenos Aires home in 1866.[3] The SRA has been since its inception a small but cohesive association of large landowners with estates in the pampas, although many of them managed their fortunes while residing in cosmopolitan Buenos Aires. The SRA was soon dominated by ranchers (estancieros) who made up the bulk of its leadership. Its members considered themselves the true national elite not just because of their wealth but also because of the pivotal role that agricultural production played in the economic development of the country. In their view, the progress of the country was intimately tied with beef and grain exports, and their claims were well grounded. (See table 7.1.)

The large landowners of the pampas quickly became, to all intents and purposes, the "aristocracy" of the young nation, and the SRA became their exclusive "club." Becoming a member was tantamount to

TABLE 7.1
Export of Major Products, 1871–1962 (percentage)

Period	Livestock Products	Agricultural Products	Other
1871–1874	95		5
1875–1879	93	2	5
1880–1884	89	7	4
1885–1889	81	16	3
1890–1894	66	29	5
1895–1899	64	31	5
1900–1904	49	46	5
1905–1909	39	58	3
1910–1914	45	51	4
1915–1919	55	39	6
1920–1924	37	58	5
1925–1929	37	59	4
1930–1934	35	60	5
1935–1939	37	57	6
1940–1944	56	26	18
1945–1949	43	50	7
1950–1954	48	43	9
1955–1958	52	40	8
1959–1962	50	45	5

SOURCE: James Scobie, *Argentina: A City and a Nation* (New York: Oxford University Press, 1964), p. 277.

joining the establishment. Ideologically, the Rural Society adhered strictly to the principle of comparative advantage theory. The theory stated (among other things) that a country should specialize in the production of those goods in which it holds a comparative advantage over competitors. Thus a country like Argentina, endowed with fertile land and abundant open spaces for cattle raising, had to concentrate on improving the efficiency of beef and grain, trading these goods for manufactured goods from Europe, which would have been too expensive to produce domestically. The SRA's liberalism in economics, however, did not spill over into the political sphere. As noted in chapter 2, its members were development-minded, "enlightened" conservatives. They advocated quick modernization, but they were also in favor of a very elitist, restrictive type of "democracy" which would leave to them, the aristocrats, the responsibility of running the country as they saw fit because "they knew best."

SRA members did not limit themselves to agricultural business. Many of them invested in industrial and financial endeavors complementary to rural production. Quite a few actually joined the UIA, the entrepreneurs' umbrella organization.[4] The SRA opposed ISI, which it perceived as economically inefficient and superfluous as long as Argentina could purchase at cheaper prices manufactured goods from abroad by adhering to the comparative advantage theory. However, the agroindustry constituted an important exception:

> Agro-industrialists naturally adopted a middle position between the agrarian liberal free traders and the industrial protectionists. They argued that it was necessary to make a distinction between "natural" and "artificial" industry. Natural industries were those which used mostly local raw materials. They included wine, sugar, flour, meat, meat by-products, leather, edible oils, dairy products, lumber, furniture, tobacco, alcohol, beer, non-alcoholic beverages. Besides using local material, such industries needed very little sophisticated machinery, hence their costs were low and their prices competitive enough to meet the standards of the law of comparative advantage. By contrast, artificial industry required much expensive imported machinery, a great deal of imported fuel, and even imported raw materials. Most heavy industry, including iron and steel, machine building, chemicals, automobiles, electrical equipment, and rubber fell into this category. The agro-industrialists joined with the *estancieros* in considering such industries unsustainable for Argentina and unworthy of protection. By contrast, some temporary protection might be justified for natural industries, in order to give them a starting push.[5]

The SRA membership grew very slowly. At the turn of the century it numbered around 2,000 affiliates. In 1940, its membership was just 2,300, but it steadily increased thereafter, rising to 3,900 in 1950, 7,500 in 1960, and 12,000 in 1975.[6] In spite of its small number of members, the SRA comprised the country's most important export producers, which allowed it unchallenged domination of the agricultural sector well into the 1930s. Its smallness and its homogeneity in terms of members' socioeconomic background and political and ideological views made the SRA extremely cohesive. Its leaders, for instance, tended to stay in office for prolonged periods. Internal elections were usually a formality, as a single list of candidates was agreed upon beforehand. An alternative list appeared first in 1908, and again in 1926, when breeders and fatteners (closely linked to foreign meat packers and shipping companies) battled for control of the SRA. They eventually won out. Only on three subsequent occasions did the SRA experience internal squabbles, and these were related to political crises affecting the whole country: in 1954 and 1955 the question was whether or not to oppose Perón; in 1962, it was whether to take a position on the conflict between the azules and the colorados; in 1972 it was over President Alejandro Lanusse's decision to lift the proscription on Peronism.[7]

As was previously mentioned, the influence of the SRA went well beyond the economic realm. The SRA became the most prestigious and powerful interest organization in the country. The oligarchs that ruled

Argentina were very often members of the SRA. In fact, the SRA and its members were the core of the PAN, which dominated Argentine political life until 1916. The PAN was in fact nothing more than the political expression of the pampas landowning interests, which were loosely allied to those of the rural elites in other provinces. SRA members could also be found among the up-and-coming Radicals. Peter Smith calculated that, in the Chamber of Deputies between 1904 and 1916, 70 percent of PAN members and 63 percent of UCR members were pampas landowners. During the Radical administrations of 1916 to 1930, these aristocrats saw their share of the UCR's congressional delegation decline to one-third. At least until 1930, contrary to the common belief that the UCR represented mainly the urban middle class, many aristocrats were involved in the party organization.[8] (Table 7.2 shows the number of SRA members in the national government.) We do not know how many aristocrats joined the UCR, but it may be assumed that many did.

Between 1916 and 1930, one president (Alvear), one vice president, and ten ministers came from the SRA, as displayed in table 7.2. Five out of nine presidents and 38 percent of the ministers belonged to the SRA. It is no surprise then that SRA affiliates were either hired as consultants or appointed as government officials by several administrations to direct rural policy prior to the creation of the Ministry of Agriculture in 1889. In that year, the SRA president, Emilio Freres, was invited to head the newly formed ministry, which remained under the direct control of SRA members until the late 1930s.[9] In the period surveyed by Smith (1910–

TABLE 7.2
SRA Members in National Government, 1910–1943

	SRA Membership		
Administration	President	Vice-president	Ministers
Sáenz Peña (1910–1914)	1	1	6
De la Plaza (1914–1916)	1	(not appointed)	3
Yrigoyen (1916–1922)	0	0	5
Alvear (1922–1928)	1	0	4
Yrigoyen (1928–1930)	0	1	1
Uriburu (1930–1932)	0	1	4
Justo (1932–1938)	1	1	3
Ortiz (1938–1941)	1	0	1
Castillo (1941–1943)	0	(not appointed)	1
Total SRA members	5	4	28
N	9	7	72

SOURCE: Peter Smith, *Politics and Beef in Argentina: Patterns of Conflict and Change* (New York: Columbia University Press, 1969), p. 49.
NOTE: All cabinets had eight members.

1943) twelve of the fourteen ministers of agriculture came from the Rural Society. Even two of Perón's three ministers of agriculture belonged to the SRA, and the third joined after having been appointed. The SRA's influence, however, did not stop with agricultural matters. In fact, as table 7.3 shows, many of its members were repeatedly in charge of the economic and foreign relations ministries as well. The SRA early on also established close links with such powers as the military and the church.[10] Another way it made its point of view known was through the yearly agricultural fair in Palermo Park, the most important fair of South America, which the SRA still organizes annually in August. The inaugural speech given by the SRA president is usually attended by the president of the republic, members of Congress, the mayor of Buenos Aires, and high-ranking officials of the armed forces, the Catholic church, and entrepreneurial interest groups. Because of the importance of agricultural exports in the national economy, it constitutes something very close to a state of the nation address.

A serious challenge to SRA dominance of the rural sector first came from previously unorganized tenant farmers. In 1912, after staging a nationwide strike, they organized the Argentine Agrarian Federation (Federación Agraria Argentina, or FAA).[11] At first the FAA was composed primarily of European immigrants or first-generation Argentines.[12] In 1914, about 58 percent of pampas farmland was cultivated by tenant farmers, of whom 78 percent were foreigners.[13] While tenant farmers and sharecroppers made up the majority of the FAA membership, a substantial segment of the federation was represented by small farmers who had emigrated from Europe to colonize the lightly settled provinces

TABLE 7.3
SRA Members in Public Office, by Regime, 1956–1983

Position	Liberating Revolution	Frondizi	Guido	Illia	Argentine Revolution	Peronism	Proceso
Ministers	3	2	3		5		1
Secretaries, undersecretaries, public managers	1	10	10	2	13		7
Provincial appointees	6	4	1		1		1
National banks	2	3	3	1	9		4
Others					2		
Total	12	19	17	3	30		13

SOURCE: Mirta de Palomino, *Tradición y poder: la Sociedad Rural Argentina* (Buenos Aires: CISEA/Grupo Editor Latinoamericano), p. 75.

north and northwest of Buenos Aires, particularly Santa Fe, Entre Ríos, and Córdoba.[14] While the big landowners of the SRA concentrated on cattle raising, tenants and small farmers developed grain cultivation, due in part to the fact that tenant farmers and sharecroppers were usually prevented by their contracts with the landowners from raising cattle. These contracts to sharecrop or to tenant the land were for five years, after which the landowner decided whether the tenant could stay another five years.[15] Although the SRA took credit for the country's great economic strides, it was mainly through the work of these small farmers that "between 1872 and 1895 cultivated land increased by fifteen times (10 million acres) and cereals from a negligible proportion in 1870 reached, in 1900, 50 percent of export value."[16]

The SRA's main concerns were to control prices and to directly market their livestock to defend against the oligopolistic practices of foreign meat packers and shipping companies. The FAA, however, battled for more basic agricultural issues: land redistribution, easy financing for the purchase of land, restrictions on tenant evictions, and an easing of the limitations on the crops tenants could raise. Because these demands jeopardized the landowning elites' privileges, the FAA and the SRA soon came into conflict and have remained a world apart on most issues ever since. While the FAA became an outspoken supporter of socioeconomic reform and usually sided with progressive sectors of the Argentine society, the SRA remained adamantly attached to the defense of the status quo and traditional values.

Lacking the political and economic power enjoyed by the SRA, the FAA tried to make its point through strikes and lobbying. A national strike boycotting land rents was successfully carried out in 1919 and helped convince Congress, two years later, to pass legislation "forbidding clauses in tenant contracts restricting what could be planted and to whom it could be sold. The law also required owners to indemnify tenants for all improvements and forbade the seizure of tenants' tools and animals to pay off a debt. These rules were tightened further in 1932, and in 1940 Congress aided tenants suffering from the Great Depression by making it extremely difficult for owners to evict them."[17] Moreover, the FAA increased its membership and organizational capabilities. By 1943, it numbered 27,000 members, who could count on strike funds in times of need. It also organized over a thousand cooperatives nationwide to increase the bargaining power of producers over that of brokers and distributors, who traditionally garnered a substantial part of the profits.[18]

The 1930 military coup led to the restoration of oligarchic rule. In 1932, after General José Uriburu stepped down, the Concordancia represented mainly the interests of the landed aristocracy.[19] Generally speaking, the SRA influence in the post-1930 period was quite obvious, as most of the ministers and two presidents were SRA members (see table 7.2). Many regarded the era of the Concordancia as one of the darkest periods in Argentina's history due to its exclusion of political adversaries and its practice of electoral fraud. Nonetheless, the regime showed remarkable skills in devising new policy strategies to mitigate the devastating effects that the Great Depression had on the country's well being. Through a combination of a strict monetary policy (implemented in 1934 by Argentina's Central Bank, modeled after the British example), exchange controls, and the introduction of an income tax, the Concordancia governments were able to take the country away, slowly but steadily, from the troubled waters of the depression years.

A key initiative was the signing of the Roca-Runciman treaty with the United Kingdom in 1933. In 1932, British Commonwealth countries had agreed to buy from each other and to erect protectionist barriers against imports from nonmember nations. Afraid of losing the British market (the largest importer of Argentine agricultural goods), President Justo, under pressure from the SRA, sent Vice President Julio Roca to London to negotiate an agreement. The Roca-Runciman treaty turned out to be highly favorable to the United Kingdom. It stipulated that London would buy roughly the same quantity of Argentine beef that it had in 1932. On the other hand, Argentina agreed to reduce import tariffs to pre- 1931 levels on about 350 British products, to transport 85 percent of beef exports in British-owned ships, to grant important concessions to British-owned rail and train companies in Argentina, and to buy British goods with the British pounds they earned with their exports.[20] The treaty was renewed three years later with even more favorable conditions for the British, who threatened to close their markets to Argentina and to import Canadian and Australian goods under the Commonwealth's special treatment provisions. Both treaties triggered a nationalistic outcry in Argentina, particularly from industrial manufacturers whose products were in direct competition with British imports.

In retrospect, Justo had virtually no other option. Raúl Prebisch, who was on the negotiating team, later asserted that many of the opposition's accusations were not supported by the facts or were exaggerated.[21] Actually, industrial output in the 1930s rose substantially, as Argentine goods began to replace European and British imports. Quietly but surely, the Concordancia governments abandoned the old free-market economic development model and switched to a Keynesian approach out of necessity. A number of measures were enforced by the Justo administration and subsequent administrations to actively support ISI in spite of the SRA's opposition. Multiple exchange rates, and even some disguised tariff barriers were used to help Argentine industrialists.[22] The same applied to the agricultural sector.

The effects of the world crisis on Argentine rural producers prompted government intervention in the commodity markets in open violation of economic liberalism. In late 1933, an executive order created the Grain Regulatory Commission, long advocated by the FAA; its goal was to defend domestic producers of wheat, flax, and maize from speculation by foreign buyers. Minimum prices for commodity exports were enforced, with the government financing the gap between domestic and international prices when the latter were lower than the former. Farmers could sell their products either to the Commission or to export companies. Moreover, in an unprecedented move, the Commission expropriated private grain elevators and built new ones to minimize storage and shipment costs.[23] Similar provisions were made for beef exports.

Until the early 1930s, foreign meat packers had set beef prices through oligopolistic practices, which were willingly accepted by cattlemen as long as business was thriving. Legislative attempts in 1923 to change this state of affairs were met with little success, but the sharp drop in sales during the depression exacerbated relations between the two groups. At the end of 1933, Congress passed a reform, based on a proposal drafted in 1931 by the SRA, establishing the National Meat Board composed of nine directors (of whom two were SRA nominees). Foreign importers had to register with the board in order to comply with a control price mechanism aimed at guaranteeing a certain income for livestock producers. The board also organized a government-subsidized stockraisers cooperative, the Corporation of Argentine Meat Producers (Corporación Argentina de Productores de Carne, or CAP), to sell up to 11 percent of the beef exports allowed into the United Kingdom under the Roca-Runciman treaty. The corporation's goal was to be a channel for Argentine producers to sell their products directly to foreign customers, thus bypassing the exporters' cartel.[24]

Because the SRA had sponsored the state's interventionist measures to rescue agricultural producers, it could hardly prevent regional rural groups from organizing to press their demands upon the Justo administration. One such regional grouping was the Confederation of Rural Associations of Buenos Aires and La Pampa (Confederación de Asociaciones Rurales de Buenos Aires y La Pampa, or CARBAP). It was set up in 1932 by small cattlemen, in competition with SRA's big ranchers. Contrary to the conventional myth that stockraisers were big property owners, in the 1920s only 25,000 ranchers of 330,000 had over 200 head of cattle.[25] In 1942, CARBAP (which a year later would boast a membership of 10,000) and three other regional organizations gave birth to the Argentine Rural Confederations (Confederaciones Rurales Argentinas, or CRA). By the early 1940s, the CRA, the CARBAP, and the FAA had eroded the SRA's authority to speak for the whole rural sector—or the *campo*, as it is usually referred to in Argentina. Through their lobbying effort, these coalitions forced the Concordancia to change economic rents and monopolistic conditions to their advantage.

In 1940 Economic Minister Federico Pinedo's plan for economic reactivation was defeated in Congress. Pinedo was a long-time SRA member and an outspoken supporter of agriculture-led rather than industry-led economic growth. He had helped draft the Roca-Runciman treaty and the interventionist policies that had helped the campo in the 1930s; with World War II in full swing, Pinedo and his close advisor Raúl Prebisch concluded that Argentina should not again be exposed to the fluctuations in world commodity prices experienced during the Great Depression. Accordingly, the Pinedo Plan was a comprehensive approach to sustained growth. It included a number of countercyclical measures to mitigate the effects of recessionary periods in times of worldwide economic crises.

First, the plan called for higher state subsidies for rural production and the purchase of excess production to keep prices high. Second, the government was to finance public works and low-income housing, which was expected to create 200,000 jobs. Third, the "natural industry" would be promoted by reorienting part of its production toward export markets. This goal was to be attained by creating a free trade zone with other Latin American countries and by giving industrialists incentives like export subsidies and reimbursements for the purchase of raw materials and technology.[26]

In the view of many commentators, the Pinedo Plan was an innovative, far-sighted approach to the economic realities of the 1940s. Initially, the plan gained the support of the UIA, which liked the industrial promotion scheme, and the SRA, which applauded the subsidization of agricultural production and saw no threat in the furthering of the "natural industry" as long as it remained subordinate to rural needs. The Pinedo Plan was approved by the Senate but sank in the Radical-controlled Chamber of Deputies, since the bill was a good opportunity for the Radicals to embarrass the Concordancia. Sounding like the most obtuse advocates of economic liberalism, the Radicals justified their stand by arguing that, as long as the "rural sector produces and exports, the country will surely keep buying what it needs at a cheaper price than the one established through custom duties in order to favor the particularistic [industrial] interests so created."[27] The CARBAP sided with the UCR and led the charge for the agricultural coalitions, which were afraid that the Pinedo Plan would jeopardize the privileged status of the campo. Eventually, the uproar became so great that even the SRA abandoned its initial stance.[28]

The SRA had clearly lost its hegemony. Concomitantly, the presence of SRA members in the last two administrations of the Concordancia diminished steadily. However, it was not until the 1943 military coup and the subsequent coming to power of Peronism that the rural sector's direct influence on policy making, particularly that of the SRA, came to

an end. The agricultural producers' myopia had defeated the mildly reformist Pinedo Plan, whose ultimate objective was the consolidation of
the rural economy. With Perón, they not only lost their influence on policy making but were forced to subsidize populist policies, a trend that
continued under the governments that followed Perón. Thus, after
World War II, while in the United States and the European Economic
Community (EEC) agriculture was sheltered and heavily subsidized
through a transfer of resources from industry and commerce, in Argentina the opposite was true.

From Military Intervention to
Peronist Dominance (1943–1955)

The 1943 coup was a historic turning point for the rural sector as a
whole. From then until 1983, the campo's relations with the government
ranged from cooperation to conflict. There was often open hostility to
democratically elected governments and collaboration in the aftermath
of military takeovers. The sector realized to its dismay that it was relegated to a secondary role, both politically and economically, to the Peronist populist coalition and new interest groups. The SRA, the CRA,
the CARBAP, and the FAA had not lost all their influence over the policy
agenda, but they had lost their hegemony. These agricultural groups
were increasingly on the defensive against Peronist and Radical policies
favoring the urban middle class and the working class, which were tied
to the industrial and service sectors. This trend was momentarily reversed in periods of authoritarian rule, when distribution lost out to
capital accumulation, which favored agricultural producers in its early
stages. It is not by chance that SRA members in official positions increased in number during these periods, compared to previous civilian
regimes. (See table 7.3.) The following SRA leaders had important government positions during 1956–1983.[29]

Eduardo Busso, interior minister, Liberating Revolution

Carlos Gómez Alzaga, Banco Nación and ambassador, Guido administration

Alfredo Gatzambide, Provincial Bank of Buenos Aires, Argentine
Revolution

Juan B. Legerén, Banco Nación, Frondizi

Alberto Mihura, subsecreatry of stock raising, Proceso

Lorenzo Sojo, Central Bank, Proceso

Ignacio Zuberbühler, minister of agricultural affairs of the Buenos Aires
province, Liberating Revolution

Members of the SRA were most numerous during the administrations of the Argentine Revolution (1966–1973) and, conversely, were to-

tally absent from the third Peronist administration (1973–1976). The large number of SRA members during the Frondizi and Guido administrations stemmed from the strong military influence upon those two presidents, in particular the second one, when some SRA members were also closely tied to high-ranking military officers.[30] The military viewed the participation of the SRA's affiliates in government as an assurance that "sound" policies would be pursued. During the 1956–1983 period, forty-nine SRA members occupied ninety-four official positions, 37 percent of them in more than one government and 40 percent occupying more than one post.[31] Some observers believe that SRA members played a decisive role during the early stages of the authoritarian governments[32] only to be later replaced by industrial entrepreneurs. Others at least agree that SRA members could be found consistently in positions related to the rural sector, such as minister, secretary, or undersecretary of agriculture at both the national level and the provincial level (most notably the Buenos Aires province) during authoritarian periods.[33] Furthermore, SRA leaders were quite involved in banking as well, which is not surprising since some of them owned or were shareholders in large financial companies. What these data suggest is that, after 1943, SRA members in official posts decreased and that their participation was greatest in governments emerging from military coups or when the armed forces had either a veto power or controlled the government machinery (under Frondizi and Guido).

The honeymoon between authoritarian governments and conservative agricultural groups like the SRA, the CRA, and the CARBAP did not last very long, partly for economic reasons. Peronist and Radical administrations were concerned with distribution and full employment, and after 1946 their economic measures had two objectives:

> The first objective [income distribution] is sought by granting larger social benefits and generous wage and salary increases. The second objective—full employment—is sought by assuring a high level of demand. Other principal instruments of expansionist, or populist, economic policies include manipulating foreign exchange rates and controlling the prices of goods and services rendered by both the private and the public sectors to keep the cost of living low. Expansionist periods frequently begin with an increase in real salaries, cheap credit, increased economic activity, and optimism in the industrial and commercial sectors. This stage seldom lasts long. The budget deficit grows, the balance of trade is thrown into disequilibrium, accelerating inflation erodes real wages, and unrest develops in the labor unions. The process culminates in the exhaustion of central bank reserves and a crisis of balance of payments. Expansion comes to a halt, and a chaotic economic situation emerges.[34]

Expansionary policies contemplated high tariff barriers to shelter domestic industry from foreign competition and to maintain a large but inefficient public bureaucracy and state-owned industrial and service sectors. In practical terms, what this economic strategy caused was a net transfer of income from the rural sector to the industrial and service sectors. Agricultural producers paid the costs of the expansionary policies in two ways. First, heavy export taxes were imposed on agricultural goods to finance welfare and industrial programs. Second, to keep the cost of living low, price controls were imposed on food, thus discouraging producers who sold to the domestic market. As a consequence, urban dwellers enjoyed higher standards of living, while people in agriculture were penalized and felt more and more estranged from the new regimes. Both Peronists and Radicals failed to address rural demands for a policy reversal.

Argentines eventually consumed more than they produced, and, when the country's external deficit could no longer be sustained by domestic financial resources (i.e., foreign reserves or additional taxation), economic crises ensued. These economic crises coincided with political crises. Authoritarian governments then would step in to restore "law and order," to reestablish a positive balance of payments, to bring down the inflation rate, and to reduce the fiscal deficit created by the expansionary policies of the Peronist or Radical administrations they had ousted. Under these circumstances economic stabilization programs were carried out by orthodox measures. This meant importing less, exporting more, removing price controls (thus reducing the purchasing power of urban dwellers), increasing interest rates, devaluing the currency, and increasing sales taxes. The authoritarian governments' policies were therefore beneficial to the sector of the economy able to export, that is, agriculture. To encourage rural exports, governments not only removed price controls on food but sometimes slashed export taxes as well. There is no mystery, then, why agricultural groups, with the exception of the FAA, tended to support military coups. Thus the SRA, the CRA, and the CARBAP clashed with populism not only because they favored a conservative political system but also because their distributive interests were incompatible with populist economic aims.

However, in Argentina, stringent stabilization policies have never lasted long, even during times of severe military repression, because labor and industrial distributional coalitions boycotted them. When these groups' pressure proved intolerable, authoritarian governments were forced to reverse some of their early decisions. Because such a reversal often negatively affected agricultural producers, the initial transfer of income from the industrial and service sectors to the rural sector was halted. In addition, the authoritarian governments' insulation of the policy-making process made things even worse. Although the initial stabilization policies proved beneficial to agricultural distributional coalitions, these coalitions still had no control over the general direction of economic policy. SRA members occupied some key government positions, but the Ministry of the Economy usually remained in the hands of technocrats, whose views did not always coincide with those of rural producers. Tensions between agricultural groups and authoritarian governments increased when the latter allowed the exchange rate to appreciate (which meant that exports became less competitive), tried to impose land taxes, and reintroduced disguised tariffs on exports. In the end, agricultural producers found their interests not as protected by authoritarian governments as they had hoped.

Tensions between government and rural interests reached their climax during the first two Peronist administrations. This trend was visible as early as 1944, when the SRA openly expressed misgivings about Perón. SRA President José María Bustillo blasted Perón's easy populism and the state's interventionism in the opening speech of the 1945 Palermo agricultural fair.[35] Perón's antioligarchic rhetoric certainly did not endear him to the SRA, but equally disturbing to the SRA (and to the CARBAP and the CRA as well) was the state's intrusion into labor and marketing relations. Perón was instrumental in freezing land rents, which, while pleasing the FAA, outraged the landowners of the SRA and the CRA. He also decreed the Statute of the Peón, which for the first time gave farm laborers a bill of rights establishing clear guidelines for minimum wages, fringe benefits, and working conditions. Arbitrary layoffs were severely curtailed and regional union boards were instituted to make sure landowners complied with the statute. Some rural unions were even set up in the west and northwest regions of Argentina among previously unorganized sugarcane, yerba mate, and wine workers.[36] Perón further infuriated agricultural groups (and angered industrial and financial associations as well) with his sweeping nationalization plans and his pivotal role in introducing wage indexation to make up for inflation and price controls.[37]

All of these factors convinced the SRA, the UIA, the Buenos Aires Stock Exchange, and the Chamber of Commerce of Buenos Aires to support the Unión Democrática, an electoral alliance (made up of Radicals, socialists, progressive democrats, and communists) that challenged Perón's 1946 presidential bid.[38] The stakes were very high; "if Perón's plan was to be carried out, economic elites had to 'give, in order not to lose everything,' not only a share of their wealth, but also a share, and a very considerable one, of their power."[39] The Peronist victory clearly signified a serious setback for the country's entrepreneurial groups. This was indeed the case for the rural distributional coalitions, which saw their darkest dreams become reality when, a few week's before Perón's inauguration, the military government, besides nationalizing the Central Bank, created the Argentine Trade Promotion Institute, or IAPI. The IAPI was a state monopoly presiding over agricultural exports. Its task was to buy cheaply from rural producers and sell at much higher prices to foreign customers, the profits supporting welfare and industrialization programs. The meat and grain boards created by the Concordancia in the mid-1930s were reorganized and put under IAPI jurisdiction, thus ending the agricultural interest groups' control over production and marketing policies. The CAP, the publicly financed producers' corporation in charge of beef sales abroad, suffered a similar fate. The IAPI severely curtailed the profits of farmers, meat-packing companies, and the country's four largest private export corporations but not foreign meat packers and grain exporters.[40]

Understandably, the IAPI was perceived by most agricultural concerns as an all-out attack on the campo. Nonetheless, by the end of 1946, agricultural producers had little choice but to go along with it. Perón had pushed the SRA, the CRA, and the CARBAP into a corner but avoided a complete falling out. Instead of exploiting the long-standing quarrel between these groups and the more progressive FAA, and gaining FAA support for agricultural reforms, Perón limited himself to satisfying some FAA demands on an ad hoc basis. To this end, in 1948 he had Congress renew the 1943 decree freezing land rents and extending tenant contracts from five to eight years. This very action showed Perón's ambiguity toward the landowning elite. He had promised to reform the land tenure structure in his 1946 campaign, but once in power he found the project too daring. Instead, he hoped that landowners would find renting unprofitable in the face of rising costs and thus would sell holdings to their tenants (who would be given generous credit from the government to purchase plots).[41]

Perón stopped short of land reform because, politically, it would have been unacceptable to landowners, who, although defeated electorally, still had considerable power.[42] Economically, breaking properties into smaller plots had a negative impact on agricultural output, something he could not afford, as agriculture was the main source of Argentina's foreign exchange earnings. Perón paid lip service to agricultural matters. His main concern remained the consolidation of the industrialization process and the success of his welfare programs, which aimed at gaining for him the support of the urban working and middle classes. According to his pragmatic approach, agriculture was to be exploited economically but not destroyed, as it performed an important function in his development plans. By the same token, rural distributional coalitions had to be emasculated but not antagonized, as the government needed rural interlocutors with whom to deal. Perón's objective was to induce the SRA, the CRA, the CARBAP, and the FAA to collaborate with him and to have at their helms sympathetic leaders. Not surprisingly, Perón did not try to replace any of these associations with new ones.

Some students of the SRA regard the 1946–1955 period as the worst experienced by that association. Others contend that the SRA reached a tacit understanding with Perón by adapting to the new circumstances.[43] It praised him occasionally, once for the commercial agreement with the United Kingdom in 1951 and later for the emergency economic plan of 1952; it even congratulated him on his successful reelection bid. Two of Perón ministers of agriculture belonged to the SRA, and other SRA members actively collaborated with the regime—which led to squabbles between collaborationists and loyalists in 1954 and 1955.[44] In spite of these individual links, "as public representatives of the Society's interests, these officers became [minor players] because they had rejected the collective position taken by the members of the Rural Society, and they served the Society only as contact men when needed."[45] SRA-Peronist relations were marked by open confrontation, whose form and content were kept within limits.[46]

The SRA resisted Perón's attempt to limit its autonomy by adapting itself to the new realities. In 1950, it changed its statutes to allow all areas of the country, not just the pampas, to be represented on the association's governing board.[47] The SRA also expanded its membership to include more differentiated economic interests to broaden its representativeness vis-à-vis the government.[48] The SRA orchestrated joint actions with the CARBAP and the FAA (which became disillusioned, as its farmers saw their profits shrink as a result of price controls and the IAPI's practices) to force some government concessions—but to no avail. By early 1955, relations between Perón and the campo were at a historic low, and to the surprise of no one, most rural associations (save perhaps the FAA) welcomed his ouster.

Agricultural Distributional Coalitions During the Peronist Proscription (1955–1966)

The conservative restoration attempted by the Liberating Revolution, following the September 1955 coup, raised hopes among the rural sector. This was indeed true for the SRA, which described it as the beginning of a new era, a "national rebirth," after the "oppression" of Peronism.[49] Soon after taking over, President Pedro Aramburu appointed a substantial number of SRA members to key positions and met some of the campo's most pressing demands. For instance, the IAPI was dismantled, the CAP was returned to private hands, most price controls on food were lifted, and a substantial devaluation of the peso was decreed to stimulate beef and grain exports.[50] However, Aramburu disappointed his rural supporters in another dimension. Although agricultural groups, and particularly the SRA, had hoped to regain control of the country's economic policy, this did not happen. The three economic ministers of the Aramburu administration, although committed to revitalizing beef and grain production and to guaranteeing good prices for it, ignored the demands of special interest groups. Substantial differences arose over tariff and rent policies. The SRA and the CARBAP bitterly objected to the government's decision to impose a 25 percent export tax, which in their view perpetuated Perón's old scheme of penalizing the only productive sector of the country. Furthermore, Aramburu's decision to prolong land rent contracts, which were due to expire, while pleasing the FAA, prompted an outcry from the SRA and the CRA. Eventually, the president was forced to give in, and the tenants were confronted with two options: to purchase the land at a price asked by landowners or to leave.[51]

Many rural organizations reorganized to be able to deal with the new political situation—for instance, the SRA and the CARBAP purged Peronist "collaborators." Moreover, the de facto government, supported by a loose coalition of anti-Peronist parties, created an anomalous situation—which would become more the rule than the exception in the years to follow. Agricultural coalitions felt that their interests were not adequately represented by the existing parties, which did not have much voice in Aramburu's plans, and they went straight to the source of power—the executive and the various branches of the public administration—bypassing the parties. This tendency was not new by any means, but until 1943 the SRA and CRA's relationship with conservative parties and moderate (antipersonalist) Radicals had been such that Congress could articulate rural interests. After 1943 this was no longer true, as conservative parties shrank electorally and the UCR adopted a proindustry, prourban bias.

The election of Arturo Frondizi in 1958 was a cause for concern within the SRA and the CRA. First, they resented Frondizi's decision to break with the anti-Peronist, multiparty coalition that had supported the Liberating Revolution in order to reincorporate the Peronists into the political process and gain their electoral support. Second, they opposed Frondizi's plan to give top priority to the development of heavy industry, which again relegated agriculture to a secondary role and turned the once powerful Ministry of Agriculture into a secretariat under the control of the Ministry of the Economy.[52] The first economic measures stiffened rural opposition against the UCRI president. High wage increases accompanied by price controls and new retentions on beef and grain exports were deeply resented. To make matters worse, a feud arose when the UCRI governor of Buenos Aires sponsored a plan to reduce tax evasion. The bill would force pampas landowners to pay property taxes according to their land's potential value rather than its usage, a practice commonly used to underestimate the taxable income of rural property owners. The SRA and the CRA, whose members were concentrated in that province, claimed that the bill was an outright violation of the constitutional right to private property, and through intense lobbying they succeeded in defeating the bill.[53]

The eventual collapse of the Frondizi alliance with Peronist labor late in 1958 and the president's adoption of a stringent economic stabilization plan supported by the IMF failed to rally rural support for the president. The SRA and the CRA welcomed this U-turn in economic policy, which veered toward the free-market path they advocated. Among other things, the peso suffered a massive devaluation, most price and exchange controls were phased out, government industrial subsidies were trimmed, and plans were made for the privatization or closure of many unprofitable state enterprises. However, the agricultural distributional coalitions in general continued to complain about export tariffs (10 percent for livestock and 20 percent for grain) and import surcharges on farm equipment and fertilizers.[54] These issues and others to follow made the SRA and the CRA suspicious of Frondizi throughout his tenure. The president's decision to reinstate the pro-Peronist CGE, banned in 1955 by the military, allowed the formation of a CGE-FAA alliance shortly thereafter. The SRA harshly criticized Frondizi's overture to the CGE, and in 1958, to counterbalance the CGE-FAA bloc, it joined the UIA and the Argentine Chamber of Commerce (CAC) in an anti-Peronist coalition, the Coordinating Association of Free Enterprise Institutions (Asociación Coordinadora de Institutciones Empresarias Libres, or ACIEL), representing the country's big capital.[55]

The appointment of conservative politician Alvaro Alsogaray as economy minister in 1959 and economist Roberto Alemann in 1961 did nothing to ease the tensions. The SRA and the CRA appreciated both ministers' commitment to free-market economics but repeatedly questioned the continuation of the 1958 industrialization plan, which they saw as an unfair transfer of resources from the rural to the industrial sector. During the chaotic Guido administration, five people alternated at the helm of the Ministry of the Economy. Of these five, only Alsogaray was not a member of the SRA. During Alsogaray's brief tenure, the agricultural coalitions rose up in arms to prevent him from reintroducing export tariffs and a land tax whose goal was to increase production.[56] At one point, Alsogaray came under fire from both agricultural groups, headed by the SRA, and industrial groups, headed by the UIA. The UIA was fighting to retain industrial credit lines that the minister wanted to cut. Eventually, this combined effort forced Alsogaray's resignation, and his measures were quickly abandoned, to the great satisfaction of both groups.[57] The SRA's presence was felt more during this period than at any other time between 1955 and 1983, and the policies that were implemented then favored agriculture over industry, although only for a short time.[58]

The Illia presidency reversed all that. Illia's economists took a Keynesian approach, which emphasized strong state intervention in the economy through heavy public spending to stimulate aggregate demand. The purpose was of course to raise the income of urban dwellers. To partially finance its programs, the Illia administration imposed a 5 percent surcharge on agricultural production and introduced new export tariffs. The social component of the administration's policy consisted of (1) a cap on the amount of beef available for export in order to satisfy domestic demand, (2) new price and exchange controls, (3) the reintroduction of a minimum salary for rural workers, and (4) the resumption of freezes on farm rents. The last two measures were openly praised by the FAA but created a storm among the SRA, the CRA, and the CARBAP, thus splitting yet again the rural front on property and income distribution issues. However, the most threatening measure of the Illia administration was a bill aimed at taxing land according to potential output. The tax attempted to force large landowners to farm productive land that otherwise would be idle.

The SRA and the CRA charged the Radical administration with being "collectivist" and "interventionist" to the point of violating individual and property rights guaranteed by the constitution. The CRA and the CARBAP organized the Coordinating Committee for Agrarian Entities, which set up a coalition of regional farm producers opposing Illia's policies. The combined action of the SRA, the CRA, and the CARBAP again proved too strong for the government to resist. In the end, Illia had to abandon price controls, beef export limits, and a proposed plan for a grain production tax.[59] The only rural support that the president had was from the FAA, but it was too little, too late. On balance, the sector's relations with the government were the worst since Perón. The government's tendency to insulate the decision-making process from the pressure of distributional coalitions was far greater than under Aramburu or Guido and quite similar to that adopted by Frondizi. Consequently, tensions between the government and the rural groups escalated. Just before the coup, the SRA accused the Illia administration of being a "minority" government lacking "constitutional legitimacy" and incapable of assuring "law and order," which was tantamount to giving the military its approval for intervention.[60] A few months later, Illia was deposed in one of the most bloodless, orderly, and widely supported coups in Argentine history.

The Argentine Revolution (1966–1973)

The SRA welcomed the Onganía regime with open arms, calling it "our government."[61] It assumed that the new administration would implement policies favorable to agriculture and that it would keep in check labor, whose militancy during the last two years of the Illia presidency had created fear among big capital, landowners included. Between 1966 and early 1967 things went as expected: the agricultural distributional coalitions recovered their income share, and repressive measures muted opposition. In early 1967, Adalbert Krieger Vasena took charge of the Ministry of the Economy for the second time.[62] Krieger Vasena quickly presented his economic plan. The agricultural groups enthusiastically approved the peso's sharp devaluation, the liberalization of prices, the foreign exchange market, and wage controls, as the general thrust of the plan was geared to opening up the economy, They were equally pleased when a month later the government issued an executive order allowing landowners to raise rents as they saw fit and evict tenants if they failed to pay.

However, these agricultural interests soon realized that Krieger Vasena had a policy agenda quite different from their own. The minister's objective was to promote certain economic structural changes long advocated by various quarters of Argentine society heretofore politically unfeasible. In Krieger Vasena's view, both public and private sectors had developed intertwined, distributive interests that discouraged competition, allowed economic rents due to monopolistic or oligopolistic arrangements, and penalized economic efficiency. If Argentina was to catch up with the industrialized societies of the Western world, it had to modernize its economic structure. This would involve stepping on the vested interests of industrialists, agricultural producers, public enterprises, and labor unions. However, Krieger Vasena believed that the discretionary powers Onganía had granted him gave him an advantage over his predecessors, allowing him to insulate the policy process from the distributional coalitions' lobbying efforts to an unprecedented level and, at the same time, enabling him to use state authority to promote economic reform. The state was not to be used as a partisan agent of specific agricultural or labor-industrial interests, as had happened under the Conservative and Radical regimes prior to 1943 and the Perón, Frondizi, and Illia administrations thereafter. The state, in Krieger Vasena's modernization scheme, was to act outside of party lines to promote what was best for the nation, following pure efficiency criteria.

Therefore, agricultural distributional coalitions were not in the center of the new capital accumulation model, nor did they have as much input into the economic decision-making process as they had hoped for in 1966.[63] The first clash between Krieger Vasena and these coalitions occurred when he imposed export tariffs and taxes on farm imported inputs in mid-1967. Although the government reduced these tariffs in 1968, the SRA and other rural interest groups demanded their complete elimination. Relations between Krieger Vasena and the rural sector as a whole became progressively more strained, even though the rural coalitions still supported the regime as a whole.[64] With Krieger Vasena showing no sign of changing his course, in order to gain concessions, agricultural groups formed a broad coalition front, including some of their traditional rivals in the industrial sector who also disliked the minister's policies.[65] Krieger Vasena reacted by denouncing the selfishess of agricultural and industrial interest groups and in December 1968 decreed a new land tax. The philosophy behind the tax was very similar to that of previous attempts by the Frondizi and Illia administrations: it aimed at discouraging tax evasion by rural producers by imposing a tax on unused land while granting tax breaks to those willing to increase production. The law increased the number of taxpayers, forcing people in low income brackets to file tax returns for the first time.

Interestingly enough, the FAA, which had previously denounced the government for the 1967 farm rent executive order came to Krieger Vasena's defense, applauding the project as instrumental in modernizing rural production and attacking the privileges of big landowners.[66] On the other side of the spectrum, the SRA and the CRA were predictably angry, and both groups switched from a position of criticism to one of blunt opposition to Krieger Vasena. The SRA's belief was that they had "to prevent the president from being cheated by his economic minister, in order to avoid the complete loss of prestige of this government."[67] "Rural spokesmen were outraged that an authoritarian government, whose creation they had cheered because of its apparent dedication to the promotion of economic growth, had ignored the wishes of the rural producers whom it had been expected to serve."[68] The SRA and the CARBAP pulled out of Onganía's Agricultural Advisory Council in protest and stepped up their attacks on the economy minister's measures, describing them as unconstitutional, confiscatory, and collectivist.[69] As in the past, agricultural distributional coalitions were very unnerved with Krieger Vasena's support for a strong capital goods industry and reasserted that the country's industrial development had to be subordinated to the needs of agriculture.

Krieger Vasena's resignation in mid-1969 and Onganía's removal a year later temporarily eased relations between the agricultural groups and the military government. But the economic policies of the Levingston and Lanusse administrations tried to stay within the boundaries traced by Krieger Vasena and therefore failed to enlist the support of the rural sector. To make things worse, policy implementation was much less consistent than during the 1967–1969 period due to the deterioration of the military regime. The profound disappointment of the rural coalitions with the Argentine Revolution was coupled with their fear of a return of Peronism. As the military regime came to a close, these coalitions retreated from the political arena. This was no coincidence: having gambled on the military option and lost, they now had no alternative but to wait and see what Peronism, after seventeen years, would bring.

The Comeback of Peronism (1973–1976)

The initial attitude of the rural interests with regard to the Cámpora administration, and the Perón administration that followed, was one of skepticism mixed with some willingness to compromise over short-term objectives. Minister of the Economy José Gelbard was well aware of the negative effects that bad relations with the rural sector had had on the Peronist economic performance of the early 1950s. Therefore, he tried to convince the SRA, the CRA, the FAA, the CARBAP, and the Confederation of Agricultural Cooperatives (Confederación de Cooperativas Agropecuarias, or Coninagro) to give external support to the CGE-sponsored social pact. Gelbard specifically asked them to comply with price controls and a substantial production increase in return for a number of concessions, including tax incentives, farm subsidies, and expanded credit.[70] All groups except the CARBAP signed the Act of Commitment with the Rural Sector in August 1973. By itself, this was a remarkable achievement if one considers that under Frondizi most of the same organizations had bitterly opposed the reinstatement of the CGE.

Unfortunately, agricultural distributional coalitions very soon mobilized against the pact, especially attacking a series of government measures dealing with minimum prices, property taxes, rent controls, and agrarian reform.[71] In May 1975, in an unprecedented showdown with the government, the CARBAP and the CRA led the rest of the agricultural groups in a twenty-four-hour strike, which, although not successful in stopping the food supply to the cities, was an embarrassment to the Peronist administration. The FAA, which had earlier adhered to the social pact, eventually pulled out and joined in the agricultural action committees that the CRA and the CARBAP were organizing nationwide. More effective strikes followed in September and October. The rapid deterioration of farm prices was the common denominator uniting the SRA, the CRA, and the CARBAP with the FAA and Coninagro—for the first time since 1955.[72]

At the same time, the SRA began to express its grievances to the newly appointed army commander, General Jorge Videla, not only about the rural sector, but also about the corruption and incompetence of the Isabel Perón administration and her inability to prevent the country from falling into chaos.[73] As the situation turned from bad to worse, the antigovernment front broadened even further. In 1975, the SRA, individual members of the UIA, and the CAC gave birth to the Permanent

Assembly of Entrepreneurial Trade Associations (Asamblea Permanente de Entidades Gremiales Empresarias, or APEGE). The APEGE was the natural heir of the ACIEL, which had been disbanded in 1973. In February 1976, driven to desperation, the APEGE called for an entrepreneurs' lockout, which paralyzed most business activity and brought the Peronist government to its knees. The military coup that took place a few weeks later was generally welcomed by the campo with the notable exception of the FAA.

The Proceso (1976–1983)

Most distributional coalitions, including those with membership in the APEGE, actively supported the armed forces' intervention in March 1976 and publicly endorsed the policies of Minister of the Economy José Alfredo Martínez de Hoz until he left office in 1981.[74] As usual when a military regime comes to power, a substantial number of SRA and CARBAP members were assigned to government posts. Martínez de Hoz himself belonged to one of the founding families of the SRA, and the secretary and undersecretary of agriculture belonged to SRA inner circles, as well. Surprisingly, Martínez de Hoz disappointed his SRA supporters in the long run. Like Krieger Vasena, he saw distributional coalitions as detrimental to the country's well-being and thought it was up to the government to impose "sound" economic measures by using its coercive powers and by insulating the decision-making process. However, in the first two years of the Proceso criticism of the government was muted. Between 1976 and 1977 the government resorted to traditional ways of fighting spiraling inflation and the balance of payment deficit, which again favored rural producers. Things seemed to be going well, except that the peso became increasingly overvalued compared to the dollar and exports lost their competitiveness.

Not until 1978 did the SRA start to make its point with Martínez de Hoz. It complained of the steady overvaluation of the peso, the reimposition of export tariffs eliminated in 1977, and other problems caused by increases in the value-added tax and the land tax.[75] As the minister of the economy was unwilling to compromise on those issues, between mid-1978 and March 1979, SRA members in the Secretariat of Agriculture resigned one by one. However, criticism was unusually mild, compared to attacks on previous civilian and authoritarian governments, perhaps because in other areas the administration did fulfill the early expectations of the agricultural groups.[76] What these coalitions criticized was not Martínez de Hoz's policy goals, but the policy tools used to achieve them. The SRA therefore defended the government's repression effort when the Organization of American States' Commission for Human Rights visited Argentina in 1979. While complaining of the heavy tax burden on the rural sector, the SRA asserted in 1980, "The Proceso has produced extraordinary results for the sake of the Republic, permitting the reconciliation of the Argentine people with their glorious traditions."[77] In the same year both the SRA and the CRA affirmed that Argentina was not yet ready for democracy.[78] The Coninagro and the FAA, on the contrary, grew increasingly critical of the military regime.

When General Roberto Viola replaced General Jorge Videla as president, the SRA and other agricultural groups praised the regime's achievements but also pointed out that mistakes had been made related to exchange and tax policies. Viola's indecisiveness and the 1981 financial crisis during his brief tenure created panic in many sectors, agriculture included. Therefore, when General Leopoldo Galtieri deposed Viola, the SRA, among others, welcomed the change even though Galtieri's economic team levied new export tariffs. These were momentarily accepted, since the government was to return to the free-market, pro-agriculture principles that had guided the Proceso's initial efforts. Like the great majority of Argentina's economic sectors, the SRA unconditionally backed Galtieri's gamble in the Falklands/Malvinas war. Only after the military debacle did the SRA and the CRA look to the restoration of democracy, which they had so often helped to deestablish, as the solution to the crisis.[79]

Before we move to the 1984–1993 period, the structural changes that have taken place among rural distributional coalitions should be noted, as well as the issues that such coalitions deem most important.

Structural Changes and Internal
Dynamics of Rural Coalitions

In recent years rural interest groups have been less concentrated in the pampas and more heterogeneous in their nature and goals.[80] Even though the interests of the pampas are still overrepresented in the most influential coalitions, all rural associations have attempted to attract regional groups with problems that are far different from those facing pampas producers. Regional associations are usually organized according to product. By inviting these associations into their provincial branches, traditional pampas groups have broadened their national-level representativeness, thus strengthening their bargaining power. For their part, regional associations have welcomed such invitations, which reduce their isolation and political vulnerability. Joining larger organizations both legitimizes them and helps them achieve their economic gains.[81]

Profound structural changes have also occurred in the economy. In the early 1950s agricultural output fell significantly, but in 1953 a recovery began, and by the mid-1960s the whole sector had reached historic levels. In the 1970s, the rural sector experienced a new boom in productivity: between 1962 and 1984 the output of the pampas tripled. Most of the growth was accounted for by cereal production; beef output became sluggish after 1978. The reason for this trend was mainly the increased use of fertilizers and machinery in the 1960s. The switch to more lucrative grain production also increased the amount of land devoted to farming. All this took place without land reform or a clear agricultural policy or, most of all, favorable international prices. For instance, while agricultural exports grew by 69 percent during the 1980–1986 period, their net value increased by only 11.9 percent, because international prices fell by 34 percent.[82]

Thus the structural changes of the 1970s and 1980s significantly altered the economic and political cleavages within the rural sector. The end of the old conflict between breeders and fatteners, the diminished role of tenant farming, and the diversification of agricultural production defused many of the old conflicts dividing interest groups representing the campo.

One of the few issues that has united the disparate agricultural groups has been the fight against the various taxes imposed on the campo. Two examples are property taxes and export tariffs. All groups complain that these are unfair burdens on the only productive sector of the economy. What is most outrageous, they feel, is that revenues so generated are used to finance the deficit created by an inefficient, expensive state bureaucracy and a money-losing industrial sector.

Price controls, taxes on capital gains and production, exchange controls, and an overvalued currency are similarly condemned as further means to extract resources from the agricultural sector. Taxation on unused land, however, has usually split the campo. Conservative distributional coalitions like the SRA, the CRA, and regional rural associations, have strongly opposed it, while the FAA and the Coninagro see it as a tool to reduce tax evasion by big landowners.

The SRA and CRA have consistently argued that any attempt toward land reform or land expropriation is unconstitutional and economically detrimental, since land fragmentation almost invariably reduces output. Attempts at land reform by the Buenos Aires and Entre Ríos provincial governments in 1984 and 1985 were thoroughly condemned by the SRA and the CARBAP, while the FAA and the Coninagro, consistent with their past stands, supported these initiatives.[83]

Because most agricultural groups see an expanded state role in economic development as heralding their socioeconomic decline, they have vigorously opposed state intervention since the early 1940s. For the SRA, the CRA, and the CARBAP, taxes, price regulation, manipulation of exchange rates, credit, and marketing operations all attack their vested interests. They have been recently joined by the more progressive Coninagro, which agrees that the state should limit itself to a few areas such as foreign policy, national defense, and basic services like justice, education, health care, and enforcement of law and order. The only dissenting voice has been that of the FAA, which advocates state regulation of marketing if it helps to break up domestic and multinational oligopolies.[84]

The SRA, the CRA, and the CARBAP thus endorsed Menem's free-market economics aimed at weakening labor's bargaining power, eliminating the public deficit, deregulating business operations, and shrinking the state's role in the economy by privatizing state enterprises. Although such policies may resemble those of Margaret Thatcher and Ronald Reagan in the 1980s, there is a difference: whereas in Britain and the United States economic freedom depends on political freedom, for the SRA and the CRA, the opposite is true. Although they favored the interventions of the Concordancia regime under the Great Depression and have welcomed state subsidies, price supports, cheap credit, tax incentives, and technological aid when they benefited them, when Alfonsín and Menem tried to allow food imports to bring down domestic prices, these groups strenuously objected.

Upon the return to constitutional democracy in 1983, the rural sector counted over half a million producers and four major national interest groups: the SRA, the CRA, the FAA, and the Coninagro, differing in size, membership, and interest.[85] The SRA remained the most powerful and prestigious of the four associations. In 1985 it represented about 9,000 members, including members of the old landed aristocracy; descendants of immigrants who made a fortune and entered elite Buenos Aires society; descendants of immigrants outside these circles; businessmen born into immigrant families who expanded their economic activities to rural endeavors; industrialists who went into agriculture to diversify their business activities or to gain social prestige; and lawyers who either defended landowners' interests or became proprietors themselves.[86] Although ranchers are still overrepresented in the SRA leadership, grain and dairy producers have become more prominent in the 1990s, reflecting the diversification of production away from cattle raising.

Two out of five SRA leaders were large landowners, and about three-quarters live in Buenos Aires. Most belonged to that city's upper class, join its exclusive clubs, and educate their children in its established preparatory schools.[87] Of the 145 leaders surveyed between 1956 and 1983, 88 were also members of limited corporations in financial and insurance (29), industrial (41), and commercial (18) companies, which testifies to their diversified business interests. Like their leaders, SRA members usually owned land in the pampas. However, commercial companies made up about 18 percent of the membership. Many of these were limited corporations, owning land for tax shelters; others are large-scale enterprises.[88] Although there were attempts after 1950 to enlarge it, SRA membership remains quite small and socioeconomically homogeneous.

The SRA regards itself as the ultimate defender of rural interests. Its political discourse is based upon a conservative vision of society. It supports those articles of the constitution that emphasize the virtues of private property, law and order, economic freedoms rather than political freedoms. By the same token, it refuses all other constitutional provisions that can conflict with these values. This double standard regarding freedom explains why the SRA supported military coups in 1955, 1966, and 1976 and why in 1980 it supported the idea of giving the military institutional access to government through the National Security Council. Besides the armed forces, the SRA has identified itself with Catholicism and has cultivated close links with the church hierarchy.

In relation to the other agricultural interest groups, the SRA has usually stressed unity, although sharp differences persist. It has a stronger affinity with the CRA and the CARBAP than with the Coninagro and the FAA. (Many SRA members are also CRA and CARBAP members and some SRA leaders, for example, have served on the ruling bodies of the CRA and CARBAP.) Ties with the Coninagro are looser; like the SRA, this group is antistatist, but it disagrees over the taxation of idle land, which the former supports while the latter does not. On the other hand, the FAA and the SRA are often on the opposite end of many issues involving the interests of the campo.

Much has been said about the incompatibility of industrial and agricultural interests, but relations between the SRA and the UIA are characterized more by agreement than conflict. They maintain formal contact and at critical junctures in Argentine history both have joined the entrepreneurial fronts created under the ACIEL and the APEGE banners. The two groups agree on the secondary role of the state with respect to private capital and the inviolability of private property. What separates them is the SRA claim that agriculture, not industry, is paramount in the growth of the economy. In the 1980s, the SRA organized opposition to government policies and was a key partner in temporary alliances with industrial, commercial, and (for the first time) labor organizations to oppose government policy.

When the government was unresponsive to its pleas, the SRA (unlike the CRA) has been nonconfrontational in its lobbying and has focused on the executive office and key ministries. For instance, during Perón's first term, the anti-Peronist president of the SRA, José María Bustillo, was replaced by the more conciliatory José A. Martínez de Hoz, and in 1984, the SRA selected as president a well-known Radical, Guillermo Alchourón. When unable to place its own people in the government, the SRA seeks access to politicians and bureaucrats through the personal connections of its members. The SRA has also tried to establish close links with officials of international organizations such as the World Bank and the EEC, not only to defend its interests in the international arena but also to enhance its status with the government and other contending distributional coalitions. The SRA's lobbying effort has also adroitly used the media to make its point with government officials, entrepreneurs, and the public.[89]

The SRA due to its very nature as an elitist distributional coalition primarily devoted to influencing public policy in defense of the preservation of the status quo has had a small bureaucratic apparatus. Only in the recent past, as a result of its effort to expand its membership beyond the pampas, has the SRA begun to provide services and technical information common to other rural organizations.

Whereas the SRA's goals were, until the early 1940s, tantamount to those of the government, the CRA and the CARBAP emerged as a reaction to government policies. The CRA represents twelve regional federations nationwide (not individual members or firms), divided into 300 rural associations, which comprise about 100,000 people. The CARBAP, with 30,000 members, is the most important regional federation and often acts independently. CRA members tend to be large and medium-sized rural producers who operate to a large extent in the pampas. This fact places the CRA in open competition with the SRA for members, and it is not uncommon for its members to also belong to the SRA. Yet in contrast to the diversification of business activities that characterizes SRA members, members of the CRA are primarily in agribusiness.

Like the SRA, the CRA lacks an extensive administrative and technical structure to assist its members the way the Coninagro and the FAA do. This is because, like the SRA, the CRA's main goal is to defend the interest of its members by exerting pressure on the state. This also explains the lack of multiple objectives and the virulence of its stands against government interventionism.[90] Both the CRA and the CARBAP have gained strength and visibility when important producers feel threatened by government policies or by other economic groups. Both have consistently scorned politicians and partly politics and have devoted their effort to lobbying the executive branch and the bureaucracy. The CRA has traditionally been much weaker than the SRA in establishing connections with political power, with some notable exceptions. Its leadership has also been more personalized. As a consequence, the CRA has conflicted with most governments, and its lobbying efforts have often been inconsistent and ineffective.[91]

While the FAA at its creation was composed largely of tenant farmers, today its members are mostly medium-sized and small farmers who cultivate crops rather than raising cattle. The increase in independent farmers over tenant farmers is partly the result of structural changes in land tenure.[92] Land rents and farm credit legislation allowed many tenants to buy land. As an organization that emerged to challenge the privileged status of SRA members, the FAA found allies in Radical and Peronist administrations. It greatly benefited from populist policies emphasizing redistribution of wealth, cheap and easy credit, cooperative farming, and a more equitable taxation system. By 1966 only 36 percent of FAA members were still tenant farmers, and its leaders were mostly large landowners.[93] Therefore, its emphasis is no longer land redistribution but land taxation and exploitation, in order to address property and income tax evasion and to counter a tendency to leave large tracts of land idle.

The FAA represents about 100,000 producers, who although heavily concentrated in the pampas play an important role in regional economies. It has exhibited the strongest commitment among rural organizations to constitutional democracy and has often been close to populist and democratic movements, under which it thrived.[94] In the 1980s, it distanced itself from the demands and intrasector alliances supported by the SRA and the CRA. Indeed, the FAA consistently sided with trade unions and small and medium-sized industrialists in direct opposition to the big capital fronts joined by the SRA and the CRA. The FAA takes a nationalist stand on political and economic issues; it justifies state intervention and is critical of free-market economics, which favors big agricultural exporters and transnational capital. As a result, FAA relations with civilian governments have been better than its relations with authoritarian ones.

The Coninagro was created in 1956 and is therefore the most recent agricultural organization. It includes thirteen federations, representing 1,278 cooperatives employing 459,000 people.[95] It is politically less influential than the other groups and its approach to government is more conciliatory perhaps due to its dependence on federal credit and technical assistance. The Coninagro's economic clout, however, has made it an important distributional coalition. In 1985 it controlled 46 percent of cereal marketing, 20 percent of grain exports, and 40 percent of milk production.[96] Because of its heterogenous composition, the Coninagro's profile is difficult to define, and its political activity is usually limited to agricultural issues, unlike the other organizations. In the 1980s it often endorsed the demands of the CRA and the SRA but was reluctant to join their protest actions.

The New Democratic Regime and Agricultural Coalitions, 1983–1993

Agricultural distributional coalitions are neither as homogeneous nor as cohesive as they were in the early 1940s. The SRA retains its leadership role, but it cannot speak for the whole sector any longer and has to counter the claims of the CRA and the FAA. However, regardless of jealousies, divisions on ideological and pragmatic issues, and differences in the socioeconomic position of their members, most of these groups put their differences aside to assert the rights of the campo over other economic sectors and to prevent its fiscal exploitation. They all share the belief that, since the campo plays such an important role in the national economy, it is, paradoxically, extremely vulnerable to the attacks of the government and industrial distributional coalitions, which conspire to take away its profits.

With a return of democracy, rural organizations witnessed interesting internal changes. Historically, the SRA, the CRA, and the FAA have experienced long leadership continuity, and internal dissent has been relatively modest compared to other entrepreneurial or labor distributional coalitions. For instance, CRA president Raúl Romero Feris won three consecutive terms, and the FAA had only five presidents between 1912 and 1986. Although the SRA presidency has changed hands regularly, the tenure of its board of directors has been quite long, and its membership has remained steady. Starting in early 1984, however, internal elections have been marked by increased competition. The old tradition of submitting a single list, common to all groups, has been broken, and competing factions have risen within the SRA, the CRA, and the CARBAP. More dissent and open discussion have been allowed than in the past, which some interpret as an effect of the democratization of the country as a whole.[97]

The campo welcomed Argentina's return to constitutional democracy. Initially, the Alfonsín administration tried to address the rural sector's problems through the National Agricultural Program (Pronagro). Despite its limitations, it was the most ambitious and comprehensive program for the rural sector since 1973, which testifies to the lack of planning assigned to agricultural policy by previous administrations. The Pronagro was meant to emphasize the role of agriculture in the national economy, both as a provider of food for the domestic market and as the major contributor to the export sector. Its immediate goals were increasing the output of cereal production by 50 percent during the 1984–1989 period, boosting export earnings, and promoting employment and better standards of living in rural areas.[98] Despite the last provision, it was clear that the Pronagro was targeted on the cereal production in the pampas, leaving out cattle production and the rural economies of the poorer provinces. The Pronagro contemplated the following policy tools to achieve its stated goals: export tariffs, to be partly used as a compensation fund during times of low international prices; new taxes on land to force greater productivity and to distribute the fiscal burden more equitably; and price supports for some commodities. In the end, the Pronagro, despite its moderate reformist nature, never materialized, save perhaps some aspects of its credit policy—due to lobbying by the rural coalitions. Given the favorable prices for Argentine exports in 1984, most rural groups did not perceive the Pronagro as a threat when it was disclosed at the end of that year. However, a 30 percent fall in international prices in 1985–1986 compared to 1983–1984 changed the initial positive reception and exacerbated distributive conflicts.

The CRA, later joined by the SRA, was the first to attack the Pronagro, arguing that the scheme was an attempt by the government to intervene in the free operation of the marketplace. More specifically, the CRA and the SRA criticized the role the National Grain Board (JNG) was to play. The program entrusted the JNG with the purchasing and marketing of cereals, to defend small producers from the large agricultural conglomerates represented by the SRA and the CRA. Support for the JNG from the Coninagro and the FAA was insufficient to save the plan.

Another issue of contention was the land tax, which was to stimulate production while not penalizing investments. Originally, the *impuesto a la tierra libre de mejoras* (ITLM) was conceived as a progressive tax whose burden was to be shouldered by large landowners. The Secretariat of Agriculture, which was in charge of the Pronagro, argued that through the efficient application of the ITLM it would be possible to phase out export tariffs, so opposed by the campo. Once more, the Coninagro and the FAA, despite some reservations, expressed their support. The CRA and SRA, on the contrary, launched a major campaign against it. The SRA proposed an alternative plan that called instead for a 5 percent tax on profit earnings. Far from being a concession, the proposal aimed at perpetuating tax evasion. In fact, in 1985 alone the government estimated that instead of the $400 million expected in revenues from profit earnings, rural producers paid only $70 million.[99] By 1986, with agricultural prices deteriorating even further, the Coninagro and the FAA joined the SRA and the CRA in convincing the Alfonsín administration to withdraw the ITLM from congressional consideration.

The failure of the Pronagro was not solely because of lobbying by the rural coalitions; lack of cooperation and coordination among the government agencies and ministries in charge of its implementation was also to blame. Although the Ministry of the Economy publicly supported the program, many of its stabilization measures contradicted the Pronagro or made its execution unfeasible. As the Secretariat of Agriculture was subordinate to the Ministry of the Economy, it had no choice but to go along with the general guidelines on macroeconomic policy. Constrained by the repayment of the foreign debt and the need for a fiscal adjustment, Alfonsín's economists forced through a number of measures, such as a price freeze, a manipulation of the exchange rate, and an increase in export tariffs, which hurt agricultural producers. At the same time, provincial and municipal administrations, unable to secure funds from the federal government, imposed taxes on agricultural producers, which worsened their fiscal burden. The fiscal drag on the campo rose substantially in the first half of the 1980s, when 45 percent of the rural sector's GDP was transferred via taxation to the public sector and other parts of the economy.[100] (See table 7.4.)

Once the Pronagro was abandoned in December 1986, the Alfonsín administration was without any clear agricultural policy. The marketing and land tenure structure remained unchanged, and the proposed plan to reform rural contracts did not take place. With the economic situation going from bad to worse, all decisions affecting agricultural policy were left to the Ministry of the Economy. Relations between the campo and Alfonsín were also severely strained by the steady deterioration of international prices for beef and cereals. In fact, even when in 1986–1987 export tariffs were dropped to an average of 13 percent and the exchange rate was made more competitive, producers still suffered a 27.3 percent reduction in prices.[101]

Of all the distributional coalitions, the CRA was the most aggressive and confrontational. Between 1985 and 1989, either alone or in collaboration with other groups, it organized five strikes and protest actions against the government.[102] The SRA, on the other hand, while subscribing to CRA demands, kept a dialogue going with the administration. It presented a counterproposal (the Informe 84), which asked for the elimination of export tariffs, a competitive exchange rate, and the development of new technologies. The SRA proposal also renewed the old plea that agricultural exports should be given priority over industrial promotion in order to reactivate the economy—which, of course, prompted a UIA protest. In order to exercise greater pressure on the government, the SRA, the CRA, and the Coninagro in 1984 joined the Group of 11, which represented the country's ten major distributional coalitions in

TABLE 7.4
Agriculture in the Argentine Economy, 1971–1991 (percentage)

Period	Agriculture in GDP	Agricultural Exports to Total Exports	Agricultural Taxation in GDP	Argentine Grain Exports to World Grain Trade
1971–1975	13.2	76.2	18.0	11.7
1976–1980	13.5	76.5	25.4	10.6
1981–1985	15.1	74.2	45.6	10.9
1986–1991	14.8	69.3		

Source: The World Bank: *Argentina: Reforms for Price Stability and Growth*, (Washington D.C.: World Bank, 1990). Figures for the 1986–1991 period are from the Argentine Rural Society.

the industrial, agricultural, commercial, and financial fields plus the CGT. This was a historic event because most of the business groups making up the Group of 11 had traditionally opposed the CGT and its involvement in entrepreneurial agreements. The CGT called for a substantial reduction in state involvement in the economic realm, while the entrepreneurs accepted the CGT's request to strengthen social programs. These concessions were of course quite contradictory, and the statement served no practical purpose, since Alfonsín refused to back down.[103] However, what was remarkable was the fact that the SRA and the CRA for the first time agreed to collaborate on a common project with the CGT. The FAA supported the government until the end of 1986, after which (partly because several of its federations demanded a more aggressive posture and partly because of Alfonsín's increasing dependence upon alliances with big capital) it became extremely critical of the Radical government and organized several strikes at the local level. The Coninagro again showed more moderation than the others and— while supporting on and off the claims of the SRA, the CRA, and the FAA—avoided collision with Alfonsín.

However, Alfonsín's shifts in alliances and strategies were not conducive to policy cooperation. In 1984, Minister of the Economy Bernardo Grinspun made it clear that the government was not willing to compromise with the rural coalitions. As the economy worsened, the Ministry of Interior and the Secretariat of Agriculture explored the possibility of an agreement with key rural coalitions. In 1985 policy talks were abandoned in favor of unilateral decision making with the support of the country's largest industrial conglomerates.[104] In early 1987, Alfonsín made substantial concessions to the rural distributional coalitions, drastically cutting export tariffs, and property taxes, refinancing the debts of small producers, and appointing an SRA member to the Secretariat of Agriculture. The improvement of the campo's relations with the government was also facilitated by a surge in the international prices for many Argentine commodities. In August 1988 the Spring Plan sanctioned Alfonsín's alliance with the UIA and the CAC, which angered the campo, as the Spring Plan implied an income transfer from the campo to the industrial sector. The dual exchange rate regime adopted for commercial transactions also openly favored the industrial sector.[105] Tension escalated: at the inauguration of the 1988 Palermo fair, Alfonsín and SRA President Guillermo Alchourón engaged in a bitter exchange.

In September, in a rare show of solidarity, the four major rural distributional coalitions staged a two-day work stoppage protesting the Spring Plan. Their opposition continued until its demise in February 1989. Alfonsín accused the rural coalitions of contributing to the collapse of the Spring Plan when, in February, many of their members refused to change the dollars earned through exports into australs. A weaker than ever Radical government was forced to make additional concessions to rural producers, which more than compensated for previous losses.[106] Nonetheless, by the time the 1989 presidential election came, they had abandoned an administration that they had warmly welcomed only five-and-a-half years earlier.

In President Menem the more conservative rural groups found an unexpected ally. Even before assuming office, Menem held talks with representatives of the SRA and the CRA to assure them that his administration would promote policies favorable to exporters. For once, he kept his word. Menem's decision to hand over the Ministry of the Economy to former executives of Bunge and Borne, the nation's largest conglomerate with important interests in agribusiness, was a clear signal of his attempt to win the campo's approval. Even after the collapse of Bunge and Born's stabilization plan in December 1989 and the withdrawal of its team from the administration, Menem's commitment to free-market economics, his rolling back of the state, and his privatization policies kept the SRA and the CRA in his camp. Yet the rural sector became increasingly restless in the face of the steady overvaluation of the austral and the heavy fiscal burden imposed on farm producers. In January 1991, the FAA, the CRA, and the Coninagro warned the government that if their plea was not taken seriously, they would urge their members to give low priority to their tax obligations, which amounted to an antitax rebellion.

In March, Minister of the Economy Domingo Cavallo came to a compromise by proposing a fiscal pact with the sector's leading organization, according to which the administration would abolish taxes on agricultural exports, which then ranged from 5 to 13 percent. In return, the SRA and the CRA urged their members to pay the new value-added tax and their property and income taxes and to increase production. Moreover, a longstanding demand by those organizations was also met when Cavallo created joint commissions with government and rural representatives to negotiate new taxes as well as transport and credit policies. Cavallo not only averted a revolt by the farm sector but actually found support for his stabilization plan, as agricultural policy became a top priority of the Ministry of the Economy.

The improved relations between the administration and the rural sector were further testified to by Menem's speech at the 105th SRA fair the following August, when the president stated that "never again will farm export duties be used to bail out a political adventure. . . . We won't tolerate discrimination against Argentine agriculture."[107] This constituted a watershed for Peronism because it reversed the policies of the first two administrations of Juan Perón. Although expressing his misgivings for some government policies, the SRA president nevertheless praised the administration's stabilization plan. To offset the losses experienced by agricultural producers due to the strength of the austral in the international financial markets, Menem tried to boost farm exports to Brazil within the context of the MERCOSUR. Moreover, it lobbied North America and Europe to end U.S. and EEC farm subsidies, which hurt Argentine producers.

The deregulation decree announced in November 1991, although eliminating farm subsidies, did incorporate many proposals advocated by the SRA and the CRA. Government regulatory agencies like the Liniers Livestock Market, the National Meat Board, the National Grain Board, the National Sugar Directorate, and the National Wine Institute were all eliminated.[108] Not only were domestic markets deregulated but so was foreign trade. The FAA criticized the deregulation decree, but to no avail. Once again conservative rural groups had gained the upper hand through government action. Their satisfaction was expressed by the SRA president, Eduardo de Zavalía: "The present economic programme has put aside those interventionist theories and has entrusted Argentine development to the sectors best able to compete abroad, letting the markets assign resources."[109] In early 1993, even though agricultural exports were hurting because of the steady appreciation of the Argentine currency vis-à-vis the U.S. dollar, the SRA continued to support Cavallo's stabilization plan and refrained from asking for a devaluation. In return, the government approved tax reductions and new credit lines for agricultural producers.

Although at this point it is hard to predict the future development of the Menem-rural sector relations, it can safely be said that some attitudinal changes seem to be taking place among the campo's most representative interest groups. The restoration of democracy has forced the SRA, the CRA, and the CARBAP to reform their internal organization and the means used to articulate their interests.[110] The SRA in particular seems inclined to accept that democracy, and not military dictatorship, can best serve its interests. Indeed, the SRA and the CRA joined the Coninagro and the FAA in openly supporting the defense of the constitutional regime during the military rebellion of 1988.

Agricultural distributional coalitions still lack confidence that parties will represent their interests, and they continue to directly lobby the government. However, they have greater confidence in democracy than before, and this attitudinal change can be greatly reinforced if Menem institutionalizes his conservative alliance. If this happens, conservative agricultural distributional coalitions may find in the PJ the political party that addresses their interests and may eventually stop looking to the military to solve the country's problems.

8

INDUSTRIAL DISTRIBUTIONAL COALITIONS

THE INDUSTRIALIZATION PROCESS took place in Argentina sooner than in most of Latin America. At its inception, the infant Argentine industry was primarily an offspring of the booming agricultural economy. By 1914 the bulk of manufacturing output was concentrated in the production of food, beverages, textiles, tobacco, wood products, and leather.[1] Given the secondary role that industry played in the early economic growth of the country, industrial entrepreneurs' needs were subordinated to those of the pampas landowners, who dominated in both the economic and political realms until 1943. While not challenging the primacy of the agricultural sector, manufacturing kept expanding and diversifying after World War I, particularly in the second half of the 1930s. By 1943 this steady growth led the industrial sector to surpass agriculture in terms of GDP, a historic event.

However, industrialists did not replace landowners as the new dominant social class. On the contrary, they accepted the traditional values of the landed oligarchy and attempted to gain admission into the old elites' most exclusive circles. Nor were industrialists able to translate their economic strength into political strength. Although Peronist and Radical administrations from 1946 on supported the continuation of the ISI process begun in the 1930s, they did so unilaterally and with little or no consultation with the sector's interest groups. These groups, finding themselves left out of the decision-making process, fought back. Deeply divided among themselves and lacking a political party that could express their grievances, industrial distributional coalitions countered by reducing investments and operations, laying off workers, and exporting their capital. When these failed, they—like their agricultural counterparts—turned to the military to create governments they hoped would promote policies favorable to them. Yet they found that the authoritarian solution was even more costly than the evil it was supposed to replace.

278

Industrial distributional coalitions are engaged in a constant struggle to limit government interference in their operations. At the same time, they fight with labor, agricultural, financial, and distributional coalitions to protect their interests. Industrial associations still lack the ability to lobby in a unified way. The overlapping structural, ideological, and attitudinal cleavages that characterize them are indicative of the malaise that has affected the country as a whole. Therefore, in this chapter the analysis will center on the roles that industrial distributional coalitions played in the political arena, which of them were most involved, what interests they represented, and what resources they used to accomplish their goals.

The Early Development of Industrial Groups

The first Argentine industrial association was organized in Buenos Aires in 1875 under the name of Industrial Club (Club Industrial) by individuals whose companies were concentrated in light manufacturing. Later on, a rival group representing entrepreneurs of the agroindustry set up the Center for Industry (Centro Industrial).[2] The two contending associations finally merged into the UIA in 1887. The bulk of the 887 original members of the UIA were foreigners who had recently arrived from Belgium, France, Germany, Italy, and the United Kingdom.[3] Since its inception, the UIA was an elitist organization, resembling a club rather than an interest group. Its members were mostly big businessmen located in metropolitan Buenos Aires.[4] Nonetheless, the UIA leadership remained firmly in the hands of Argentines well into the twentieth century: Argentine-born leaders from the ruling oligarchy had political and financial connections that foreign members did not have, spoke Spanish fluently, and knew how to work within the government bureaucracy.[5]

Why then was the early industrialization process carried out by immigrants? To begin with, when the first waves of foreign immigration came to Argentina at the end of the nineteenth century, most of the best land had already been taken, and many newcomers settled in the cities, particularly in Buenos Aires (the port of arrival in Argentina), and started small businesses.[6] Second, as some scholars have argued, the landowning ruling class that shaped Argentine politics from 1880 until 1916 was ideologically against a national industry.[7] The Conservatives' economic base was the rural economy, which promoted the country's economic growth through its exports. This meant strict compliance with the theory of comparative advantage, which in principle prevented the creation of a local manufacturing sector, as Argentina would be better off to trade its agricultural products for industrial goods that could be purchased at cheaper prices abroad. Therefore, not only was industrialization absent from the ideology of the oligarchs, but for many of them it was counterproductive. As Juan Bautista Alberdi said, "One of the causes of the South American crisis . . . has been the ignorant and blind anxiety to create a South American manufacturing industry to rival European industry through protective legislation. . . . With respect to big industry . . . such an attempt is of the same nature as the crazy battle of Don Quixote against the windmills."[8]

Following this reasoning, some scholars conclude that "the first industrialists [found themselves] in a situation of objective weakness with respect to an 'establishment' whose economic project [was] based upon agricultural exports and whose conception of democracy [was] highly restrictive."[9] There is widespread consensus that the emerging industrial sector in the first quarter of this century was economically, politically, and socially subordinated to the landowning elite. For instance, the industrialists' political apathy has been explained by arguing that, because foreign entrepreneurs could freely pursue their business interests without applying for Argentine citizenship, they lacked the incentive to participate in domestic politics through political parties.[10] The fact that the majority of the country's industrialists were foreign-born lends some support to the assertion that the oligarchy scorned any manufacturing not linked to agriculture as not legitimate entrepreneurial activity.[11] Argentines owned only 19 percent of the country's industrial establishments in 1895, a share that increased in the twentieth century, reaching 32 percent in 1914, and 39 percent in 1935.[12] These data are not all that surprising if one considers that in 1914, 43 percent of the economically active population of metropolitan Buenos Aires, where most of Argentine industry was located, was foreign-born.[13] The small increase in Argentine ownership may have been caused by the fact that some of the Argentine offspring of the foreign-born industrialists had taken over their parents' companies by 1935. Additionally, by 1935 many landowners had begun to invest in manufacturing to diversify their business activities.

Taking all these factors together, it is no wonder that foreign-born industrialists (whose companies were primarily in manufacturing), although constituting the majority of the UIA's membership, left the representation of their concerns to Argentine agroindustrialists—who as both landowners and members of the most influential political circles had direct access to the source of power.[14] Under the leadership of the agroindustrialists, the UIA accepted the secondary role that the Conservative governments had in mind for domestic industry. As a consequence, the nation's entrepreneurs rather passively accepted the agriculture-led development model.[15] The UIA had more realistic and less ambitious goals, like securing passage in Congress of modest tariff protection measures and the stopping of prolabor legislation, both of which could be acceptable to the oligarchy. The UIA strongly lobbied Congress against the right to strike, the right to organize, the eight-hour workday, collective bargaining, and protection of working youth. It also sponsored the right-wing Liga Patriótica Argentina.[16]

Some scholars have contended that, at the turn of the century, the industrialists missed the opportunity to take national leadership away from the landowning aristocracy by exploiting the social unrest among the urban middle sectors, who were asking for active participation in the political system.[17] Instead of supporting the national movement for political enfranchisement and forging a new class alliance between capital and the petit bourgeoisie, the entrepreneurs backed off, afraid that such support would antagonize the oligarchy. As a result, the potential constituency for a proindustry, urban-based political party was stolen away by the Radicals, who had very little interest in promoting industrialization, as some of their most prominent leaders were landowners themselves.[18] In other words, the Radical administrations under Yrigoyen and Alvear were more concerned with the redistribution of the spoils of power among their followers rather than the creation of an alternative capital accumulation model based upon industrial expansion. Between 1916 and 1930 the Radicals kept endorsing the agricultural development model created by the Conservatives while paying lip service to the demands of the manufacturing sector. The Radicals did not have much sympathy for the industrialists, nor did the opposition parties in Congress. Conservatives looked down on manufacturing and feared that protectionist measures to defend it could jeopardize their own special trade relation with the United Kingdom. The socialists regarded the industrial bourgeoisie as reactionary and an enemy of the working class.

Besides the lack of a party linkage, structural and sociological factors kept industrialists from playing a significant political role. From a structural standpoint, the heterogeneous makeup of the industrial establishment was one of the main obstacles to its being a unified actor. First, there was a split between a few big entrepreneurs, many linked to the agroindustrial sector, and the large number of small businessmen, almost invariably from humble beginnings and concerned with their own well-being rather than with that of the sector as a whole.[19] The UIA represented big business and ignored the needs of the small entrepreneurs. Second, individualism coupled with ethnic division created suspicion and rivalry among foreign-born entrepreneurs. Third, small-scale, foreign-born industrialists, unlike the agroindustrialists, had no access to credit and financing. Jewish banks as well as local branches of Spanish, Italian, German, French, Belgian, Dutch, and British banks were set up to meet this money-starved entrepreneurial class.[20] Yet this only reinforced their tendency to turn to their own national group for help and slowed the process of unifying them with large industrialists. Finally, the agroindustrialists and manufacturing entrepreneurs were split.[21]

From a sociological viewpoint, it has been argued that the oligarchs' ideological bias against industrialization and the limits imposed on the manufacturing sector until 1930 affected the behavior of entrepreneurs. Unlike the big industrialists in Europe and North America, their Argentine counterparts did not develop their own class consciousness, preferring to emulate the landowning elite's life-style and to adopt its conservative political values. Thus, instead of becoming an element of social transformation, the country's most important industrial entrepreneurs remained politically very conservative and prone to endorse authoritarian solutions.[22] Some scholars cite as a typical example the custom of successful manufacturing entrepreneurs to buy ranches and join exclusive landowners' associations, like the SRA and the Jockey Club of Buenos Aires. The assimilation of some emerging entrepreneurs within the old socioeconomic establishment was facilitated to some degree by business and personal ties with the agroindustrialists, many of whom, as we have seen, were part of the oligarchy.[23]

In spite of the fact that the country lacked an industrialization policy until the late 1930s, some tariff protection schemes were enforced, although unevenly, for some manufacturing sectors.[24] Between 1900 and 1930, industrial output grew steadily; and the portion of the economically active population engaged in industrial activities increased from a fourth in 1895 to a third by 1914.[25] Between 1900–1904 and 1925–1929 manufacturing expanded at an estimated rate of 5.4 percent of GDP, a growth caused not by the production of import substitution products but by an increase in agroindustrial exports (meat packing and dairy products, milling, etcetera) and domestic demand for Argentine-made goods.[26] Before the Great Depression, light industry made up the great majority of the sector's output. The bulk of entrepreneurial activity was carried out by thousands of small, labor-intensive shops and a few very large enterprises.

In the 1920s (and more so in the 1930s) the participation of the manufacturing sector in the national economy continued to increase. As agricultural growth began to slow, a heated debate revolved about the need to strengthen and diversify the industrialization process. In the proindustry camp, Alejandro Bunge, a renowned economist and public figure from one of the country's wealthiest families, emerged as the dominant ideologue.[27] In spite of his oligarchic origin, Bunge spoke out against the old agriculture-led development model through the *Revista de Economía Argentina*, a periodical he founded in 1918.[28] In addition, Bunge also worried about the steady economic decline of the British

Empire, Argentina's main trading partner, and the rise of the United States. He believed that, had Argentina been forced to replace the United Kingdom with the United States as its main supplier of industrial goods, it would have found itself in dire straits, as the latter was self-sufficient in primary goods production.

Bunge urged the government to design and finance an industrial policy aimed at creating a new manufacturing sector, protected through import tariffs, which would produce previously imported goods.[29] However, if Bunge's endorsement of ISI and economic nationalism constituted a challenge to the economic ideology of the oligarchy, in political matters he was as much an elitist as the establishment he criticized. Although Bunge had supported Yrigoyen early on, he later became dissatisfied with democratic politics in general and specifically with the Radicals' corruption and lack of resolve in tackling Argentina's problems. Not only did he welcome the 1930 coup, he was also adamantly against unionism and publicly expressed his sympathies for fascism.[30] Bunge was essentially "a productivist who believed that all classes would benefit as rising productivity created a bigger economic pie."[31] This was in fact the general attitude of the proindustry movement, which, while advocating structural reform, remained uninterested in reshaping the political system to suit the changed socioeconomic conditions.

Many of Bunge's proposals were adopted by several industrial associations as their own, among them the Argentine Confederation of Commerce, Industry, and Production (Confederación Argentina del Comercio, la Industria y la Producción, CACIP), founded in 1916. The CACIP included foreign railway and utility corporations, exporters, financiers, and agroindustrialists, in order of importance. Its leadership was dominated by large enterprises, both domestic and foreign. British-owned—and to a lesser extent, North-American-owned—companies were prominent in the CACIP and alone accounted for 95 percent of its industrial membership.[32] The CACIP's main argument was that conflicts among agriculture, industry, and commerce were artificial, and it proposed diversification of the economy along Bunge's lines. But in the end, the CACIP was supportive mainly of those industries that could export and was lukewarm about ISI due to the smallness of the Argentine market.[33]

A much more vocal Bunge supporter was Luis Colombo, chairman of the UIA throughout the 1925–1946 period. Colombo personified the new brand of up-and-coming businessmen who had steadily replaced the agroindustrialists at the helm of the UIA. Although the UIA did not represent exclusively industrial interests, it was the entrepreneurial association in which manufacturing was most heavily concentrated:

manufacturing made up 50 percent of the capital it represented compared to only 10 percent of the CACIP's.[34] Foreign capital was important to the UIA, but not as much as it was to the CACIP.

Colombo did not limit himself to convincing politicians and the general public that no fundamental contradiction existed between industry and agriculture. He tirelessly called for better protection and financing of entrepreneurs as a means to boost the domestic market and attain greater economic independence. He organized massive rallies in 1933 to denounce the Roca-Runciman treaty, which gave British manufacturers privileged access to the Argentine market. Two years later, under Colombo's guidance, the UIA released a document entitled *Seis Leyes Económicas*, in which the association renewed its appeal for greater protection, claiming that "it had been industry rather than agriculture that had rescued the country after the depression by overcoming a host of legal and economic obstacles to expand its operations and absorb 400,000 of those unemployed in 1931."[35] Unlike CACIP leaders, Colombo discounted the old argument favoring "natural industry" as opposed to "artificial industry." Like Bunge, he was a "productivist" for whom the more industry there was, the better. Like Bunge, he had supported the 1930 coup against the Radicals.[36]

The third association comprising small entrepreneurs was the Argentine Federation of Entities Defending Commerce and Industry (Federación Argentina de Entidades Defensoras del Comercio y la Industria, or FAEDCI), set up in 1932 to protest the government's policy of taxing businessmen's incomes and commercial transactions. Similar to the CACIP, the FAEDCI included diverse interests; but if the CACIP was the expression of big business, the FAEDCI represented small- and medium-sized commercial and industrial companies (some located outside of Buenos Aires) producing for the local economy. It had no agricultural members. While it agreed with the UIA on the necessity of more industrial protectionism, the FAEDCI vehemently opposed foreign capital as well as large companies—which they accused of monopolistic practices, a position that took the FAEDCI and the CACIP a world apart. Thus the only common beliefs binding these three interest groups were their repression of labor and their opposition to taxes.

Mutually exclusive economic interests, internal squabbles, intrasector rivalries, and ideological differences over free trade made it impossible for industrial distributional coalitions to act as a common front and led the UIA, the CACIP, and the FAEDCI to influence government policy individually. The structural heterogeneity of industrial interests (e.g., big capital as opposed to medium-sized and small industries) in part explains why entrepreneurs failed to create a strong representative association like the SRA for the agricultural sector. The lack of such a group had a lot to do with the industrialists' peculiar relationship with the state (the state was responsible for maintaining protective barriers and was both an important consumer and a producer of industrial goods).[37] Because of such heterogeneity in this period, "we cannot strictly speak of an industrial bourgeoisie but rather of sectors of the bourgeoisie with interests in industry."[38]

Furthermore, the fact that industrialists gained more concessions during the Concordancia years than in the 1920s did not mean that they had a well-defined alternative strategy of development. Indeed, their demands concentrated on very specific matters (import tariffs, tax breaks, easy credit) to promote economic growth through expansion and diversification of the manufacturing sector, without questioning the pivotal role played by agriculture.[39] In other words, many industrialists aspired to become partners with rather than rivals of the landed elites in the development of the nation's economy. Indeed, the only coherent industrialization program put forward during the Concordancia was the government-sponsored Pinedo Plan, which conceived the promotion of industry as complementary to agriculture as it: "emphasized the need to stimulate not all industries indiscriminately but those only that had a reasonable chance of developing efficiently and at a low cost. The programme envisaged in particular the development of the so-called 'natural industries,' that is, those that processed the agricultural raw materials which Argentina produced cheaply."[40]

Why did the Concordancia enforce policies that ultimately favored the ISI process? For Guillermo O'Donnell, this was a logical consequence of the coalition of agricultural exporters and agroindustrialists supporting that regime: ISI policies were designed to reward agroindustrialists. On the other hand, to Gilbert Merkx ISI policies "were not undertaken for the *specific* purpose of aiding the industrial sector, but rather were intended to safeguard the export market, aid agricultural production, and maintain Argentina's ability to meet her international obligations." Following Merkx's line of argument, Benjamin Most also refuted O'Donnell's thesis, adding that "if the agriculturalists were engaging in defensive modernization to protect their own interests, the export-related industrialists need not have been involved in the policy formulation and execution process."[41]

Merkx's and Most's interpretations seem more realistic than O'Donnell's. It seems that the growth of the industrial sector in the 1930s was triggered by the Great Depression rather than by a deliberate plan to change the nature of the Argentine economy. The economic teams of the Concordancia resorted to exchange controls, import permits, and tariff barriers to shelter selected manufacturing sectors as a response to the collapse of international trade. Entrepreneurs took full advantage of these favorable circumstances: the drop in foreign imports (either because of protectionist measures or the unavailability of foreign supplies) coincided with a rise in domestic demand in the second half of the 1930s. It is not unlikely that industrial associations shaped some government initiatives, but there is no clear evidence that agroindustrialists designed plans or were targeted by them. Throughout the Concordancia, the well-being of the agricultural sector remained the number-one priority. The end result, though, was undeniably positive for Argentine industry.

> Between the triennial averages of 1927–1929 and 1941–1943, manufacturing grew at an annual rate of 3.4 percent, as against only 1.5 percent in the rural sector and 1.8 percent in gross domestic product. Imports of manufactured consumer goods, around 40 percent of total imports before 1930, had fallen to less than 25 percent by the late 1940s. The 1914 census had catalogued some 383,000 industrial workers; by 1935 the number had risen to 544,000, by 1941 to around 830,000, and by 1946 to over 1 million. Similarly, the number of industrial firms grew from less than 41,000 in 1935 to more than 57,000 in 1940, and to around 86,000 by 1946. In 1935 the value of industrial production was still 40 percent below that of the agrarian sector; in 1943 industry surpassed agriculture for the first time.[42]

Interestingly enough, most of the expansion took place in manufacturing sectors that existed prior to 1930. The bulk of industrial production remained concentrated in the labor-intensive, light consumer goods industries, namely textiles, foods, and beverages. Neither the internal composition nor the location of manufacturing experienced much change. Myriad small companies coexisted with a few large industrial establishments (which accounted for almost two-thirds of the sector's employment). The Buenos Aires metropolitan area hosted about 70 percent of manufacturing in 1939.[43] As industry grew, so did the membership of its representative associations. The UIA, which in 1946 was the sector's largest entrepreneurial organization, comprised ninety-one chambers, representing 3,000 firms—compared to six chambers and 300 firms in the early 1930s.[44] Still, small industrialists continued to be excluded from representative associations: in 1941 the UIA represented only 3 percent of Argentine industrialists, most of whom were from big firms in the Buenos Aires area.[45]

From Military Intervention to Peronist Dominance (1943–1955)

Soon after the 1943 coup, the new military authorities made it explicit that ISI was to become a top priority. That year, for the first time in the country's history, industry's share of GDP surpassed that of agriculture. This policy was the culmination of the trend of the previous two decades, but by 1943 the war had made self-sufficiency more important than ever. Further, the military leaders were uneasy about the close military and economic ties between Brazil and the United States, which threatened their ambition to become the dominant South American power.[46]

The military governments considerably enlarged the size of the public bureaucracy, invested in new defense-related industrialization and infrastructure, strengthened tariff protection, and created an industrial credit bank. The increase in government spending spurred demand for consumer goods, which was for the most part satisfied by domestic industries, given that foreign imports had declined due to the disruptive effects of World War II on international trade. Thus, the 1943–1946 period saw business activity thriving as a consequence of exceptionally favorable exogenous factors and government expansionary policies. Manufacturers were among the big winners, especially those owning small and medium-sized companies that produced previously imported consumer goods. Many of these people had quickly risen from humble working class or commercial backgrounds; others were immigrants and for the most part not politically active.

These events were interpreted by O'Donnell as the policy outcome of the new populist coalition headed by the armed forces which also included labor, producers of nonexportable primary goods, and small and medium sized industrialists in the import substitution sector. What O'Donnell suggested was that, because these industrialists kept the benefits themselves, they were part of the populist coalition.[47] However, other researchers have convincingly argued that this was not the case. Most pointed out that there was no evidence of any appreciable participation by the industrialists in the decision-making process. Torcuato Di Tella added that, although many small entrepreneurs owning import substituting factories welcomed the military policies and a few may have had some influence over some measures, they did so on an individual basis rather than as representatives of the whole sector. Carlos Díaz Alejandro hypothesized that ISI served the purpose of creating jobs for Perón's base of support, urban workers, rather than the boosting of entrepreneurs' well-being. Samuel Bailey believed that the initial ISI policies were crafted by the conservative military leaders first in control of government, who did so for national security reasons; only later, did these policies take on a populist content, targeting labor, an event that coincided with Perón's ascendancy to power between mid-1944 and early 1946.[48] What can be said with some degree of certainty is that in the early days of the military regime industrialists were supportive but not actively involved.

However, as time went on many entrepreneurs, particularly in the UIA, became worried about the military's economic nationalism.[49] One of their concerns was the armed forces' use of state powers to interfere in the operation of the market. Some private companies were nationalized, and restrictions were imposed on credit, investments, prices, wages, and the use of fuel and raw materials.[50] Moreover, the pro-Axis military stance until two months before the end of the war angered the United States, the main source of capital equipment.

In 1944 Perón tried to lure the UIA into his camp to be his industrial counterpart of the CGT, but UIA President Colombo refused. Perón then bypassed the UIA, making ad hoc deals directly with companies and industrial sectors. In 1945, he made a further move to draft the support of organized interests for his plans by setting up the Postwar Socioeconomic Council, a corporatist institutional arrangement that was to bring together representatives of the military, labor, industry, and agriculture. But once more Perón's plans were frustrated by UIA and SRA refusal to cooperate, and the Council never worked out. Why was the UIA opposed to Perón's overtures if his proindustry rhetoric indicated a convergence of interests? Misgivings about bad relations with the United States were part of the reason, but more important for entrepreneurs were Perón's prounion policies.[51] Closely linked to this point was the perception that Perón's policies of "social justice" and state intervention were devised to emasculate the old economic elite, both economically and politically—economically, because such policies forced landowners and industrialists to share their profits with previously marginalized urban classes; politically, because Perón wanted to subordinate the power of the economic elite to his own personal authority so he could impose new rules upon the economic establishment.[52]

Some members of the UIA, most noticeably Miguel Miranda, joined Perón, but they were a minority. In 1945, the UIA led an anti-Peronist entrepreneurial bloc made up of the SRA, the Chamber of Commerce, and other trade associations to support the Democratic Union candidate who challenged Perón's 1946 presidential bid.[53] After the election, the UIA paid dearly for its defiance. Soon after Perón became president, the UIA convened its congress to select a new leadership. Three main lists were presented: "collaborationists" were headed by Miranda and supported Perón's economic plan; the "blue list" was vehemently anti-Peronist and allegedly endorsed by Colombo, who had retired due to failing health; the "white list" was made up of moderate members searching for compromise between the other two positions. When the votes were cast, the blue list was victorious, but it was a short-lived success; in August 1946, Perón officially dissolved the UIA on the pretext that it had illegally used its funds for political purposes.[54]

I have already argued that O'Donnell's thesis that a populist coalition dominated the political arena between 1943 and 1952 was not well supported for at least the military regime (1943–1946), but what about when Perón was in power (1946–1955)? Were the industrialists part of his coalition, and to what extent did they have an impact on policy making? Certainly, some members of the entrepreneurial class were selected to head important government posts, the most symbolic being Miranda, Perón's main economic adviser between 1946 and 1949. Nonetheless, these people joined Peronist administrations not as members of industrial distributional coalitions but as individuals. Perón himself tried to create an entrepreneurial organization (with little success) during his first administration. Why? In an interview, former Minister of the Economy Alfredo Gómez Morales said, "While Perón had frequently suggested that it might be useful to develop and institutionalize private-sector collaboration with the government, he was too much in a hurry to complete his economic reforms to expend the effort needed to build such collaboration. Instead, he preferred either to speak directly with individual cattlemen and industrialists when help was needed or, more often, just to ignore them and trust in the ability of his subordinates to get the job done."[55]

With the UIA gone, in late 1946 Perón set up a more docile entrepreneurial organization, the Association of Production, Industry, and Commerce (Asociación de la Producción, Industria y Comercio, AAPIC). The AAPIC included not only industry but also other major business activities in order to make it as high-powered as the CGT. However, the attempt was a dismal failure. Most UIA members refused to join, as did agricultural and commercial businessmen, who preferred to remain with the SRA and the Chamber of Commerce, respectively. In 1949, Perón tried once more to convince entrepreneurs to join his labor and military supporters by dissolving AAPIC and creating from its ashes the Argentine Economic Confederation (Confederación Económica Argentina, or CEA). The CEA made some strides in improving its representativeness, compared to the AAPIC, but still fell short of Perón's expectations, since most big business ignored it.

The breakthrough finally came when Perón turned his attention to the small and medium-sized businesses of the provinces, some of which had in 1950 organized the Argentine Confederation of Production, Industry, and Commerce (Confederación Argentina de la Producción, Industria y Comercio, or CAPIC), under the leadership of José Gelbard.[56] The CAPIC's main feature was that its companies were concerned with the domestic market, relatively weak in self-financing, and were labor-intensive. Because they had developed primarily as a consequence of ISI, CAPIC companies were extremely concerned with a possible return to a free-market economic regime. Due to their geographical location, they constantly faced problems of credit financing and marketing, which were dominated by Buenos Aires' companies. Therefore, the

CAPIC offered to Perón his long-awaited business support, while it would receive government protection, subsidies, and perhaps institutionalized access to policy making.

In 1951 the CAPIC began talks with the CEA for a possible merger, which took place in 1953, when Gelbard was put in charge of the CGE. The large entrepreneurs of metropolitan Buenos Aires were eventually forced to join the CGE when Perón made membership compulsory. To their dismay, they had little say in the confederation, as its operations were dominated by Gelbard and his associates. Thus, early in his second term in office, Perón succeeded in bringing into his coalition a business counterpart for labor. Both the CGE and the CGT were umbrella organizations, or associations of the fourth degree. In theory, both were supposed to persuade their members to comply with the policies these organizations agreed upon with the government—according to Perón's corporatist scheme, which, however, he never implemented.

In organizational terms, the CGE was divided into three branches: the General Confederation of Production (agriculture) (Confederación General de la Producción), the General Confederation of Industry (Confederación General Industrial, CGI), and the General Confederation of Commerce (Confederación General del Comercio). Each confederation was based upon regional federations, which in turn were made up of individual chambers. Representation was not determined according to a company's size or location but according to the simple rule of one man, one vote. However, companies contributed to the CGE a fixed percentage of their capital. In practice, this meant that the small and medium-sized companies, thanks to their number, dominated the confederation, while most of the bill was paid by large businesses.[57]

Thus, the CGE received state protection and guidance. However, although Gelbard and other CGE officials were appointed to several important posts and Gelbard himself was often invited to cabinet meetings, it is doubtful that his influence over socioeconomic policy was appreciable. In the end, what brought Perón and Gelbard together had more to do with personal convenience than shared ideals. The evidence suggests that Perón was always afraid to institutionalize the access of interest groups into the decision-making process. The CGE, like labor, by accepting Perón's patronage, had limited ability to change the Peronist power structure from within. Domestic entrepreneurs were favored by the government's import restrictions (imposed to solve the 1949 foreign exchange crisis), but by the time the CGE came about the expansion of light consumer goods had reached its apex. In fact, Perón's tight austerity program announced in 1952 put pressure on both labor and capital to accept government measures for wage and price restraints. More to the point, the 1953 foreign investment law and the 1955 agreement with the California Petroleum Company to exploit Argentine oil resources reversed the regime's early nationalistic stance and upset the CGE.

This policy U-turn was probably prompted by the realization of a number of problems. First, the horizontal ISI process had produced a large industrial base, but one that was scarcely integrated and still needed foreign technology and raw materials to function. Second, the DGFM had proved incapable of developing a high-quality heavy industry that could supply the domestic market, and even more troublesome, most DGFM companies were poorly managed, overstaffed, and required continuous injections of money which further compounded the precarious situation of the fiscal deficit. Last, the expansionary policies of the mid-1940s had drained domestic credit, and it was hoped that a slow opening up to foreign capital could alleviate the problem.[58] This is not to say that Perón returned to a free-market economic development model. Indeed, Argentina remained a semiclosed economy dominated by heavy protectionism. But it seems clear that between 1952 and 1955 the administration was trying to keep its supporting coalition together while adopting a more pragmatic approach to the external imbalance situation, which ran against the interests of both the CGT and the CGE. During this period, the contradictions of the Peronist movement came into the open and eventually led to the end of the populist coalition.

Industrial Distribution Coalitions During the Peronist Proscription (1955–1966)

With the coming to power of the Aramburu government, the map of entrepreneurial associations was redrawn again, but this time at the expense of the Peronists. The UIA regained its legal status and was left with a near monopoly on industrial representation, as the new administration dissolved the CGE because of its close ties with the previous regime. This of course deepened the old cleavages between the entrepreneurial class. The small producers who had supported the CGE and had thrived under the protectionist policies of Perón found themselves at the mercy of an administration with little sympathy for their concerns. Conversely, the large domestic and foreign companies felt that their moment had finally come and a drastic reversal of economic policies was on the horizon.

Initially, Aramburu seemed to please these large companies. Besides reinstating the UIA, Aramburu appointed Eugenio Blanco, a respected academician, to head the Ministry of the Economy. To strengthen support for his policies, the president consulted representatives of entrepreneurial groups over specific measures. But Aramburu found it increasingly difficult to undo almost ten years of Peronist economic policy, due to the opposition of the constituencies that had grown around them. The provisional nature of the government and the president's personal commitment to allow new elections in a relatively short time prevented the development of any long-term structural reform of the Argentine economy. On the other hand, the Radicals, who constituted the single most important party now that the Peronists were disbanded, although they had supported the 1955 coup, shared many of Perón's nationalistic policies and were opposed to any sweeping changes that would imply a return to a free-market economy.[59]

Thus, Aramburu chose a middle-of-the-road approach that could hold together the fragile coalition backing the Liberating Revolution.[60] He retained many state powers created under Perón to enable him to manipulate economic variables with a freer hand. Deficit-ridden state enterprises were kept and so were most public employees in the overstaffed public administration. Price controls, multiple exchange rates, import quotas, export taxes, and consumption subsidies were also retained. The Liberating Revolution tried to eliminate Peronist control over labor unions through political repression, but Aramburu was careful to prevent the stabilization measures from overly penalizing blue-collar and white-collar workers, (whose real salaries in 1957 were the same as in 1954).[61] The economy as a whole, and manufacturing in particular, grew at a sustained pace. (See table 8.1).

Notwithstanding these positive results, toward the end of his brief tenure Aramburu came under fire from both agricultural and industrial coalitions. The UIA and the SRA became disenchanted with Aramburu over time. In fact, they perceived his administration as unwilling to dismantle government controls over economic activity, to reform the operation of state corporations and the bureaucratic apparatus, and to open the economy to foreign capital and technology.

If Aramburu failed to fulfill the expectations of the UIA, his successor, Arturo Frondizi, promised even more trouble for UIA interests. The interest groups representing big capital (the UIA, the SRA, the CAC, the Buenos Aires Stock Exchange, and the CARBAP) resented Frondizi's campaign promises to reincorporate Peronism.[62] Adding to the strain between these groups and the Radical administration was Frondizi's decision, soon after his election, to decree large wage increases, to legalize the CGE, and to permit many trade unions to be recaptured by Peronist labor leaders who had been purged by Aramburu. These steps further alienated big capital, which interpreted them as a betrayal of the objectives of the Liberating Revolution—the eradication of Peronism.

These were mainly political quarrels, but economically Frondizi did not fare much better. This may appear, at first glance, a little puzzling. After all, Frondizi was proposing a development plan to address some of the shortcomings of the early ISI strategy. Import substitution, save for the DGFM, had concentrated almost exclusively on consumer goods;

TABLE 8.1

Composition of GDP, by Economic Sector, 1945–1972 (percentage)

Year	GDP: Change from Previous Year	Agriculture	Manufacturing	Construction	Commerce	Banking	Public Services	Mining
1945	-4.8	20.3	22.8	5.8	16.2	7.1	26.6	1.2
1946	8.3	19.4	23.7	5.7	17.0	7.0	26.2	1.0
1947	13.8	18.8	24.5	5.2	18.1	6.5	25.9	1.0
1948	1.1	18.0	23.7	6.4	18.3	6.5	26.7	0.9
1949	-4.5	16.8	23.0	7.2	17.2	7.0	27.9	1.0
1950	1.5	18.0	27.9	4.8	19.4	4.0	25.3	0.9
1951	3.9	18.5	27.5	4.7	19.4	4.0	25.1	0.6
1952	-5.1	16.7	26.5	4.6	19.0	4.4	26.1	0.6
1953	5.4	20.7	26.9	4.3	17.7	4.2	15.4	0.7
1954	4.1	19.8	27.8	4.0	18.1	4.2	15.4	0.7
1955	7.1	19.3	29.2	3.8	19.5	4.1	14.5	0.7
1956	2.8	17.9	20.4	3.6	18.9	4.0	14.7	0.7
1957	5.1	16.9	31.2	4.0	19.1	3.9	14.1	0.7
1958	6.1	16.7	31.8	4.6	19.0	3.9	23.4	0.7
1959	-6.4	17.6	30.5	3.6	18.1	4.2	25.1	0.9
1960	7.8	16.6	31.1	4.0	18.9	4.0	24.3	1.1
1961	7.1	15.4	31.9	4.0	19.6	3.8	23.9	1.4
1962	-1.6	16.3	30.6	3.7	19.2	4.0	24.6	1.6
1963	-2.4	16.9	30.1	3.6	18.1	4.2	25.5	1.6
1964	10.3	16.5	32.5	3.4	17.9	3.8	24.4	1.5
1965	9.1	16.0	33.9	3.2	18.1	3.6	23.8	1.4
1966	0.6	15.3	33.9	3.4	17.8	3.7	24.4	1.5
1967	2.7	15.5	33.5	3.7	17.6	3.7	24.4	1.6
1968	4.3	14.1	34.3	4.2	17.7	3.7	24.3	1.7
1969	8.6	13.7	35.0	4.6	18.1	3.6	23.3	1.7
1970	5.4	13.7	35.2	4.5	17.8	3.5	23.2	1.8
1971	3.6	12.5	36.8	4.4	18.1	3.5	23.0	1.7
1972	1.6	11.1	37.9	4.5	18.2	3.5	23.1	1.7

SOURCE: Guido Di Tella and Rudiger Dornbusch, eds., *The Political Economy of Argentina, 1946–83* (Pittsburgh: University of Pittsburgh Press, 1989), pp. 325, 326.

it had accelerated under Perón but eventually led to a recurrent balance of payments deficit, creating the stop-and-go economic cycle. The heart of the problem lay in the fact that Argentine manufacturing needed to produce capital equipment rather than import it. Given that domestic consumer goods were hardly exportable because of their high costs, domestic industry was unable to generate the foreign exchange necessary to import this capital equipment. This task was left to agricultural exports, whose revenues kept manufacturing operating.

However, from the late 1940s on, the import needs of manufacturing exceeded the capacity of the agricultural sector to generate foreign exchange. Rural sector growth was sluggish in the late 1940s and 1950s partly because of unfavorable weather and fluctuating international prices. Perhaps equally important was that many agricultural producers refrained from investing as long as the government heavily taxed their profits and used them to finance an inefficient industry and a bankrupt bureaucracy. The situation became a vicious circle. When a foreign exchange imbalance occurred, government officials curtailed imports and domestic consumption and tried to stimulate agricultural exports. Once a positive balance of payments was achieved, expansionary policies were prompted to spur the economy, and again income was transferred to manufacturing and services, as agricultural prices lagged behind industrial prices. Frondizi thought he had the formula to stop all that. His plan called for the creation of a heavy domestic industry like petroleum, chemicals, car manufacturing, and steel, which would make the country self-sufficient in many imported capital goods, thus eliminating the structural bottleneck that had impaired previous ISI. Since Argentina had not enough capital for such an ambitious program, Frondizi looked to foreign investors—whom he had previously despised—for help. North American and European multinationals were invited to invest in the country with very favorable government concessions.

Although many of the policies adopted by Frondizi had been long advocated by the UIA, the SRA, and the CAC, these policies failed to gain support for the president when he announced them upon taking office in May 1958. The following December, after his alliance with Peronist labor unions turned into overt confrontation, Frondizi made a further move that had been sought by big capital for many months: he agreed on a strict stabilization program, with the assistance of the IMF. The UIA, while expressing its pleasure with the decision, remained skeptical about Frondizi. One reason rested simply on the fact that Frondizi had changed his political and economic views from one side to another in a matter of a few months, and most entrepreneurs were uncomfortable supporting a man so unpredictable. Frondizi's dealings with Perón and his occasional overtures toward labor and the CGE reinforced their skepticism. A second reason was that, while the development program and the stabilization policies implemented between 1959 and March 1962 met with UIA approval, the president never consulted the UIA on them. As a matter of fact, Frondizi kept interest groups at arm's length. However, due to this ambiguous behavior, neither the Peronists, nor big capital, nor the military trusted him, and eventually the president alienated everyone.

The CGE was equally resentful of the fact that Frondizi did not involve it in crafting economic policy, but for different reasons. The CGE attacked the government's stabilization plan to partially open the economy, which it feared would jeopardize the weak and scarcely competitive firms it represented. A related complaint was that the tight monetary and credit policies were driving many small entrepreneurs out of business, because unlike big business, they could not rely on self-financing or foreign loans. By the same token, the CGE denounced the IMF agreement as a selling of the country's sovereignty and a denationalization of the domestic economy, because the new policies permitted foreign capital to take over financially troubled Argentine companies.

The profound division between the CGE and the UIA on almost every socioeconomic issue polarized the industry. From an economic standpoint, the CGE wanted a strong state; the government was to draft economic policy in concert with both labor and capital. This trilateral policy was guaranteed by a permanent bargaining institution, the Social and Economic Council (Consejo Económico Social, or CONES), made up of representatives of the three groups. In practice, the CONES was a corporative institution whose antecedents went back to the Peronist regime (although, as we saw, Perón never put the scheme to work). The CGE believed that the CONES would safeguard its interests against those of big domestic capital and multinational corporations, which in an unregulated market were likely to gain the upper hand over small and medium-sized entrepreneurs. As in the early 1950s, the CGE stood for a closed economy, opposed the oligopolistic practices of big companies, and wanted strict regulation of multinationals.[63] To put pressure on the government, the CGE resorted to on-again, off-again tactical alliances with labor, usually following economic cycles—being "on" during recessions and "off" when growth resumed.[64] This erratic pattern once more demonstrated that convenience more than anything else had brought the CGE into the Peronist coalition in 1953. In fact, many members of the CGE leadership were not Peronists, and quite a few were actually Radicals belonging to the UCRP.[65] Without Perón's mediation, the CGE and Peronist labor leaders were often unable to resolve their feuds when economic downturns affected them in conflicting ways.

The irreconcilable nature of CGE and UIA demands made clear once more the inability of the industrial sector to act in a unified way. In 1958, the UIA joined the SRA and the CAC in creating the ACIEL. What

ACIEL's members had in common was that they represented big capital, demanded a reduction of state interventionism, despised any kind of social pact, welcomed foreign investments and technology, and opposed labor unions, the CGE, and anything reminiscent of the Peronist era. They were also bound by the shared conviction that a free-market economic system was most beneficial to the country. Although official statements by all three associations pointed in this direction, in practice, as far as the UIA was concerned, some cracks did exist. Although UIA members believed that free-market economics would let them import without restrictions, those who produced for the domestic market did not want foreign companies to compete in their markets. In the Argentine economy, domestic conglomerates enjoyed monopolistic or oligopolistic privileges, and Frondizi's policies were particularly favorable to these conglomerates. The oldest ones, Bunge and Born (agribusiness) and Alpargatas (textile and shoes), had started back in the 1880s, but by 1963 several others had risen to prominence, like Techint (steel and construction), Pérez Companc, Bridas, and Astras (petrochemicals). The younger groups took advantage of heavy industrialization programs and flourished under the auspices of government contracts, tax incentives, and oligopolistic concessions. These conglomerates tended to buy foreign technology or to form joint ventures with foreign multinationals, which put them ahead of the competition and allowed them to form cartels to exploit the domestic market.[66]

The typical strategy of large Argentine companies was to support free-market policies to lower import duties on needed inputs, thus permitting them to buy cheaply from abroad. However, they also strived to maintain or increase tariff barriers protecting their products so that they could sell dearly in the domestic market under conditions of little competition from foreigners. Legislation requiring the state and its companies to buy from domestic suppliers, enacted under the Illia administration, reinforced the monopolistic position of national conglomerates. Such legislation was against the principles of the free market, but UIA members who benefited from it were far from denouncing it. Similarly, foreign companies that came in during the Frondizi period (some of which joined the UIA) did invest, thanks to heavy government subsidies and the assurance that they would operate in an oligopolistic market. Thus, while the SRA and the CAC squarely backed the free-market system, the UIA's double standard made its commitment much more questionable. In effect, industrialists liked the free market as long as it did not have deleterious effects on them personally.[67] With ACIEL often reflecting the opinion of SRA and CAC free marketeers, the UIA found itself at odds with its partners on numerous occasions. These tensions would linger on throughout the existence of the ACIEL and was one of the main reasons for its dissolution in 1973.

TABLE 8.2
Composition of Industrial GDP, by Economic Sector, 1950s, 1960s (percentage)

Sector	1950	1958	1964	1966
Traditional	52.5	43.4	35.3	34.9
Dynamic	29.8	41.3	52.1	51.9
Intermediate	10.9	10.1	8.0	8.8
Other	6.8	5.2	4.6	4.4

SOURCE: William C. Smith, "Crisis of the State and Military-Authoritarian Rule in Argentina." Ph.D. diss, Stanford University, 1980, p. 176.

Big capital needed an organization of the fourth degree that could oppose the CGE on an equal footing.[68] The ACIEL served the function of forming a conservative business block that could prevent the CGE from regaining its dominance within the entrepreneurial sector. Therefore, the scope of ACIEL activities was confined to coordinating member association responses with respect to government policies, labor militancy, and CGE initiatives. The SRA, the UIA, and the CAC retained much of their institutional autonomy and independence of action, which should not come as a surprise given that what held them together was a common threat more than a common ideology. The structural transformation that took place with the arrival of multinational corporations consolidated the differences between big capital and small and medium-sized industry in terms of technology, financing, management, and productivity. Multinationals and domestic conglomerates began to dominate the most dynamic sectors of the Argentine economy while expanding their output. This trend can be observed both in terms of GDP composition and the shift in import substitution in different industrial branches. (See tables 8.2 and 8.3.)

Frondizi's proindustry policies had a very positive impact on heavy industry but neglected traditional manufacturing, which experienced a substantial decline in its share of the nation's industrial GDP, much to the resentment of the CGE. In the end, the president's develop-

TABLE 8.3
Composition of GDP, by Economic Sector, 1980s, 1990s (percentage)

Year	Agriculture	Manufacturing	Construction	Services	Other	Mining
1980	11.1	21.8	5.8	44.6	14.5	2.2
1985	14.0	20.0	2.8	45.0	15.8	2.4
1990	16.7	18.1	1.9	42.9	17.6	2.8

SOURCE: Central Bank of Argentina and Instituto de Estadística y Censos.

ment program, or *desarrollismo*, fell into a political vacuum. It could not draft the support of either the UIA or the CGE, nor did it create a political constituency of its own, as Frondizi continued to be ostracized for most of his term by the same union movement he initially hoped would help him.[69]

The election of Arturo Illia to the presidency in 1963, after the brief parenthesis of the Guido administration, marked a further evolution in the strategy to attain socioeconomic development. Frondizi had tried to solve the stop-and-go cycle by combining a stabilization plan with an ambitious investment program carried out through foreign capital. Illia and his advisers took a more nationalistic, Keynesian approach. After repudiating the IMF agreement, the president began slowly to promote expansionary fiscal, monetary, and income policies. Investments allocated to state companies and social programs grew, as did salaries for public workers. Easy terms of credit were also designed to help revitalize traditional light industry. The objective was to lift the country out of the 1962 recession by pumping in money and moderately redistributing income in favor of salary and wage earners, who had suffered the most in the previous two years.

The CGE first welcomed Illia's policies, which reintroduced greater industrial protectionism, stricter controls over foreign capital, easier terms of credit, and a tougher stand in the renegotiation of the foreign debt. Retrospectively, the CGE acknowledged that the Illia presidency was "the most progressive of all postwar governments," but while he was in office the CGE hesitated to publicly forge an alliance with the Radicals.[70] This lack of cooperation was partly Illia's fault. His party had a longstanding tradition of rejecting compromises with other political forces and considered interest groups as solely interested in taking advantage of the state. Illia, like Frondizi, insulated the decision-making process, but at the same time he hoped that interest groups would realize how beneficial his policies were to them and would accordingly comply with his administration's guidelines. To his dismay, this reasoning was no more than wishful thinking. The CGE, although sympathizing with many government policies, wanted to be actively involved or at least consulted on key policy issues. As Illia was unwilling to do so, the CGE adopted a wait-and-see attitude, and its relations with the government cooled as the president became increasingly isolated. Afraid that supporting Illia was tantamount to betting on a losing horse, the CGE kept its options open by talking to the administration while avoiding being identified with its policies.

The UIA and the ACIEL, on the other hand, had little hesitation in deciding that the administration's policies were detrimental to the interests of the nation—and of course of their own. Illia's emphasis on a state-led rather than a market-led economic development model and his reinstatement of many government controls over the private sector were antithetical to both organizations' tenets. The president's economic incrementalism and nonconfrontational approach to problem solving did not induce tolerance on the part of opposition parties, labor unions, and big capital. Quite the opposite, his moderation was interpreted by the UIA and the ACIEL as a sign of weakness and ineptness, which they used to convince the military that a president elected with only one-fourth of the total vote could not effectively rule the country. The inflationary upsurge and balance of payments difficulties encountered by the administration between the end of 1965 and early 1966 certainly were of great concern to industrialists regardless of their size. Yet what seems to have worried the ACIEL and the UIA the most was their perception that the mounting militancy of Peronist labor unions (which hoped that by destabilizing the Radical government they could speed up Perón's return) threatened the very nature of Argentine capitalism.[71] The Peronist triumph in the 1965 midterm congressional elections fueled the anxiety of these groups, and it became even worse when Illia, in spite of his supporters' defeat at the polls, announced that he would change neither his expansionary policies nor his nationalistic position with regard to foreign investments and the foreign debt.[72] When the military finally deposed Illia, the ACIEL was among the first of the interest groups to applaud the coup. Illia's removal sanctioned the end of the Argentine experiment with limited democracy begun under Frondizi.

The political stalemate that characterized this period of Argentine history resulted from a combination of factors. On the one hand, the Intransigent Radicals first, and the Popular Radicals later, were incapable of building support for their political and economic programs. This inability was compounded by the polarization between Peronist and anti-Peronist camps. Frondizi and Illia found themselves caught in an "impossible game."[73] This referred to the zero-sum mentality among the political players, which left no ground for compromise: if an administration tried to please the Peronists, they would trigger reactions from the military, the ACIEL, and the conservative parties, while if they leaned toward the conservative bloc, the CGT and the CGE would sabotage their policies. Finally, when they opted for a middle-of-the-road approach, they were attacked by both camps.

By mid-1966 the entrepreneurial class represented by the ACIEL and the military seemed to have reached an agreement that although based on different premises, had at least on one point in common: democracy and party politics were unsuitable for Argentina. They thought that what the country needed was a strong government that could maintain law and order and assure the conditions conducive to a good business climate. The 1966 crisis highlighted the chronic weaknesses of industrial distributional coalitions—that is, internal division, lack of meaningful leadership, and lack of political vision (seeking instead confrontation and short-term benefits over long-term strategies). The absence of a party to articulate its demands induced the UIA to look to the military to protect the interests of its members, which tarnished its democratic credentials and widened the gulf dividing political parties from Argentina's most important businesses for many years thereafter.

The Argentine Revolution (1966–1973)

The UIA and the ACIEL's active support for the regime set up by the 1966 military coup led O'Donnell to hypothesize a causal relationship between economic development and authoritarian rule. The "easy" phase of the ISI focused upon the production of consumer goods. The following phase brought with it an industrial "deepening," concentrating on capital goods production. This transition, however, exacerbated political conflict. The deepening process, he posited, implied an economic restructuring that penalized the working class and the middle class, who had acquired substantial privileges during the easy phase in the Peronist era. The unwillingness of these classes to restrain their socioeconomic demands caused a polarization in the political arena. The stalemate that ensued convinced the "propertied classes" to join the military to exclude the popular sectors. This process, he argued, resulted in a new ruling coalition of development-minded officers, bourgeois technocrats, foreign capitalists, domestic conglomerates, and agricultural exporters.[74] That the UIA and the ACIEL were active members of the coup coalition is generally accepted, but once the new regime was installed, these organizations had no institutionalized access to the new regime's decisions, even though some of their members were appointed to official positions.[75]

President Onganía insulated the decision-making process from external pressure even more than Aramburu, Frondizi, and Illia. At first the entrepreneurial class was not disturbed by this attitude because the administration met its expectations. Their optimism was reinforced by the announcement in March 1967 of a stabilization package designed by Minister of the Economy Adalbert Krieger Vasena. The UIA and the ACIEL welcomed most of Krieger Vasena's anti-inflationary measures, including freezing wages and salaries, even though this went against the principles of free-market economics they pretended to support. In return, these industrialists agreed to limit price increases.[76]

The goal of the stabilization package, in addition to defeating inflation, reducing the fiscal deficit, and stabilizing the country's external accounts, was to restructure the Argentine economy. Krieger Vasena's intention was to revive economic growth through new investments and a transfer of industrial resources from low-productivity activities to high-productivity ones. This implied a reorientation of part of industrial production from the domestic market to the foreign market—which, it was hoped, would ease the foreign exchange bottleneck, because industry could finance its own operations through exports. Krieger Vasena swiftly moved to improve economic efficiency by opening up the economy to foreign competition and encouraging capital investment from Europe and the United States.[77] The government invested heavily in infrastructure projects and worked to rationalize the operations of the deficit-ridden state companies and the public bureaucracy. In sum, Krieger Vasena's plan had elements of orthodox economic policy but avoided relying exclusively on market forces. Instead, it used income and price policies to enable the government to retain an active role in shaping economic development. As the 1960s drew to a close, foreign enterprises dominated the most dynamic industrial sectors (machinery, automotive, chemicals, basic metals) and accounted for 30 percent of manufacturing production. Seven of the country's ten largest companies were foreign-owned.[78]

The CGE bitterly protested the stabilization package, citing arguments similar to those used under Frondizi. It accused Krieger Vasena of purposely "denationalizing" the Argentine economy by leaving its small and medium-sized entrepreneurs defenseless against the more technologically advanced and better financed and organized foreign firms. The UIA praised Krieger Vasena's policies that transferred income to economic groups linked to transnational capital but "cried foul as soon as the [tariff reduction] policy took effect, claiming . . . that the high cost of industrial goods was due primarily to the country's inflated social security system, high taxes and interests rates, extravagant contracts, and an appalling economic infrastructure, all conditions that competition with cheaper imported goods would not alleviate."[79]

The abrupt changes imposed by Krieger Vasena brought to the surface the lingering internal contradictions within the UIA. They also exposed the differences separating the UIA from the industrial branch of the CGE, the CGI. However, those UIA members supplying the domestic market and feeling threatened by aggressive foreign competitors came to sympathize with CGI demands for strict regulation of foreign corporations and a limit on their investments to fields that would not affect the domestic industry. This was a far cry from the position of the ACIEL, the SRA, and those UIA members integrated with transnational capital (domestic conglomerates). Divisions also appeared within the CGE:

> [CGI] industrialists were much less positive toward labor unions than was the CGE as a whole. Most significant, perhaps, was the expressed desire of a large majority of both UIA and C[G]I members for a merging of the two bodies so as to enhance industry's political influence. Many members vol-

unteered the opinion that the only reason for the separation was personal antagonism between the leaders, and not any great difference in ideology.[80]

One of the most serious matters of contention between CGE and ACIEL leaders was representation. The CGE insisted that industrial, agricultural, financial, and commercial entrepreneurs be represented by only one umbrella organization, a position refused by the ACIEL because its members (UIA, SRA, CAC, etcetera) were jealous of their independence. A closely related controversy was over monopoly of representation: that is, was the CGE or the ACIEL the more important umbrella organization, deserving of a closer relationship with government officials? Squabbles between the two arose over the criteria to assess membership strength. The CGE based its count on the number of affiliated members, which of course gave it an edge over the ACIEL. In the late 1960s the CGE comprised 61.5 percent of registered firms, as opposed to 20.7 percent for the ACIEL.[81] Geographically, the CGE represented businesses across the country more evenly, having only 39.5 percent of its firms in the Buenos Aires province as opposed to ACIEL's 48.9 percent. The CGE accounted for 53.5 percent of the industry, compared to only 32.1 percent for the ACIEL.

The ACIEL charged that CGE figures were misleading and that the economic importance of the firms represented, rather than their number, was the best parameter. The ACIEL's strength using the economic importance criterion was overwhelming. In the industrial sector alone the UIA, an ACIEL member, included 90 percent of industrial sales, 95 percent of employed personnel, 90 percent of industrial production, 95 percent of wages and salaries, and 85 percent of capital goods production.[82] Complicating measurement was the tendency by many firms to have memberships in both the UIA and the CGI in order to maintain good relations with both.

The resignation of Krieger Vasena in the aftermath of the Cordobazo in mid-1969, and the removal of Onganía from power a year later, created great uncertainty about the economy, which was again plagued by high inflation and balance of payments problems. General Roberto Levingston, who succeeded Onganía, lacked a power base of his own and was incapable of restoring public confidence in the Argentine revolution's ability to gain control of the situation, which was steadily getting worse. Even the charismatic General Alejandro Lanusse, who ousted Levingston in March 1971, was unable to stop the negative trend. Lanusse initially attempted to build support by announcing a new political project, the Great National Accord (GAN), which was to harness political and economic forces to fight subversion and economic instability. In return, Lanusse promised to encourage participation by socioeconomic groups in decision making by creating the CONES and to lay out a timetable for a quick return to democracy. In reality, the GAN aimed at creating a conservative bloc that could endorse Lanusse's presidential bid in an honest election against the Peronists.

The weakening of the regime in the face of mounting economic difficulties, labor militancy, and guerrilla warfare, convinced an important sector of the UIA—the Association of Metallurgic Industrialists (Asociación de Industriales Metalúrgicos, or ADIM) and provincial chambers—to disengage the UIA from the GAN.[83] The intent of the ADIM was to gain control of the UIA leadership and pull it out of the ACIEL. The argument was that the economic liberalism advocated by the SRA and the CAC within ACIEL was counter to industry's interests. Perhaps more important, it believed that staying with the ACIEL meant sure political isolation from La Hora del Pueblo (see chap. 2), a multiparty front that was likely to frustrate Lanusse's presidential ambitions and return to power once the military quit.[84]

In 1971, in UIA internal elections the anti-ADIM bloc prevailed, forcing the ADIM to withdraw its membership; but in the process, the UIA became quite weakened. Conversely, the CGE position gained in strength. In 1971 Lanusse granted the CGE greater representation than the UIA in the newly created CONES, hoping that he could gain CGE cooperation in his plans. Ironically, the CGE gained more from Lanusse than vice versa. Although the CONES never became an effective policy-making tool, it gave the CGE prominence within the industrial distributional coalitions.

When in 1972 Lanusse refused to grant the CGE more concessions, its president, José Gelbard, forged alliances with the CGT and political parties to establish himself, rather than Lanusse, as the country's most effective power broker. In September of that year the CGE, after receiving the CGT's blessing, outlined its plan for a social pact—which later became, with a few changes, the basis for the political platform of the Peronist presidential candidate, Héctor Cámpora, in the March 1973 election. With Cámpora's victory, the CGE reached the pinnacle of its success. Unlike the second Peronist administration (1952–1955), Gelbard was given free rein to design and execute the economic policies of the social pact, which the CGE had sought all along.

The Comeback of Peronism (1973–1976)

The rapid ascendancy of the CGE pushed the UIA into a corner. Realizing that by remaining attached to the conservative, free-market approach of the ACIEL it risked having its bargaining power curtailed by the CGE-Peronist bloc, the UIA abandoned the ACIEL in October 1972.

However, the results of the March 1973 election left the UIA with no option but to accept CGE policies. In June 1973 the UIA formally supported the social pact between the CGT and the CGE, but this did not stop defections by many of its chambers to the CGE. Having estranged its former allies in the ACIEL (dissolved in 1973) and under increasing pressure from its affiliates to avoid being cut off from the new political authorities, the UIA, after months of negotiations, merged in August 1974 with the CGI to form the Argentine Industrial Confederation (Confederación Industrial Argentina, or CINA), which became part of the CGE.

Many UIA members saw the CINA as their lesser-evil option, but the honeymoon did not last long.

Former UIA members complained that Gelbard had secured CINA leadership positions for people loyal to him and that the new association was organized to maximize the power of the former CGI. However, the main point of contention was the economic situation and compliance with the social pact's price agreement. Perón's death in July 1974 was a severe blow to Gelbard's position within the government, as he could no longer count on the late president to restrain labor demands and to defend him from the attacks of right-wing Peronists like Social Welfare Minister José López Rega. In October Gelbard was forced to resign, and with his departure the social pact began to crumble.

The CGE was trapped. On the one hand, it lost control over policy making. On the other hand, its pledge of support for the administration of Isabel Perón prevented it from breaking with the government even when it abandoned the social pact, thus jeopardizing the entrepreneurs it represented. While the CGE appealed for calm and self-restraint, industrialists grew restless under price controls that did not keep up with escalating labor and production costs. The unraveling of the economic picture led former UIA members as well as many former CGI affiliates to reject CGE leadership.

In August 1975, three distinct movements emerged within the CINA in open opposition to the CGE: the Entrepreneurial Movement of the Interior (Movimiento Empresario del Interior, or MEDI) and the Movement of Industrial Unification (Movimiento de Unificación Industrial, or MUI) were splinter groups of the old CGI, while the Argentine Industrial Movement (Movimiento Industrial Argentino, or MIA) brought together former UIA members.[85] By late 1975, entrepreneurial unity within the CGE and the CINA ceased to exist, as both organizations passively watched the country fall into chaos. However, a group of former UIA members teamed up with the SRA, the CAC, the CRA, and the Buenos Aires Stock Exchange to set up the APEGE in 1975 with the explicit aim of boycotting government policies—paving the way for the military coup.

The Proceso (1976–1983)

The military, after deposing President Isabel Perón, launched a major campaign to attack terrorism and all those associated with the past administration. The CGE and the CINA were first taken over by government officials and then dissolved by decree in July 1977. The UIA regained its assets and independent status but was not completely spared, as the new authorities, conscious of the organization's past association with the CGE, put it under government control pending internal reform. One of the crucial objectives of the military administration was to cripple any lobbying organization that might obstruct its plans. The insulation of the decision-making process under Minister of the Economy José Martínez de Hoz (1976–1981) was far greater than under Krieger Vasena and Onganía. The military authorities and the minister of the economy shared the conviction that the political polarization and economic crisis plaguing the country was the fault not only of "corrupt and inept" political parties but of "greedy and selfish" distributional coalitions that had prevented the crafting and implementation of "sound" economic policies under previous authoritarian regimes. Consequently, during the first five years of the Proceso the military government disbanded Peronist-linked associations and weakened others by fragmenting their representation, redefining their role and structure, and intimidating them.

Martínez de Hoz used economic policy not as an end in itself but as a means to transform society to neoconservativism. The Peronist and Radical programs, which had emphasized economic nationalism, forced industrialization, income redistribution, and state intervention, came to be perceived as the cause of all the country's problems. The reestablishment of a market-dominated economy became Martínez de Hoz's top priority. Imposing "discipline" on the marketplace was a natural complement to the military's attempt to regiment the whole Argentine society.[86] Accordingly, the military regime sought not support but compliance. One of the main casualties was domestic industry, which had been sheltered from foreign competition. It was reasoned that the high prices of domestically manufactured products were the result of such artificial conditions as tariff protection and labor-management deals in which labor accepted entrepreneurs' price markups in return for wage increases. Martínez de Hoz believed the only way to break this cycle was to open the economy to foreign competition, a policy attempted many times before but only half-heartedly implemented due to labor and industrial opposition. Thus entrepreneurs were faced with two options: cut down production costs to improve efficiency or go out of business.

Big entrepreneurial interests were initially very supportive of Martínez de Hoz's plan, as shown by public statements by the APEGE (which was itself dissolved shortly after the coup). Many industrialists welcomed the return of the free-market model and government policies designed to slash the deficit, sell unprofitable state corporations, cut government bureaucracy, and destroy labor's power. The fact that the minister was an entrepreneur himself led many industrialists to conclude that the economy was finally in the hands of "one of ours."[87] Even those unimpressed by the minister's credentials and economic philosophy had been driven to such desperation by the instability preceding the coup that they were willing to give him the benefit of the doubt.

The stabilization program of 1976–1977 followed a conventional approach and achieved rather quickly a positive balance of payments, thus strengthening the position of the regime both domestically and internationally. Entrepreneurial backing began to dwindle when the effects of the deregulation and exchange policies adopted in 1978 began to be felt in 1980. Manufacturers complained about high interest rates and the combination of import liberalization and an overvalued exchange rate, which provoked a large influx of cheap foreign goods and a drastic fall in exports. However, their interest organizations having shut down, entrepreneurs were unable to articulate their demands in any organized fashion. Divided among themselves and affected unevenly by the liberalization measures, industrialists reacted to the abrupt economic changes individually rather than collectively and lobbied the government on specific issues rather than criticizing the whole economic plan. "Those entrepreneurs who could count on self-financing or foreign credit, . . . capital accumulation, and technological innovation took advantage of the new conditions and modernized their equipment. Others managed to survive by reducing fixed costs, cutting the level of production, and converting their industrial activities into import or commercial ones. Some made up for their small operations . . . by resorting to speculative operations. . . . Many entrepreneurs . . . had to lay off their employees and close down their businesses."[88]

The losers in the new economic regime were the small and medium-sized firms, many of which were acquired at bargain prices by domestic and foreign conglomerates. The concentration of capital in the hands of big corporations increased considerably, helped along by the deregulation of financial transactions. By 1984, the eight largest domestic conglomerates accounted for over 50 percent of manufacturing production, compared to less than 45 percent ten years earlier.[89] Manufacturing's share of GDP dropped from 37.9 percent in 1973 to 24.7 percent in 1984. Within the same period 15 percent of industrial establishments were closed down, and 10 percent of manufacturing employees were laid off.[90] In other words, under the Proceso Argentina suffered what many analysts have labeled a "deindustrialization" process, as many entrepreneurs either went bankrupt or switched their assets from investment to more profitable speculative ventures.

The first sign of open industrial dissent with Martínez de Hoz came in September 1980 when Eduardo Oxenford, a leading figure of big domestic capital who had been appointed by the military to reform the UIA and prepare for its internal elections, denounced the minister's ill-advised policies that had led to the bankruptcy of many firms. In 1981, government receivership of the UIA ended, and the organization was returned to officials elected by its membership. UIA representation now included both regional and sectoral interests. With the CGE still illegal, some former CINA members joined the new UIA. In 1982, former members of the MEDI and the MUI teamed up as the National Industrial Movement (Movimiento Industrial Nacional, or MIN), the strongest minority block within the UIA. In turn, the Industrial Union gained almost a monopoly of representation, which enhanced its overall prestige and bargaining power. The inclusion of regional chambers with ties to the old CGE upgraded the UIA's political discourse. Although the industrial groups of Buenos Aires continued to dominate the UIA's leadership, less emphasis was placed on free-market rhetoric and more attention was given to the needs of small and medium-sized provincial firms and to preventing further deterioration of domestic capital's control over the economy. This was quite a departure from earlier attitudes.[91] The deepening economic crisis between 1981 and 1983 and the piecemeal responses attempted by the three administrations following the Martínez de Hoz era widened the gulf between the UIA and the regime and convinced industrialists to push for a quick return to constitutional democracy.

The UIA came out of the Proceso as the leading association of industrial interests. A minor rival association, which has often taken issue with the UIA since its creation in 1982, was the Argentine Industrial Council (Consejo Argentino de la Industria, or CAI), comprising small and medium-sized domestic firms from the provinces (particularly Córdoba) that felt inadequately represented by the UIA. Another rival was the CGE (including its industrial branch, the CGI), which was legalized again in 1984 in an effort by the Alfonsín administration to divide the entrepreneurial front opposing its policies. Yet after 1983 the UIA's strength was more apparent than real. The Alfonsín and Menem administrations' unwillingness to promote a social pact and the continuing divisions between big and small entrepreneurs significantly narrowed the UIA's bargaining power and led to a piecemeal approach to solving problems. On the other hand, regional and sectoral chambers were encouraged by civilian administrations to deal directly with them, rather than through the UIA, to settle price, tax, subsidy, and labor issues. On the other hand, representatives of the big domestic conglomerates, commonly referred to as the captains of industry, occasionally defected from the UIA by making separate deals with the government. Thus although in theory the UIA was unchallenged, its cohesiveness was questionable at best.

Structural, Ideological, and Strategic Development

Before we proceed to analyze the 1984–1993 period, a summary of the structural, ideological, and strategic development of the industrial coalitions is in order.

Structural Development

Heterogeneity of interests has always troubled the industrial associations. Early on, agroindustry was pitted against traditional manufacturing. Later it was domestic corporations against multinational corporations, big businesses against small and medium-sized companies, industries in Buenos Aires province against those in other regions. These three factors led to the creation of rival associations articulating different interests. The CGE came to defend small and medium-sized provincial business, while the UIA represented, for the most part, large domestic and foreign corporations of the Buenos Aires region. To complicate matters, even these groups found it difficult to reconcile conflicting interests, as internal disagreements cut across traditional cleavages. Intrasector priorities emerged within the CGE, as well as conflicts over the usefulness of tactical alliances with labor and the Isabel Perón administration. The UIA experienced splits between domestic and multinational interests. Moreover, UIA members disagreed on trade liberalization, production subsidies, and state intervention.

This situation impeded the creation of an umbrella organization representing the whole industrial sector. Equally, damaging was the fact that the CGI and the UIA loyalty were often unable to secure compliance from their members. In fact, loyalty was strongest at the chamber level, which could take care of bread-and-butter issues more effectively.[92] All these factors make it clear why it has been so difficult to create cohesive associations sharing common interests, objectives, and norms of behavior, and why Argentine industrial associations as a whole have rarely developed a strong leadership.

These structural defects were routinely exploited by successive civilian and military governments, which tried divide-and-rule tactics to overcome entrepreneurial opposition. Although industrial coalitions could, at times, veto initiatives by weak governments, they lacked the strength to impose their will. On the other hand, from the 1930s on the state could affect business interests by manipulating macroeconomic variables. Exchange controls, production and export subsidies, investment credit, and tariffs were used to reward and penalize different interests, depending on who was in power. In addition, the UIA's inability to establish a party link made big business prone to join other organizations with links to the military regimes and to endorse authoritarian solutions to socioeconomic crises. Unfortunately, the authoritarian governments' disdain for institutionalized interest mediation forced industrialists to lobby government officials directly, which in turn weakened entrepreneurial associations during the Proceso.

Ideological Development

Most analysts agree that Argentine entrepreneurs have lacked an industrial ideology. This was partly the result of the ideological bias of the conservative ruling class during the nineteenth century favoring agriculture over industry. As time went by, industrialists organized. The UIA embraced free-trade economics, whereas the CGE adhered to a nationalist, state-led economic development model that favored corporatist arrangements among state, capital, and labor. Both approaches mirrored the structural cleavages we have discussed, but neither gained lasting public acceptance. To confuse matters further, advocates of either free-market economics or economic nationalism have used them selectively, leading to many contradictions—witness the fact that many UIA members supported free trade when it allowed them to import cheap inputs but opposed foreign competitors in their markets.

A related issue is the apparent absence of an entrepreneurial class consciousness. At the beginning of the twentieth century, industrialists from immigrant groups tried to gain social acceptance by imitating the values and living standards of the landed elite. This trend continued even after first-generation immigrants were replaced by their Argentine-born children. It became fashionable for newly rich entrepreneurs to purchase land, which made them eligible to joint the prestigious SRA and the country's most exclusive clubs. Owning a ranch is still regarded as *the* most Argentine thing to do: "Entrepreneurs have been absorbed by the preoccupation of reaching the highest status possible, for the sole, exclusive, and personal benefit of themselves, their families, their group, their enterprise, but not for the entity, corps, institution, or social sector outside their own domain."[93]

Many contend that younger-generation industrialists lack the entrepreneurial spirit of earlier generations, that in search of riches they resort to speculative operations—whether in finance, real estate, or trade—rather than risking money and time in less lucrative, more long-term, investments in manufacturing. Even those willing to invest are often averse to taking risks due to the great instability of the economy. Traditionally, they support protected markets in which their investments bring assured high returns and face little competition, thanks to government protection.[94] In the early sixties, a scholar remarked,

> Argentine industrial managers (and business in general) seem to be sitting in a glass cage, watching the day-to-day deterioration of industrial relations, blaming labor and government for Argentina's economic retardation, but at the same time discharging their burden of responsibility for solving the industrial problem on the already overloaded shoulders of the state. They know that, in the past, government has been conspicuously unable to manage the nation's industrialization process. But they still insist that the state should not only provide the necessary protectionist climate to foster industrialization, but also (perhaps by magic!) provide industry with a docile, obedient, disciplined, productive labor force. Industrialists in general do not seem to have given thought to the fact that the productivity, motivation, and cooperation of labor are simply determined by the management which employs it and not by the more or less enlightened social and economic policies of government.[95]

While these generalizations may go too far, there is little doubt that much of Argentine society held this view in the 1960s and 1970s. The very nature of Argentine industry at the time—characterized by high rents, heavy protection, and dependence on rural exports and geared primarily toward supplying the domestic market—reinforced the old conservative anti-industry bias and eventually materialized in the stabilization policies of Martínez de Hoz, explicitly aimed at penalizing these protected and inefficient industrial sectors. Ironically, these policies had the unintended effect of penalizing investors rather than speculators.

Strategic Development

From an economic standpoint, big Argentine entrepreneurs have manifested an oligopolistic strategy proper to distributional coalitions. This was accentuated when the country restricted foreign competition as a result of the development of ISI. Schvarzer notes that entrepreneurs "could not export to the world markets, for different reasons, and needed to create a cartel to divide up the domestic market."[96] Domestic conglomerates, which began to emerge in the 1950s, needed much the same. Their strategy was to attain an oligopolistic control over selected markets, which invariably tended to be the most dynamic and lucrative. Moreover, despite their professed adherence to free-market economics, captains of industry succeeded through generous government tax breaks and subsidies and through lucrative contracts for public works.[97]

Like their agricultural counterparts and political parties, industrial distributional coalitions viewed relations with each other, with labor, and with other economic sectors in terms of a zero-sum game. This view was the direct result of the profound political polarization that occurred between the 1940s and the 1970s. The economic crisis that ensued, coupled with the alternation in power of widely different governments enforcing ever changing policies, made it impossible for industrialists to make long-term investment plans. Chronic instability led entrepreneurs and their interest groups to adopt short-term approaches that maximized immediate benefits but exacerbated relations with other economic groups (even within industry) over the distribution of political and economic power.[98] This situation fed the already strong individualism and suspiciousness of Argentine entrepreneurs and translated into strategies according to which "entrepreneurs obtain benefits exclusively for their own enterprises, whether these benefits pertain to customs, tariffs, credit, or taxes. They negotiate, petition, and bring influence to bear until they get the favorable decision for themselves and their business, but not for their industry as a whole."[99]

Thus the optimal solution to any economic problem became gaining control of, or at least influence over, the levers of power. The representative of a major conglomerate stated that once he was appointed to chair a state bank, he suddenly gained easy access to policy makers and, with it, the ability to promote his group's interests.[100] This explains why cooperation and compromise were considered second-best options if a given interest group found it possible to control decision making. Only on isolated occasions, when competitive behavior could no longer solve the socioeconomic crisis (as in 1973), did cooperation materialize (this time in the form of a social pact). Yet going it alone remained common and explains why Argentine industrial associations like the UIA and the CGI have functioned more as pressure groups and movements rather than bargaining institutions.[101] However, they were so weakly institutionalized that their members had considerable freedom of action and could abandon them once their objectives were met or when it was more convenient to deal with labor or government one-on-one rather than collectively.

The New Democratic Regime and Industrial Coalitions, 1983–1993

In the first year of his administration, Alfonsín, strong from his landslide victory, tried to enforce policies that did little to meet the demands of socioeconomic actors. The new Minister of the Economy Bernardo Grinspun immediately made it clear that government consultation with distributional coalitions was out of the question. This attitude was partly the result of an economic crisis that left little room for bargaining but certainly was reinforced by the Radical tradition of acting on behalf of the common citizen against the interests of capital and labor. Martínez de Hoz's policies had transferred massive economic resources from the state and wage earners to the most powerful distributional coalitions like domestic conglomerates, large agricultural exporters, and foreign banks. Some of the means used to effect such transfers were to nationalize most of the private debt held by conglomerates, government subsidies to promote industrial exports and provide credit, lenient tax policies, and price gouging by conglomerates in providing goods and public services.

The threat that these special concessions could end aroused big capital's suspicions about Alfonsín's real intentions. Thus, the president could not count on the support of key distributional coalitions, large industrialists included. Grinspun's unilateral decision-making style also unnerved the UIA. His expansionary policies, which, along with other measures emphasizing economic nationalism, increased business taxation, fueled the budget deficit, and exacerbated relations between government and entrepreneurs. It was at this time that the UIA and the other nine distributional coalitions joined the CGT to create the Group of 11 specifically to present a unified bloc vis-à-vis Alfonsín. For the first time, labor and capital had united in a common cause. Moreover, the UIA and the CGT issued joint plans as alternatives to the administration's. Why would the UIA, which had traditionally opposed making policy in concert with labor, now support it? Two reasons often mentioned are (1) that, in the absence of collective bargaining legislation, this would avoid union unrest and (2) that this would guarantee them involvement in fiscal, trade, monetary, and wage policy decisions, which the government previously kept as its exclusive prerogative.

Relations eased somewhat after a new economic team headed by Juan Sourrouille, who replaced Grinspun in early 1985, executed the Austral Plan in June of that year. The plan marked the beginning of a close relationship between the Alfonsín administration and the captains of industry, who had gained such economic clout in the last fifteen years that they now dealt directly with the government, bypassing the UIA (of which they were members). The conglomerates were assured that their interests would not be damaged if they would comply with the government's economic guidelines and promote investments.

The UIA grudgingly accepted the Austral Plan and the price freeze that came with it as a necessary short-term measure to break the hyperinflation spiral. It also backed the changed approach of the administration, which replaced many of Grinspun's policies with fiscal and monetary austerity, a slow opening of the economy, less state intervention, and more emphasis on the market for allocating resources. The success of the Austral Plan enabled Alfonsín to take the initiative and again divide his opposition. In August 1985, he convened the Social Economic Conference (Conferencia Económica Social, or CES) to which only selected representatives of industry and labor were invited. The administration's goal was not to make policy in concert with socioeconomic groups but rather to split the entrepreneurial front and break its tenuous alliance with labor. Faced with the options of staying away or having a say in shaping economic policy, the UIA accepted the invitation. This caused the dissolution of the Group of 11, as militant Peronist labor unionists like CGT leader Saúl Ubaldini rejected the CES, while agricultural groups felt left out of the new institutional arrangement.

With the beginning of the second stage of the Austral Plan in March 1986, the government tried to grant some of the industrialists' requests, including ending the price freeze and lowering interest rates. However, despite some concessions, it did not grant the UIA's request for institutionalized input in economic decision making. Moreover, a series of government concessions to labor, which were perceived as contradicting early statements by the president, alienated the UIA.[102] The weakening of the Alfonsín administration after the September 1987 congressional and gubernatorial elections was accompanied by a steadily deteriorating economy.

The UIA multiplied its attacks on government policy until August 1988, when Sourrouille negotiated a six-month pact (the Spring Plan) with the UIA and the CAC. The latter agreed to price restraints in return for credit and tax concessions, a reduced fiscal deficit, and currency devaluation. The unraveling of the Spring Plan in February 1989 cut short the alliance, and both the UIA and the CAC rescinded the agreement. Indeed, the conglomerates Alfonsín had chosen as the government's entrepreneurial interlocutors took the lead in the run to the dollar, forcing the depletion of most of the Central Bank's reserves and a massive devaluation in March. These conglomerates quickly jumped on the Peronist bandwagon headed by Carlos Menem.

After his electoral victory, Menem intensified his talks with representatives of big capital and reassured them of his policy intentions. Menem's alliance with the Bunge and Born conglomerate, whose managers helped elaborate the administration's economic policy, identified his administration with some of the most influential representatives of Argentine capitalism. It also set the tone for the new capital accumulation model, which implied a dramatic reconfiguration of the power structure across distributional coalitions. The Bunge and Born plan would transfer capital from speculative operations to exporters. In other words, industrial coalitions that had grown thanks to government sponsorship now had to depend on their own resources. Not by chance, a substantial number of Bunge and Born's petrochemical and agribusiness companies were export-oriented.

The UIA's reaction to these policies was mixed. It applauded the privatization of state enterprises, the attempt to break union power, the reduction in the state bureaucracy, and the commitment to free-market policies. However, the government's emphasis on agricultural and petrochemical production and industrial exports threatened powerful UIA groups that produced for the domestic market and now faced foreign competition. Moreover, the end of state subsidies, fat government contracts, and opportunities for financial speculations were equally dangerous to many. Thus although deregulation and the opening of the economy benefited export-oriented conglomerates like Bunge and Born, Techint, Pérez Companc, and Alpargastas, those that had grown under economic protectionism and depended on government contracts, such as Bulgheroni and Massuh, found themselves on the losing side. Finally, the recession induced by a series of austere economic packages squeezed credit and demand, causing in the first eight months of 1990 a 9 percent drop in manufacturing output. Along with it came a loss of one million jobs.[103] Thus, the policies that the UIA had long advocated came to be regarded as too bitter medicine. In early 1991 the UIA asked Menem for economic relief. Later, it demanded antidumping regulations and specific import duties for some products.

However, the sudden improvement of the economy by midyear eased relations between industrialists and the administration. In September, Minister of the Economy Domingo Cavallo and delegates from the UIA, the CGE, and other smaller industrial associations signed a formal agreement. Under this "productivity pact," the industrial sector pledged to meet its tax obligations, increase employment and investments, and hold down prices. In return the administration made a number of concessions that included lowering energy costs, special credit lines for small and medium-sized businesses, cuts in shipment costs, a new foreign trade law, and labor legislation.

By 1992, the restructuring reforms introduced in 1989 had further concentrated economic power in the hands of a few foreign corporations and the largest domestic conglomerates. The ten largest firms increased their output from $4 million to $7 million between 1981 and 1990, employed 12 percent of the work force, and owned over sixty of the top 100 domestic companies. Conversely, the weaker and smaller companies lost ground. A key factor that strengthened some distributional coalitions over others was the sweeping privatization carried out in the first three years of the Menem administration. At the end of 1992, conglomerates like Techint, Bunge and Born, Bridas, Zarraquín, Pérez Companc, Macri, and Astra accounted for 40 percent of government revenues from privatized companies. This assured the oligopolistic or monopolistic control in very lucrative markets in the service sector, such as telephones, highways, railways, oil, gas, electricity, and the media.[104] Privatized companies were also offered at bargain prices to conglomerates whose incomes were cut by the end of government contracts and subsidies.

In 1993, the government's probusiness stance was further exemplified by its attempt to meet entrepreneurial requests to cut labor costs (which are much higher than those of its Latin American neighbors) by introducing a bill in Congress. To the same end, Menem proposed a new social security reform less onerous for business.

Like other distributional coalitions, industrialists seem to have concluded that military governments, with their erratic and unpredictable behavior, are too risky. They have come to appreciate the virtues of democracy: during the military mutinies, the UIA, the CGE, the CAC, and other business associations pledged their loyalty to the constitutional government. Further, they no longer perceive labor and the Peronists as menacing industrial interests—thus eliminating a key reason for backing authoritarian political solutions. The general thrust of Alfonsín's and Menem's reforms pleased the most powerful industrial distributional coalitions, as the emphasis shifted toward a capitalist accumulation model that favored them.[105]

The role that industrial distributional coalitions will play in consolidating Argentine democracy will depend not only on the political parties' ability to carry out reforms but also on strengthening their own organizational structures so that they truly represent their sectors vis-à-vis both labor and government. The CGE came out of the Proceso much weakened, as many of its members switched to the UIA. Although this trend in theory gave more credibility to the UIA, the go-it-alone attitude of its most important members undermined the UIA's bargaining power vis-à-vis the government and other distributional coalitions. In fact, the true winners were the domestic conglomerates that by 1993 had achieved a socioeconomic clout that overshadowed that of the UIA.[106]

9

ON THE PROSPECTS FOR ARGENTINE DEMOCRACY

THE PREVIOUS CHAPTERS have described the evolution of Argentine government institutions and distributional coalitions. I have argued that the weak Argentine political system made strong distributional coalitions possible. The increasing institutional power vacuum enabled these coalitions to pursue their monopolistic or oligopolistic interests, but in so doing they furthered Argentina's socioeconomic decline.

The election of Raúl Alfonsín in 1983 opened new opportunities for establishing a democratic form of government with solid foundations. The debacle of the Proceso and the deep economic crisis convinced many distributional coalitions that had once looked to the military to solve their problems that a plural society, with all its defects, best served their interests—a dramatic departure from the past. At least initially, many coalitions came to realize that the burden of foreign debt and the disarray of government finances left Alfonsín little room to effect redistributive policies. The old zero-sum mentality gave way to a more tolerant approach to conflict resolution. For the first time in the country's history, labor and big capital held joint meetings and formulated alternatives to government policies.

After electoral defeat in 1983, the Peronists played the role of loyal opposition, thus strengthening the young democracy. The acceptance of Peronism by conservative distributional coalitions as a legitimate, responsible political force was also a crucial change. The support shown by virtually all groups for Alfonsín and later for Menem during the carapintada rebellions were remarkable events in Argentine history. Solidarity among government, political parties, and distributional coalitions was a sign of agreement that democracy had to stay and that military rule was no longer viable.

Many hoped that the emergence of the UCD would satisfy another requirement for the consolidation of democracy: the creation of a strong conservative party to represent the interests of big capital. However, the

UCD's constituency barely reached beyond the province of Buenos Aires, and its leaders failed to enlist the support of big business.

In spite of these positive signs, the young Argentine democracy failed to meet many of the expectations it had raised. A fundamental task facing the new government in 1983 was to redefine the key institutions of democratic pluralism: the party system, the Congress, and the judiciary. The democratization of the Justicialist party and the adoption of primary elections for presidential candidates by both the UCR and the PJ were positive steps in this direction. However, the emphasis gradually shifted to charismatic leadership and mobilization by political movements—hardly the best means to institutionalize interest group representation.

Alfonsín's and Menem's tendency to raise expectations that they could find quick solutions to socioeconomic crises and their failure to deliver on campaign promises has made the public skeptical. The unwillingness of both presidents to use their parties to channel the claims of citizens, while conceding to the demands of powerful distributional coalitions, has encouraged the idea that a president's failure is tantamount to the failure of the democratic system as a whole. By 1993, most parties were so plagued by internal squabbles and corruption that their public standing had dropped to its lowest point since the return to democracy. "The crisis of Argentine political parties is a phenomenon related to their incapacity to generate political representation. It is the consequence of a party system whose leaders look for power for themselves rather than channelling voters' expectations."[1] Although survey research indicates that people desired true democracy for Argentina, less power for the strongest distributional coalitions, more openness in government decisions, and more economic opportunities, party politicians failed to translate such aspirations into concrete reform programs.[2]

Confidence in the Congress and the judicial system was also shaky. Although Alfonsín made an effort early in his term to respect the autonomy of both the legislature and the judiciary, toward the end he often ruled by executive order. Menem's first four years saw the pardon of military officers and terrorists convicted of human rights violations, packing the Supreme Court, and the use of controversial executive orders—all reinforcing the general impression that the rule of law applies to some but not to others.

Argentines are not convinced that checks and balances must be weakened to enable the government to act quickly in an emergency; they see that such means were used to cover up widespread government corruption implicating members of the president's inner circle. Menem's closest ministers and advisers have been caught in documented cases of corruption involving hundreds of millions of dollars, yet none of these cases went to trial. The press, one of the few political forces that is still independent, played a pivotal role in reporting scandals. In return, Menem vehemently defended his associates while accusing journalists of plotting against his administration.

According to former state prosecutor Moreno Ocampo, while there was corruption under Alfonsín, under Menem it has become *the* system of government.[3] Allegedly no major privatization was completed in 1990–1991 without kickbacks to the ministers involved. Horacio Verbitsky reported in a 1992 best-seller that former Interior Minister José Luis Manzano justified his conduct by saying, "I steal for the crown."[4] In another article Verbitsky revealed that since 1989 Menem's personal friends had been soliciting cash contributions from businesses to "supplement" the low salaries of ministers and top bureaucrats in monthly amounts of $5,000 to $10,000.[5]

Menem skillfully survived these scandals, trusting that Argentines, happy with long sought economic stability, would overlook his misconduct and that of his cronies. By late 1992, however, with the economic situation improving, opinion polls showed that corruption had become the number one public concern. Given the sacrifices asked of many citizens in the name of economic stability, government corruption was no longer tolerated. This was particularly true for the middle class, whose vote was crucial in Menem's 1991 victory and whose support now seemed in doubt. In 1992, his popularity plunged from 50 to 37 percent. Much the same occurred to Cavallo, whose ratings dropped from 48 to 34 percent.

The task of political forces in a democratic consolidation is to create institutional arrangements capable of mediating conflicting claims and to turn interest maximizing into interest optimizing. Optimizing an interest involves "the acceptance of a level of goal accomplishment short of the maximum perceived by the decision-maker, who often finds it convenient to avoid clarification of goals so as to facilitate agreement among factions with quite different motives and expectations."[6] Argentina's political institutions have fallen short of giving citizens and distributional coalitions institutional channels for solving their problems.

In view of the weakenesses of the country's institutions, in the mid-1980s many analysts and politicians in Argentina, as in other Latin American countries facing similar situations, advocated the creation of a three-party social pact involving government, business, and labor. Such a pact was regarded as essential to consolidating the young democracy and broadening opportunities for participation and coalition building. Yet it never materialized.

Unlike military leaders in Brazil, Chile, and Uruguay, the Argentine military was unable to negotiate its exit from power after the debacle of the Falklands/Malvinas war. The high level of popular mobilization during the transition process, combined with the absence of a pact between the Afonsín administration and key distributional coalitions, compounded the situation. In Terry Karl's view, "Such a mixed scenario, while perhaps holding out the greatest hope for political democracy and economic equity, may render a consistent strategy of any type ineffectual and thus lead to the repetition of Argentina's persistent failure to consolidate any type of regime."[7]

While one could argue that the hopes for democracy are brighter in Argentina than in other Latin American countries, many clouds still persist. Giorgio Alberti observes that the young democracies of the region were crippled by the economic crises inherited from outgoing military regimes. The 1980s was a "lost decade" that produced "democracy by default: a political regime that survives because no other alternatives are available . . . but one which loses progressively the elan of the democratic ideal and the hope for the future."[8] The deepening economic crisis has tarnished the idea held by many Latin Americans that democracy brings better standards of living and social change. Thus, writes Alberti, "A democracy that cannot accomplish its mission is not worthy of support. It may, at best, survive, but precisely by default."[9]

Other observers argue that institutional reforms are sorely needed to rescue Argentina from its socioeconomic crisis. However, as we have seen, these institutions have not developed: neither political parties nor social pacts have emerged to meet the demands for governability voiced by a population frustrated by decades of official mismanagement, corruption, and partisanship.

Since 1983 the democratic regime has been faced with increasing popular demands in a climate of scarce resources. The response has been a return to movimientismo, slowing the reform of democratic institutions that could mediate conflicting social interests. Alfonsín in 1983 and Menem in 1989 responded to the unfolding socioeconomic crisis by attempting to reestablish charismatic leadership. Consistent with Max Weber's theory, the debacle, first, of the Proceso and then the Radical administration created situations ripe for the emergence of a charismatic bond.[10] The "return of the leader" was portrayed as the cure to all ills. Menem's campaign slogan, "Follow me! I am not going to betray you!" exemplifies the situation. However, this approach has made interest mediation dependent upon the arbitrary decision of a charismatic leader. The political game has been reduced to "a messianic vision of the solitary leader who, without a political-institutional support, is called upon by the 'demand for government' to solve the pressing economic and social problems that afflict society. The leader, in his solitude, invites a technocratic team to dictate the economic measures that it considers most appropriate to solve the crisis."[11]

Unfortunately, charismatic leadership by itself is usually incapable of sustaining political power in the long run; thus policies have been shaped in an institutional vacuum. Furthermore, although both Alfonsín and Menem recognized the need to build institutions, they perceived institutional reforms as means to keep themselves in power and, instead of backing reforms, preserved the movement type of political mobilization that initially made their fortunes. Alfonsín, for instance, began to talk about turning Argentina from a presidential into a parliamentary system, following the European model, so he could remain in office as prime minister after his term expired. Menem, on the other hand, proposed a presidential system like that of France, envisioning a prime minister responsible to Congress and a presidential term of four years with the possibility of reelection.

In short, as long as a strong president dominates Argentine politics, political instability will persist, as scholars so eloquently point out.[12] Menem's strategy of purposely excluding parties, Congress, and the judicial system from all major decisions and ascribing to himself the role of ultimate mediator undermines the very tenets of democracy and its institutions. Moreover, whereas some of Menem's economic reforms have emasculated several distributional coalitions (for example, unions, government contractors, the military, and businesses previously protected from foreign competition), they have increased the socioeconomic clout of others (some domestic conglomerates, multinationals, and agricultural exporters) by creating conditions conducive to new cartels and monopolies. Rather than ending the negative effects of vested interests, the Menem "revolution" has simply trimmed the number of distributional coalitions, making them potentially much stronger. In fact, with the state retreating to a more subordinate role, the prospects of rule by entrenched monopolistic or oligopolistic interests are quite real, posing a serious menace to the achievement of a more efficient economy.

In the name of social justice, Menem has forced a redistribution of resources from some distributional coalitions to others. Conspicuously absent from his agenda is any reference to a social policy. This fact has triggered criticism not only from the left but even from Pope John Paul II, as austerity policies have further concentrated wealth in the hands of a few and forced more and more people into poverty.[13] The return to democratic government that was welcomed in 1983 has by now shattered the hopes of many.

> A democracy that excludes politically because it reduces politics to a cold government technique entrusted to "operators" and condemns the sovereign people to the role of spectator; a democracy that marginalizes economically and socially because it demonstrates that it feels no obligation toward

the poor and the weak and ignores their fate; a democracy that manipulates justice to protect the powerful and political cronies while allowing the law of the jungle in the suburbs; can a democracy with such characteristics consolidate itself at the ballot box?[14]

When this chapter was written, Menem and his Minister of the Economy Domingo Cavallo were being praised for their bold efforts at economic restructuring. Yet things cannot be reduced to numbers, nor can a charismatic leader mediate conflict forever. History proves that charisma is an unstable and transitory phenomenon whose survival hinges upon its "routinization"—that is, the transfer of authority from the leader to the party. In the first four years of his administration, Menem made no effort toward such an institutionalization, for reasons explained in chapter 3. As past leaders have done, Menem claims legitimacy on the basis of his economic objectives. However, drastic economic changes are no panacea. They must be accompanied by political changes made through institutional channels.

The institutions Argentines decide to create or modify are up to them. One difference between the 1990s and the past is that the people of Argentina are now fully conscious of their rights and they have come to cherish democracy as never before. Public outcries for more transparent, representative government linking citizens with their representative institutions have become more and more common, as indicated by survey research. In this, the people are far ahead of their leaders, and leaders who do not understand this are doomed sooner or later to suffer a serious problem of legitimacy, with all its political consequences.

Future governments have to take this new trend quite seriously. Institutions, new or reformed, must instill in the average citizen a trust in government and in one's fellow citizens. Adam Przeworski writes, "Establishing democracy is a process of institutionalizing uncertainty."[15] Nothing could be more true in today's Argentina. Establishing democracy is not an easy task, particularly in a conflict-ridden country. Argentina needs to develop institutions that can reduce uncertainty and thwart the excesses of the past. Only in this way can a collective rationality develop, one based upon clear rules of the game so often lacking in the Argentine political game.

NOTES
INDEX

NOTES

CHAPTER 1: *Introduction*

1. Carlos Díaz Alejandro, *Essays on the Economic History of the Argentine Republic* (New Haven: Yale University Press, 1970), p. 1n.

2. Carlos Waisman, *Reversal of Development in Argentina: Postwar Counterrevolutionary Policies and their Structural Consequences* (Princeton: Princeton University Press, 1987), p. 6.

3. Juan José Llach, *Reconstrucción o Estancamiento* (Buenos Aires: Tesis, 1987), p. 25.

4. *Economist*, "Nearly Time to Tango," 18 April 1992, p. 17.

5. Similar circumstances led Samuel Huntington, *Political Order in Changing Societies* (New Haven: Yale University Press, 1968), to define his now famous "praetorian society" thesis:

> In all societies, specialized social groups engage in politics. What makes such groups seem more "politicized" in a praetorian society is the absence of effective political institutions capable of mediating, refining, and moderating group political action. In a praetorian society social forces confront each other nakedly; no political institutions, no corps of professional political leaders are recognized or accepted as legitimate intermediaries to moderate group conflict. Equally important, no agreement exists among the groups as to the legitimate and authoritative methods for resolving conflict. . . . In a praetorian society . . . not only are the actors varied, but also the methods used to decide upon office and policy. Each group employs means which reflect its particular nature and capabilities. The wealthy bribe; students riot; workers strike; and the military coup. (p. 196)

6. Quoted from Samuel Huntington, "Political Development and Political Decay," *World Politics* 17 (1965): 386.

7. Drawing on de Tocqueville, Huntington replaced the "art of associating together" with the term *institutionalization,* and "equality of conditions" became *participation.* For Huntington, "it is useful to distinguish political development from modernization and to identify political development with the institutionalization of political organizations and procedures. Rapid increases in mobiliza-

tion and participation, the principal political aspects of modernization, undermine political institutions. Rapid modernization, in brief, produces not political development but political decay" (ibid.).

8. Peter Smith, *Argentina and the Failure of Democracy: Conflict among Political Elites* (Madison: University of Wisconsin Press, 1974), says "though charged with some legislative responsibilities, the Chamber [of Deputies] seems to have initiated and promulgated very few laws of its own. One reason for this weakness was simply the historical preeminence of the presidency, and the wide-ranging authority of executive decrees" (p. 18). Note that throughout the text, when capitalized *Conservative* refers to a coalition of conservative parties; otherwise, it refers to political conservatism.

9. Díaz Alejandro, *Essays*, 108.

10. Douglas Madsen and Peter G. Snow, *The Charismatic Bond: Political Behavior in Time of Crisis* (Cambridge: Harvard University Press, 1991).

11. Daniel James, "The Peronist Left, 1955–1975," *Journal of Latin American Studies* 8 (1976): 294.

12. Gary Wynia, *Argentina: Illusions & Realities* (New York: Holmes and Meier, 1986), p. 199.

13. Guillermo O'Donnell, *Un juego imposible. Competición y Coaliciones entre Partidos Políticos en Argentina 1955–1966* Documento de Trabajo (Buenos Aires: Instituto Torcuato Di Tella, 1977).

14. Guillermo O'Donnell, "Modernization and Military Coups: Theory, Comparisons, and the Argentine Case," in *Armies and Politics in Latin America*, ed. Abraham Lowenthal and Samuel Fitch (New York: Holmes and Meier, 1986), p. 101.

15. William Smith, *Authoritarianism and the Crisis of the Argentine Political Economy* (Stanford: Stanford University Press, 1989), p. 5.

16. O'Donnell, "Modernization and Military Coups," p. 101.

17. Late in the campaign, a conservative publisher distributed a pamphlet entitled *Vote al mal menor*.

18. *El Informador Público* (Buenos Aires), 16 March 1990.

19. José Luis de Imaz, *Los Que Mandan* (Those Who Rule) (Albany: State of New York University Press, 1970), p. 225.

20. "Any good can be viewed as a collective good for some set of individuals if, once it is supplied by one or more individuals in the set, it is automatically available for consumption by *all* individuals in the set." Terry Moe, *The Organization of Interests: Incentives and the Internal Dynamics of Political Interest Groups* (Chicago: University of Chicago Press, 1980), p. 22. Defense policy, social security, and public services, for instance, are all public goods.

21. Here public choice is understood as an approach "involved in measuring and evaluating the goals of public policy." Dennis Palumbo, "Organization Theory and Political Science," in *Handbook of Political Science: Micropolitical Theory*, ed. Fred Greenstein and Nelson Polsby, vol. 2 (Reading Mass.: Addision-Wesley, 1975), p. 320.

22. Mancur Olson, *The Logic of Collective Action* (Cambridge: Harvard University Press, 1971); Mancur Olson, *The Rise and Decline of Nations* (New Haven: Yale University Press, 1982).

23. Olson, *The Rise and Decline*, p. 237. The following passages are based on this work.

24. The free-ride problem arises for unions (as well as for other groups) when individuals avoid joining the union because they are not compelled to do so in order to receive the benefits of unionization. The larger the union or group, the more serious the free-ride problem. See Dennis Mueller, *Public Choice II: A Revised Edition of Public Choice* (New York: Cambridge University Press, 1989), pp. 34–35.

25. Ibid., p. 74.

26. Olson, *Rise and Decline*, p. 165.

27. In Latin America, following the European tradition, the *state* refers to the bureaucratic and legal institutions composing the various branches of government and its corporations. Thus, the *state* comprehends "the head of state and the immediate political leadership that surrounds the head of state, as well as the public bureaucracy, legislature, judiciary, public and semipublic corporations, legal system, armed forces, and the incumbents of these institutions." Ruth Berins Collier and David Collier, *Shaping the Political Arena* (Princeton: Princeton University Press, 1991), p. 789.

28. On the overlapping interests of labor and the industrial sector producing for the domestic economy in Argentina, see Adolfo Canitrot, "Discipline as the Central Objective of Economic Policy: An Essay on the Economic Programme of the Argentine Government Since 1976," *World Development* 8 (1980): 920.

29. Samuel Beer, *Britain Against Itself* (New York: Norton, 1982), p. 27.

30. Albert Hirschman, *Essays in Trespassing Economics: Economics to Politics and Beyond* (New York: Cambridge University Press, 1984), p. 193.

31. Smith, *Authoritarianism*, p. 6.

32. Mueller, *Public Choice II*, p. 319.

33. José Nun and Mario Lattuada, *El Gobierno de Alfonsín y las Corporaciones Agrarias* (Buenos Aires: Manantial, 1991), p. 163.

34. William Smith, "State, Market and Neoliberalism in Post-Transition Argentina: The Menem Experiment," *Journal of Interamerican Studies and World Affairs* 33 (1991): 50.

CHAPTER 2: *Political Development*

1. For an excellent description of the colonial era in Argentina, see David Rock, *Argentina 1516–1987: From Spanish Colonization to Alfonsín*, 2d ed. (Berkeley: University of California Press, 1987): pp. 6–78; James Scobie, *Argentina: A City and a Nation* (New York: Oxford University Press, 1964), pp. 36–87; H. S. Ferns, *Argentina* (New York: Pracgcr, 1969).

2. Scobie, *Argentina*, p. 61.

3. William White and Allan Holmberg, *Human Problems of U.S. Enterprises in Latin America* (Ithaca: New York State School of Industrial and Labor Relations, Cornell University, 1956), p. 3.

4. Rock, *Argentina 1516–1987*, p. 104.

5. Ferns, *Argentina*.

6. Cited in Eduardo Crawley, _A House Divided: Argentina 1880–1980_ (London: Hurst, 1984), pp. 10–11.

7. Peter G. Snow, _Political Forces in Argentina,_ rev. ed. (New York: Praeger, 1979), p. 8.

8. Carlos Díaz Alejandro, _Essays on the Economic History of the Argentine Republic_ (New Haven: Yale University Press, 1970), pp. 2–8.

9. Rock, _Argentina 1516–1987,_ p. 141.

10. David Rock, _Politics in Argentina, 1890–1930: The Rise and Fall of Radicalism_ (London: Cambridge University Press, 1975), p. 11.

11. Ibid., pp. 8–15.

12. Juan Bautista Alberdi, _Bases y puntos de partida para la organización política de la República Argentina,_ 4th ed. (Buenos Aires: Plus Ultra, 1981). On the elitist political ideas of early Argentine thinkers, see Nicolas Shumway, _The Invention of Argentina_ (Berkeley: University of California Press, 1991).

13. Carl Solberg, _Immigration and Nationalization in Argentina and Chile, 1890–1914_ (Austin: University of Texas Press, 1970), pp. 81–83; see also Rock, _Politics in Argentina,_ p. 17.

14. Peter G. Snow, _Argentine Radicalism: The History and Doctrine of the Radical Civic Union_ (Iowa City: University of Iowa Press, 1965), pp. 4–5; Alberto Ciria, _Parties and Power in Modern Argentina (1930–1946)_ (Albany: State University of New York Press, 1974), pp. 123–29.

15. Rock, _Politics in Argentina,_ p. 25.

16. José Luis Romero, _A History of Argentine Political Thought_ (Stanford: Stanford University Press, 1963), pp. 156–59; Darío Cantón, _Elecciones y partidos políticos en la Argentina_ (Buenos Aires: Siglo Veintiuno, 1973), p. 45; Peter Smith, _Argentina and the Failure of Democracy_ (Madison: University of Wisconsin Press, 1974), p. 136; Natalio Botana, _El Orden Conservador: La política argentina entre 1880 y 1912_ (Buenos Aires: Sudamericana, 1977); Rock, _Argentina 1516–1987,_ pp. 130–31, 154–55, 157.

17. Peter G. Snow, "Argentina: Politics in a Conflict Society," in _Latin American Politics and Development,_ ed. Howard Wiarda and Harvey Kline, 2d ed. (Boulder: Westview, 1985), p. 153.

18. Daniel Poneman, _Argentina: Democracy on Trial_ (New York: Paragon, 1987), p. 127.

19. Quoted in Rock, _Politics in Argentina,_ p. 27.

20. Snow, "Argentina," p. 154.

21. Ysabel Rennie, _The Argentine Republic_ (New York: Macmillan, 1954), p. 166.

22. For an excellent discussion of Yrigoyen's inclination toward movement-like popular mobilization, see David Rock, "Political Movements in Argentina: A Sketch of Past and Present," in _From Military Rule to Democracy in Argentina,_ ed. Mónica Peralta Ramos and Carlos Waisman (Boulder: Westview, 1987), pp. 8–9.

23. Rock, _Argentina 1516–1987,_ p. 86.

24. Snow, _Political Forces in Argentina,_ p. 11.

25. Ibid., p. 10; see also Gino Germani, _Política y sociedad en una época de transición: de la sociedad tradicional a la sociedad de masas_ (Buenos Aires: Paidós, 1965), p. 225; and Cantón, _Elecciones y partidos políticos,_ p. 45.

26. Peter Smith, "The Breakdown of Democracy in Argentina, 1916–1930," in *The Breakdown of Democratic Regimes: Latin America*, ed. Juan Linz and Alfred Stepan (Baltimore: Johns Hopkins University Press, 1978), p. 14.

27. According to Díaz Alejandro, *Essays*, p. 95, in a single four-year period one of five rural dwellers moved to an urban center; most of them chose metropolitan Buenos Aires.

28. Snow, *Political Forces in Argentina*, p. 12.

29. Carlos Waisman, *Reversal of Development in Argentina: Postwar Counterrevolutionary Policies and Their Structural Consequences* (Princeton: Princeton University Press, 1987), pp. 166–71.

30. Scobie, *Argentina*, p. 233.

31. Joseph Page, *Perón: A Biography* (New York: Random House, 1983), p. 89.

32. John W. Sloan, *Public Policy in Latin America* (Pittsburgh: University of Pittsburgh Press, 1984), p. 183.

33. Robert Kaufman and Barbara Stallings, "The Political Economy of Latin American Populism," in *The Macroeconomics of Populism*, ed. Rudiger Dornbusch and Sebastian Edwards (Chicago: University of Chicago Press, 1991), p. 16.

34. Domingo Cavallo, describing Argentina in 1990.

35. Cited in Poneman, *Argentina*, p. 65.

36. Aside from naming streets, squares, towns, and even whole provinces after themselves, the Peróns began a process of indoctrination starting with schoolchildren. Evita's autobiography, an apology for Perón's achievements, became standard reading in elementary school. Moreover, Eva Perón, when her membership was rejected by the Sociedad de Beneficencia run by Buenos Aires upper-class women, created her own charitable institution (named after herself), which became famous by granting favors and money to whomever she pleased "in the name of Perón."

37. James W. Rowe, "Onganía's Argentina: The First Four Months," *AUFS Reports* 12 (1966): 2.

38. For an excellent account of the 1966–1973 military period, see Guillermo O'Donnell, *Bureaucratic Authoritarianism: Argentina, 1966–1973, in Comparative Perspective* (Berkeley: University of California Press, 1988).

39. Snow, *Political Forces in Argentina*, pp. 139–40.

40. Fernando Abal Medina, the first montonero leader, had been a leader of Catholic Action, and his successor, Mario Firmenich, came from the ranks of Catholic Student Youth. The inspirational leader of these young revolutionaries was Juan García Elorrio, editor of *Cristianismo y Revolución*. Elorrio was an outspoken advocate of the radical interpretation of liberation theology, and his thoughts had been heavily influenced by the writings of the Colombian guerrilla-priest Camilo Torres. Donald C. Hodges, *Argentina, 1943–1976: The National Revolution and Resistance* (Albuquerque: University of New Mexico Press, 1976), p. 54.

41. Daniel James, "The Peronist Left, 1955–1975," *Journal of Latin American Studies* 8 (1976): 284.

42. James Kohl and John Litt, *Urban Guerrilla Warfare in Latin America* (Cambridge: MIT Press, 1974), p. 391.

43. Snow, *Political Forces in Argentina*, p. 142.

44. Ibid., p. 145.

45. *Latin America Political Report* 9 (6 June 1975): 172.

46. Guillermo O'Donnell, *Modernization and Bureaucratic-Authoritarianism: Studies in South American Politics* (Berkeley: Institute of International Studies, University of California, 1973).

47. Adolfo Canitrot, "Discipline as the Central Objective of Economic Policy: An Essay on the Economic Programme of the Argentine Government Since 1976," *World Development* 8 (1980): 916.

48. For a stylized model of neoconservative policies in the southern cone, see Joseph Ramos, *Neoconservative Economics in the Southern Cone of Latin America, 1973–1983* (Baltimore: Johns Hopkins University Press, 1986). The literature on Martínez de Hoz's policies is extensive. Among some of the finest analyses are Larry Sjaastad, "Argentine Economic Policy, 1976–81," in *The Political Economy of Argentina, 1946–83*, ed. Guido Di Tella and Rudiger Dornbusch (Pittsburgh: University of Pittsburgh Press, 1989); Rudiger Dornbusch, "Argentina after Martínez de Hoz," in *The Political Economy of Argentina, 1946–83*, ed. Di Tella and Dornbusch; Jan Wogart, "Combining Price Stabilization with Trade and Financial Liberalization Policies," *Journal of Interamerican Studies and World Affairs* 25 (1983): 445–76; Roberto Frenkel and Guillermo O'Donnell, "The Stabilization Programs of the International Monetary Fund," in *Capitalism and the State in U.S.–Latin American Relations*, ed. Richard Fagen (Stanford: Stanford University Press, 1979).

49. Inter-American Development Bank, *Economic and Social Progress in Latin America* (Washington, D.C.: IDB, 1981), p. 12.

50. William Smith, *Authoritarianism and the Crisis of the Argentine Political Economy* (Stanford: Stanford University Press, 1989), p. 232.

51. *Latin America Political Report* 11, (29 April 1977): 125.

52. Snow, *Political Forces in Argentina*, p. 147.

53. National Commission on the Disappeared, *Nunca Más* (New York: Farrar, Straus, Giroux, 1986), p. 3.

54. Ibid., p. 4.

55. Ibid., p. 448.

56. The leaders forming the Multipartidaria came from the Radical Civic Union, the Justicialist party, the Movement for Integration and Development, the Intransigent party, and the Christian Democratic party.

57. *Latin American Weekly Report*, 8 January 1982.

58. Ibid., 6 February 1982.

59. See Andrés Fontana, *Fuerzas Armadas, Partidos Políticos, y Transición a la Democracia en Argentina* (Buenos Aires: Estudios CEDES, 1984), pp. 27–34.

60. Ibid. Also see Gary Wynia, *Argentina: Illusions and Realities* (New York: Holmes and Meier, 1986), p. 11; David Pion-Berlin, "The Fall of Military Rule in Argentina: 1976–1983," *Journal of Interamerican Studies and World Affairs* 27 (1985): 69–71; *Latin American Weekly Report*, 26 March 1982. For a detailed analysis of the conflict, see Max Hastings and Simon Jenkins, *The Battle of the Falklands* (New York: Norton, 1983); Virginia Gamba, *El peón de la reina* (Buenos Aires: Sudamericana, 1984); and Oscar Raúl Cardoso, Ricardo Kirschbaum, and Eduardo van der Koy, *Malvinas: la trama secreta* (Buenos Aires: Sudamericana, 1983).

61. Paul Lewis, *The Crisis of Argentine Capitalism* (Chapel Hill: University of North Carolina Press, 1990), p. 476.

62. The literature on transition to democracy is quite large. Among the most comprehensive collections of essays are Guillermo O'Donnell, Philippe Schmitter, and Lawrence Whitehead, eds., *Transition from Authoritarian Rule: Prospects for Democracy* (Baltimore: Johns Hopkins University Press, 1986); Paul Drake and Eduardo Silva, eds., *Elections and Democratization in Latin America, 1980–1985* (San Diego: Center for US-Mexican Studies, Institute of the Americas, University of California at San Diego, 1986); and Barbara Stallings and Robert Kaufman, eds., *Debt and Democracy in Latin America* (Boulder: Westview, 1989). On the unpopularity of compromise, see Edgardo Catterberg, *Argentina Confronts Politics: Political Culture and Public Opinion in the Argentine Transition to Democracy* (Boulder: Lynne Rienner, 1991), p. 6. For a detailed analysis of the Argentine transition, see Eduardo Viola and Scott Mainwaring, "Transitions to Democracy: Brazil and Argentina in the 1980s," Working Paper 21 (Notre Dame: Helen Kellogg Institute for International Studies, University of Notre Dame, July 1984).

63. Carlos Waisman, "The Argentine Paradox, *Journal of Democracy* 1 (1990): 94.

64. On this point, see Carlos H. Acuña, Mario dos Santos, Daniel García Delgado, and Laura Golbert, "Relación estado/empresarios y políticas concertadas de ingresos. El caso argentino," in *Política económica y actores sociales. La concertación de ingreso y empleo*, ed. Patricio Silva (Santiago de Chile: PREALC-OIT, 1988): Juan Carlos Portantiero, "La concertación que no fue: de la ley Mucci al Plan Austral," in *Ensayos sobre la transición democrática en la Argentina*, ed. José Nun and Juan Carlos Portantiero (Buenos Aires: Punto Sur, 1987).

65. Marcello Cavarozzi and María Grossi, "From Democratic Reinvention to Political Decline and Hyperinflation," paper prepared for the Fifteenth Latin American Studies Association Congress, Miami, 4–6 December 1989, p. 8.

66. Wynia, *Argentina*, pp. 186–87.

67. For an excellent analysis of the political economy of the Alfonsín administration, see Smith, "Breakdown of Democracy," pp. 6–34.

68. For a detailed analysis of the merits and shortcomings of the Austral Plan, see the essays by José Luis Machinea and José María Fanelli, Alfredo Canavese and Guido Di Tella, Daniel Heymann, Juan Carlos de Pablo, Carlos Alfredo Rodríguez, and Sylvia Piterman in *Inflation Stabilization*, ed. Michael Bruno, Guido Di Tella, and Rudiger Dornbusch (Cambridge: MIT Press, 1988).

69. On the negotiations between the IMF and the Alfonsín administration, see Kendall Stiles, "Argentina's Bargaining with the IMF," *Journal of Interamerican Studies and World Affairs* 29 (1987): 55–85.

70. Alfonsín's belief about the feasibility of a third national movement can be seen in his famous Parque Norte address, where he outlined his plans for a new Argentina. Luis Aznar et al , *Alfonsín: Discursos Sobre el Discurso* (Buenos Aires: EUDEBA, 1986).

71. See Juan Carlos Torre, "Economics and Politics: The Dilemmas of the Democratic Transition in Latin America" (Buenos Aires: Instituto Torcuato Di Tella, 1989).

72. Half of the congressional seats (127) were at stake. Of the twenty-one governorships contested, the UCR was able to keep only Córdoba and Río Negro, three went to provincial parties, and the remaining sixteen were won by

the PJ. According to the proposed constitution, the prime minister would be the prominent political figure, with no restriction on reelection, which would have enabled Alfonsín to stay in office (impossible under the 1853 constitution, which forbids a president to run for two consecutive terms). On Argentine voters' attitudes, see Catterberg, *Argentina Confronts Politics*, pp. 75–88.

73. Convictions of ten former junta members and a few high-ranking officers were left unchanged. See also chap. 5.

74. The attack was carried out by the previously unknown Frente de Resistencia Popular (Popular Resistance Front). Some of the twenty-eight terrorists killed were later identified as former members of the old ERP.

75. The more salient concessions were a 3 percent cut on the value-added tax, the reduction of tariff barriers for some 3,000 items, the establishment of a dual exchange rate, and the free negotiation of salaries and wages by private entrepreneurs. All these measures represented an income transfer from the state sector to the private sector, represented by the UIA and Argentine Chamber of Commerce affiliates. See Carlos H. Acuña, "Política y Economía en la Argentina de los 90 (O porqué el futuro ya no es lo que solía ser)," paper prepared for the Conference Democracia, Mercados y Reforma Estructurales en América Latina, Fundación Simón Rodríguez, Buenos Aires, 25–27 March 1992.

76. On the Spring Plan, see Mónica Peralta Ramos, *The Political Economy of Argentina: Power and Class Since 1930* (Boulder: Westview, 1992), pp. 135–41.

77. Adolfo Canitrot, *Noticias de la Fundación Arturo Illia* (Buenos Aires: Fundación Arturo Illia, 1989), p. 7.

78. For a pessimistic evaluation of the Alfonsín administration, see Guillermo O'Donnell, "Argentina, de Nuevo," Working Paper 152, Hellen Kellog Institute for International Studies, University of Notre Dame, February 1991. A more sympathetic view is expressed by Wynia, *Argentina*.

79. On Menem's nationalism prior to his election see Martín Granovsky, "Politica exterior: Las relaciones carnales con E.E.U.U.," in Atilio Borón et al., *El Menemato* (Buenos Aires: Letra Buena, 1992) p. 177.

80. On Menem's admiration for Reagan and Thatcher, see Atilio Borón, "Los Axiomas de Anillaco. La Visión de la Política en el Pensamiento y en la Acción de Carlos Saúl Menem," in *El Menemato*, ed. Borón et al., p. 58. Economy Minister Domingo Cavallo admitted, "Menem is changing all that Perón did after World War II," *La Nación*, 11 February 1992. In the case of Mexico, the surprise is not President Salinas de Gortari, who was an outspoken advocate of free-market economics even before assuming office, but rather the acceptance of his party, the Institutional Revolutionary party (PRI), to the policy change. In fact, the PRI until the early 1980s drew from economic nationalism and state-led development two of its main political issues aimed at legitimizing its hold on power. For a controversial interpretation on the reasons behind Menem's policy U-turn, see Borón, "Los Axiomas de Anillaco."

81. Ricardo Sidicaro, "La centralità del mercato," *Politica Internazionale* 6 (1991): 33–42; and Oscar Landi and Marcelo Cavarozzi, "Menem: El fin del peronismo? (Crisis y postransición en la Argentina)," *Cuaderno CEDES* 66 (1991): 23.

82. Landi and Cavarozzi, "Menem,"p. 18.

83. For analyses of Menem's economic policies, see William Smith, "State, Market and Neoliberalism in Post-Transition Argentina: The Menem Experiment," *Journal of Interamerican Studies and World Affairs* 33 (1991): 45–82; Peralta

Ramos, *Political Economy of Argentina;* Acuña, "Política y Economía"; Adolfo Canitrot, "La Destrucción del Estado Argentino y los Intentos Posteriores de Reconstrucción," paper prepared for the conference Democracia, Mercados y Reformas Estructurales en América Latina, 25–27 March 1992, Buenos Aires, Fundación Simón Rodríguez; Arnaldo Bocco and Naum Minsburg eds., *Privatizaciones: Reestructuración del Estado y la Sociedad (Del Plan Pinedo a "Los Alsogarays")* (Buenos Aires: Letra Buena, 1991).

84. Smith, "State, Market, and Neoliberalism," p. 55.

85. On the Argentine tax reform, see Richard Bird, "Tax Reform in Latin America: A Review of Some Recent Experiences," *Latin American Research Review* 27 (1992): 7–36.

86. Testifying to international investors' optimism about Argentina's future was the fact that the secondary market price of the country's foreign debt rose from 13 percent of its face value in December 1989 to 45 percent in 1991. *Nederlandsche Middenstendbank N.V.*

87. *Foreign Broadcast Information Service*, 23 September 1991, p. 26. See also Borón, "Los Axiomas," p. 72.

88. In August 1991, in return for its help, Argentina received US$100 million worth of contracts from the Kuwaiti government.

89. In 1990, Foreign Minister Di Tella, referring to his attempt to improve Argentine-U.S. relations, said, "We want to maintain good relations. Carnal relations"; see Granovsky, "Política Exterior," p. 184; see also speech by Di Tella, *Noticias Argentinas*, 24 August 1991.

90. The CIA and the State Department had long feared that the CONDOR could be purchased by Iraq or other "unreliable" Third World nations.

91. On Menem's foreign policy, see Roberto Russell and Laura Zuvanic, "Argentina: Deepening Alignment with the West," *Journal of Interamerican Studies and World Affairs* 33 (1991): 113–34; and Rut Diamint, "Un Año de la Iniciativa de las Américas. El Caso de Argentina" (Buenos Aires, 1991).

92. The deception, if one looks back at the statements Menem made prior to assuming office, appears quite clear; here are some reported by the daily *La Razon*. On the prosecution of military crimes: "No to the Full Stop Law. No forgiveness. No impunity. It is a moral and ethical duty to bring to justice those who violated the constitution and led Argentina to decay" (19 September 1986); "The only way to close for good the doors of a horrific past is to abstain from interfering with the judicial system" (19 September 1986); on political coherence: "I believe that a politician has to comply with what he promises" (17 September 1987); on the campaign trail: "For the poor hungry children, for the rich children who are sad, for the brothers without a job, for the homes without a roof, and for the bread that is not on the table of many Argentines, follow me, I am not going to betray you" (24 February 1989). After being elected, he said, "I do not understand why they criticize me for my contradictions. Tell me one, at least one."

93. In fact, the government's waning popularity could be seen in the local elections of the Tucumán and Santa Fe provinces (the latter is Argentina's third largest electoral district) held in November 1989, when Peronist candidates were soundly defeated by minor parties. In July 1991 the Radical governor of Rió Negro confiscated federal funds to pay provincial employees and was nearly impeached.

94. *Buenos Aires Herald*, 20 January 1991.

95. "Qué Piensa la Gente," *Somos,* December 1989: *Latin American Regional Reports: Southern Cone,* 14 March 1991.

96. The first such incident happened when Emir Yoma, the second in command in the Foreign Ministry and brother-in-law of the president, came under fire for having asked a U.S.-owned company, Swift Armour (belonging to Campbell Soup Co.), to pay him a "fee" in order to hasten the importation of capital equipment. U.S. Ambassador to Argentina Terence Todman, told Menem that Argentine officials had asked for bribes from other U.S. companies wanting to invest in Argentina. See the daily *Página* 12. Subsequently, Emir Yoma's sister, Amira, who served as the president's private secretary, was charged, along with her former husband, of laundering drug money. Both Yomas quit their posts by August 1991.

97. Prior to Cavallo's plan, the daily volume of trading on the stock market averaged $5 million. In August 1991 it reached $115 million. *Buenos Aires Herald,* 25 August 1991. The blue chip share index jumped from 100 in 1989 to 761 at the end of 1991.

98. In March 1991, the Secretariat of the General Agreement on Tariffs and Trade, an enforcer of Western capitalism, went out of its way to praise the Menem administration for its economic achievements.

99. Argentine companies and wealthy citizens began to invest capital abroad during the military dictatorship of the 1980s. The trend continued as the economic crisis turned worse under Alfonsín. It is estimated that Argentine foreign assets ranged between $50 and $60 billion. Smith, "State, Market and Neoliberalism," p. 47.

100. The Brady plan was an emergency package devised by U.S. Treasury Secretary Nicholas Brady to provide debt relief to debtor countries that showed they were making concrete efforts to reform their economies. Contrary to the Reagan administration's "muddling through" and its Baker plan—which emphasized full repayment of the outstanding debt—the Brady plan acknowledged that the current size of the debt was not manageable and that a substantial discount should be granted. Accordingly, the Brady plan cut the debt owned by private banks by 35 percent. The United States, Japan, and some European governments, in collaboration with the IMF, the World Bank, and the Inter-American Development Bank, also supplied financial assistance, for a total of $30 billion, to help the debt-restructuring process.

101. *Foreign Broadcast Information Service,* 19 November 1991, p. 14.

102. Smith, "State, Market and Neoliberalism," pp. 67–68.

103. The sensitivity of the issue led Cavallo to go on television to defend the administration's record on social spending. To rebuff the Catholic church's accusations, Cavallo argued that funding for education, housing, health, and social security had actually increased by $7.8 billion above that of the Alfonsín administration.

104. *Buenos Aires Herald,* 23 February 1992.

CHAPTER 3: *The Political Party System*

1. E. E. Schattschneider, *Party Government* (New York: Rinehart, 1942), p. 1; Rudolf Wildenmann, "The Problematic of Party Government," in *Visions and Re-*

alities of Party Government, ed. Francis Gastels and Rudolf Wildenmann (Berlin: de Gruyter, 1986), p. 6; emphasis added. For some of the most influential works on the role of parties, see V. O. Key, Jr., *Politics, Parties, and Pressure Groups,* 5th ed. (New York: Crowell, 1964); Maurice Duverger, *Political Parties* (New York: John Wiley, 1954); Gabriel Almond, "Comparative Political Systems," *Journal of Politics* 18 (1956): 391–409; Austin Ranney and Willmoore Kendall, *Democracy and the American Party System* (New York: Harcourt Brace, 1956); Gabriel Almond and Bingham Powell, *Comparative Politics,* 2d ed. (Boston: Little, Brown, 1978); Giovanni Sartori, *Parties and Party Systems* (New York: Cambridge University Press, 1976); Samuel Eldersveld, *Political Parties: A Behavioral Analysis* (Chicago: Rand McNally, 1964); Frank Sorauf, *Party Politics in America,* 3d ed. (Boston: Little, Brown, 1976); Bingham Powell, *Democracies: Participation, Stability, and Violence* (Cambridge: Harvard University Press, 1982); and Angelo Panebianco, *Political Parties: Organization and Power* (New York: Cambridge University Press, 1988).

2. Alessandro Pizzorno, "Interest and Parties in Pluralism," in *Organizing Interests in Western Europe: Pluralism, Corporatism, and the Transformation of Politics,* ed. Suzanne Berger (New York: Cambridge University Press, 1981), p. 72; emphasis added.

3. Larry Diamond and Juan Linz, "Introduction: Politics, Society, and Democracy in Latin America," in *Democracy in Developing Countries: Latin America,* ed. Larry Diamond and Juan Linz (Boulder: Lynne Reinner, 1989).

4. Robert Dix, "Democratization and the Institutionalization of Latin American Political Parties," *Comparative Political Studies* 24 (1992): 450.

5. Daniel Poneman, *Argentina: Democracy on Trial* (New York: Paragon, 1987), pp. 18–19.

6. Pizzorno, "Interests and Parties in Pluralism."

7. Hans Daalder, "Parties, Elites, and Political Development in Western Europe," in *Political Parties and Political Development* ed. Joseph La Palombara and Myron Weiner (Princeton: Princeton University Press, 1966), p. 43.

8. Ibid., p. 44

9. For an analysis of the nineteenth-century agrarian liberal parties, see Duverger, *Political Parties,* p. 285.

10. Joseph La Palombara and Myron Weiner, "The Origin and Development of Political Parties," in *Political Parties,* ed. La Palombara and Weiner, p. 4.

11. Giovanni Sartori, "Political Development and Political Engineering," *Public Policy* 17 (1968): 292.

12. Seymour Lipset and Stein Rokkan, "Cleavage Structures, Party Systems, and Voter Alignments," in *Party Systems and Voter Alignments: Cross-National Perspectives,* ed. Seymour Lipset and Stein Rokkan (New York: Free Press, 1967).

13. This is not at all surprising, as many anarchist and syndicalist leaders were Italian and Spanish immigrants.

14. Sartori, "Political Development," p. 292.

15. According to Sartori, *Parties and Political Systems,* "Political movements and associations may become parties: But qua mere movements and associations they are not yet parties" (p. 61).

16. David Rock, "Political Movements in Argentina: A Sketch from Past and Present," in *From Military Rule to Liberal Democracy in Argentina,* ed. Mónica Peralta Ramos and Carlos Waisman (Boulder: Westview, 1987), p. 3.

17. For an analysis of political movements in comparative perspective, see Kay Lawson and Peter Merkl, eds., *When Parties Fail: Emerging Alternative Organizations* (Princeton: Princeton University Press, 1988).

18. Duverger, *Political Parties*, pp. 42–43.

19. Peter G. Snow, *Argentine Radicalism: The History and Doctrine of the Radical Civic Union* (Iowa City: University of Iowa Press, 1965), p. 23; David Rock, *Politics in Argentina 1890–1930: The Rise and Fall of Radicalism* (New York: Cambridge University Press, 1975), pp. 49–51.

20. Rock, "Political Movements," p. 4.

21. Giorgio Alberti, Franco Castiglioni, and Paolo Munini, "Política e ideología en la industrialización argentina," *Boletín Informativo Techint*, no. 239 (1985): 17.

22. Ibid.

23. Douglas Madsen and Peter G. Snow, *The Charismatic Bond: Political Behavior in Time of Crisis* (Cambridge: Harvard University Press, 1991), p. 5.

24. Alberti, Castaglioni, and Munini, "Política e ideología," p. 17.

25. Panebianco, *Political Parties*, p. 147, makes this point in discussing the charismatic parties of Western Europe.

26. For the case of externally created parties, see La Palombara and Weiner, "Origin and Development," p. 5.

27. Snow, *Argentine Radicalism*, p. iii.

28. Giorgio Alberti, "Democracy by Default, Economic Crisis, *Movimientismo* and Social Anomie in Latin America," paper prepared for the Conferenza Internazionale: Le Sfide delle Transizioni Democratiche: Est-Ovest e Nord-Sud, Forlì, 30–31 May 1991, p. 13.

29. The need for a powerful party of the economic right as a means to bring political stability is advanced in Torcuato Di Tella, *Latin American Politics: A Framework of Analysis* (Austin: University of Texas Press, 1990), p. 148.

30. On the weaknesses of the Argentine party system vis-à-vis powerful distributional coalitions, see Marcelo Cavarozzi, "Los partidos argentinos: subculturas fuertes, sistema débil," paper prepared for Conference on Political Parties and Redemocratization in the Southern Cone, Wilson Center, Washington D.C., 16–17 November 1984.

31. Liliana De Riz and Catalina Smulovitz, "Los actores frente al cambio institucional" (Buenos Aires: CEDES, 1988).

32. Rock, "Political Movements," pp. 16–17.

33. Max Weber, *Economy and Society* (New York: Bedminster, 1968).

34. Alberti, Castiglioni, and Munini, "Política e ideología," p. 17.

35. Panebianco, *Political Parties*, p. 147.

36. Ibid., p. 55.

37. Ibid., p. 56.

38. Sartori, "Political Development," p. 290.

39. On Alfonsín's movimientismo, see Guillermo O'Donnell, "Argentina de Nuevo," Working Paper 152 (Notre Dame: Helen Kellog Institute for International Studies, University of Notre Dame, February 1991), p. 4.

40. Oscar Landi and Marcelo Cavarozzi, "Menem: El fin del peronismo?" *Cuaderno CEDES*, no. 66 (1991): 23, 31.

41. Ricardo Gallo, *Balbín, Frondizi y la división del radicalismo* (Buenos Aires: Belgrano, 1983).

42. Although the split was formalized in early 1957, in the aftermath of the December 1956 Party Congress of the UCR, squabbles between Balbín and Frondizi had emerged much earlier. According to Frondizi, a few months after the 1955 coup Aramburu invited both Balbín and him for a business luncheon to discuss the possibility of an agreement. Aramburu pledged the support of the provisional government for the UCR candidate in future presidential elections in return for a promise from them to uphold the anti-Peronist ban established by his administration. While Balbín agreed, Frondizi did not. Interview with former president Frondizi, Buenos Aires, August 1987.

43. Ruth Berins Collier and David Collier, *Shaping the Political Arena* (Princeton: Princeton University Press, 1991), p. 722.

44. Peter Snow, *Political Forces in Argentina*, rev. ed. (New York: Praeger, 1979), pp. 18–19.

45. Ricardo Guardo, *Horas difíciles* (Buenos Aires: Peña Lillo, 1963), p. 97.

46. Marcelo Cavarozzi, *Sindicatos y política en Argentina* (Buenos Aires: CEDES, 1984), pp. 98–99.

47. The most recent analysis of Frondizi's desarrollismo can be found in Cathryn Sikkink, *Ideas and Institutions* (Ithaca: Cornell University Press, 1990).

48. Richard Mallon and Juan Sourrouille, *Economic Policymaking in a Conflict Society: The Argentine Case* (Cambridge: Harvard University Press, 1975), p. 20.

49. An excellent analysis of Frondizi's policymaking can be found in Gary Wynia, *Argentina in the Postwar Era* (Albuquerque: University of New Mexico Press, 1978), pp. 112–35.

50. Ibid., p. 107.

51. See Carlos Floria and César García Belsunce, *Historia política de la Argentina contemporánea, 1880–1983*, 2d ed. (Buenos Aires: Alianza Universidad, 1988), pp. 182–83. According to one interpretation, Frondizi's advisers convinced him that polls taken in Buenos Aires indicated a likely UCRI victory in Buenos Aires province, the most important gubernatorial race. See Kvaternik Eugenio, "Sobre partidos y democracia en la Argentina entre 1955 y 1966," *Desarrollo Económico* 18 (1978): 37. Others argue that, although fearful of being defeated, Frondizi could no longer justify a ban on the Peronists. The military, for instance, refused to take a stance partly because hard-line officers were counting on a Peronist victory as an excuse to remove Fronidizi. Most officers, though, felt it was in the best interests of the armed forces to stay out of politics and let things run their course. See Robert Potash, *The Army and Politics in Argentina, 1945–1962* (Stanford: Stanford University Press, 1980), pp. 357–58. For a detailed discussion of this debate, see Collier and Collier, *Shaping the Political Arena*, p. 727.

52. In the legislative elections, the Peronists polled 2,530,000 votes, the UCRI, 2,423,000, and the UCRP, 1,730,000. The Peronists won ten of the fourteen governorships at stake, including Burenos Aires. The UCRI lost its majority in the Chamber of Deputies, retaining only seventy-four seats, as opposed to fifty-seven for the UCRP, forty-five for the Peronists, and sixteen divided among minor parties. Floria and Belsunce, *Historia política*, p. 183.

53. Gary Wynia, *Argentina: Illusions and Reality* (New York: Holmes and Meier, 1986), p. 129.

54. Floria and Belsunce, *Historia política*, p. 189.

55. Samuel Baily, "Argentina: Reconciliation with the Peronsits," *Current History* 49 (1965): 357; and Wynia, *Argentina in the Postwar Era*, p. 125; Arthur

Whitaker, "Argentina Struggle for Recovery," *Current History* 48 (1965): 16–17. On Illia's economic policies, see Wynia, *Argentina in the Postwar Era*, pp. 112–35; and Alieto Guadagni, "Economic Policy during Illia's Period in Office, 1963–1966," in *The Political Economy of Argentina, 1946–1983*, ed. Guido Di Tella and Rudiger Dornbusch (Pittsburgh: University of Pittsburgh Press, 1989).

56. Figures from Electoral Department, Ministery of Interior.

57. On Balbín's dramatic turnaround, see Marcelo Cavarozzi, "Peronism and Radicalism: Argentina's Transitions in Perspectives," in *Elections and Democratization in Latin America, 1980–85*, ed. Paul Drake and Eduardo Silva (San Diego: Center for Iberian and Latin American Studies, University of California, San Diego, 1986); and Marcelo Luis Acuña, *De Frondizi a Alfonsín: la tradición política del radicalismo/2* (Buenos Aires: Centro Editor de América Latina, 1984), pp. 201–07.

58. Cavarozzi notes that Perón at his death was aware of his wife's shortcomings and unsuccessfully tried to find a way for Balbín to succeed him in order to maintain the diffiuclt equilibrium. Cavarozzi, "Peronism and Radicalism," p. 166.

59. The Multipartidaria included the Radicals, the Peronists, the Christian Democrats, the MID, and the Intransigent party.

60. The MRC was composed for the most part of Buenos Aires Radicals and obtained the support of the Junta Coordinadora Nacional (National Coordinating Board, an influential university students organization) and anti-Balbinist factions in Córdoba and Santa Fe. At the 1972 party convention, the Alfonsín-Storani ticket polled 126,204 votes, to 165,140 for Balbín-Gammond. See Acuña, *De Frondizi a Alfonsín*, pp. 205–06.

61. Proof of the plot was never disclosed, but past collaboration betwen Peronist labor leaders and the military made the speculations highly plausible among weary Argentines. See Wynia, *Argentina*, pp. 139–43.

62. See Cavarozzi, "Peronism and Radicalism," pp. 169–70; and Wynia, *Argentina*, pp. 136–42.

63. On Alfonsín's ability to give political expression to the demands arising from society, see Manueal Mora y Araujo, "The Nature of the Alfonsín Coalition," in *Elections and Democratization*, ed. Drake and Silva, pp. 175–88; Edgardo Catterberg, *Argentina Confronts Politics: Political Culture and Public Opinion in the Argentine Transition Process* (Boulder: Lynne Reinner, 1991); Luis González Estévez and Ignacio Llorente, "Elecciones y preferencias políticas en la Capital Federal y Gran Buenos Aires el 30 de Octubre de 1983," in *La Argentina electoral*, ed. Natalio Botana et al. (Buenos Aires: Editorial Sudamericana, 1985): Leticia Maronese, Ana Cafiero de Nazar, and Víctor Waisman, *El voto peronista '83. Perfil electoral y causas de la derrota* (Buenos Aires: El Cid Editor, 1985). Catterberg notes that the leadership factor helped Alfonsín particularly among the more affluent strata of the working class. Catterberg, *Argentina Confronts Politics*, p. 84.

64. On the Coordinadora and the third historical movement, see Carlos Altamirano, "La Coordinadora: elementos para una interpretación," in *Ensayos sobre la transición democrática en la Argentina*, ed. José Nun and Juan Carlos Portantiero (Buenos Aires: Punto Sur, 1987). For a critical evaluation of the third historical movement, see Cavorozzi, "Peronism and Radicalism," p. 172; and Liliana De Riz, "Alfonsin's Argentina: Renewal of Parties and Congress" (Buenos Aires: CEDES, July 1989), p. 23.

65. Marcelo Cavarozzi and María Grossi, "From Democratic Reinvention to Political Decline and Hyperinflation," paper prepared for the Fifteenth Latin American Studies Association Congress, Miami, 4–6 December 1989, p. 8. For an excellent discussion of movimientismo, see Rock, "Political Movements in Argentina."

66. According to the Carta Orgánica (the charter) of the UCR, radical officials taking government posts were required to quit their party posts. In 1984 Alfonsín had the rule changed, enabling him to retain his party leadership and also avoid competition among party factions, which Alfonsín saw as potentially destabilizing for the UCR. Cavarozzi, "Peronism and Radicalism," p. 172.

67. Carlos Floria, "Dilemmas of Consolidation of Democracy in Argentina," in *Comparing New Democracies,* ed. Enrique Baloyra (Boulder: Westview, 1987), p. 158; and Catterberg, *Argentina Confronts Politics,* pp. 89–95.

68. On this point, see Torcuato Di Tella, *Hacia una Estrategia de la Socialdemocracia en la Argentina* (Buenos Aires: Punto Sur, 1989), p. 111.

69. For an analysis of the UCR debacle, see Cavarozzi and Grossi, "From Democratic Reinvention," pp. 11–12.

70. *La Prensa,* 20 February 1992.

71. James McGuire, "Peronism without Perón: Unions in Argentine Politics, 1955–1966," Ph.D. diss., University of California, Berkeley, 1989, pp. 55–57.

72. Torcuato Di Tella, *Latin American Politics,* pp. 138–40; Manuel Mora y Araujo, "Populismo, laborismo y clases medias: política y estructura social en la Argentina," *Criterio* 1775–76 (1977): 9–12.

73. James McGuire, "Political Parties and Democracy in Argentina," in *Building Democratic Institutions: Parties and Party Systems in Latin America,* ed. Scott Mainwaring and Timothy Scully (Stanford: Stanford University Press, 1994).

74. Cavarozzi, *Sindicatos y política,* pp. 89–90.

75. Torcuato Di Tella, "La situación argentina: fin de la integración y comienzo de la coexistencia," *Cuadernos Americanos* 124 (1962): 56–57.

76. Collier and Collier, *Shaping the Political Arena,* p. 721.

77. Ibid., pp. 731–32.

78. Snow, *Political Forces in Argentina,* p. 24.

79. McGuire, "Political Parties and Democracy," p. 25.

80. Collier and Collier, *Shaping the Political Arena,* p. 735.

81. David Rock, *Argentina 1516–1987: From Spanish Colonization to Alfonsín* (Berkeley: University of California, 1987), p. 359; Joseph Page: *Perón: a Biography* (New York: Random House, 1983), pp. 421–22.

82. Page, *Perón,* p. 404.

83. On why Perón selected Cámpora, see Wayne Smith, "El diálogo Perón-Lanusse," in *Racionalidad del Peronismo,* ed. José Enrique Miguens and Frederick C. Turner (Buenos Aires: Planeta, 1988), pp. 138–39.

84. Ibid., pp. 150–51.

85. Floria and Belsunce, *Historia política,* p. 204.

86. The UOM was one of the sixty-two unions making up the "62 organizations" commonly regarded as representative of Peronist unionism. Guido Di Tella, *Argentina under Perón, 1973–76* (New York: St. Martin's, 1983), pp. 76–77.

87. Cavarozzi, "Peronism and Radicalism," p. 156; and Manuel Mora y Araujo, "La estructura social del peronismo, 1983–1987," in *Racionalidad del peronismo*, ed. Mingues and Turner, pp. 168–69.

88. On the Renovation, see Emilio de Ipola, "La difícil apuesta del peronismo democrático," in *Ensayos*, ed. Nun and Portantiero.

89. De Riz, "Alfonsin's Argentina," pp. 18–21.

90. Perón notoriously patronized Cafiero in public, referring to him as Cafierito, or "little Cafiero."

91. See Alfredo Leuco and José Antonio Díaz, *El heredero de Péron* (Buenos Aires: Planeta, 1989); Cavarozzi and Grossi, "From Democratic Reinvention," pp. 18–20; and Gary Wynia, "The Peronists Triumph in Argentina," *Current History* (January 1990): 13–14.

92. Three examples of amateur politicians strongly backed by Menem were businessman Jorge Escobar in San Juan, singer Ramón "Palito" Ortega in Tucumán, and former car racer Carlos Reutemann in Santa Fe. All won close gubernatorial races in 1991.

93. Snow, *Political Forces in Argentina*, p. 25.

94. Karen Remmer, *Party Competition in Argentina and Chile* (Lincoln: University of Nebraska Press, 1984), pp. 99–100, 103–04.

95. Di Tella, *Latin American Politics*, p. 148.

96. Snow, *Political Forces in Argentina*, p. 25.

97. Ibid.

98. Ibid.; and William Smith, *Authoritarianism and the Crisis of the Argentine Political Economy* (Stanford: Stanford University Press, 1989), p. 219.

99. Smith, *Authoritarianism*, p. 219.

100. For an excellent analysis of the UCD, see Edward Gibson, "Democracy and the New Electoral Right in Argentina," *Journal of Interamerican Studies and World Affairs* 32 (1990): 177–288.

101. Rosendo Fraga and Gabriela Malacrida, *Argentina en las Urnas 1916–1989* (Buenos Aires: Centro de Estudios Unión para la Neuva Mayoría), p. 53.

102. Gibson, "Democracy," pp. 202–03.

103. These parties were the Partido Demócrata Progresista (Santa Fe), the Partido Liberal and the Partido Autonomista (Corrientes), the Partido Demócrata (Mendoza), the Unión Demócrata de Centro (Córdoba), and a federation of smaller parties in other provinces. Alvaro Alsogaray headed the thicket, while Alberto Natale (Santa Fe) was his running mate. The Alianza received 6.2 percent of the vote.

104. Fraga and Malacrida, *Argentina en las Urnas*, p. 27.

105. Alvaro Alsogaray became foreign debt adviser to the president, while his daughter was appointed to head the state telephone corporation and to make plans for its privatization. Both Alsogarays joined the administration as individuals, not party members.

106. *Buenos Aires Herald*, 23 October 1991.

107. *La Prensa*, 10 September 1991. One of the UCD's most important leaders commented that the alliance to back Porto heralded the end of the UCD as an independent party. *Buenos Aires Herald*, 29 February 1992. For a critique of the long-term failure of the UCD from the standpoint of one of its former leaders, see Manuel Mora y Araujo, *Ensayo y Error* (Buenos Aires: Planeta, 1991), p. 135.

108. For a portrayal of Rico, see *Somos*, 23 September 1991. See also Deborah Norden, "From Military Movement to Political Party," paper prepared for the Seventeenth Latin American Studies Association Congress, Los Angeles, 24–27 September 1992.

109. *La Prensa*, 1 March 1992. On the background of MODIN's deputies, see *Somos*, 6 January 1992.

110. Snow, *Political Forces in Argentina*, p. 26.

111. Ibid., p. 106.

112. Rock, *Argentina 1516–1987*, p. 187.

113. Snow, *Political Forces in Argentina*, p. 25.

114. *Clarín*, 10 August 1991.

115. Fraga and Malacrida, *Argentina en las Urnas*, pp. 30–31.

116. Deputies are elected for four-year terms: half of the seats are up for re-election every two years. The federal district has two senators as well, but having no legislature of its own, its senators are selected by an electoral college voted on by popular vote. Tierra del Fuego gained representation in the Chamber of Deputies in 1991. Under a direct system of election, the provinces of Buenos Aires and Santa Fe plus the federal district have enough votes to select the president.

117. Catterberg, *Argentina Confronts Politics*, pp. 50–54.

118. *Somos*, 20 December 1989.

119. Dix tried to measure factionalization using the less sophisticated Rae-Taylor index and obtained a score of .663 for the 1982–1989 period, the sixth highest among the eighteen Latin American countries surveyed. The first five were Ecuador (.835), Guatemala (.821), Chile (.808), Panama (.780), and Bolivia (.757). Dix, "Democratization," p. 503.

120. For the discussion of Laakso and Taagpera's index and its usefulness in determining the "effective number of parties," see Arend Lijphart, *Democracies: Patterns of Majoritarian and Consensus Government in Twenty-one Countries* (New Haven: Yale University Press, 1984), pp. 119–23.

121. Sartori, *Parties and Party Systems*, p. 314. One can also use Blondel's classification scheme, yet the result is very much the same. Argentina would be classified as a multiparty system with one party (the PJ), getting at least two-fifths of the vote. Jean Blondel, "Party Systems and Patterns of Government in Western Democracies," *Canadian Journal of Political Science* (1968): 180–203.

122. Mark Jones, "A Comparative Study of Popular Confidence in Democratic Institutions in Argentina, Chile, and Mexico," paper prepared for the Seventeenth Latin American Studies Association Congress, Los Angeles, 24–27 September, 1992.

123. Pizzorno, "Interests and Parties," pp. 270–71; Paul Allen Beck, "A Socialization Theory of Partisan Realignment," in *The Politics of Future Citizens*, ed. Richard Niemi et al. (San Francisco: Jossey Bass, 1974).

124. Pizzorno, "Interests and Parties," p. 271.

CHAPTER 4: *Political Culture,*
Public Opinion, and Voting Behavior

1. Tómas Roberto Fillol, *Social Factors in Economic Development: The Argentine Case* (Cambridge: MIT Press, 1961), pp. 46–47.

2. Ibid., p. 3.

3. Thomas McGann, *Argentina: The Divided Land* (Princeton: Van Nostrand, 1966), pp. 101–05.

4. Daniel Poneman, *Argentina: Democracy on Trial* (New York: Paragon, 1987), p. 170.

5. Manuel Mora Araujo, *Ensayo y Error* (Buenos Aires: Planeta, 1991), pp. 63–64.

6. John Johnson, *Political Change in Latin America: The Emergence of the Middle Sectors* (Stanford: Stanford University Press, 1958).

7. Mora y Araujo, *Ensayo y Error*, p. 68.

8. Fillol, *Social Factors in Economic Development;* McGann, *Argentina;* Susan Calvert and Peter Calvert, *Argentina: Political and Cultural Instability* (Pittsburgh: University of Pittsburgh Press, 1989), pp. 172–75.

9. Lars Schoultz, *Politics and Culture in Argentina* (Ann Arbor: Center for Political Studies, Institute for Social Research, University of Michigan, 1988), p. 10.

10. Gary Wynia, *Argentina: Illusions and Realities* (New York: Holmes and Meier, 1986), p. 35. Perhaps in an effort to improve the country's image in this regard, President Menem ordered the release of the secret files that the Argentine government had kept on the many German Nazis who had migrated to Argentina at the end of World War II.

11. José Ortega y Gasset, *Obras Completas*, 3d ed., 2 vols. (Madrid: Espasa-Calpe, 1943), 2:670; Jeane Kirkpatrick, *Leader and Vanguard in Mass Society: A Study of Peronist Argentina* (Cambridge: MIT Press, 1971), p. 120; Ezequiel Martínez Estrada, *X-Ray of the Pampa* (Austin: University of Texas Press, 1971); Calvert and Calvert, *Argentina*, p. 134; Schoutz, *Political and Culture*, p. 12.

12. Laura Randall, "Economic Development Policies and Argentine Economic Growth," in *Economic Development: Evolution or Revolution?*, ed. Laura Randall (Boston: Heath, 1964), p. 125; see also Richard Mallon and Juan Sourrouille, *Economic Policymaking in a Conflict Society: The Argentine Case* (Cambridge: Harvard University Press, 1975), p. 156.

13. Schoultz, *Politics and Culture*, p. 16.

14. Ibid., p. 3.

15. Poneman, *Argentina*, p. 127.

16. Justices Rodolfo Barra and Mariano Cavagna Martínez hired their own daughters. On the politicization of the Supreme Court under Menem, see Laura Koch, "Old Democratic Pitfalls Dog the New Argentina," *Wall Street Journal,* 27 March 1991.

17. An instance of this the free-ride behavior can be seen in the 1989 government estimates of people riding free on the national railway, which was put at 40 percent of total ridership. These people either held special passes or simply did not pay, since conductors often did not check passengers' tickets. The cost of government subsidies to private enterprises and individuals was estimated at $3–4 billion a year. *New York Times,* 30 September 1989.

18. *New York Times,* 23 January 1989; World Bank, *Argentina: Reforms for Price Stability and Growth* (Washington D.C.: World Bank, 1990), p. 39.

19. Schoultz, *Politics and Culture*, p. 20.

20. Kirkpatrick's survey excluded about 15 percent of rural dwellers and the inhabitants of the Patagonian provinces, or 3 percent of Argentina's population. Kirkpatrick, *Leader and Vanguard*.

21. José Luis de Imaz, *Motivación electoral* (Buenos Aires: Instituto de Desarrollo Económico y Social, 1963), pp. 29–33.

22. José Luis de Imaz, *La clase alta de Buenos Aires* (Buenos Aires, UNBA, 1965), p. 15.

23. Kirkpatrick, *Leader and Vanguard*, p. 85.

24. Instituto de Sociologia de la Universidad del Litoral, *Political Apathy in Rosario* (Rosario: Instituto de Sociología, 1963).

25. Peter G. Snow, *Political Forces in Argentina*, rev. ed. (New York: Praeger, 1979), p. 50. The survey he cites is "Voting Attitudes," 1,383 persons interviewed in metropolitan Buenos Aires and the cities of Mar del Plata and Bahia Blanca (both in the province of Buenos Aires) in 1963 by José Enrique Miguens and the Centro de Investigaciones Motivacionales y Sociales.

26. There has been speculation that the military intelligence conducted its own polls, but results have never been published.

27. Menem's drop in popularity was linked to the pardon of those officers and civilians still in jail who had been convicted during the Alfonsín administration for human rights violations (22.8 percent), corruption in government circles (22 percent), the economic recession (13.8 percent), and the sending of a naval task force to support UN sanctions against Iraq without congressional approval (12 percent). *Buenos Aires Herald*, 20 January 1991.

28. Mora y Araujo, *Ensayo y Error*, p. 148.

29. Ibid., p. 29.

30. Positive attitudes toward the military increased after the Tablada attack by left-wing guerrillas. Mora y Araujo, *Ensayo y Error*, p. 77.

31. Edgardo Catterberg, *Argentina Confronts Politics* (Boulder: Lynne Reinner, 1991), pp. 11–20.

32. Mora y Araujo, *Ensayo y Error*, p. 59.

33. Ibid., p. 72.

34. Ibid.

35. *Buenos Aires Herald*, 1 September 1991.

36. Mora y Araujo, *Ensayo y Error*, p. 18.

37. Catterberg, *Argentina Confronts Politics*, p. 41.

38. Cited in Howard Wiarda, *Finding Our Way? Toward Maturity in U.S.-Latin American Relations* (Washington D.C.: American Enterprise Institute), pp. 72–73.

39. Catterberg, *Argentina Confronts Politics*, pp. 42–43. This finding is consistent with findings of Seymour Lipset and Gino Germani, in their early works, which hypothesize that people with low socioeconomic and educational levels are likely to hold authoritarian values.

40. Ibid., pp. 39–48.

41. Charles Anderson, *Politics and Economic Change in Latin America* (New York: Van Nostrand, 1967), pp. 87–114.

42. Mora y Araujo's typological definitions are as follows: *social democrat*, "preference for a liberal democratic political system, with a strong emphasis on 'welfare state' policies"; *corporatist*, "preference for a social order in which organized sectors and institutions play a central role in major collective decisions,

promoted by a very active state"; *liberal*, preference for an order which supports individual initiative and property rights, with a limited role for the state"; *traditional*, "preference for traditional values independent of other considerations with an emphasis on 'morality' and a frequently 'authoritarian perception of social order"; *leftist*, "preference for a decidedly collectivist order, whether or not it is explicitly Marxist." Manuel Mora y Araujo, "The Nature of the Alfonsín Coalition," in *Elections and Democratization in Latin America, 1980–85*, ed. Paul Drake and Eduardo Silva (San Diego: Center of Iberian and Latin American Studies, University of California, San Diego, 1986)," p. 186.

43. Mora y Araujo, *Ensayo y Error*, p. 74.

44. Edgardo Catterberg, *Los Argentinos frente a la politicia: Cultura política y opinión pública en la transición argentina a la democracia* (Buenos Aires: Planeta), p. 35.

45. Mora y Araujo, *Ensayo y Error*, pp. 87–88.

46. Catterberg, *Los Argentinos*, p. 34.

47. Andrés Fontana, "Seguridad, fuerzas armadas y percepciones sociales" (Buenos Aires: April 1991). Fontana's unpublished study was done in collaboration with Catterberg and was based on a sample of 500 respondents. Of the remaining people, 26 percent believed that a coup was still possible, while 10 percent reported no opinion.

48. Catterberg, *Argentina Confronts Politics*, p. 58.

49. Manuel Mora y Araujo, Graciela Di Rado, and Paula Montoya, "La política exterior y la opinión pública Argentina," mimeographed, Buenos Aires, 1991.

50. The First World country mentioned most often was the United States (45 percent), particularly by those in the upper and lower socioeconomic groups. The reason given was usually the U.S. position as world leader. Japan (16 percent) and Europe (9 percent) were chosen because of their advanced technology. For Europe, historic and affective ties were also factors (ibid., pp. 35–39).

51. Ibid., pp. 32–33.

52. Gino Germani, *La estructura social de la Argentina* (Buenos Aires: Editorial Raigal, 1955), pp. 253–55; Pedro Huerta Palau, *Análisis electoral de una ciudad en desarrollo* (Córdoba: Universidad Nacional de Córdoba, 1963), p. 27.

53. Snow, *Political Forces*, p. 33.

54. Lars Schoultz, "The Socio-Economic Determinants of Popular-Authoritarian Electoral Behavior: The Case of Peronism," *American Political Science Review* 71 (December 1977): 1426.

55. Luis González Estévez, Ignacio Llorente and Manuel Mora y Araujo, *El voto peronista* (Buenos Aires: Sudamericana, 1980).

56. Huerta Palau, *Análisis electoral*, p. 19.

57. Schoultz, "Socio-Economic Determinants," p. 1429.

58. Snow, *Political Forces*, pp. 35, 40. The same conclusions were reached by Schoultz in his study of Peronism between 1946 and 1973. Lars Schoultz, *The Populist Challenge: Argentine Electoral Behavior in the Postwar Era* (Chapel Hill: University of North Carolina Press, 1983), p. 85.

59. Manuel Mora y Araujo, "La Estructura Social del Peronismo, 1983–1987," in *Racionalidad del Peronismo*, ed. José Enrique Miguens and Frederick C. Turner (Buenos Aires: Planeta, 1988), p. 167.

60. Mora y Araujo, "The Nature of the Alfonsín Coalition," pp. 180–83.

61. However, women (who cast their ballots separately from men) voted overwhelmingly for Alfonsín.

62. Mora y Araujo, *Ensayo y Error*, p. 22; Oscar Landi and Marcelo Cavorozzi, "Menem: El Fin del Peronismo? (Crisis y Postransición en la Argentina," *Cuaderno CEDES*, no. 66 (1991): 31; and interview with Julio Aurelio, pollster for the Peronists during the 1989 elections, Buenos Aires, June 1989.

63. Catterberg, *Los Argentinos*, pp. 130–33.

64. *Somos*, 22 July 1991.

65. *Buenos Aires Herald*, 15 September 1991.

CHAPTER 5: *The Armed Forces*

1. Robert A. Potash, "The Impact of Professionalism on the Twentieth Century Argentine Military" (Amherst: Program in Latin American Studies, University of Massachusetts, Amherst, Occasional Paper 3, 1977), p. 16.

2. Samuel P. Huntington, "Political Development and Political Decay," *World Politics* 17 (April 1965): 419.

3. Alain Rouquié, *The Military and the State in Latin America* (Berkeley: University of California Press, 1989), p. 275.

4. Karen Remmer, *Military Rule in Latin America* (Boston: Uwin Hyman, 1989), p. 32.

5. Rouquié, *The Military*, p. 291.

6. Samuel Huntington, *The Soldier and the State* (Cambridge: Harvard University Press, 1957), pp. 80–97. In Huntington's definition professionalism has three components: expertise, social responsibility, and corporate loyalty. On the impact of professionalism on the Argentine military, see Marvin Goldwert, "The Rise of Modern Militarism in Argentina," *Latin American Research Review* 48 (May 1968): 189–205.

7. Potash, "Impact of Professionalism," p. 6.

8. Robert Wesson, "Foreign Influences," in *The Latin American Military Institution*, ed. Robert Wesson (New York: Praeger, 1986), p. 98.

9. Andrés Fontana, "Percepción de amenazas y adquisición de armamentos: Argentina 1960–1989," *Cuaderno CEDES* 48 (1990): 37.

10. Jean Meyneaud, "Les Militaires et le Pouvoir," *Revue Francaise de Sociologie* 2 (April–June 1961): 81.

11. While many may dispute such a comparison between the Aramburu and Onganía administrations, it should be stressed that, under Aramburu, few military men were appointed to government positions. Aramburu needed the support of anti-Peronist parties, and some of their members were appointed to cabinet positions. See José Luis de Imaz, *Los Que Mandan (Those Who Rule)* (Albany: State University of New York Press, 1970), p. 51.

12. The selection of the German training pattern was allegedly influenced not only by the Prussian victories over Austria and France but also by the excellent performance by the Prussian-trained Chilean army against Bolivia and Peru in the War of the Pacific (1879–1983). On this issue see Goldwert, "Rise of Modern Militarism," p. 190; and de Imaz, *Los Que Mandan*, p. 56–57.

13. Robert Potash, *The Army & Politics in Argentina, 1928–1945* (Stanford: Stanford University Press, 1969), pp. 10–28.

14. Eduardo Crawley, *A House Divided: Argentina 1880–1980* (London: Hurst, 1984), p. 42.

15. Potash, *Army & Politics in Argentina, 1928–1945*, p. 77.

16. Quoted in Crawley, *House Divided*, p. 51.

17. Potash, *Army & Politics in Argentina, 1928–1945*, p. 64.

18. Former Minister of the Economy Federico Pinedo stressed that, while Uriburu was undoubtedly influenced by the appeal of some of the corporatist institutions proposed by European fascists and Catholic nationalists, he did not believe that the former general could easily transplant them to Argentina. Cited in Alberto Ciria, *Parties and Power in Modern Argentina (1930–1946)* (Albany: State University of New York Press, 1974), p. 191.

19. Cited in Ciria, *Parties and Power*, p. 192.

20. Cited in Crawley, *House Divided*, pp. 50–51.

21. The last blow to Uriburu's credibility came in early 1931 when partial elections were held in the Buenos Aires province—where the president was confident that his candidates would score an easy victory. On the contrary, the UCR won by a wide margin.

22. Alain Rouquié, *Poder militar y sociedad política en la Argentina*, vol. 1 (Buenos Aires: Emecé, 1981), pp. 276–77; and Benjamin Most, *Changing Authoritarian Rule and Public Policy in Argentina, 1930–1970* (GSIS Monograph Series in World Affairs, University of Denver and Lynne Reinner, 1991), pp. 88–89.

23. Potash, *The Army & Politics in Argentina, 1928–1945*, pp. 182–83.

24. S. E. Finer, *The Man on Horseback* (New York: Praeger, 1962), p. 120.

25. David Rock, *Argentina 1516–1987: From Spanish Colonization to Alfonsín*, 2d ed. (Berkeley: University of California Press, 1987), p. 250.

26. Edwin Lieuwen, *Arms and Politics in Latin America* (New York: Praeger, 1960), p. 71.

27. Marvin Goldwert, *Democracy, Militarism, and Nationalism in Argentina, 1930–1966* (Austin: University of Texas Press, 1972), p. 103.

28. Military expenditures declined from its all-time high of 43.3 percent of the federal budget in 1945 to 24.9 percent in 1949. Robert Potash, *The Military & Politics in Argentina, 1945–1962* (Stanford: Stanford University Press, 1980), p. 83. To endear himself to the air force, Perón allowed it to develop an Argentine-made Puma jet fighter. The navy received a carrier from the United Kingdom which was renamed *21 de Mayo*.

29. Alain Rouquié, "Adhesión militar y control político del ejército en el régimen peronista (1946–1955)," *Aportes* 19 (1971): 74–93.

30. Guillermo O'Donnell, *Un juego imposible. Competición y coaliciones entre partidos políticos en Argentina 1955–1966*, Documento de Trabajo (Buenos Aires: Instituto Torcuato Di Tella, 1977). For a critique of O'Donnell's thesis, see Catalina Smulovitz , "En busca de la fórmula perdida: Argentina 1955–1966," paper prepared for the Fifteenth Latin American Studies Congress, Miami, 4–6 December 1989.

31. Guillermo O'Donnell, "Modernization and Military Coups: Theory, Comparisons, and the Argentine Case," in *Armies & Politics in Latin America*, 2d ed., ed. Abraham Lowenthal and Samuel Fitsch (New York: Holmes and Meier, 1986), p. 102.

32. According to Rogelio Frigerio, Frondizi's chief economic adviser, there were more than twenty coup attempts during Frondizi's term. Interview, Buenos Aires, July 1987.

33. Oscar Alende, *Entretelones de la trampa* (Buenos Aires: Santiago Rueda, 1964), pp. 116–17.

34. Potash, "Impact of Professionalism," p. 14.

35. Philip Springer, "Disunity and Disorder: Factional Politics in the Argentine Military," in *The Military Intervenes: Case Studies in Political Development*, ed. Henry Bienen (New York: Russell Sage, 1968), p. 150.

36. Ibid.

37. For some, however, Onganía's stress on institutional autonomy, renewed professionalism, and apolitical behavior was counterproductive for the military. It expanded and multiplied roles, furthered intraservice conflicts, and in the end increased the armed forces' politicization (Fontana, "Percepción y amenazas," p. 7).

38. Ibid., pp. 8–19.

39. Guillermo Osiris Villegas, *Políticas y estrategias para el desarrollo y la seguridad nacional* (Buenos Aires: Pleamar, 1969), p. 109.

40. O'Donnell, "Modernization and Military Coups," p. 105.

41. Ibid., pp. 96–133; Alfred Stepan, "The New Professionalism of Internal Warfare and Military Role Expansion," in *Armies & Politics*, ed. Lowenthal and Fitch, pp. 134–50.

42. David Pion-Berlin, "Latin American National Security Doctrines: Hard- and Softline Themes," *Armed Forces and Society*, 15 (1989): 411–29.

43. See Deborah Norden, "Democratic Consolidation and Military Professionalism in Argentina," paper prepared for the Fifteenth Latin American Studies Association International Congress, Miami, 6–7 December 1989, p. 6.

44. Cited in Brian Loveman and Thomas M. Davies, eds., *The Politics of Antipolitics: The Military in Latin America*, 2d ed. (Lincoln: University of Nebraska Press, 1989), pp. 194–95.

45. Rouquié, *The Military*, p. 294.

46. José Nun, "The Middle Class Military Coup," in *The Politics of Conformity in Latin America*, ed. Claudio Veliz (New York: Oxford University Press, 1967), p. 106.

47. See Guillermo O'Donnell, *Modernization and Bureaucratic-Authoritarianism: Studies in South American Politics* (Berkeley: Institute of International Studies, University of California, 1973); O'Donnell, "Reflections on the Patterns of Change in the Bureaucratic-Authoritarian State," *Latin American Research Review* 13 (1978): 3–38; O'Donnell, *Bureaucratic Authoritarianism: Argentina, 1966–1973* (Berkeley: University of California Press, 1988).

48. William Smith, *Authoritarianism and the Crisis of the Argentine Political Economy* (Stanford: Stanford University Press, 1989), p. 54.

49. Ibid., p. 68.

50. According to Krieger Vasena, Lanusse intentionally refused to allow the Third Army Corps stationed in Córdoba to put down the first riots when the police chief asked for help. On top of that, Onganía for a few days did not have a clear idea of the seriousness of the events and failed to act appropriately. Interview, Buenos Aires, August 1987.

51. Guido Di Tella, *Argentina under Perón, 1973–76* (New York: St. Martin's, 1983), pp. 79–80; Crawley, *House Divided*, pp. 417–20.

52. Andrés Fontana, "Political Decision Making by a Military Corporation, Argentina, 1976–1983," Ph.D. diss., University of Texas, 1987, pp. 92–93.

53. Andrés Fontana: "Armed Forces and Neoconservative Ideology: State Shrinking in Argentina, 1976–1981," in *State Shrinking*, ed. William Glade (Austin: University of Texas Press, 1986), p. 71.

54. Andrés Fontana: "Notas sobre relaciones cívico-militares y el proceso de consolidación democrática en la Argentina," *Cuadernos Simón Rodríguez*, no. 10 (Buenos Aires: Biblos, 1987), p. 18.

55. Ibid., p. 15.

56. Ibid., p. 17; Carlos Floria and César García Belsunce: *Historia política de la Argentina contemporánea, 1880–1983*, 2d ed. (Buenos Aires: Alianza Universidad, 1989), pp. 242–56.

57. Rock, *Argentina, 1516–1987*, pp. 370–71.

58. Edward Milensky, "Arms Production and National Security in Argentina," *Journal of Interamerican Studies and World Affairs* 22 (1980): 267–87; see also Andrés Fontana, "El Sector de Producción para la Defensa: Origen y Problemas Actuales" (Buenos Aires: CEDES, 1986).

59. International Institute for Strategic Studies, *The Military Balance 1981–1982* (London: IISS, 1982), pp. 92–93.

60. See Silvio Waisbord, "Politics and Identity in the Argentine Army: Cleavages and the Generational Factor," *Latin American Research Review* 26 (1991): 157–70.

61. Max Hastings and Simon Jenkins, *The Battle for the Falklands* (New York: Norton, 1983), pp. 322–25.

62. Alfred Stepan, *Rethinking Military Politics: Brazil and the Southern Cone* (Princeton: Princeton University Press, 1988), p. 87.

63. Felipe Agüero, "The Assertion of Civilian Supremacy in Post-Authoritarian Contexts, Spain in Comparative Perspective," Ph.D. diss., Duke University, 1991, pp. 20–21.

64. The law was approved in August 1984. See Andrés Fontana: "La política militar del gobierno constitucional argentino," in *Ensayos sobre la transición democrática en la Argentina*, ed. José Nun and Juan Carlos Portantiero (Buenos Aires: Punto Sur, 1987). For an analysis of the Alfonsín administration's military policy, see Rut Diamint, "La cuestión militar en el gobierno del Dr. Alfonsín" (Buenos Aires, September 1991).

65. Fontana, "La política militar," pp. 383–84.

66. Ibid., pp. 385–86.

67. The first junta members were General Jorge Videla (president), General Roberto Viola (army), Admiral Emilio Massera (navy), and Bigadier Orlando Agosti (air force). The second junta was made up of Viola (president), General Leopoldo Galtieri (army), Admiral Armando Lambruschini (navy), and Brigadier Omar Graffigna (air force). The third junta included Galtieri (president and army commander), Admiral Jorge Isaac Anaya (navy), and Brigadier Basilio Lami Dozo (air force).

68. Andrés Fontana: "La política militar en un contexto de transición. Argentina 1987–1989," *Cuaderno CEDES* 34 (1990): 24.

69. See David Pion-Berlin, "Between Confrontation and Accommodation: Military and Government Policy in Democratic Argentina," *Journal of Latin America Studies* 23 (October 1991): 555–56; Rosendo Fraga, *La Cuestión Militar* (Buenos Aires: Centro Estudios Unión para la Nueva Mayoría, 1989), pp. 97–103; and Fontana: "La política militar," p. 13.

70. UN Institute for Disarmament Research, *National Security Concepts and States: Argentina* (Geneva: United Nations, 1992), p. 54.

71. Fraga, *La Cuestión Militar*, p. 165. In 1991, the minister of defense stated that the military budget had not improved much. "In real terms it does not even amount to one percent of the gross national product. . . . The problem is that in our budget we must include military pensions of high-ranking officers and some thirty companies that lose money." *Buenos Aires Herald*, 17 November 1991.

72. Fraga, *La Cuestión Militar*, p. 166.

73. Ibid., pp. 173–74.

74. Deborah Norden: "Rebels with a Cause? The Argentine Carapintadas," paper prepared for the annual meeting of the Midwest Political Science Association, Chicago, 5–7 April 1990, p. 8.

75. For a detailed description of these events, see Fontana, "La política militar," pp. 383–418.

76. Norden, "Democratic Consolidation," p. 13.

77. Norden, "Rebels with a Cause?" p. 11.

78. On Rico's version of the alleged pact with Alfonsín, see *Buenos Aires Herald*, 18 June 1991.

79. Fraga, *La Cuestión Militar*, p. 117.

80. Norden, "Rebels with a Cause?" p. 12.

81. Fraga, *La Cuestión Militar*, p. 117.

82. Regarding the fulfillment of a pact among Caridi, Cáceres, and Seineldín see ibid., p. 116; and Norden, "Rebels with a Cause?" p. 15.

83. Norden, "Rebels with a Cause?" p. 15.

84. Allegedly, Menem and Seineldín held a secret meeting during the presidential campaign that led to a pact between the two, according to which Menem was going to make major concessions to the carapintadas in return for political support. *Somos*, 31 December 1990, pp. 4–7.

85. On the carapintadas support for Menem see Mónica Peralta Ramos, *The Political Economy of Argentina: Power and Class Since 1930* (Boulder: Westview, 1992), p. 146. Moreover, the carapintadas hoped that had Menem been elected 432 of their comrades sentenced or facing indictments for the 1987–1988 mutinies would be freed immediately.

86. Carlos H. Acuña and Catalina Smulovitz, "Ni olvido ni perdón? Derechos humanos y tensiones cívico-militares en la transición argentina," *Cuaderno CEDES*, no. 69 (1991): 43–44. See also Rosendo Fraga and Eduardo Ovalles, *Menem y la Cuestión Militar* (Buenos Aires: Centro Estudios Unión para la Nueva Mayoría, 1991), pp. 145–50.

87. The 270 who benefited from the pardon were 39 senior officers charged with crimes committed during the dirty war; the 3 members of the last junta who had decided to invade the Falklands/Malvinas; 164 rebels of the three military mutinies; and 64 left-wing terrorists. Excluded from the pardons were the members of the first junta, General Carlos Suárez Masón, montonero leader

Mario Firmenich, and former Buenos Aires police chiefs Oliviero Ricchieri and Ramón Camps. *Buenos Aires Herald,* 1 October, 1989.

88. Allegedly, the plot was supported by Menem's estranged wife Zulema and her family, the powerful Yoma clan. Other families of Arabic descent, such as the Saadis, the Samids, and the Salims (all of whom are rivals of the Menems), were reportedly participants in the coup coalition. *Latin American Regional Reports: Southern Cone,* 13 September 1990, p. 1.

89. *Buenos Aires Herald,* 9 December 1990. See also Fraga and Ovalles, *Menem y la Cuestión Militar,* pp. 127–43.

90. According to an unofficial report by the army chief of staff, the makeup of the rebels was as follows: 34 officers of 5,800 total (0.6 percent), 550 NCOs of 23,800 total (2.3 percent), plus 18 civilians. *Somos,* 31 December 1990. That the carapintada leadership had been taken over by lower-ranking officers is testified to by the fact that among officers who headed the coup the most prominent were majors Hugo Abete and Jorge Mones Ruiz, and Captain Gustavo Breide Obeid; colonels Luis Baraldini and Oscar Vega seemed to have taken orders from the former. *Buenos Aires Herald,* 9 December 1990.

91. *Buenos Aires Herald,* 13 January 1991. Actually, Seineldín did not physically take part in the coup, as he was serving a sixty-day jail term in the province of La Pampa, but he was considered the mastermind behind the rebellion. Rico was not involved. On 15 August 1991 the SCAF sentenced twenty-six noncommissioned army officers to terms ranging from six months to nine years. This brought the number of sentenced officers to 58 since the trials began in early 1991. Some 328 officers and NCOs were also acquitted. On 2 September, the Federal Court of Appeals upheld the SCAF's life sentence for Seineldín but substantially reduced the sentences for the other officers. Although the SCAF handed out cumulative sentences of 301 years (counting 30 years for a life term), the Federal Court of Appeals reduced them to 202 years. The Menem administration immediately appealed the sentences, claiming they had been too lenient. *Buenos Aires Herald,* 8 September 1991.

92. Buenos Aires Herald, 6 January 1991.

93. Acuña and Smulovitz, "Ni olvido ni perdón?" pp. 53–54.

94. *Somos,* 22 July 1991. See also Daniel Poneman, *Argentina: Democracy on Trial* (New York: Paragon, 1987), p. 101.

95. *Clarín,* 22 January 1992.

96. The list included Zapla Blast Furnaces, Somisa (steel), Bahía Blanca Petrochemical Co., General Mosconi Petrochemical Co., Río Tercero Petrochemical Co., Carboquímica Argentina, AFNE (state shipyards and naval factories), Córdoba Material Aérea, Sulphuric Acid Co., Synthetic Toulene Co., Former Meteor Co., Polisur, Vinylic Monomers, Petropol, Induclor, Tanador (North Basin shipyards), Hipasam, and Forja. A complete list can be found in *Latin American Finance Supplement,* March 1992, p. 50.

97. *La Prensa,* 3 January 1992.

98. Peralta Ramos, *Political Economy,* p. 126.

99. Fraga, *La Cuestión Militar,* p. 140.

100. Gary Wynia, *The Politics of Latin American Development,* 2d ed. (New York: Cambridge University Press, 1984), p. 86.

101. Pion-Berlin, "Between Confrontation and Accommodation," p. 557.

102. Fontana, "La Política Militar," p. 21.

103. Pion-Berlin, "Between Confrontation and Accommodation," pp. 569–70.

104. Acuña and Smulovitz, "Ni olvido ni perdón?" p. 1.

105. Norden, "Democratic Consolidation," p. 1.

106. David Pion-Berlin and Ernesto López, "A House Divided: Segmented Professionalism and Role Perceptions in the Argentine Army," in *The New Democracy in Argentina*, ed. Edward Epstein (New York: Praeger, forthcoming), pp. 31–36.

107. To give an idea of the drastic changes that took place with the restoration of democracy, suffice it to say that, of the high-ranking officers of the armed forces at the end of the Proceso, by January 1989 only three admirals and two brigadiers were left. Fraga, *La Cuestión Militar*, p. 124.

108. Acuña and Smulovitz, "Ni olvido ni perdón?" p. 2. A related point was made by Federal Appeal Court prosecutor Luis Moreno Ocampo, who represented the Argentine government in the most important trials against the military between 1985 and 1991. In an interview, Ocampo stated that even if the sentences were not served, which hurt the process, the staging of the trial itself was of value. "We aired judicial proof of crimes that had been covered up in Argentina." *Buenos Aires Herald*, 15 September 1991.

109. Most of the coast guard leadership was cashiered. About a third of its remaining 12,000 troops were transferred to the Ministry of Interior. Leaders of both the coast guard and border guard bitterly protested the measures, leading to the resignations of their commanders. *Buenos Aires Herald*, 5 January 1992. The pay hikes of April 1992 ranged from 29.6 percent ($3,000) for high-ranking officers to 7 percent for the lower ranks ($330). The gap between senior officers and noncommissioned officers was estimated at around 700 percent. *Buenos Aires Herald*, 15 April 1991.

110. For the 1989 figures, see Fraga, *La Cuestión Militar*, pp. 171–73. In 1991 the armed forces strength was: army, 30,000 officers and NCOs; navy, 16,000; and air force, 13,000. Recruits were dropped to 20,000 annually. The army had four NCOs for every officer (24,000 to 6,000). *Folha de São Paulo*, 1 June 1991.

111. The CONDOR middle-range missile project began under the Videla administration but was later continued and expanded into the CONDOR II during Alfonsín's term. Its cost has been estimated at $300 million. The United States strongly feared that this missile could be sold to unreliable Third World nations. After the war in Iraq in 1991, the United States increased its pressure upon the Argentine government to terminate the project. *Buenos Aires Herald*, 16 February 1992.

112. For the first argument, see Deborah Norden, "Democratic Consolidation and Military Professionalism: Argentina in the 1980s," *Journal of Interamerican Studies and World Affairs* 32 (1990): 151–76; for a synthesis of Atilio Borón's argument, that the rebels intended a coup, see Norden, "Rebels with a Cause?" p. 2.

113. *Clarín*, 17 November 1991.

114. For a discussion of coup conditions, see Fontana, "Notas sobre relaciones cívico-militares," p. 12.

115. Poneman, *Argentina: Democracy on Trial*, p. 83.

116. Not surprisingly, Seineldín immediately praised the Venezuelan coup and stressed its similarities (some of them gratuitous) to the carapintada rebellions. *La Prensa*, 17 February 1992.

117. Buenos Aires Herald, 31 March 1991.

CHAPTER 6: *The Labor Movement*

1. Julio Godio and Héctor Palomino, *El movimiento sindical argentino hoy: Historia, organización y neuvos desafíos programáticos* (Buenos Aires: Fundación Friedrich Ebert, 1987), p. 50. A count of effective union membership is made very difficult by the tendency of unions to claim more affiliated members than they actually have in order to obtain more welfare benefits for their obras sociales (union welfare services) and political weight within the union movement. The most reliable way to assess union strength is the effective number of workers eligible to vote in union elections. These statistics are reported by individual unions and federations to the Ministry of Labor. Unfortunately, the Ministry of Labor has not released these figures in recent years for public scrutiny. Thus, the numbers here are gross approximations based upon interviews with specialists in union affairs, pundits, and individual union leaders.

2. Rural workers are scarcely organized with the exception of sugar workers in Chaco, Jujuy, Salta and Tucumán; fruit packers in Neuquén, Entre Ríos, Misiones, and Río Negro; and wine workers in La Rioja and Mendoza.

3. Juan Carlos D'Abate, "Trade Unions and Peronism," in *Juan Perón and the Reshaping of Argentina*, ed. Frederick Turner and José Enrique Miguens (Pittsburgh: Pittsburgh University Press, 1983), pp. 69–69.

4. Pablo Pozzi, "Argentina 1976–1982: Labour Leadership and Military Government," *Journal of Latin American Studies* 20 (1988): 132.

5. Tomás Roberto Fillol, *Social Factors in Economic Development: The Argentine Case* (Cambridge: MIT Press, 1961), p. 76.

6. Gilbert Merkx, "Sectoral Clashes and Political Change: The Argentine Experience," *Latin American Research Review* 4 (1969): 83.

7. The nation's first workers' organization was set up in 1857 under the name of Buenos Aires Printers' Society (Sociedad Tipográfica Bonarense). This was primarily a self-help organization; it was created by immigrants from Italy and Spain and resembled workers' associations in those two countries.

8. Enrique Dickmann, *Recuerdos de un militante socialista* (Buenos Aires: La Vanguardia, 1949); Jacinto Oddone, *Gremialismo proletario argentino* (Buenos Aires: La Vanguardia, 1949); Luis Cerruti Costa, *El sindicalismo, las masas y el poder* (Buenos Aires: Trafac, 1957); Sebastián Marotta, *El movimiento sindical argentino. Su génesis y desarrollo*, vols. 1 and 2 (Buenos Aires: Lacio, 1960); Hobart Spalding, *La clase trabajadora argentina (Documentos para su historia, 1890–1916)* (Buenos Aires: Galerna, 1970); Rubens Iscaro, *Historia del movimiento sindical*, vol. 2, *El movimiento sindical argentino* (Buenos Aires: Fundamento, 1973); David Rock, *Politics in Argentina, 1890–1930: The Rise and Fall of Radicalism* (London: Cambridge University Press, 1975); and Richard Walter, *The Socialist Party of Argentina, 1890–1930*, Latin American Monograph 42 (Austin: Institute of Latin American Studies, University of Texas, 1977).

9. Alberto Belloni, *Del anarquismo al peronismo (Historia del movimiento obrero Argentino)* (Buenos Aires: A. Peña Lillo, 1960), pp. 22–23.

10. Robert J. Alexander, *Organized Labor in Latin America* (New York: Free Press, 1965), p. 36.

11. Rock, *Politics in Argentina*, p. 80.

12. Ruth Berins Collier and David Collier, *Shaping the Political Arena* (Princeton: Princeton University Press, 1991), pp. 92–93; and Paul Lewis, *The Crisis of Argentine Capitalism* (Chapel Hill: University of North Carolina Press, 1990), pp. 100–01.

13. The social defense law also prevented anarchists from holding rallies, using propaganda, and entering the country. Samuel Baily, *Labor, Nationalism and Politics in Argentina* (New Brunswick: Rutgers University Press, 1967), p. 26. See also Alexander, *Organized Labor*, p. 37.

14. Rock, *Politics in Argentina, 1890–1930*, p. 84.

15. The new anarchist organization was dubbed the FORA of the Quinto Congreso referring to the 1905 FORA Congress, which had accepted anarchic communism as its guiding principle. See ibid., p. 90.

16. According to Madsen and Snow, "1916, in the twenty wards of the Federal Capital the rank order correlation between the percentage of the registered voters who were manual workers and the percentage of the vote received by the UCR was −81; in 1928 that correlation was +.54." Douglas Madsen and Peter G. Snow, *The Charismatic Bond: Political Behavior in TIme of Crisis* (Cambridge: Harvard University Press, 1991), p. 41.

17. Between 1915 and 1922, the FORA increased its following from 51 affiliated unions with perhaps, 3,000 members to 734 affiliates with about 70,000 members.

18. Between 700 and 800 people died during the Semana Trágica, and 1,000 to 2,000 in the Patagonian repression. On the Semana Trágica see Hugo del Campo, "La Semana Trágica," *Polémica* 53 (1971) and Collier and Collier, *Shaping the Political Arena* pp. 145–46. On the Patagonian repression, see Osvaldo Bayer, *La Patagonia Rebelde* (Buenos Aires, Nueva Imagen, 1980); and Sandra McGee, "The Liga Patriótica Argentina and Its 'Practical Humanitarianism': A Right-Wing Response to Social Change," paper prepared for the Eighth National Meeting of the Latin American Studies Association, Pittsburgh, April 1979.

19. Upon the creation of the CGT, the Socialist Argentine Labor Union (Unión Sindical Argentina, or USA) and the Syndicalist Argentine Workers' Confederation (Confederación Obrera Argentina, or COA) were dissolved. James McGuire, "The Cause of Strikes in Alfonsín's Argentina, 1983–1989: New Ideas, New Data, and a Quantitative Analysis," paper presented for the American Political Science Association Meeting, San Francisco, 31 August through 2 September, 1990, p. 6.

20. Luis Ramicone, *La organización gremial obrera en la actualidad. Apuntes para la historia* (Buenos Aires: Bases, 1963), pp. 66–67.

21. Collier and Collier, *Shaping the Political Arena*, p. 155.

22. Baily, *Labor, Nationalism and Politics*, p. 64. See also Alberto Ciria, *Parties and Power in Modern Argentina (1930–1946)*, (Albany: State University of New York Press, 1974), pp. 263–68.

23. For instance, the socialists kept insisting on the necessity of using legislative means to push social reforms, while the syndicalists argued that the most effective way to accomplish such reforms was to lobby the government directly to ensure union influence in the decision-making process. James McGuire, "Peronism without Perón: Unions in Argentine Politics, 1955–1966," Ph.D. diss., University of California, Berkeley, 1989, pp. 24–25.

24. Collier and Collier, *Shaping the Political Arena*, p. 336.

25. United Nations, *Report on the World Social Situation* (New York: United Nations, 1957), p. 175.

26. Gino Germani, "El surgimiento del Peronismo: El rol de los obreros y de los emigrantes internos," *Desarrollo Económico* 13 (1973): 479.

27. David Rock, *Argentina 1516–1987: From Spanish Colonization to Alfonsín*, 2d ed. (Berkeley: University of California Press, 1987), p. 255. In 1940, these two unions along with the Unión Tranviaria accounted for 115,000 members, that is, a fourth of the country's union membership. Benjamin Most, *Changing Authoritarian Rule and Public Policy in Argentina: 1930–1970*, (GSIS Monograph Series in World Affairs, Boulder: University of Denver and Lynne Reinner, 1991), p. 61.

28. Ciria, *Parties and Power*, p. 257.

29. Cited in Eduardo Crawley, *A House Divided, Argentina 1880–1980* (London: Hurst 1984), p. 73.

30. Ibid., p. 88.

31. Rubens Iscaro, *Origen y desarrollo del movimiento sindical argentino* (Buenos Aires: Ateneo, 1958), p. 228.

32. Collective bargaining allows workers to have union representatives negotiate their wages, benefits, and working conditions with management. Before 1943 such agreements were limited to a handful of industries: management usually dealt with each worker individually. With Perón, collective bargaining became the norm. Fillol, *Social Factors*, p. 66. See also Javier Slodky, *La negociación colectiva en la Argentina* (Buenos Aires: Fundación Friedrich Ebert, 1987).

33. A detailed list can be found in D'Abate, "Trade Unions and Peronism," pp. 59–60.

34. Cited in Ciria, *Parties and Power*, p. 272.

35. Robert Alexander, *The Perón Era* (New York: Columbia University Press, 1951), p. 31.

36. Edward Epstein, "Labor Populism and Hegemonic Crisis in Argentina," in *Labor Autonomy and the State in Latin America*, ed. Edward Epstein (Boston: Unwin Hyman, 1989).

37. Joseph Page, *Perón: A Biography* (New York: Random House, 1983), p. 292. On rank-and-file behavior, see Collier and Collier, *Shaping the Political Arena*, p. 339.

38. Rock, *Politics in Argentina*, 1890–1930, pp. 255, 263. The new unions were in communications, oil, plastics, automotives, textiles, shoes, clothing, rubber, chemicals, food processing, tobacco, shipping, health care, construction, utilities, paper, glass, and others. D'Abate, "Trade Unions and Peronism," p. 57. The textile workers and metal workers unions each had about 2,000 members in 1943; by 1946 they had 85,000 and 100,000, respectively. Roberto Carri, *Sindicatos y poder en la Argentina* (Buenos Aires: Editorial Sudestada, 1967), p. 27.

39. Madsen and Snow, *Charismatic Bond,* p. 48. See also Fillol, *Social Factors,* p. 83; Gino Germani, *Política y sociedad en una época de transición: De la sociedad tradicional a la sociedad de masas* (Buenos Aires: Paidós, 1965), pp. 230–31; and Baily, *Labor, Nationalism, and Politics,* p. 82.

40. Peter Smith, "The Social Bases of Peronism," *Hispanic America Historical Review* 52 (1972): 55–73; Spencer Wellhofer, "The Mobilization of the Periphery: Perón's 1946 Triumph," *Comparative Political Studies* 7 (1974): 239–51: pp. Tulio Halperín Donghi, "Algunas observaciones sobre Germani, el surgimiento del peronismo y los migrantes internos," *Desarrollo Económico* 14 (1975): 765–79; Walter Little, "The Popular Origins of Peronism," in *Argentina in the Twentieth Century,* ed. David Rock (Pittsburgh: Pittsburgh University Press, 1975), pp. 162–78. For a synthesis on the debate, see José Enrique Miguens, "Las interpretaciones intelectuales del voto peronista: los prejuicios académicos y las realidades," in *Racionalidad del peronismo: Perspectivas internas y externas que replantean un debate inconcluso,* ed. José Enrique Miguens and Frederick Turner (Buenos Aires: Planeta, 1988), pp. 209–32.

41. Collier and Collier, *Shaping the Political Arena,* p. 335.

42. The CGT ruling committee's call for a general strike was not an easy one (twenty-one leaders voted for, nineteen voted against). Nor was the general strike calling explicitly for Perón's release. Rather, it made six demands, all accepted by President Farrell.

43. Alexander, *Perón Era,* p. 43; and Baily, *Labor, Nationalism, and Politics,* pp. 91–92.

44. Bertram Silverman, "Labor Ideology and Economic Development in the Peronist Epoch," *Studies in Comparative International Development* 4 (1968–69): 245.

45. Rock, *Politics in Argentina,* pp. 263, 285.

46. Because of the power and money involved in labor representation, many young and ambitious workers were lured into the union hierarchy. Eventually, taking advantage of their status and the lack of control over their operations, many labor leaders were involved in corruption scandals, manipulating their unions' financial resources for personal use. To maintain their acquired wealth and privileges, they rigged elections to perpetuate themselves in office. These crimes tarnished the image of the union leaders as true representatives of the workers. Paul Lewis, *The Crisis of Argentine Capitalism* (Chapel Hill: University of North Carolina, 1990), pp. 402–14.

47. During sixteen legal strikes workers were not compensated by the employers.

48. This was the fate of some of the older unions in the textile, shipbuilding, shoe, banking, food processing, telephone, printing, and railway sectors.

49. McGuire, "Causes of Strikes," p. 6.

50. Adolfo Canitrot, "Discipline as the Central Objective of Economic Policy: An Essay on the Economic Programme of the Argentine Government Since 1976," *World Development* 8 (1980): 920; and Eduardo Feldman, "Wage Industrial Negotiation and Protectionism in Argentina 1946–1976: The Tragedy of the Commons," M.A. thesis, University of North Carolina at Chapel Hill, 1992.

51. McGuire, "Peronism without Perón," pp. 43–44.

52. Alexander, *Organized Labor,* p. 46.

53. Silverman, "Labor Ideology," p. 245.

54. Baily, *Labor, Nationalism and Politics*, p. 116; Rock, *Politics in Argentina*, pp. 257, 313.

55. A minority of older unions also resisted the Peronist hegemony. In September 1951, Perón declared a state of siege to break a strike by La Fraternidad railway workers.

56. Gary Wynia, "Workers and Wages: Argentine Labor and the Incomes Policy Problem," in *Juan Perón and the Reshaping of Argentina*, ed. Turner and Miguens, pp. 36–37.

57. Juan Carlos Torre, "El movimiento sindical en la Argentina," (Buenos Aires: Instituto Torcuato Di Tella, 1979).

58. Gary Wynia, *Argentina: Illusions & Realities* (New York: Holmes and Meier, 1986), p. 72.

59. Epstein, "Labor Populism," p. 13.

60. James McGuire, "Union Political Tactics and Democratic Consolidation in Alfonsín's Argentina, 1983–1989," *Latin American Research Review* 27 (1992): 37–74.

61. Cited in Rock, *Politics in Argentina*, p. 286.

62. Cited in Page, *Perón*, p. 89.

63. McGuire, "Union Political Tactics," pp. 38–39.

64. The best example of labor leadership self-perpetuation is the UOM. Between 1958 and 1990 this union had only two leaders, Vandor and Miguel.

65. Epstein, "Labor Populism," p. 19.

66. However, since the revolutionary government banned from union office all those who had held office between 1946 and 1955, an entirely new generation of union leaders emerged.

67. Marcelo Cavarozzi, *Sindicatos y política en Argentina* (Buenos Aires: CEDES, 1984), pp. 74–83. The word normalization when applied to the CGT in Argentina means the return of the organization to its legal representatives who are elected by union delegates.

68. Ibid., pp. 158–74.

69. Collier and Collier, *Shaping the Political Arena*, pp. 730–31.

70. Vandor's effort to gain control of the Peronist party apparatus and the eventual defeat of Vandor's candidate in the Mendoza gubernatorial election of 1966 constitute an important backdrop to this division of the "62," in which Alonso's "62 de pie" were Perón's labor operatives in his struggle to block Vandor.

71. About all that the Independents had in common was opposition to Peronism and to the claim of that group that the CGT was simply the labor branch of the Peronist movement.

72. On this period, see also William Smith, *Authoritarianism and the Crisis of the Argentine Political Economy* (Stanford: Stanford University Press, 1989), pp. 100–26.

73. Epstein, "Labor Populism," p. 19.

74. Ibid., p. 23.

75. Although Vandor is generally described as an orthodox Peronist, his willingness to compromise made him an important ally of the participationist Peronists on several occasions. Indeed, differences existed between Vandor and

the more accommodating union leaders of the collaborationist faction of the labor movement. Yet, these differences mainly rested upon the issue of how separate unions were to be from government policies, with Vandor supporting autonomy. According to one author, Vandor and the participationists agreed on "a show of 'responsibility' designed to appeal to the political apparatus, nationalist officers, and middle-class groups opposed to Krieger's economic policies. The contrast with the 'revolutionary' option defended by the CGT could hardly have been more clearly delineated." Smith, *Authoritarianism*, p. 120.

76. The percentage of union members needed to call a meeting was doubled, ordinary assemblies were cut to one every two years, and the rank and file were excluded from running for the most important union positions.

77. Guido Di Tella, *Argentina under Perón, 1973–76* (New York: St. Martin's, 1983), pp. 106–09.

78. The Group of 8 was expelled from the "62" when it refused to join a strike called by Perón in 1969. The *antiverticalistas* emerged in 1975 when they challenged the leadership of Isabel Perón and horenzo Miguel. Loyalists to the latter were called, in turn, *verticalistas*.

79. Pozzi, "Argentina 1976–1982," p. 114.

80. Ibid., p. 124.

81. See Rock, *Politics in Argentina*, pp. 352–57, and Juan Carlos Portantiero, "Clases dominantes y crisis política en la Argentina actual," in *El capitalismo argentino en crisis*, ed. Oscar Braun (Buenos Aires: Siglo XXI, 1973), pp. 101–03.

82. Andrés Fontana, "Armed Forces and Neoconservative Ideology: State Shrinking in Argentina, 1976–1981," in *State Shrinking*, ed. William Glade (Austin: University of Texas Press, 1986.

83. Pozzi, "Argentina 1976–1982," p. 118.

84. The Story of Triaca's rise from obscurity to wealth and power (and alleged corruption) can be found in *Somos* 30 (1992): 4–9.

85. Pozzi, "Argentina 1976–1982," pp. 120–21.

86. Ibid., p. 129.

87. Epstein, "Labor Populism," p. 21.

88. CGT-Brasil and CGT-Azopardo were the streets in Buenos Aires where the two organizations' offices were located.

89. Santiago Senén González, *Diez años de sindicalsimo argentino* (Buenos Aires: CEAL, 1984), pp. 165–66.

90. Charles Blake, "The Rise and Fall of Saúl Ubaldini: Peronism at the Crossroads," paper prepared for the annual meeting of the Midwest Political Science Association, Chicago, 18–20 April 1991, p. 6.

91. McGuire, "Union Political Tactics," pp. 51–65.

92. Alejandro Francisco Lamadrid, *Política y alineamientos sindicales: opiniones del nuevo cuadro gremial* (Buenos Aires: Punto Sur, 1988), p. 123.

93. Héctor Palomino, "Los sindicatos bajo el gobierno constitucional: de la confrontación a la alianza," in *Ensayos sobre la transición democrática en la Argentina*, ed. José Nun and Juan Carlos Portantiero (Buenos Aires: Punto Sur, 1987), p. 187.

94. Lamadrid, *Política y alineamentos sindicales*, pp. 123–24.

95. Ibid., p. 187.

96. McGuire, "Union Political Tactics," p. 16.

97. Lamadrid, *Política y alineamientos sindicales,* pp. 125–26.

98. Ricardo Gaudio and Héctor Domeniconi, "Las primeras elecciones sindicales en la transición democrática," *Desarrollo Económico* 26 (1986): 437.

99. Palomino, "Los sindicatos," p. 188; Lamadrid, *Política y alineamientos sindicales,* pp. 128–29.

100. Palomino, "Los sindicatos," p. 187.

101. The co-direction of the CGT by four general secretaries was an uneasy compromise. Besides Ubaldini and Triaca, the CGT-Brasil and the CGT-Azopardo added each one of their people too. It took three years to organize a CGT congress to elect a new leadership, because each faction first wanted to gain the upper hand. Blake, "Rise and Fall of Saúl Ubaldini," p. 9.

102. McGuire, "Union Political Tactics," p. 53.

103. Ibid., p. 16.

104. Palomino, "Los sindicatos," p. 186.

105. McGuire, "Union Political Tactics," p. 47.

106. In May 1987 the Group of 15 was the largest labor faction within the CGT and could count on the support of a substantial number of nonaligned unions. Estimates put its overall strength at 2 million members. Palomino, "Los sindicatos," p. 186.

107. Epstein, "Labor Populism," p. 29.

108. McGuire, "Union Political Tactics," p. 49.

109. ANSSAL's importance rested on its administration of $350 to $450 million available for union welfare programs. Barrionuevo made quite public his having provided $1 million for Menem's presidential campaign in 1989. His candor led him into a political storm when in November 1990 he confessed that it was customary for union leaders to use their official positions for personal profit. A few weeks later he was forced to resign. *Buenos Aires Herald,* 25 November 1990.

110. The decree explicitly covered "basic social services" like health, transport, education, telecommunications, water supply, electricity, gas and fuels, and the administration of justice. The decree prevented wildcat strikes. It called for a two-month negotiation period to solve labor-management disputes prior to notification of the date a strike would be staged. Essential services were to be maintained during a strike, and if a dispute remained pending after compulsory conciliation talks, the government was to step in and enforce compulsory arbitration. Equally important was the fact that, because of its vague language, the decree's provisions could be extended to other sectors, as all activities threatening the "life, health, freedom, and security of the community" were included.

111. Historically, Peronism always had a difficult time with strikes when in power and repeatedly attempted to limit their use. In 1945 with Perón's assent the military government issued Decree 536 outlawing strikes in the public sector. Interestingly, the right to strike was incorporated in the Argentine Constitution only in 1957 under the anti-Peronist administration of President Aramburu. Again under Perón in 1974, Law 20.638 authorized the executive branch to impose compulsory government arbitration of labor conflicts affecting "economic activity and the security and well-being of the community."

112. *Buenos Aires Herald,* 15 October 1989.

113. Blake, "Rise and Fall of Saúl Ubaldini," p. 24.

114. *La Prensa*, 12 July 1991. The new "62" could count on the support of 111 unions and 67 regional labor delegations.

115. *Buenos Aires Herald*, 18 September 1991.

116. *La Prensa*, 17 November 1991. Under the new law, companies could hire up to 30 percent of their work force on six-month to eighteen-month contracts; six-month to twenty-four-month contracts were allowed to get new enterprises off the ground; youths under twenty-five years old could be hired on training contracts from four months to two years. The government justified the law as a way to provide jobs for 800,000 unemployed and over a million underemployed people.

117. *Clarín*, 1 November 1992.

118. The five general secretaries were José Rodríguez, Oscar Lescano, José Pedraza, Aníbal Martínez, and Ramón Baldassini. Rodríguez (auto workers) and Pedraza (power workers) were pro-Menem, Lescano was an independent, Baldassini (a former CGT-Azopardo leader) was close to Ubaldini, and Martínez was from the UOM.

119. *Latin America Regional Reports: Southern Cone* 8 (1990): 8.

120. Blake, "Rise and Fall of Saúl Ubaldini," pp. 9, 11.

121. William Smith, "Democracy and Distributional Conflict in Argentina: Constraints on Macroeconomic Policymaking During the Alfonsín Government," in *Latin America and Caribbean Contemporary Record, vol. 8, 1988–89*, ed. James Malloy and Eduardo Gamarra (New York: Holmes and Meyer, forthcoming), table 10, graph 5.

122. *Buenos Aires Herald*, 11 March 1990.

123. A so-called silent majority march on 6 April 1990 was held to support Menem's economic and state reform policies after Ubaldini-led strike of 60,000 state workers two weeks before. The march, which drew to Buenos Aires's main square about 150,000 people, was supposedly a "spontaneous" demonstration. In fact, the march was conceived by conservative journalist Bernardo Neustadt, one of the country's leading political analysts, and was organized by pro-Menem labor leader Luis Barrionuevo and Buenos Aires Vice Governor Luis María Macaya.

124. Lewis, *Crisis of Argentine Capitalism*, p. 409.

125. Furthermore, CGT's financial resources are considerably smaller than those of its largest and most powerful member unions.

126. Interview with Héctor Palomino, Buenos Aires, May 1990.

127. CGT statutes approved in March 1992 include some important provisions: minority representation within each union; union independence from political parties and philosophical and religious ideologies; permission for the labor movement to create its own party; and permission for unions with less than 500 members to send delegates to the CGT congress. Distribution of delegates was organized as follows: unions having 300 to 2,000 members, one delegate; those with 2,000 to 3,000 members, two delegates; those with 3,000 to 15,000 members, five delegates; and unions exceeding 15,000 members, five delegates plus an additional delegate for every 3,000 members.

128. Ubaldini's candidacy for governor of Buenos Aires in 1991 was not an attempt to form a labor party. It was more a reaction to the events of late 1990

than a long-term strategy. Having been abandoned by most unions, Ubaldini was trying to realize his ambition for power through the only route left, the ballot box.

129. McGuire, "Union Political Tactics," pp. 68–72.

CHAPTER 7: *Agricultural Distributional Coalitions*

1. World Bank: *Argentina: Reforms for Price Stability and Growth* (Washington D.C.: World Bank, 1990), p. 185.

2. *Buenos Aires Herald,* 14 March 1992.

3. Mirta L. de Palomino, *Tradición y poder: la Sociedad Rural Argentina (1955–1983)* (Buenos Aires: CISEA/Grupo Editorial Latinoamericano, 1988), p. 20. The charter of the association was signed by sixty individuals of whom fifteen were Britons and two were Italians. José Luis de Imaz, *Los Que Mandan* (Albany: State University of New York Press, 1970), p. 98.

4. Dardo Cúneo, *Comportamiento y crisis de la clase empresaria* (Buenos Aires: Pleamar, 1967), pp. 50–62.

5. Paul Lewis, *The Crisis of Argentine Capitalism* (Chapel Hill: University of North Carolina, 1990), p. 82.

6. De Palomino, *Tradición y poder,* p. 30.

7. Ibid., pp. 21, 65.

8. Peter Smith, *Politics and Beef in Argentina: Patterns of Conflict and Change* (New York: Columbia University Press, 1969), pp. 30–31. Between 1910 and 1943, there were five presidents, three vice presidents, twelve agriculture ministers, five foreign ministers, four economy ministers, three public works ministers, three ministers of justice and education, three maritime ministers, two army ministers, and one interior minister.

9. De Palomino, *Tradición y poder,* p. 71.

10. The president, the vice president, presidents of the Chamber of Deputies and the Senate, the chief justice of the Supreme Court, ministers or secretaries of agriculture, provincial governors, and the mayor of Buenos Aires were all granted ex officio honorary membership in the SRA upon taking office. Ibid., pp. 28–29.

11. Gary Wynia, *Argentina in the Postwar Era* (Albuquerque: University of New Mexico Press, 1978), p. 23.

12. Lewis, *The Crisis,* p. 23.

13. Carlos Waisman, *Reversal of Development in Argentina: Postwar Counterrevolutionary Policies and Their Structural Consequences* (Princeton: Princeton University Press, 1987), p. 53.

14. James Scobie, *Argentina: A City and a Nation* (New York: Oxford University Press, 1964), pp. 112–35; David Rock, *Argentina 1516–1987: From Spanish Colonization to Alfonsín,* 2d ed. (Berkeley: University of California Press, 1987), pp. 131–33, 140–43.

15. Carl Taylor, *Rural Life in Argentina* (Baton Rouge: Louisiana State University Press, 1948), p. 195; Lewis, *The Crisis,* p. 22.

16. Wynia, *Argentina in the Postwar Era,* p. 23.

17. Lewis, *The Crisis*, p. 23.

18. Ibid.

19. The Concordancia technically started with the administration of President Augustín Justo in 1932 and was supported early on by conservatives, independent socialists, and anti personalist radicals. See Peter Smith, *Argentina and the Failure of Democracy: Conflict Among Political Elites* (Madison: University of Wisconsin Press, 1974), p. 37.

20. Rock, *Argentina 1516–1987*, p. 224.

21. Raúl Prebisch, "Argentine Economic Policies since the 1930s: Recollections," in *The Political Economy of Argentina, 1880–1946*, ed. Guido Di Tella and D. C. M. Platt (New York: St. Martin's, 1986), pp. 142–43. See also Robert Potash, *The Army & Politics in Argentina, 1928–1945* (Stanford: Stanford University Press, 1969), p. 83; Carlos Floria and César García Belsunce, *Historia política de la Argentina contemporánea, 1880–1983*, 2d ed. (Buenos Aires: Alianza Universidad, 1988), p. 126.

22. Lewis, *The Crisis*, p. 91. From 1948 until his retirement Prebisch was the intellectual force behind the ISI policy advocated by the UN Economic Commission for Latin America.

23. Roger Gravil, "State Intervention in Argentina's Export Trade between the Wars," *Journal of Latin American Studies* 2 (1970): 157–58.

24. Ibid., pp. 158–64.

25. Ibid., p. 159.

26. Rock, *Argentina, 1516–1987*, pp. 239–40; Guido Di Tella, "Economic Controversies in Argentina from the 1920s to the 1940s," in *The Political Economy of Argentina, 1880–1946*, ed. Di Tella and Platt, pp. 128–29.

27. Juan Llach, "El Plan Pinedo de 1940: su significado histórico y los orígenes de la economía política del peronismo," *Desarrollo Económico* 23 (1984): 529–30.

28. Wynia, *Argentina in the Postwar Era*, p. 31.

29. De Palomino, *Tradición y poder*.

30. Ibid., p. 76.

31. Ibid., p. 74.

32. Jorge Niosi, *Los Empresarios y el Estado Argentino (1955–1969)* (Buenos Aires: Siglo Veintiuno, 1974).

33. De Palomino, *Tradición y poder*, p. 74.

34. Marcelo Diamand, "Overcoming Argentina's Stop-and-Go Economic Cycles," in *Latin American Political Economy*, ed. Jonathan Hartlyn and Samuel A. Morley (Boulder: Westview, 1986), p. 129.

35. Lewis, *The Crisis*, p. 153.

36. Ibid., p. 142. See also Samuel Baily, *Labor, Nationalism, and Politics in Argentina* (New Brunswick: Rutgers University Press, 1967), p. 77.

37. Lewis, *The Crisis*, p. 148.

38. Cúneo, *Comportamiento y crisis* pp. 153–58, 174–78; Tulio Halperín Donghi, *Argentina: la democracia de masas* (Buenos Aires: Paidós, 1972), p. 53; Félix Luna, *El 45: Crónica de un año decisivo* (Buenos Aires: Sudamericana, 1975); Robert Potash, *The Army & Politics in Argentina, 1945–1962* (Stanford: Stanford University Press, 1980), pp. 15–46.

39. Waisman, *Reversal of Development*, p. 175.

40. Wynia, *Argentina in the Postwar Era*, p. 49; Rock, *Argentina, 1516–1987*, p. 274.

41. Wynia, *Argentina in the Postwar Era*, pp. 50, 59.

42. Moreover, it is said that the army would not have allowed expropriation of land because most generals aspired to become landowners after retirement; some were also married to daughters of SRA members.

43. Jorge Newton, *Historia de la SRA* (Buenos Aires: Gancourt, 1966); Cúeno, *Comportamiento y crisis*; de Imaz, *Los Que Mandan*.

44. Lewis, *The Crisis*, p. 163.

45. De Imaz, *Los Que Mandan*, p. 120.

46. De Palomino, *Tradición y poder*, p. 24.

47. Nonetheless, pampas producers, specially fatteners, remained firmly in control of the SRA.

48. De Palomino, *Tradición y poder*.

49. Ibid., p. 113.

50. Wynia, *Argentina in the Postwar Era*, p. 157. De Imaz, *Los Que mandan*, p. 106, also notes that the board of the CAP, once it was returned to private ownership in 1961, was heavily staffed with SRA members. In 1961, four of the sixteen members of the board of directors belonged to the SRA.

51. Wynia, *Argentina in the Postwar Era*, p. 158. The SRA also convinced the government to abandon its projects to create regulatory commissions for milk and wool production and marketing. De Palomino, *Tradición y poder*, p. 113.

52. On the shortcomings of Frondizi's agricultural policies, see Clarence Zuvekas, "Argentine Economic Policy 1958–1962: The Frondizi Government's Development Plan," *Inter-American Economic Affairs* 22 (1968): 45–74. On the same period, see also Alberto Petrecolla, "Unbalanced Development, 1958–62," in *The Political Economy of Argentina, 1946–83*, ed. Guido Di Tella and Rudiger Dornbusch (Pittsburgh: Pittsburgh University Press, 1989), pp. 108–25.

53. Lewis, *The Crisis*, p. 294; de Palomino, *Tradición y poder*, p. 116.

54. Wynia, *Argentina in the Postwar Era*, p. 105.

55. On ACIEL formation as a response to Frondizi's policies, see Carlos H. Acuña, *Intereses empresarios, dictadura y democracia en la Argentina actual, Documento CEDES* (Buenos Aires: CEDES, 1990), p. 15; Marcelo Cavarozzi, *Sindicatos y política en la Argentina* (Buenos Aires: CEDES, 1984), p. 101; William Smith, *Authoritarianism and the Crisis of the Argentine Political Economy* (Stanford: Stanford University Press, 1989), pp. 37–38.

56. The five ministers were Jorge Wehbe (30 March–6 April 1962), Federico Pinedo (6 April–25 April 1962), Alvaro Alsogaray (30 April–10 December 1962), Eustaquio Méndez Delfino (10 December–15 May 1963), and José Alfredo Martínez de Hoz (21 May–12 October 1963).

57. Lewis, *The Crisis*, p. 295.

58. De Palomino, *Tradición y poder*, p. 123; Niosi, *Los Empresarios*.

59. Niosi, *Los Empresarios*, p. 128; Lewis, *The Crisis*, p. 295.

60. De Palomino, *Tradición y poder*, pp. 125–27.

61. Ibid., p. 127.

62. His first term of office was under Aramburu between March 1957 and May 1958.

63. Smith, *Authoritarianism,* pp. 85–86.

64. De Palomino, *Tradición y poder,* p. 132.

65. Smith, *Authoritarianism,* p. 87.

66. Ibid., p. 89.

67. SRA *Memorias of 1969,* cited in de Palomino, *Tradición y poder,* p. 134.

68. Wynia, *Argentina in the Postwar Era,* p. 181.

69. Smith, *Authoritarianism,* p. 88.

70. Lewis, *The Crisis,* p. 425.

71. De Palomino, *Tradición y poder,* pp. 142–49.

72. For a detailed description of these events, see Lewis, *The Crisis,* pp. 443–45.

73. De Palomino, *Tradición y poder,* p. 150.

74. Acuña, *Intereses empresarios,* pp. 22–23.

75. De Palomino, *Tradición y poder,* p. 157.

76. Ibid., p. 160.

77. SRA *Memorias of 1980,* cited in ibid., p. 162.

78. José Nun and Mario Lattuada, *El Gobierno de Alfonsín y las Corporaciones Agrarias* (Buenos Aires: Manantial, 1991), p. 112.

79. Ibid., pp. 166, 167.

80. Roberto Martínez Nogueira, "Las organizaciones corporativas del sector agropecuario: notas para un ensayo interpretativo de sus comportamientos," Working Paper 10, CISEA, Buenos Aires: December 1985, p. 3.

81. Ibid., pp. 4–5.

82. Nun and Lattuada, *El Gobierno de Alfonsín,* p. 119.

83. Martínez Nogueira, "Las organizaciones corporativas," p. 6.

84. Ibid., p. 8.

85. Ibid., p. 5.

86. See de Palomino, *Tradición y poder,* p. 30; de Imaz, *Los Que Mandan,* p. 96.

87. De Imaz, *Los Que Mandan,* p. 97.

88. De Palomino, *Tradición y poder,* pp. 51–54, 27–28. A few people are given honorary memberships to further political connections. The following passages are based on de Palomino, *Tradicion y poder;* pp. 95–99, 108–09, 90, 101–02.

89. One of Argentina's most important newspapers, *La Nación,* has consistently expressed the SRA's point of view. Furthermore, the SRA has publicized its policy proposals through conservative think tanks like the Fundación de Investigaciones Latinoamericanas.

90. Martínez Nogueira, "Las organizaciones corporativas," pp. 26–28.

91. Mirta de Palomino, "El agro frente al Gobierno Constitucional," *El Bimestre* 28 (1986): 5. De Palomino also notes that Jorge Aguado, president of the CARBAP, was governor of the Buenos Aires province in 1981 and that the current CRA president, Raúl Romero Feris, is a prominent member of the Autonomist party of Corrientes.

92. Martínez Nogueira, "Las organizaciones corporativas," p. 20.

93. Wynia, *Argentina in the Postwar Era,* p. 182; de Imaz, *Los Que Mandan,* p. 109.

94. De Palomino, "El agro frente," p. 5.

95. Nun and Lattuada, *El gobierno de Alfonsín,* p. 71.

96. Ibid.

97. De Palomino, "El agro frente," p. 10–11.

98. Nun and Lattuada, *El gobierno de Alfonsín*, p. 27.

99. Ibid., p. 35.

100. World bank, *Argentina: Reforms for Price Stability and Growth* (Washington D.C.: World Bank, 1990), p. 186.

101. Nun and Lattuada, *El gorbierno de Alfonsín*, pp. 118–19.

102. Twice in March 1985 (once alone and once with the SRA); April 1986 (with the SRA, the FAA, and the CONINAGRO); once in June 1986 (with the SRA); and once in March 1989. Ibid., p. 155.

103. Acuña, *Intereses empresarios*, p. 30.

104. The change of economic teams in 1985 failed to mute the rural sector's criticism of official policy. In March 1985, the CRA and the SRA called for a strike, the first one since 1976, which drew the moral support of the FAA, the CONINAGRO, the CGT, the UCD, and provincial parties. The implementation of the Austral Plan the following May did not appreciably change the sector's stance with regard to government policies. Agricultural groups praised the Austral Plan's bold attempt to attack hyperinflation but maintained their opposition to the price freeze on food and the persistence of very high export tariffs.

105. The gap between the two exchange rates was around 25 percent. In practice, the government subsidized the industrial sector's import-export operations by subsidizing its exchange rate with dollars primarily from agricultural exports, which was unacceptable to the rural distributional coalitions.

106. In April 1989, with exchange reserves running dangerously low, Alfonsín had no option but to ask the economic team that had been in charge since 1985 to resign. A new minister of the economy reunified the exchange rate and rushed through a series of measures highly favorable to agricultural exporters in order to induce them to exchange their dollars for local currency. Nun and Lattuada, *El gobierno de Alfonsín*, p. 149.

107. *Buenos Aires Herald*, 11 August 1991.

108. *La Prensa*, 1 November 1991.

109. *Buenos Aires Herald*, 14 March 1992.

110. De Palomino, "El agro frente," p. 12.

CHAPTER 8: *Industrial Distributional Coalitions*

1. Carlos Díaz Alejandro, *Essays on the Economic History of the Argentine Republic* (New Haven: Yale University Press, 1970), p. 212.

2. Paul Lewis, *The Crisis of Argentine Capitalism* (Chapel Hill: University of North Carolina Press, 1990), p. 81.

3. José Luis de Imaz, *Los Que Mandan* (Albany: State University of New York Press, 1970), p. 156.

4. Ibid., p. 247.

5. De Imaz, *Los Que Mandan*, p. 156.

6. Jorge Schvarzer, *Los Industriales* (Buenos Aires: Centro Editor de América Latina, 1981).

7. Giorgio Alberti, Franco Castiglioni, and Paolo Munini, "Política e ideología en la industrialización argentina," *Boletín Informativo Techint* 239 (1985): 7–

20; Natalio Botana, *El orden conservador: La política argentina entre 1880 y 1916* (Buenos Aires: Sudamericana, 1977), pp. 53–53. According to these scholars, this bias could be seen in the thought of Juan Bautista Alberdi, one of the intellectual and political leaders of the oligarchy. Politically, in Alberdi's view, the new immigrants were to be granted civil liberties because such liberties were the basis of the socioeconomic mobility these newcomers were looking for by coming to Argentina. By not restricting an individual's pursuit of a better life, Alberdi's argument went, these people would engage in entrepreneurial activities beneficial to the country's economic development. However, political rights, such as the right to vote and hold public office, were to be restricted to the "enlightened" oligarchy, who knew what was best for the country. Consequently, Alberdi's ideas justified a restricted democracy based on a collective good principle determined by the few; the landowning elite.

8. Cited in Antonio Brailovsky, *1880–1982: Historia de las crisis argentinas* (Buenos Aires: Universidad de Belgrano, 1982), p. 15.

9. Alberti, Castiglioni, and Munini, "Política e ideología," p. 8.

10. Oscar Cornblit, "Inmigrantes y empresarios en la política argentina," in *Los fragmentos del poder,* ed. Torcuato Di Tella and Tullio Halperín Donghi (Buenos Aires: Jorge Álvarez, 1969).

11. Alberti, Castiglioni, and Munini, "Política e ideología"; Torcuato Di Tella, *Latin American Politics: A Framework of Analysis* (Austin: University of Texas, 1990); Adolfo Dorfman, *Historia de la industria argentina,* 2d ed. (Buenos Aires: Solar Hachette, 1970); Aldo Ferrer, *The Argentine Economy* (Berkeley: University of California Press, 1967); Tómas Roberto Fillol, *Social Factors in Economic Development: The Argentine Case* (Cambridge: MIT Press, 1961); and Ricardo Ortiz, *Historia económica de la Argentina, 1860–1930,* 2 vols. (Buenos Aires: Raigal, 1955).

12. Díaz Alejandro, *Essays,* p. 215.

13. Gino Germani, *Política y sociedad en una época de transición: de la sociedad tradicional a la sociedad de masas* (Buenos Aires: Paidós, 1965), pp. 185–88.

14. The first UIA president was Antonio Cambaceres, a rancher and plantation owner who had interests in meat-salting, railway, and banking businesses. His successors had similar backgrounds, and their investments included cattle raising, meat packing, wine production, shipping, and finance. Some of these people were also congressmen and often members of the SRA. Lewis, *The Crisis,* pp. 81–83; De Imaz, *Los Que Mandan,* p. 156; and Dardo Cúneo, *Comportamiento y crisis de la clase empresaria* (Buenos Aires: Pleamar, 1967), pp. 63, 75.

15. Jorge Schvarzer, *Empresarios del pasado: La Unión Industrial Argentina* (Buenos Aires: CISEA, 1991), p. 265.

16. Gary Wynia, *Argentina in the Postwar Era* (Albuquerque: University of New Mexico Press, 1978), pp. 28, 32.

17. Alberti, Castiglioni, and Munini, "Política e ideología," p. 9.

18. Ibid., p. 8; Cornblit, "Inmigrantes y empresarios"; Di Tella, *Latin American Politics;* Alain Rouquié, *Poder militar y sociedad política en la Argentina,* vol. 1 (Buenos Aires: Emecé, 1981).

19. Roberto Cortés Conde, "Problemas del crecimiento industrial," in *Argentina, sociedad de masas,* ed. Torcuato Di Tella and Gino Germani (Buenos Aires: EUDEBA, 1965); Eduardo Jorge, *Industria y concentración económica: desde principios de siglo hasta el peronismo* (Buenos Aires: Siglo Veintiuno, 1971).

20. De Imaz, *Los Que Mandan*, pp. 157–58.

21. Many economists contend that the agriculture-led development model delayed industrialization because manufacturing prior to 1930 was concentrated in the agroindustrial sector, which was subject to erratic growth due to fluctuations in international demand, making industrial development uneven and causing it to concentrate on a few goods produced by a large number of small companies. See Guido Di Tella and Manuel Zymelman, *Las etapas del desarrollo económico argentino* (Buenos Aires: EUDEBA, 1967); Lucio Geller, "El crecimiento industrial argentino hasta 1914 y la teoría del bien primario exportable," *El Trimestre Económico* 37 (1970): 763–811; and Roberto Cortés Conde, *El progreso argentino* (Buenos Aires: Sudamericana, 1979).

Others, on the other hand, argue that there was nothing inherently wrong with the development of early Argentine industry—that it expanded according to demand and thus simply used the opportunities and the resources open to it at the time. See Díaz Alejandro, *Essays;* Carlos Díaz Alejandro, "No Less Than One Hundred Years of Argentine Economic History, Plus Some Comparisons," Discussion Paper 392 (New Haven: Economic Growth Center, Yale University, 1973); and Ezequiel Gallo, *Agrarian Expansion and Industrial Development in Argentina (1880–1930),* (Buenos Aires: Instituto Torcuato Di Tella, 1970). See also Vicente Vázquez Presedo, *Crisis y retraso. Argentina y la economía internacional entre las dos guerras* (Buenos Aires: ADEBA, 1978); and Arturo O'Connell, "Free Trade in One (Primary Producing) Country; the Case of Argentina in the 1920s," in *The Political Economy of Argentina, 1880–1946*, ed. Guido Di Tella and D. C. M. Platt (New York: St. Martin's, 1986). A summary of this debate can be found in Juan José Llach, *La Argentina que no fue* (Buenos Aires: IDES, 1985), pp. 28–34; and Juan Carlos Korol and Hilda Sabato, "Incomplete Industrialization: An Argentine Obsession," *Latin American Research Review* 25 (1990): 7–30.

22. Alberti, Castiglioni, and Munini, "Política e ideología," p. 9.

23. Recent research rejects this interpretation. Carlos Acuña, for instance, argues that there is no clear evidence of much class consciousness among industrialists in Europe and the United States either. The lack of class consciousness among Argentine industrialists is based on casual observations rather than hard data and is therefore more a myth than fact. See Carlos H. Acuña, "The Bourgeoisie as a Political Actor: Theoretical Notes for a Research of an Old and 'Forgotten' Topic" (Chicago: University of Chicago, April 1991).

24. Díaz Alejandro, *Essays*, p. 217. For a different view on the Argentine tariff protection policies of the 1920s, see O'Connell, "Free Trade," pp. 86–91.

25. Carlos Waisman, *Reversal of Development in Argentina: Postwar Counterrevolutionary Policies and Their Structural Consequences* (Princeton: Princeton University Press, 1987), pp. 60–61.

26. Díaz Alejandro, *Essays*, pp. 209, 211–12.

27. Bunge's ideas influenced contemporary writers like Rafael Herrera Vegas, María Luisa Tornquist de Muñiz Barreto, and Alejandro Shaw. As a professor at the universities of Buenos Aires and La Plata, Bunge counted among his disciples Raúl Prebisch, a close collaborator of Federico Pinedo and director, in 1948, of the United Nation's Economic Commission for Latin America. Bunge was also director of the Department of Labor (1913–1915) and of the National Institute of Statistics (1915–1920 and 1923–1925), adviser to the minister of the

treasury during the Alvear administration, minister of the treasury and public works for the province of Santa Fe (1931–1932), and chairman of the Banco de la Nación. See Llach, *La Argentina*, p. 18.

28. In Bunge's view, since 1914 the Argentine agricultural output had been stagnant as a result of (1) a backward land tenure system, (2) an ill-advised government credit policy, (3) the lack of new investments for the expansion of the commercial railway network, (4) the extreme specialization of agricultural production, (5) a substantial fall in foreign investments, and (6) the sluggish growth of international demand after World War I coupled with European and North American economic protectionism.

29. Bunge was far from advocating the state interventionism that characterized Argentina from 1946 on. In his view government should promote private initiative rather than replace it. Similarly, he was against the closed economy later created by Perón, while he never mentioned the development of a heavy industry, which marked the Frondizi period. Llach, *La Argentina*, pp. 22–23. Some of Bunge's most important essays on these matters are contained in Alejandro Bunge, *Una nueva Argentina* (Buenos Aires: Guillermo Kraft, 1940); For an analysis of Bunge's thought, see José Luis de Imaz, "Alejandro E. Bunge, economista y sociólogo (1880–1943)," *Desarrollo Económico* 14 (1974): 545–67; and Llach, *La Argentina*, pp. 9–38.

30. Llach, *La Argentina*, p. 16.

31. Lewis, *The Crisis*, p. 87.

32. Javier Lindenboim, "El empresariado industrial argentino y sus organizaciones gremiales entre 1930 y 1946," *Desarrollo Económico* 16 (1976): 179.

33. Lindenboim, "El empresariado industrial," p. 196; Llach, *La Argentina que no fue*, p. 25; Lewis, *The Crisis*, p. 90.

34. Between 1930 and 1946 the board of directors of the UIA was dominated by manufacturing: textile, 30 percent of the posts; metallurgy, 26 percent; food processing, 17 percent. The other major group was financial companies. Lindenboim, "El empresariado industrial," pp. 170, 177.

35. Wynia, *Argentina in the Postwar Era*, p. 29.

36. Lewis, *The Crisis*, pp. 88–90.

37. Acuña, "The Bourgeoisie as a Political Actor."

38. Lindenboim, "El empresariado industrial," p. 197.

39. Schvarzer, *Empresarios del pasado*, p. 407.

40. Guido Di Tella, "Economic Controversies in Argentina from the 1920s to the 1940s," in *The Political Economy of Argentina, 1880–1946*, ed. Di Tella and Platt, p. 129.

41. Guillermo O'Donnell, *Modernization and Bureaucratic-Authoritarianism: Studies in South American Politics* (Berkeley: Institute of International Studies, University of California, 1973); Gilbert Merkx, "Sectoral Clashes and Political Change: The Argentine Experience," *Latin American Research Review* 4 (1969): 89–90; Benjamin Most, *Changing Authoritarian Rule and Public Policy in Argentina, 1930–1970*, GGIS Monograph Series in World Affairs, University of Denver (Boulder: Lynne Reinner, 1991), pp. 47–48.

42. David Rock, *Argentina 1516–1987: From Spanish Colonization to Alfonsín*, 2d ed. (Berkeley: University of California Press, 1987), p. 232.

43. Ibid., p. 233.

44. Lindenboim, "El empresariado industrial," p. 170.

45. Lewis, *The Crisis*, pp. 88, 123.

46. Most, *Changing Authoritarian Rule*, pp. 84–89.

47. O'Donnell, *Modernization and Bureaucratic Authoritarianism*.

48. Most, *Changing Authoritarian Rule*, pp. 48–49; Torcuato Di Tella, "Populism and Reform in Latin America," in *Obstacles to Change in Latin America*, ed. Claudio Veliz (New York: Oxford University Press, 1965), p. 71; Díaz Alejandro, *Essays*, pp. 113, 129; Samuel Baily, "Argentina: Search for Consensus," *Current History* 51 (1967): 301–06; Peter Snow, "The Class Basis of Argentine Political Parties," *American Political Science Review* 63 (1969): 163–67; Peter Smith, "Social Mobilization, Political Participation, and the Rise of Juan D. Perón," *Political Science Quarterly* 84 (1969): 30–49; and Eldon Kenworthy, "Argentina: The Politics of Late Industrialization," *Foreign Affairs* 45 (1967): 463–76.

49. Torcuato Di Tella, "Stalemate or Coexistence in Argentina?" in *Latin America: Reform or Revolution?* ed. James Petras and Maurice Zeitlan (Greenwich: Fawcett, 1968); and Eldon Kenworthy, "Did the 'New Industrialists' Play a Significant Role in the Formation of Perón's Coalition?" in *New Perspectives on Modern Argentina*, ed. Alberto Ciria (Bloomington: Indiana University Press, 1972).

50. Lewis, *The Crisis*, p. 94.

51. Felix Luna, *El 45* (Buenos Aires: Sudamericana, 1971), pp. 22–30.

52. Waisman, *Reversal of Development in Argentina*, p. 175.

53. This coalition took the name of Comisión Permanente de la Industria, el Comercio y la Producción.

54. Cúneo, *Comportamiento y crisis*, pp. 178–79; Kenworthy, "Did the 'Industrialists' Play a Significant Role?" pp. 15–28; Lewis, *The Crisis*, pp. 155–57.

55. Wynia, *Argentina in the Postwar Era*, p. 57.

56. Companies from the northwest were dominant; Gelbard himself was from Catamarca.

57. Cúneo, *Comportamiento y crisis*, pp. 187–89; Lewis, *The Crisis*, p. 172.

58. Most, *Changing Authoritarian Rule*, pp. 91–99. A polemical interpretation of Perón's economic policies can be found in Pablo Gerchunoff, "Peronist Economic Policies, 1946–55," in *The Political Economy of Argentina, 1946–1983*, ed. Guido Di Tella and Rudiger Dornbusch, pp. 59–85.

59. The Radicals were not the only ones against the return of the old economic regime. Provincial conservatives representing interests that had benefited from ISI as well as important economic groups of the Buenos Aires area were also opposed.

60. Wynia, *Argentina in the Postwar Era*, p. 160.

61. Gerchunoff, "The 'Revolución Libertadora,'" in *The Political Economy of Argentina*, p. 107.

62. Guillermo O'Donnell, *Bureaucratic Authoritarianism: Argentina, 1966–1973 in Comparative Perspective* (Berkeley: University of California Press, 1988), pp. 33–34.

63. Unlike the UIA, the CGE did not allow foreign companies to join its board of directors.

64. William Smith, *Authoritarianism and the Crisis of the Argentine Political Economy* (Stanford: Stanford University Press, 1989), p. 38.

65. Gelbard did not consider himself a Peronist but agreed with many Peronist socioeconomic policies and the need for a social pact.

66. Eduardo Sguiglia, *El club de los poderosos* (Buenos Aires: Planeta, 1991), p. 38.

67. These double standards were common among industrialists, even in advanced industrialized countries; what makes Argentina different is that they were enforced for a prolonged period.

68. For an analysis of the ACIEL-CGE conflict, see Carlos H. Acuña, "Intereses empresarios, dictadura y democracia en la Argentina actual," *Cuaderno CEDES* 39 (1990): 15–16.

69. Alberti, Castiglioni, and Munini, "Política e ideología," p. 11.

70. Wynia, *Argentina in the Postwar Era*, p. 268.

71. The "perception of threat" hypothesis was put forward by O'Donnell, *Bureaucratic Authoritarianism*, p. 25.

72. Jorge Niosi, *Los Empresarios y el Estado Argentino (1955–1969)* (Buenos Aires: Siglo Veintiuno, 1974), chap. 5; Wynia, *Argentina in the Postwar Era*, p. 125; Smith, *Authoritarianism*, p. 43.

73. Guillermo O'Donnell, *Un 'juego imposible.' Competición y coaliciones entre partidos políticos en Argentina, 1955–1966.* Documento de Trabajo (Buenos Aires: Instituto Torcuato Di Tella, 1972).

74. O'Donnell, *Modernization*, pp. 51, 72.

75. "In the 1955–69 period, around 75 percent of all businessmen in high posts were affiliated with the ACIEL; the only exception was during the Illia administration, when ACIEL members held 50 percent of the top posts. During the Onganía regime, members of the ACIEL occupied 34 out of 42 top-level offices, or 81 percent. The CGE, by contrast, only had two representatives, whose tenure was limited to the first six months of the new regime. Moreover, ACIEL businessmen were not only dominant in the economic ministries, but also accounted for half of the top posts in the Defense Ministry." Smith, *Authoritarianism*, p. 94. However, most of these people joined government as individuals rather than representatives of their entrepreneurial organization, leading Smith to conclude that ACIEL was a "paper tiger."

76. This agreement required firms to keep prices steady for at least six months. The government gave special privileges to conforming firms in the form of state purchases, credit, and tax breaks. Juan Carlos De Pablo, *Política anti-inflacionaria en la Argentina 1967–1970* (Buenos Aires: Amorrotu, 1970).

77. To signal the changed attitude of the new administration toward foreign capital, Krieger Vasena created the Office for Foreign Investment to attract business from abroad. Tariff protection on many items was substantially lowered, and most of Illia's restrictions and regulations on foreign investments were lifted.

78. Oscar Braun, *El desarrollo del capital monopolista en la Argentina* (Buenos Aires: Tiempo Contemporáneo, 1970); Richard Mallon and Juan Sourrouille, *Economic Policymaking in a Conflict Society: The Argentine Case* (Cambridge: Harvard University Press, 1975); Guillermo Martorell, *Las inversiones extranjeras en la Argentina* (Buenos Aires: Galerna, 1969); and Jorge Schvarzer, "Las empresas más grandes en la Argentina: Una evaluación," *DE 17*, no. 66 (1977): 319–38.

79. Wynia, *Argentina in the Postwar Era*, p. 180.

80. Lewis, *The Crisis*, p. 342.

81. The industrial organizations of the CGE and the ACIEL, CGI and UIA, had different organizational structures. The CGI was organized by both regions and branches. In the UIA regional representation was almost absent. Individual chambers joining the UIA did so as representative of specific economic sectors or branches without any regional subdivision. Moreover, unlike the CGI, the UIA allowed on its board of directors members representing individual firms. Much of the following analysis draws on conversations with Carlos H. Acuña, Franco Castiglioni, and Jorge Schvarzer. I am particularly grateful to Acuña, whose works inform much of my thinking about the topic.

82. Smith, *Authoritarianism*, pp. 92–93; Niosi, *Los empresarios*, p. 170.

83. Acuña, "Intereses empresarios," p. 18.

84. Additionally, the ADIM put forward a plan to give greater representation on the UIA board of directors to small industry in regions other than the Buenos Aires region.

85. The MEDI represented mostly businesses from the northwest, while the MUI grouped firms of the Córdoba province. For details, see Giorgio Alberti, Laura Golbert, and Carlos H. Acuña, "Intereses industriales y gobernabilidad democrática en la Argentina," *Boletín Informativo Techint* 235 (1985): 111.

86. Adolfo Canitrot, "Discipline as the Central Objective of Economic Policy: An Essay on the Economic Programme of the Argentine Government Since 1976," *World Development* 8 (1980): 913–28. See also Jorge Schvarzer, *Martínez de Hoz: La lógica política de la política económica* (Buenos Aires: Ensayos y Tesis CISEA, 1983).

87. Alberti, Castiglioni, and Munini, "Política e ideología," p. 13.

88. Acuña, "Intereses empresarios," p. 24. Acuña also reports that, given the inflexibility of the economy ministry, entrepreneurs often appealed to other departments to intercede in their behalf with Martínez de Hoz.

89. Sguiglia, *El Club*, p. 44; and Eduardo Basualdo and Daniel Azpiazu, *Cara y contracara de los grupos económicos: estado y promoción industrial en la Argentina* (Buenos Aires: Cántaro, 1989), pp. 176–77. According to the latter, some of these conglomerates gained additional advantage through government contracts and through their foreign debts being taken over by the state in 1982. Such private debt passed on by the military regime to the Alfonsín administration amounted in 1984 to $11.5 billion, of which 85 percent belonged to a few conglomerates. Acuña, "Intereses Empresarios," p. 27.

90. Basualdo and Azpiazu, *Cara y contracara*, p. 176.

91. Alberti, Golbert, and Acuña, "Intereses industriales," p. 113.

92. Chambers representing specific sectors (associations of second degree) showed more bureaucratic and higher organizational skills because they had to face unions in collective negotiations. Voicing demands at the national level (a typical function of the UIA) was not enough; they had to be able to discuss with union leaders, to negotiate, and to impose agreements on their members. Acuña, "Bourgeoisie as a Political Actor."

93. De Imaz, *Los Que Mandan*, p. 166.

94. Lewis, *The Crisis*, p. 331.

95. Fillol, *Social Factors in Economic Development*, p. 75.

96. Schvarzer, *Empresarios del pasado*, p. 267.

97. Sguiglia, *El Club*, p. 47.

98. Carlos H. Acuña, Mario dos Santos, Daniel García Delgado, and Laura Golbert, "Relación estado/empresario y políticas concertadas de ingresos. El caso argentino," in *Política Económica y Actores Sociales: La Concertación de Ingreso y Empleo*, ed. Patricio Silva (Santiago de Chile: PREALC OIT, 1988), pp. 1–55.

99. De Imaz, *Los Que Mandan*, p. 166.

100. Interview with Pérez Companc, in Sguiglia, *El Club*, p. 93.

101. Alberti, Castiglioni, and Munini, "Intereses industriales," p. 99.

102. A first point of friction came when the ADIM, which at first was encouraged by Sourrouille to take a tough stand in renegotiating the metal workers' contracts, was later pressed by the government to come to a settlement that the ADIM judged unsatisfactory. Additionally, the appointment of union leader Carlos Alderete to head the Labor Ministry in early 1987 was interpreted by the UIA as a clear sign of the administration's double-talk. Finally, the approval of a collective bargaining law highly favorable to labor in the aftermath of the Radical defeat in the 1987 congressional and gubernatorial elections further complicated government-UIA relations. See Acuña, "Intereses empresarios," pp. 40–50.

103. *Latin American Monitor: Southern Cone* 7 (1990): 822.

104. Sguiglia, *El Club*, pp. 88, 102; see also Jorge Schvarzer, *La reestructuración de la economía argentina en nuevas condiciones políticas, 1989–92* (Buenos Aires: CISEA, 1992).

105. These points are also made by Acuña, "Intereses empresarios," pp. 56–61.

106. Luis Majul, *Los Dueños de la Argentina: La Cara Oculta de los Negocias* (Buenos Aires: Sudamerica, 1992).

CHAPTER 9: *On the Prospects for Argentine Democracy*

1. Manuel Mora y Araujo, *Ensayo y Error* (Buenos Aires: Planeta, 1991), p. 138.

2. Ibid., pp. 12–13.

3. Interview with Moreno Ocampo, Buenos Aires, November 1992.

4. Horacio Verbitsky, *Robo para la corona: Los frutos prohibidos del árbol de la corrupción* (Buenos Aires: Planeta, 1991).

5. *Latin American Regional Reports: Southern Cone Report* (London, 24 December 1992), p. 3.

6. Richard Mallon and Juan Sourrouille, *Economic Policymaking in a Conflict Society: The Argentine Case* (Cambridge: Harvard University Press, 1975), p. 164.

7. Terry Karl, "Dilemmas of Democratization in Latin America," *Comparative Politics* 23 (1990): 14.

8. Giorgio Alberti, "Democracy by Default, Economic Crisis, Movimientismo, and Social Anomie in Latin America," paper prepared for the Interna-

tional Conference on Le Sfide delle Transizioni Democratiche: Est-Ovest e Nord-Sud, University of Bologna, 30–31 May 1991, pp. 6–7.

9. Ibid., p. 6.

10. Atilio Borón, "Los Axiomas de Anillaco. La Visión de la Política en el Pensamiento y en la Acción de Carlos Saúl Menem," in *El Menemato*, ed. Atilio Borón et al. (Buenos Aires: Letra Buena, 1991), p. 55.

11. Ibid., p. 19.

12. Liliana De Riz, "Transitions to Democracy in Argentina: A Questioning of Presidentialism (1983–1989)," paper prepared for the Symposium on Transition to Democracy in Argentina, Yale University, March 1990, p. 17.

13. William Smith, "State, Market, and Neoliberalism in Post-Transition Argentina: The Menem Experiment," *Journal of Interamerican Studies and World Affairs* 33 (1992): 67–68.

14. Borón, "Los Axiomas," p. 78.

15. Adam Przeworski, "Some Problems in the Study of the Transition to Democracy," in *Transitions from Authoritarian Rule: Comparative Perspectives*, ed. Guillermo O'Donnell, Philippe Schmitter, and Lawrence Whitehead (Baltimore: Johns Hopkins University Press, 1986), p. 58.

INDEX

PITT LATIN AMERICAN SERIES
James M. Malloy, Editor

ARGENTINA

Argentina Between the Great Powers, 1936–1946
Guido di Tella and D. Cameron Watt, Editors

Argentina in the Twentieth Century
David Rock, Editor

Argentina: Political Culture and Instability
Susan Calvert and Peter Calvert

Argentine Workers: Peronism and Contemporary Class Consciousness
Peter Ranis

Discreet Partners: Argentina and the USSR Since 1917
Aldo César Vacs

The Franco-Perón Alliance: Relations Between Spain and Argentina, 1946–1955
Raanan Rein

The Life, Music, and Times of Carlos Gardel
Simon Collier

Institutions, Parties, and Coalitions in Argentine Politics
Luigi Manzetti

The Political Economy of Argentina, 1946–1983
Guido di Tella and Rudiger Dornbusch, Editors

BRAZIL

Capital Markets in the Development Process: The Case of Brazil
John H. Welch

External Constraints on Economic Policy in Brazil, 1899–1930
Winston Fritsch

The Film Industry in Brazil: Culture and the State
Randal Johnson

Kingdoms Come: Religion and Politics in Brazil
Rowan Ireland

The Manipulation of Consent: The State and Working-Class Consciousness in Brazil
Youssef Cohen

The Politics of Social Security in Brazil
James M. Malloy

Politics Within the State. Elite Bureaucrats and Industrial Policy in
Authoritarian Brazil
Ben Ross Schneider

Unequal Giants: Diplomatic Relations Between the United States and Brazil,
1889–1930
Joseph Smith

COLOMBIA

Economic Management and Economic Development in Peru and Colombia
Rosemary Thorp

Gaitán of Colombia: A Political Biography
Richard E. Sharpless

Roads to Reason: Transportation, Administration, and Rationality in Colombia
Richard E. Hartwig

CUBA

Cuba After the Cold War
Carmelo Mesa-Lago, Editor

Cuba Between Empires, 1878–1902
Louis A. Pérez, Jr.

Cuba Under the Platt Amendment, 1902–1934
Louis A. Pérez, Jr.

Cuban Studies, Vols. 16–21
Carmelo Mesa-Lago, Louis A. Pérez, Jr., Editors

Cuban Studies, Vol. 22
Jorge I. Domínguez, Editor

Cuban Studies, Vol. 23
Jorge Peréz-López, Editor

The Economics of Cuban Sugar
Jorge F. Pérez-López

Intervention, Revolution, and Politics in Cuba, 1913–1921
Louis A. Pérez, Jr.

Lords of the Mountain: Social Banditry and Peasant Protest in Cuba, 1878–1918
Louis A. Pérez, Jr.

MEXICO

The Expulsion of Mexico's Spaniards, 1821–1836
Harold Dana Sims

The Mexican Republic: The First Decade, 1823–1832
Stanley C. Green

Mexico Through Russian Eyes, 1806–1940
William Harrison Richardson

Oil and Mexican Foreign Policy
George W. Grayson

The Politics of Mexican Oil
George W. Grayson

Voices, Visions, and a New Reality: Mexican Fiction Since 1970
J. Ann Duncan

PERU

Domestic and Foreign Finance in Modern Peru, 1850–1950: Financing Visions of Development
Alfonso W. Quiroz

Economic Management and Economic Development in Peru and Colombia
Rosemary Throp

The Origins of the Peruvian Labor Movement, 1883–1919
Peter Blanchard

Peru and the International Monetary Fund
Thomas Scheetz

Peru Under García: An Opportunity Lost
John Crabtree

CARIBBEAN

The Last Cacique: Leadership and Politics in a Puerto Rican City
Jorge Heine

A Revolution Aborted: The Lessons of Grenada
Jorge Heine, Editor

To Hell with Paradise: A History of the Jamaican Tourist Industry
Frank Fonda Taylor

The Meaning of Freedom: Economics, Politics and Culture After Slavery
Frank McGlynn and Seymour Drescher, Editors

CENTRAL AMERICA

At the Fall of Somoza
Lawrence Pezzullo and Ralph Pezzullo

Black Labor on a White Canal: Panama, 1904–1981
Michael L. Conniff

The Catholic Church and Politics in Nicaragua and Costa Rica
Philip J. Williams

Perspectives on the Agro-Export Economy in Central America
Wim Pelupessy, Editor

OTHER NATIONAL STUDIES

The Overthrow of Allende and the Politics of Chile, 1964–1976
Paul E. Sigmund

Military Rule and Transition in Ecuador: Dancing with the People
Anita Isaacs

Primary Medical Care in Chile: Accessibility Under Military Rule
Joseph L. Scarpaci

Rebirth of the Paraguayan Republic: The First Colorado Era, 1878–1904
Harris G. Warren

Restructuring Domination: Industrialists and the State in Ecuador
Catherine M. Conaghan

US POLICIES

The Hovering Giant: U.S. Responses to Revolutionary Change in Latin America
Cole Blasier

Illusions of Conflict: Anglo-American Diplomacy Toward Latin America
Joseph Smith

Unequal Giants: Diplomatic Relations Between the United States and Brazil, 1889–1930
Joseph Smith

The United States and Latin America in the 1980s: Contending Perspectives on a Decade
of Crisis
Kevin J. Middlebrook and Carlos Rico, Editors